PENGUIN BOOKS

# BECOMING A HEROINE

Rachel M. Brownstein was born in New York City, where she attended Hunter College High School and Barnard College. She obtained her doctorate at Yale University and now teaches English at Brooklyn College. Her essays and reviews have appeared in *The Yale Review*, *Partisan Review*, *The New York Times Book Review*, and *Modern Language Quarterly*. This is her first book. Ms. Brownstein lives with her husband and three sons in New York City.

# BECOMING

## ~A~

# HEROINE

## Reading about Women in Novels

RACHEL M. BROWNSTEIN

PENGUIN BOOKS

Penguin Books Ltd, Harmondsworth, Middlesex, England
Penguin Books, 40 West 23rd Street, New York, New York 10010, U.S.A.
Penguin Books Australia Ltd, Ringwood, Victoria, Australia
Penguin Books Canada Limited, 2801 John Street, Markham, Ontario, Canada L3R 1B4
Penguin Books (N.Z.) Ltd, 182–190 Wairau Road, Auckland 10, New Zealand

First published in the United States of America by
The Viking Press 1982
Published in Penguin Books 1984
Reprinted 1984, 1985

LIBRARY OF CONGRESS CATALOGING IN PUBLICATION DATA
Brownstein, Rachel M.
Becoming a heroine.
Reprint. Originally published: New York: Viking Press, 1982.
Bibliography: p.
Includes index.
1. English fiction—History and criticism.
2. Heroines in literature.   3. Women in literature.
4. Women—Books and reading.   I. Title.
[PR830.H4B76   1984]   823'.009'352042   83-13080
ISBN 0 14 00.6787 6

Printed in the United States of America by
R. R. Donnelley & Sons Company, Harrisonburg, Virginia
Set in Goudy Old Style

"My Life in Fiction" appeared originally in *Columbia Forum*, and "An Exemplar to Her Sex" appeared originally in *The Yale Review*.

Grateful acknowledgment is made to the following for permission to reprint copyrighted material.

Cambridge University Press: A selection from "Jane Austen in the Novel" by Mary Lascelles, from *Jane Austen: Bicentenary Studies*, edited by John Halpern.

Doubleday & Company, Inc., and Curtis Brown Ltd: Selections from *Literary Women* by Ellen Moers. Copyright © Ellen Moers, 1963, 1972, 1973, 1974, 1975, 1976.

Harcourt Brace Jovanovich, Inc., and Edward Arnold (Publishers) Ltd: A selection from *Aspects of the Novel* (p. 85) by E. M. Forster. Copyright 1927 by Harcourt Brace Jovanovich, Inc. Copyright © renewed E. M. Forster, 1955.

Harcourt Brace Jovanovich, Inc., and The Hogarth Press Ltd: A selection from *A Room of One's Own* by Virginia Woolf. Copyright 1929 by Harcourt Brace Jovanovich, Inc. Copyright © renewed Leonard Woolf, 1957. A selection from *Jacob's Room* by Virginia Woolf. Copyright 1923 by Harcourt Brace Jovanovich, Inc. Copyright renewed 1950 by Leonard Woolf.

Hill and Wang, a division of Farrar, Straus and Giroux, Inc., and Jonathan Cape Ltd: Selections from *S/Z* by Roland Barthes, translated by Richard Miller. Copyright © Editions du Seuil, Paris, 1970. Translation copyright © Farrar, Straus and Giroux, Inc., 1974.

*To my parents,*
*Rose and Joseph Mayer*

The title women and fiction might mean . . . women and what they are like; or it might mean women and the fiction that they write; or it might mean women and the fiction that is written about them; or it might mean that somehow all three are inextricably mixed together. . . .

—Virginia Woolf,
*A Room of One's Own*

This is a vast commonplace of literature: the Woman copies the Book. In other words, every body is a citation: of the "already-written." The origin of desire is the statue, the painting, the book. . . .

—Roland Barthes,
*S/Z*

Millions of presumptuous girls, intelligent or not intelligent, daily affront their destiny, and what is it open to their destiny to *be*, at the most, that we should make an ado about it? The novel is of its very nature an "ado," an ado about something, and the larger the form it takes the greater of course the ado.

—Henry James,
Preface to *The Portrait of a Lady*

# Acknowledgments

I have been assisted and encouraged in this project by two grants from the City University Faculty Research Awards Program, and by the MacDowell Colony.

It is impossible to acknowledge all the personal debts I have incurred in the course of writing this book over a long period of time. Even if I exclude the friends who helped me only to live, and not to work, the list remains long, and also uncertain. Hundreds of comments and conversations I cannot recall partially shaped the ideas I have developed here. Were I to attempt to be exhaustive in giving credit where I know it is due, I would have to list all the colleagues, students, editors, friends, and relations who have talked with me about literature and life, recommended books and articles, corrected some of my errors, provided useful information, allowed me to teach the right courses, signed up for them, and made sympathetic sounds over the phone when I despaired. I am very lucky; I cannot. The following people, who talked and listened, or read and made suggestions, or generally, generously, let themselves be depended on, or did, somehow, all of the above, were the most help: Marylin Arthur; Georges Borchardt; Peggy Brawer; Richard Brickner; Daniel, Ezra, Gabriel, and Shale Brownstein; Myriam Chapman; Lore and Morris Dick-

## Acknowledgments

stein; Diana and Lawrence Fane; Sally Fisher; Carolyn Heilbrun; Elisabeth Jakab; Nancy Miller; Geoffrey Nunberg; Judith Johnson Sherwin; Erik Wensberg; and Andrew Wright. To them and to my editor, Elisabeth Sifton, I am very grateful.

R.M.B.

# Contents

# Introduction

"I think a higher voice is more tragic: it is more feminine: and the more feminine a woman is, the more tragic it seems when she does desperate actions."

"There may be something in that," said Mrs. Davilow, languidly. "But I don't know what good there is in making one's blood creep. And if there is anything horrible to be done, I should like it to be left to the men."

"Oh mamma, you are so dreadfully prosaic! As if all the great poetic criminals were not women! I think the men are poor cautious creatures."

"Well, dear, and you—who are afraid to be alone in the night—I don't think you would be very bold in crime, thank God."

"I am not talking about reality, mamma," said Gwendolen, impatiently.

> —George Eliot,
> *Daniel Deronda*

My brother is two years younger than I, and at the time I was doing the complete works of Frank Yerby he was reading everything about Napoleon. You can interpret that in one of several ways: (1) he was marching on Moscow while I was being raped; or (2) he was the scruffy little Corsican who conquered the world, while I was a half-breed beauty; or (3) he was the emperor while I was victim and vanquisher in succession, or even both at once. George Eliot wrote this about reading novels when she was a girl:

> I shall carry to my grave the mental diseases with which they have contaminated me. When I was quite a little child I could not be satisfied with the things around me; I was constantly living in a world of my own creation, and was quite contented to have no companions that I might be left to my own musings and imagine scenes in which I was chief actress.

The critic Richard Ellmann, noting the words "contamination," "disease," and "to my grave," remarks: "To use these weighty words lightly is not in character for George Eliot. If they have any serious meaning at all, then, she is declaring that she has been contaminated by novels which have aroused in her erotic fantasies as opposed to the merely megalomaniac ones of childhood." That George Eliot thought back on her early love of romances as if reading them had been a sort of carnal indulgence is hard to dispute. But it is equally hard, I think, to draw a line between "erotic" and "merely megalomaniac" fantasies. Admiration of the heroine of a romantic novel—beautiful, wise, beloved, and lucky—is love for an idealized image of oneself. Freud writes that "an intensification of the original narcissism" normally occurs in a girl's early adolescence:

> there arises in the woman a certain self-sufficiency (especially when there is a ripening into beauty) which compensates her for the social restrictions upon her object-choice. Strictly speaking, such women love only themselves with an intensity comparable to that of the man's love for them. Nor does their need lie in the direction of loving, but of being loved; and that man finds favour with them who fulfils this condition.

Freud disclaims any tendency to depreciate women "in this description of the feminine form of erotic life." I am not myself disposed to accuse him; indeed, I think the idea of autoeroticism as compensation for social restriction has real interest for feminists.

George Eliot ascribed her feelings not to women but to "every fellow-creature," and of course men read novels, have fantasies, as well as women. Rather, it is not a matter of men and women, but of boys and girls. Girls, enjoined from thinking about becoming generals and emperors, tend to live more in novels than boys do, and to live longer in them. It is not megalomaniacal to want to be significant; it is only human. And to suspect that one can be significant only in the fantasy of fiction, to look for significance in a concentrated essence of character, in an image of oneself, rather than in action or achievement, is, historically, only feminine. Or mostly.

The marriage plot most novels depend on is about finding validation of one's uniqueness and importance by being singled out among all other women by a man. The man's love is proof of the girl's value, and payment for it. Her search for perfect love through an incoherent, hostile wilderness of days is the plot that endows the aimless (life) with aim. Her quest is to be recognized in *all* her significance, to have her worth made real by being approved. When, at the end, this is done, she is transformed: her outward shape reflects her inner self, she is a bride, the very image of a heroine. For a heroine is just that, an image; novel heroines, like novel readers, are often women who want to become heroines.

To want to be a heroine is to want to be something special, something else, to want to change, to be changed, and also to want to stay the same.


The poets boast that brave men were living before Agamemnon, but because no poet sang their praises we do not call them heroes. A claim that novelists invented heroines would have to be phrased rather differently. But if the epic poet makes a man a hero, by writing him down, writing him up, the novelist, surely, creates the heroine. That is, if we mean by "heroine" more than a notable woman who was written about, Agamemnon's wife or his sister-in-law, or a brave woman, a female hero. The classic hero takes shape in an epic poet's imagination, where a brave man is central; the heroine at the center of a novel is informed by a novelist's vision of character and destiny. She is made in the image of an integral, aesthetically and morally coherent unique individual, a signifying self. Her special relation to this image distinguishes her from other women; in effect, it is what makes her a heroine. Tony Tanner has described the bourgeois novel as concerned more with "problems of tenure and maintenance" than with adventure and exploration. The tenure and mainte-nance of the integral self is a theme in novels about heroines—which is to say they are about becoming a heroine.

The history of both women and fiction has been influenced by the fact that the self has been identified, in novels, with the feminine. The idea of becoming a heroine marries the female protagonist to the marriage plot, and it marries the woman who reads to fiction. Many observations have been made about both of these long problematic marriages as critics have analyzed the ways already written texts and social realities influence literature, and as feminism has altered perspectives on literary and other history. Nice points about women and fiction have been pro-liferating since Virginia Woolf asked what the connection be-tween them was in 1929. It is necessary to make clear now whether we are talking about the fiction of Woman or the fiction of women, or about women in fictions; about women's relation to the arts or about women as art objects; about why there have been great women novelists or about whether women's art is distinctive or about whether, if it is, that is a function of nature or nurture. The most pressing question, it seems to me, is whether it is possible to have any one of these interesting dis-cussions without being tendentious—without either polarizing Woman and Art, or identifying them with one another.

In the past twenty years women have written a great deal about women, and as women. Feminists, like many others in our time, have been keenly conscious of what it means to write and to be written; they have been generously frank about their rela-tionships with their own and other people's pens. Women writers of the past have been rediscovered and reevaluated; literary and social critics have commented extensively about women and literature, and women seen from a literary perspective; feminist theorists, poets, journalists, and novelists have charged and even changed some of the connections between women and the arts by writing about and rewriting them. The heroine of *The Edible Woman* (1969), the first novel of the Canadian Margaret Atwood, bakes a cake in her own image and leaves this sweet mock self for an eager lover while she escapes out the back door; in Atwood's *Lady Oracle* (1976), the heroine writes cheap romances in secret, projecting her fantasies of great love as literary trash. The Englishwoman Margaret Drabble's early novels about contemporary young women making their way recall past Emmas and Claras, who also sought the hero and the variation on the marriage plot that was right for them: "What can it have been like, in bed with Mr. Knightley?" a liberated Jane Austen reader wonders in *The Waterfall* (1972). The popular rebel heroines of Erica Jong and Marilyn French, closer to home, are women who studied English literature in graduate school, who were marked for life, as I was, by having been English majors.

As a student of English literature in college I learned that the marriage plot in, say, Jane Austen's and George Eliot's novels, significantly adumbrates "larger" themes, such as the individual's conflict with society, or the city's with the country. When I reread those novels years later, in a feminist climate, the story about a girl's getting married seemed obviously the most important part. For the marriage plot poses questions about how the sexual is bound up with the moral life, about the coexistence of intimacy and identity, about how very odd it is to choose another so as to choose a self, about whether one can be who one is while living a generic woman's life, about the possibility of managing and shaping and comprehending the point of a determined female destiny. These themes of the classic English novel precisely echoed my own preoccupations, and those that other women were articulating. I recognized that for years I had thought about being a woman and being literary—caring for language, and watching for life to shape up like a novel—as if the two were intrinsically knotted together. I began to wonder why. I had always given novels about women a different kind of attention than I had given other books, and now it seemed possible, necessary, to say so. It seemed clear that the classic English novels about maidens choosing were urgently relevant reading for young women who could admit (as I had not quite been able to do, as a maiden) an interest in themselves as women.

Every English major knows the novel has been involved with women since the novel began. There have been great women novelists, and more not-so-great ones, and there have been even more novels about women. Innumerable women have bought, borrowed, and read novels, and novels, in return, have determined women's lives. Generations of girls who did not read much of anything else, whose experience was limited by education, opportunity, and convention, have gone to fiction to escape a stifling or a boring or a confusingly chaotic reality, and have come back with structures they use to organize and interpret their feelings and prospects. Girls have rushed right from novels, headlong and hopeful, into what they took to be happy endings: the advice they have given their friends, their gossip about their enemies, their suspicions and interpretations of the actions of others, and their notions about themselves have run along lines derived from fiction. Women who read have been inclined since the eighteenth century to understand one another, and men, and themselves, as characters in novels.

Of course men have also read fiction, and have been affected by what they read. But for women, I think, novels have been particularly preoccupying. Girls have learned from novels about the most important things in their lives, sexual and personal relations, in training for marriage, "the one great profession open to our class since the dawn of time," as Virginia Woolf described it, "the art of choosing the human being with whom to live life successfully." The disciplines that might prepare them for such an art or profession were not taught in schools (when girls went to school)—except, of course, in those too-warm classrooms where a young woman might encounter a master who would thrillingly respond as she did to language, and there the ground would shift perilously from literature to life, as it did for Charlotte Brontë when she fell in love in Brussels with M. Héger.

The classic English novels that center on heroines confronting a specifically female destiny seem to me singularly worth rereading at a time when women's "role models" and options are subjects of discussion. These novels do not merely contribute to the discussion of woman's place and nature: they have wise or provocative things to say about the whole phenomenon of thinking simultaneously about what it is to be a woman and how to choose what and who and how to be. The novel about a chaste heroine and her gender-determined destiny raises and ponders such still-pressing questions as whether intimacy and identity can be achieved at once, and whether they are mutually exclusive, entirely desirable, and, indeed, other than imaginary. It explores the connections between the inner self and its outward manifestations—between the personal and the social, the private and the public—by focusing on a woman complexly connected to others, who must depend, to distinguish herself, on the gender that delimits her life. The protagonist of the classic English novel is at the center of a web of questions about how much her fate is just a woman's, or characteristically a heroine's, or authentically her own. Her self-consciousness is compelling because it mirrors the posture of the reader who looks in a novel for a coherent image of herself. The operative fantasy dominating both reader and novel, I think, is of becoming a heroine.

To want to become a heroine, to have a sense of the possibility of being one, is to develop the beginnings of what feminists call a "raised" consciousness: it liberates a woman from feeling (and therefore perhaps from being) a victim or a dependent or a drudge, someone of no account. The domestic novel can be credited with strengthening and shaping the female reader's aspirations to matter, to make something special of herself. But the self-consciousness that novels encourage has its own dangers. The idea of becoming a heroine, which can organize the self, can also enclose it. In the interest of order and beauty and even truth, it can lie. I think the image of the heroine is worth examining right now because it makes multiple contradictory suggestions about the illusion of an ideal feminine self.

My approach to the subject of women and novels is on the one hand unorthodox and on the other old-fashioned. The impulse behind this book, and the mode of it—the splicing together of autobiographical and literary-critical discourse—could not have been without the contemporary feminist movement. My ideas developed in the climate of opinion it warmed; I have read feminist criticism with interest and profit. But I make no attempt to articulate a theory or to follow a particular method of feminist criticism here. And while the novels about heroines I have chosen to write about compose a sort of personal version of The Great Tradition, only in the fullest, most ambiguous sense of that word do I propose them as models. I have chosen these familiar texts because they are rich works of art that invite rereadings, and because they are books I think in terms of when I think about being a woman. They seem to me to be tied together by a set of themes and images that is suggestive about the relations of women with fictions, about women's inscription in language and literature. They are works written by both women and men; each centers on a single heroine's character and destiny. In their self-consciousness, I think, these classic heroine-centered novels comment on how literary conventions partly determine images of women in (and out of) literature.

Even I know that there are women who don't and never did read novels. They will probably not be interested in this book. But I think I am writing about them, too. An addiction to fiction, to getting as it were high on heroines, seems to me a metaphorical as well as an actual phenomenon. All women with a hungry susceptibility to a comprehensible self-image can be said to suffer from it. Of course men may, too; but—my subject being quite broad enough—I am not writing about men. Yet the truth is that while part of my intention is to warn women against the seductive idea of the heroine and to recommend to feminist attention insights developed through a rich literary tradition, I don't think mine a strictly feminine subject. Having the idea of becoming a heroine is a mode of self-awareness. I am writing about how the self and self-consciousness are mutually and problematically involved, and involved in literary form and in language.

The paradigmatic heroine of courtly love poetry and aristocratic romance is a creature of art and idea. She is unlike all other women, being important and unique, but she is also quintessentially feminine, therefore rightly representative of her sex. A paragon of paradoxes, she is both chaste and suggestive of erotic ecstasy, famous and private, embowered and imperiled; while she is pure idea, her outlines are hard and clear. Beautiful and virtuous as real people never are, she is the Ideal incarnate. Therefore, in romance, the Lover seeks her. He represents yearning, aspiring Man. In a novel, a "realistic" rewriting of romance, a conscious female protagonist takes the quester's place. It is a she who is the representative of searching humanity: and she also continues to represent the obscure and vulnerable beautiful ideal. In the woman-centered novel she represents specifically the ideal of the integral self. What the female protagonist of a traditional novel seeks—what the plot moves her toward—is an achieved, finished identity, realized in conclusive union with herself-as-heroine. Her marriage or death at the end of the narrative signifies this union. When he continued *Pamela* past the wedding, Samuel Richardson made the point that the aim of the female protagonist of a novel is not a husband but a realized identity, which is only real, for Pamela, when all the neighbors and their servants acknowledge her as her husband's wife.

The novel rose in England with a rising class that could neither simply accept nor simply repudiate the values of the aristocracy it sought to replace. Middle-class eighteenth-century writers were disposed to inquire into, to weigh, to adapt old values, to measure the distances between old ideals and the new realities they saw and made, and ultimately to posit their kind of literary discrimination, their own language, as a value. The power of the rising class was linked to the new power of the press: it matters that the author of *Pamela* was a printer, whose first published work was a collection of model letters that told the literate but socially maladroit what was the right thing to write on various social occasions. The young, beautiful, virtuous model heroines of Richardson's novels are also model letter-writers. The heroine of the middle-class novel is designed to appeal to readers who are suspicious but also envious of aristocratic ideals. While the heroine of romance stands for a spiritual absolute, the novel heroine figures in a critical inquiry into absolutes. Sensitivity and self-awareness, energy, a fine ear for language and its ambiguities, and a keen wit distinguish her. With them she wrestles with the idea of becoming a heroine; ultimately they make her one. Her vivid inner life, her quickness, and her way with words equip the bourgeois heroine to represent process and suspicion of appearances. What real power she has derives from her ability to recognize and to deal well with fictions. But in the critical act of becoming a heroine, she perfects herself into art, out of life.

The woman-centered novel in the Richardsonian tradition claims to be realistic, but in effect it contradicts itself when it makes a woman and her inner life central as they are not, in fact, in the bourgeois real world—but as they are in aristocratic romance. This paradox reflects and generates others involved in becoming a heroine. The novel heroine is both a representation (a girl trembling on the brink of a sexual and moral decision) and a metaphor (for an erotic-moral-aesthetic-psychological ideal). She is not only a believable image of a person but also the image of an ideal. This is emphasized when she is identified with art, with the novel which often bears her name. In her metaphorical aspect, a heroine stands for an integral self that can be located, defined, defended. This image is outlined by the story about how her self is realized. Therefore there is often some irony involved in the relationship of the novel heroine to her story. The self-awareness that makes her see herself as other—as a heroine—leads her to choose a fate that, while perfectly a heroine's, is rather too simplifying to be perfectly hers. This irony makes the reader have a pleasant (as in *Pride and Prejudice*) or (as in *The Portrait of a Lady*) an uncomfortable consciousness of what completeness implies when her story ends. The heroine's achievement of a coherent, integral self must be critically regarded by the reader, who is invited by a "realistic" fiction to weigh and measure whether such a thing is a real possibility.

In one sense this doubleness of a novel heroine is perfectly obvious. Every good reader recognizes a heroine as a representation of an actual woman and, at the same time, as an element in a work of art. She does not regard a woman in a novel as if she were one of her acquaintances; she experiences how the context of the fiction limits a character's freedom and determines her style. "I don't see how you can call Elizabeth Bennet a sensible girl," a young student said to me recently. "I mean, she's marrying Darcy and she hardly knows him, she's never even slept with the guy." My student's approach to Elizabeth is clearly naïve: everyone over twenty knows that for girls like Elizabeth in Jane Austen's day it was neither usual nor acceptable to sleep with the guy first. And that is clear to a good reader of *Pride and Prejudice* even if she knows nothing at all about Jane Austen's day: not Elizabeth's character but the novel's makes that much clear. The reader identifies with Elizabeth, and as she does so accepts the rules involved in being Elizabeth, and at the same time she sees how the rules determine that Elizabeth be as she is—not merely the rules of the society Jane Austen's novel represents, but also the rules that govern the representation of it, the novel. Elizabeth Bennet marries, in other words, because marrying was all a girl of her time and class could do, and because she loves Mr. Darcy, and also because the novel requires that she marry. Reading well, we read Elizabeth not only as a representation of a person but also as the creature of a romantic novel.

The idea of the heroine haunts the novel because aristocratic romance haunts it: the "realism" the early novelists boasted of is a matter of observing the real effects of romance, and of such romantic fantasies as the illusion of a self. When it shows how people around her see a heroine in simplifying conventional terms, and how she herself sees herself that way, the novel takes up the subject of the effects on real people of images. It is an important subject. No need to invoke the true stories of those tragic Victorian murderesses enraged by life's failure to live up to romantic fictions: literature, clearly, directly influences life. The history of women has been seriously affected by the history of the novel. Many writers have complained that novel-readers have been distracted from the affairs of a man's world, and lulled into "feminine" passivity, and spoiled by impossible visions of gentleman lovers. I think we have been affected most deeply by the tantalizing, misleading illusion of the self perfected through a resolution of the female destiny—by the idea of becoming a heroine. The novels I discuss simultaneously generate and anatomize this illusion.

Young women like to read about heroines in fiction so as to rehearse possible lives and to imagine a woman's life as important—because they want to be attractive and powerful and significant, someone whose life is worth writing about, whose world revolves around her and makes being the way she is make sense. The reader can see a heroine of a novel and be her, too, as she wishes she could simultaneously be and critically see herself. Richardson held the mirror up to this in his great second novel, *Clarissa*, which is about a girl's dying to be a heroine or, as he calls it, an exemplar to her sex. Read right, *Clarissa* brilliantly contradicts itself, giving both a model for readers to imitate and a tragic account of the destiny of a girl who aimed to enclose herself within a model self. The reader of *Clarissa* is forced to measure the distances between the character, who is a fictitious representation of a young woman, and the heroine, the exemplar, whom the young woman tries to become.

It is traditional for women in fiction to be aware of images of women, and of their power. Chaucer's feisty Wife of Bath observed long ago that women in literature influence the attitudes and behavior of readers, which was why she ripped the offending leaves out of her husband's book, an antimarriage manual warning against wicked, worthless wives. The effect of novel heroines on women readers is a comic subject in Charlotte Lennox's *The Female Quixote* (1752), E. S. Barrett's *The Heroine* (1815), and Jane Austen's *Northanger Abbey* (1818), novels about girls who confuse literature and life, and aim to become heroines like those they have read about. These novels satirize the grandiose aspirations of ordinary girls, and echo moralists' attacks on fiction for misleading readers, even while they exploit the novel's potential for being entertaining as well as instructive, and mimic as they mock romance. A woman's desire to be a heroine is less explicit but equally important, I think, in nonparodic woman-centered fiction, where the protagonist's circumscription in an ideal self and a preordained plot is presented as problematic or ironic—that is, in the self-consciousness of the novel.

Feminists today are interested in the mutual modifications of images and truths, ideals and society, literature and life, prejudice and pride: there is much to learn about these matters from the realistic novel, which invites awareness of how they change and shape one another. This awareness can, I think, help one avoid an obscure, present danger. When feminists (like many others) idealize a fully articulated meaningful identity, they often end by redefining "exemplary" instead of examining the idea of an exemplar. The best novels in the self-conscious Richardsonian tradition subtly caution against the habit of assessing women in literary terms, as heroines. Readers who do that today generally do not idealize virtuous virgins, but instead measure women with a yardstick marked off in degrees of achieved fulfillment, or identify the essentially feminine with "hunger, rebellion, and rage," in Matthew Arnold's words about Charlotte Brontë—with desire, in more fashionable terms, and subversiveness. To do this is to invert the old order in which Woman was identified with artistic decorum and genteel good form; but it is to continue to insist on a fantastic feminine absolute. The self-reflexive heroine-centered novel usefully explores the paradoxes involved in pursuing such an objectified, coherent, gender-based, essential self. It makes the reader feel the seductive power of this idea, and it also encourages analysis of it. Adrienne Rich has reiterated one of Henry James's favorite ideas, revision, and redefined it as a feminist project, arguing that women must re-read, re-see, re-vise. As novels acknowledge that the heroine's importance, and character, and fate are determined by the book she inhabits, they too encourage re-vision, and make subtly revisionary suggestions about real women and the fictions that are the matrix of their lives. The implicit message of the heroine-centered novel is double: the novel proposes a sophisticated version of the ideal of romance as the heroine comes to transcendent closure, but that ideal is undercut as transcendence and closure are characterized as romantic, as proper to Art, not Life.

About George Eliot's heroines, Virginia Woolf wrote that "the ancient consciousness of women, charged with suffering and sensibility, and for so many ages dumb, seems in them to have brimmed and overflowed and uttered a demand for something—they scarcely know what—for something that is perhaps incompatible with the facts of human existence." The heroine figure in literature is traditionally a metaphor for "something that is perhaps incompatible with the facts of human existence," an ideal or a romantic or a literary value; when the exquisite consciousnesses of novel heroines brim and overflow and simultaneously seem to utter "a demand for something—they scarcely know what," they represent both transcendence and the desire for transcendence. We find this moving, I think, because it reflects our own condition—the state of the reader reading. Like Charlotte Lennox's Arabella and Richardson's Clarissa, the reader feels for, and feels her distance from, the literary-feminine ideal she confronts. Reading about heroines, one experiences the double jeopardy of Jane Austen's Catherine Morland, who foolishly imagined herself a heroine, and even more foolishly believed she could entertain the real evils of a woman's situation as if they could only threaten someone else—in safety, as if she were reading a novel. In her doubleness, as she coexists with the illusion of her more coherent self's metaphorical meaning, the novel heroine is a clue to the novel-reader's state of mind.

I am not sure if it is possible to distinguish between the ancient consciousness of women and the consciousness that has been imagined to be theirs. I am not sure, therefore, whether feminist critics can succeed in the aim of defining the shape of the distinctively feminine sentence, and the tone of the female voice uttering what has been unutterable. Novels imply—and so do the best critics—that this will require not a new language or a literature freed of convention, but a language and literature expressive of a keen critical awareness of language and convention, and of their links with gender. Possibly, as Nancy K. Miller has suggested, the distinctively female text is characterized by an idiosyncratically feminine emphasis or inflection—the sign of an ironic apprehension of conventional concepts of character and plot.

The works I discuss here are novels in English by both men and women. Except for *The Portrait of a Lady*, they are English novels; except for *Mrs. Dalloway*, they were written in the eighteenth and nineteenth centuries. Their remoteness in time and place—the foreignness of the novel world—is important to my argument. For my American reader's sense of the necessary Englishness of English novels is a part of my subject: the best way I know to characterize it is to point to my inclusion of Henry James only— that is to say, not even of Edith Wharton. My first, autobiographical introductory chapter encourages the reader *not* to avert her eyes politely from the discrepancy between the genteel society the novels present as normal and the place where I have read them, in the course of my life in the twentieth century in New York City. That irony seemed right to start off with, in a book about the relationship of "real" character to "mere" fiction. There is another irony, or half one, implicit in my organization. Although the novels are discussed in the order of their appearance in the world, this is not a chronological study of development. I am not attempting to trace the growth of the English novel or the English heroine, any more than I am trying to detail the fatal consequences of girlish literary dreams of Being Perfect, of Getting Married, of Thinking It Over and seeing the grand design of one's life clearly making sense. On the contrary, I insist on the power of unchanged images, and their influence on becoming. My discussions of novels are meant to describe a circle. Richardson's *Clarissa*, the first work I consider, is about a girl who is too good, too beautiful, too exquisitely conscious, too perfectly symbolic of perfection, to be happy on earth; the heroine of *The Portrait of a Lady*, the subject of my last chapter but one, is gifted and burdened like Clarissa by a heroine's appearance and assets. Between Richardson's time and James's the idea of the heroine was much explored in English fiction. Redefining the terms by positing perfection as the couple and not the maiden, Jane Austen could substitute (ambiguously) marriage for death as the promised end a heroine is made for. Charlotte Brontë's protofeminist *Villette* deliberately rejects the idea of the novel heroine; George Meredith's pseudofeminist *The Egoist* archly revises it, by rewriting the courtship plot; George Eliot's *Daniel Deronda* ponders the heroine's meaning and importance by placing its female protagonist in a broader context than the one a heroine conventionally dominates, and giving her only half a novel to queen it over. Virginia Woolf's *Mrs. Dalloway*, as I read it, looks retrospectively at the tradition of the novel and its heroine.

There are other English novels that have heroines at their centers. Some of them are very different from the novels I write about, and some (*Middlemarch*, for instance) are arguably better books. I have chosen novels that develop the ideas about heroines that interest me. And I talk about myself, to begin with, so as to admit outright that that interests me, and to suggest that some of my interpretations have been determined by my life at least as much as my life has been determined by novels. My first chapter acknowledges that what Freud nicely termed "the family romance"—the fantasy of being the son or daughter of royalty, in other words a more special person of a higher social class—is involved in the appetite for romances. By starting off with a sketch of where I come from, I also want to emphasize that the idea of becoming a heroine is private and personal, and to insist that just as realistic novels depend on real life, life may depend on novels.

# PART ONE

## Being Perfect

# ⟨ 1 ⟩

# My Life in Fiction

Of all the departments in literature, fiction is the one to which, by nature and circumstances, women are best adapted.

—G. H. Lewes,
"The Lady Novelists"

The good ended happily, and the bad unhappily. That is what Fiction means.

—Miss Prism, in
*The Importance of Being Earnest*

In my house novels were *weibische sachen*, women's things. My father used to read Gibbon, Churchill, the paper, while my mother read a good book. My brother was to be a scientist but I was to major in English, which is not too dangerously far from typing (words on paper, after all), because literature is the high road to assimilation, because culture is okay for the Jewish wife-in-training, because poetry is decorative and harmless, but more profoundly because novels are for women. Most novels. Of course my father's face darkened with respect at the names Tolstoy, Dostoevski, and Mann. Over Balzac, Flaubert—maybe Dickens—he supposed men and women might sometimes meet. But George Eliot? Henry James? Charlotte Brontë and Jane Austen? Kathleen Winsor and Margaret Mitchell? The distinction is made with words like "serious." Women and Englishmen, from my father's Austro-Hungarian perspective, were not serious.

He was an underachieving businessman who cheered himself up by explaining why Rome (also) fell, an armchair philosopher and a connoisseur of hard facts, and deep inside him lived a frustrated foxhunter. He very much admired the English. His attitude toward women, whom he affected to despise, was more complicated than he let on. My father assumed that Thackeray and Henry James were not serious, were not for him, but he thought they were subtle and sensitive and other good things. They were The Finer Things. Dostoevski, whose subjects were lust and hatred, jealousy and greed, wrote about what my father considered The Facts. The English novelists wrote, he supposed, about delicate and elevated feelings, the feelings women have or should have: social, not religious, ecstasies. A misconception, you say, and you are right. But it is also true that reading Henry James, that not-English apogee of English novelists, inspired in me a passion for a social life of complex and rarefied meaning. This aspiration my father dimly imagined to be British, frivolous, feminine, unrealistic, but commendable, an excellent, even a necessary thing in a woman. For while men studied the tragic course of history and read the novelists who revealed the horrors that underlie it, women had to keep alive that aspiration toward Fineness without which both the pleasantness and meaning of private life would disappear. My father luxuriated in his tragic vision from the depths of a doilied armchair. My mother, he vaguely presumed, plumped up the cushions, crocheted and disposed the doilies, because of a countervision of coherence and comfort he needed her to continue to have. He was not wrong to think she derived some of her respect for the value of private life from her novelists.

Susan Ferrier (an English woman) wrote a novel called *Marriage* in 1818, and prefaced it with this epigraph from Dr. Johnson (an English man):

Life consists not of a series of illustrious actions; the greater part of our time passes in compliance with necessities—in the performance of daily duties—in the removal of small inconveniencies—in the procurement of petty pleasures; and we are well or ill at ease, as the main stream of life glides on smoothly, or is ruffled by small and frequent interruption.

A sentiment to which my father would subscribe. On the one hand, there is the important world of "illustrious actions," to which his heart thrilled but from which his false friend History had barred him; that world is grand, male, and real. On the other hand, there is ordinary life, and ordinary life is all most of us have. That is the life novels describe, and by giving it form and connecting it with dreams, they make it extraordinary—something no man with visions of Higher Things would stoop to do but something any sensible man is happy to have someone else do, while she's doing for him generally.

So this Jewish daughter listened to her father and became an English major at about eleven. (My neighbors gave to "English major" the stresses proper to, say, "French lieutenant.")

Reading the novels of Henry James at fifteen I experienced a miracle. Behind the locked bathroom door, sitting on the terry-cloth-covered toilet seat, I was transformed into someone older, more beautiful and graceful. I moved subtly among people who understood delicate and complex webs of feeling, patterned perceptions altogether foreign to my crude "real" life. Mealtimes, encounters, conversations were precisely as significant in James's world as they were insignificant in mine; and as I read more and more novels, what happened in my actual family came to seem less and less important. My parents were proud of my reading and encouraged it, but I knew this was because they were ignorant of what I felt while I read. For commitment to the world of Henry James—a world ineffably *goyish*—was betrayal of them. I hugged my secret knowledge that they were harboring a viper in their bathroom.

Not until I was twenty did I find out that *The Wings of the Dove* is about money; God knows what I thought it was about.

All I knew was that its world was the antithesis of the vulgar one in which I was eating lamb chops and mashed potatoes, overhearing gossip about my aunts in Yiddish, fighting with my brother, and going to school. That my father connected reading Henry James with going to school—that he sanctioned it—was an aspect of the central Miracle in the Bathroom in which I turned into Isabel or Kate or Milly. It enabled me to betray him in safety. We lived in a small apartment; in novels I had a universe, not just a room of my own. I remember knowing I was lucky in having two worlds at once. I could relish my lamb chops as Milly Theale never could hers, and at the same time I could be Milly. I, not she, seemed to me the great creation of Henry James.

The English novelists cannot be said to inflame the girlish heart to rebellion. But they do move the mind to make and to value such distinctions as put one's family in its place. Learning from novels about life and love and goodness and beauty, I learned at the same time the difference between a gentleman and a man whose father was in trade, between a lady and the niece of an earl, and these points seemed implicated in the abstractions. English novelists flatter the reader by assuming she has a sense of class distinctions and their importance, even a sense of their being—in their subtler ramifications—a little absurd. "English fiction without the nieces of Earls and the cousins of Generals would be an arid waste," Virginia Woolf wrote. "It would resemble Russian fiction. It would have to fall back upon the immensity of the soul and upon the brotherhood of man."

In the 1950s, when we were both undergraduates at Columbia, my brother spent a lot of time complaining that he was not Prince Hamlet nor was meant to be. I was envious because I couldn't say that without sounding grotesque, and there was no analogous quotation available. What wrung those lines from my brother's lips, in addition to the desire to show he knew them, was of course a feeling that he *had* been meant to be Prince Hamlet, and that circumstances beyond his control, unkinder than the circumstances beyond Hamlet's, made it impossible. A college boy in the 1950s had not even the faded possibilities of Julien Sorel, but he did have Julien to be rueful over, and the phrase about Hamlet, and anti-heroes were coming out as fast as Anchor Books. I rifled the library but found no specific image I could mention to accommodate me. To claim Elizabeth Bennet outright seemed unbecoming.

I never took a course in The Novel. Too snobbish. In the bathroom I moved from Thomas B. Costain to Henry James; because I was an English major I could delight in doing what I pleased. I could gobble up *Forever Amber* without feeling too sinful (it was literature in a way, therefore required). I could allow myself three bathroom readings of *Gone with the Wind*. But on the outside I had to prove that studying English literature was not just loving novels and gossiping about the characters in them. (Graduate students argue the question of Mr. Knightley's sex appeal as if he had made them a proposition. Gossip, like novels, is a way of turning life into story. Good gossip approximates art; criticism of novels is mostly gossip.*) By my sophomore year in college I already had myself a century, the solid eighteenth. Impressed with the New Criticism, I concentrated on the ambiguities of poetry, on the theory of satire, but not on novels. Fielding was fun, and Fanny Burney was background, but Pope and Swift were compellingly other, lean and clean and demanding and available to the kind of analysis academics respected. I read *Clarissa* and was strangely moved—and I moved away. I was to be a professional, and *The Memoirs of Martinus Scriblerus* was much more the right sort of thing.

As a specialist in Augustan satire, I could read a lot, stay long in libraries, get good grades, and be in the company of serious men. All of which I loved. I could look like a lady to my father,

---

* See, *e.g.*, William Wordsworth to R. P. Gillies, 25 April 1815: "Infinitely the best part of *Waverley* is the pictures of Highland manners at MacIvor's castle, and the delineation of his character, which are done with great spirit. The Scotch baron, and all the circumstances in which he is exhibited, are too peculiar and *outré*. Such caricatures require a higher condiment of humour to give them a relish than the author of *Waverley* possesses. But too much of this gossip."

and unknown to him be engaged in something that my false fathers, my professors, deemed as serious as science, or nearly. My father could suspect this (which pleased him, for he didn't want his daughter to be like all the other women) and still avoid owning up to a daughter's unseemly professionalism.

Behind the arras of my seriousness, however, I was depriving myself of air, the breath of my life: novels.

There are many heroines of novels who read, with intensity, about heroines. Consider Rachel Vinrace in *The Voyage Out* (1915), Virginia Woolf's first novel. Rachel, whose forty-year-old sophisticated aunt, Helen, can "hardly restrain herself from saying out loud what she thought of a man who brought up his daughter so that at the age of twenty-four she scarcely knew that men desired women and was terrified by a kiss," begins under the tutelage of the aunt to learn about life. She goes to South America, and meets men; she also reads fiction, this way:

> her eyes were concentrated almost sternly upon the page, and from her breathing, which was slow but repressed, it could be seen that her whole body was constrained by the working of her mind. At last she shut the book sharply, lay back, and drew a deep breath, expressive of the wonder which always marks the transition from the imaginary world to the real world.
>
> "What I want to know," she said aloud, "is this: What is the truth? What's the truth of it all?" She was speaking partly as herself, and partly as the heroine of the play she had just read. The landscape outside, because she had seen nothing but print for the space of two hours, now appeared amazingly solid and clear, but although there were men on the hill washing the trunks of olive trees with a white liquid, for the moment she herself was the most vivid thing in it—an heroic statue in the middle of the foreground, dominating the view. Ibsen's plays always left her in that condition. She acted them for days at a time, greatly to Helen's amusement; and then it would be Meredith's turn and she

became Diana of the Crossways. But Helen was aware that it was not all acting, and that some sort of change was taking place in the human being.

Rachel is given a copy of *Persuasion* by a Mrs. Dalloway, and she cannot get through the Gibbon she is loaned by a young man who seeks to educate and/or taunt her: the conventional lines between men and women, fact and fiction, are clearly drawn in the background. The description of Rachel reading, however, is of something strange: when she looks up from the page her own image nearly obliterates her view of the world; she speaks (to herself) partly as herself and partly as the heroine she has become; her aunt sees that her acting effects as well as reflects some sort of change in her from an unformed girl to a person with a decided identity. Chaperoned by her aunt, Rachel has opportunities to stay out late and speak intimately with young men, opportunities that heroines of nineteenth-century fiction lacked. But even in 1915 she learns about life partly by doing mysterious solitary researches into her own importance by becoming, as she reads fiction, a heroine. It is a crucial stage in the young woman's coming of age.

In Anthony Trollope's *Can You Forgive Her?* (1864–65), Alice Vavasor cannot decide to marry the man she loves and is engaged to because "she had gone on thinking of the matter till her mind had become filled with some undefined idea of the importance to her of her own life." The issue of marrying has made her life seem too important to be determined by that issue's resolution. Analyzing the problem, Trollope blends Alice's thoughts with his own: "What should a woman do with her life? There had arisen round her a flock of learned ladies asking that question, to whom it seems that the proper answer has never yet occurred." He is unsympathetic with feminists, the "learned ladies," and Alice herself is no feminist. Still, the question of the relationship of feminism to Alice's predicament must occur. This is because Alice's idea, the idea of her own importance to herself, is a basis of feminism. In her world, women are supposed to subordinate themselves gladly to men, to renounce, to please, to find their importance only as it is reflected by another's choice, approval, esteem, love. Alice's presumption in becoming "filled with some undefined idea of the importance *to her* of her own life" is protofeminist, at least.

Trollope makes a little speech about the importance of a woman's life as he sees it:

> A woman's life is important to her,—as is that of a man to him,—not chiefly in regard to that which she shall do with it. The chief thing for her to look to is the manner in which that something shall be done. It is of moment to a young man when entering life to decide whether he shall make hats or shoes; but not of half the moment that will be that other decision, whether he shall make good shoes or bad. And so with a woman;—if she shall have recognized the necessity of truth and honesty for the purposes of her life, I do not know that she need ask herself many questions as to what she will do with it.

But the reason Alice is making a fuss about whom to marry is that she has suddenly "recognized the necessity of truth and honesty for the purposes of her life." As she jilts the man she is attracted to and engages herself to another man, she seems deliberately to deny that marriage is a sexual choice, denying her own sexual feelings. Marriage presents itself to Alice as a moral question. Trollope's condescending comparison of a woman to a young man about to decide whether to make hats or shoes, rather than to a young man of Alice's own class, is perhaps a clue to his confusion. His Alice is rich and independent. She is not obliged to marry for the reasons that force young men to make either hats or shoes, good or bad. What obliges her to make a decision that will once for all determine her life and its character, and her own character, too, is not economic necessity, or biology, or even social convention. The only reason Alice must marry is that she must decide how and who to be once for all; it is about time for her to do so; and to marry is the only decision she can make.

Of *Can You Forgive Her?*, Henry James snorted, "Of course, and forget her too." He was right: Alice is not at the novel's center and therefore the importance of her life, that very importance which she has just discovered and found so awesome, is unconvincing. Trollope is not convinced of it, and we, as we read about Alice, do not believe she is important, either. One big reason for this is that Trollope's novel has three courtship plots, not one. The heroine-centered novel that makes what James called an "ado" about the disposition of a girl's life affirms her importance as *Can You Forgive Her?* cannot. The novel that centers on a single heroine and her deciding whom to marry always implies it is important to decide carefully, and possible to choose correctly, and that a lot depends on deciding.

It is much easier to say why girls gobble up gothics than to explain their passion for Jane Austen. The tallness and darkness of Darcy and Knightley are for the most part left to a reader's imagination. Yet young women devour those cool novels; they rush through them in something like suspense. I pretended I wasn't doing that; I pretended I wasn't really hot to be as cool as Jane Austen, cool as reading Jane Austen made me feel; I pretended to have been cool all along, cool to the core, cover to cover.

For years I made a crude distinction between emotional, sloppy-minded people (female) who read love stories for emotional reasons, and the rational sorts like me. Not only were the novels I and the others read very different, I grandly supposed; the natures of our appetites for novels were, too. In the process of defining my self through fictitious women, I imagined that what I chose to read, the reasons for the choices, and whatever lay behind the reasons were as different from most girls' as Austen was different from Charlotte Brontë, Elizabeth Bennet from Jane Eyre. The image of the passionate heroine suits girls who feel they are better than others because they are kinder and more sensitive and maybe even crazier, because of private characteristics that cannot be tested for. I was good at tests; my heroine was Elizabeth Bennet. This may have had something to do with *Pride and Prejudice*'s being—my friend D. contributes the thought—Jane Austen's Jewish novel. He means by this that contemporary American Jewish writers have claimed the theme of the bright young person stuck, as Elizabeth is, in an uncontrollable, embarrassing family, helplessly loyal to it and defensively aware that the mandatory escape from its suffocating confines will look to an observer like social climbing. Not to mention Mrs. Bennet's commitment to getting her daughters married, or Mr. Bennet's tired, passive, amused detachment in his library.

I was determined to be a comic, not a tragic, heroine. It was logical: I liked to make jokes and I wanted to be happy. To be a heroine and happy, too, seemed to be the perfect blend of art and life. At college a boyfriend and I played Benedick and Beatrice. Freshmen flocked to hear our witty exchanges in the cafeteria; in secret there was love-talk, but audiences drew out the rapiers of our wits, and we were Man and Woman, antagonists. In graduate school an avuncular professor pitted me against another boyfriend by setting us up in a seminar argument about—what else?—women and comedy.

The comic heroine has it all over the tragic: she is applauded for venting a lot of nastiness, and no matter how sharp her tongue she gets the best man in the end, contradicting my mother, who claimed I'd never get married if I didn't stop making wisecracks. Although the heroine's great wit might seem to scare all men, it actually frightens off only the ones you wouldn't want. It tests men, like Portia's caskets in *The Merchant of Venice*; it is armor against fools. I placed more confidence in my wit than ever beauty was fool enough to vest in her body, and I never thought it vanity. The comedies I read, about Millamant and Célimène, Rosalind and Beatrice, confirmed my rightness. A Misanthrope, an Alceste who would have been her best accolade, is of course incorrigible; but Benedicks succumb. That comedies traditionally end in marriage was, to my mind, altogether on comedy's side.

I remember a lecture Professor Gilbert Highet gave at Barnard when I was an undergraduate. Among the things he said was that women cannot understand tragedy, and to prove it he conjectured that when Penelope looked round at the bodies of all the slain suitors, she knew all wasn't over, because the potential for new life was within her. Of course it was not possible at Barnard in the 1950s to question the probability of parthenogenesis in Greek ladies of a certain age, or for that matter immaculate conception, religion and sex being out of bounds in the College Parlor on Thursdays at noon, when the lunchtime lectures had a faint but distinct classy Protestant flavor. Not that I, in the flowering of my Comic Heroinism, would want to raise such questions. The Anthon Professor's words fell like fertilizer from heaven into the furrows of my earthy brain: women cannot comprehend tragedy, they are the agents of comedy. That's me.

In his *Essay on Comedy*, George Meredith identifies woman with the comic spirit, and says that comedy comes close to being the essence of civilization itself. With spectacular British snobbishness, he opines, "There has been fun in Bagdad. But there never will be civilization where comedy is not possible; and that comes of some degree of social equality of the sexes." Dizzy with delight, I read and reread Meredith's best novel, *The Egoist*, not because I felt for the heroine who agonizes in the egoist's embrace, but because I felt with Meredith, the wit who saw through Willoughby the Insufferable Man. He mocks him as only he or a woman could:

"Laetitia Dale!" he said. He panted. "Your name is sweet English music! And you are well?" The anxious question permitted him to read deeply in her eyes. He found the man he sought there, squeezed him passionately, and let her go.

*The Egoist* was hard to find then, and few of my friends could tolerate its stylistic excesses. But every girl I knew knew Jane

Austen. Jane Austen, chaste and clear, herself seemed to us a comic heroine. To take her view of life was to transcend life, to float far above a woman's place, inflated by irony. Like Beatrice, Jane Austen translated vitality into reason, wit, language. The six novels are about girls who must choose, by a single decision, how to make femaleness the foundation of a life: which man to marry. By linking her life to a man's, the heroine defines her singularity. By reconciling opposites, transforming the complex into the simple—by marrying, in other words—she makes herself all she is, complete. Reading Jane Austen, you believe it can happen to you; you believe you can watch while it does; you believe it is worth writing a book about. You may even go so far as to imagine you can write it.

The ruling fiction goes that when the right man proposes, and she accepts, a girl is set right; it unnaturally follows that when the wrong man does, and she rejects him, she is somehow in the wrong. Jane Austen's Emma, forced to hear the presumptuous proposals of the Rev. Mr. Elton, realizes she has misled him and suffers painful remorse; Elizabeth Bennet, who has been too amused by Mr. Collins, is punished by having to endure his proposals. Eleanor Bold of Trollope's *Barchester Towers* recognizes when the deplorable Mr. Slope asks her to marry him that her refusal to join the general league against him was interpreted as a sexual invitation. Novelists agree that from a man's petition that she marry him a woman learns to know herself.

My first semester at college I got two proposals of marriage, perhaps only half-serious and yet made, distressingly, as if they were not unimaginable. I felt guilty, not for rejecting them but for allowing them to happen. One hidden ruling fiction is that women are the shapers as well as the shapes of men's desire. Both boys were a few inches taller than I, and entirely presentable. As they proposed I saw myself: middle-sized, plausibly an embryo wife. If I had known the later usage of the word I would have realized I had to change my style; but I would have rejected such an idea as hypocritical. I was fanatically natural. I wore the clothes my mother picked off the racks in her flying visits to Ohrbach's because I was above troubling with clothes; if it had occurred to me that mine clearly marked me as my mother's daughter, a middle-class girl from the borough of Queens, I would have scorned the idea of pretending to be richer or poorer, uglier or prettier, more or less intellectual or "arty," as we said then. Like every heroine worth a novel, I deplored tricking men by artifice, looking like what I was not; but it was confusing to learn that if I did what was easiest and most natural, I was per-force engaged in masquerade. If they had been aware of the real me, I knew, those two boys would not have proposed; they would have been horrified; they would have known what I had most prominently in my mind was mockery, derision of all they held sacred.

In terror, after a while, I got around to pretending: it seemed most honest to pretend to be anonymous. I wore a black tur-tleneck, black skirt, black stockings, black shoes, and a black coat, occasionally enlivened by something gray. The man who recognized me would prove it, I figured, by seeing through my cloud; noticed, found, recognized in spite of all I could do to prevent it, I would assume the true form of my self. It was much easier to disabuse Lotharios of the notion that I was morbid and suffering than it was to convince nice boys I was made for some-thing more than moving hand in hand with them from the Dean's List to the altar and on to the suburbs.


Every heroine worth a hero has "a collection of views on the subject of marriage" rather like those of Isabel Archer: "The first on the list was a conviction of the vulgarity of thinking too much of it." But marriage, nevertheless, is inescapably the subject in view. James says Isabel affronts her destiny; a simpler point to make is that she is affronted by it.


"Get married, Antigone!" Peter Newman thundered sternly from Macmillan Theater's stage. Peter was a senior; the *Antigone* was

15

Anouilh's, perfect for 1956. The war was over, in Europe as in Thebes; Eisenhower was President; and the fashionable butt of campus sneerers at Columbia was the Citizenship Campaign, which was urging students to help the community. Ten years later, no one would remember Anouilh (is it fair to say not many would remember Antigone?), and students would have discovered their feelings of solidarity with their black and Puerto Rican neighbors. But in 1956 "community" was a laughably pious term, evoking Mom and Dad and Apple Pie, Grayson Kirk and Norman Rockwell and semiclassical music and Levittown. In our hearts we lived in Paris, my friends and I, thinking and inhaling deeply (Gitanes) at the Deux Magots, confronting Life. Retreat was what Peter Newman was advising Antigone, retreat to the suburbs.

The glib existentialism fashionable in my crowd was strongly infused with a sociological world view: while we scorned sociology as a discipline or a college course, we swallowed it whole. David Riesman, *The Lonely Crowd*. We laughed at joiners; it kept us joined. From our literature and history courses we learned the dangers of becoming part of a crowd, and how joining intensified existential loneliness. We talked laughingly, fearfully, about how it would be in ten years, when the boys would have been changed by their gray flannel suits and we by our kitchens, by diapers. We knew how the outer life wrecked the soul; we knew that if one gave in just a little, one slid all the way. We had also learned in literature classes that the mockers always end up mocked. Get married, Antigone, Creon was saying in scorn. Give up your heroics, your egotism. See where it got your brothers: dead, both of them, in spite of your nice distinction they're equally dead. And so will you be, Antigone, someday dead. So stop fighting me. I speak for the world. You know, there's something unprincipled in your passion for principles—something you yourself don't like about it. You're an intelligent girl, Antigone; I know you see my point.

His message sank in that night (I was reviewing the performance for the *Barnard Bulletin*) because Peter Newman was awfully good, because he happened to be engaged to my best friend, and because for all his rich, manly voice he sounded just like my mother. The reason he could sound just like her, this Creon-Peter, this young man, was that my mother had never made his point out loud. It was simply, completely, implied, had been from the beginning: I had to get married. It was as if I had got myself pregnant at nine, a unique ten-year pregnancy: just being a girl I was in trouble.

Marriage for the purpose of saving one's family's good name was not, of course, what Creon was advising Antigone, or what Peter was offering my friend. But that night, in my mind, they coalesced clearly. Creon's blunt, reasonable pragmatism was my mother's, and as he hustled the pleasant life he sounded like Peter, who I knew had in mind a succession of agreeable evenings in the embrace of the intellectual community, little gourmet dinners with imported wines and Bach on the record player. The tomb was what they were pushing, the lot of them. And Antigone was fighting to choose a tomb of her own. Peter Newman was never so seductive in real life as he was that night onstage; body and mind, I was with him; but it was Antigone I loved. I knew the actress only slightly; she looked intense and distraught and very private as she rushed to and from her classes; it made sense for her to be obsessed with burying her brother, just as it made sense that Peter Newman was pushing marriage. No, I was not with him at all, I loathed him, I was with Antigone, who wore black clothes just like mine, a Barnard girl in mourning for her life, weighing Creon's advice for her own reasons. Antigone knew life involved being *engagée*, involved in ultimate moral issues; she didn't give a fig for being lovely and engaged. But was it not, as Creon said, foolhardy, wrong, to martyr oneself for truth? Peter Newman had played in *Murder in the Cathedral* the previous semester, and advised that the greatest treason was to do the right thing for the wrong reason.

Submission to "The Right Thing"—what Creon, convention, and one's mother advised—was submission to tyranny; but wasn't one's own idea of right a tyrant, too? And what about the possibility of doing what everyone else did, but for different reasons? It began to seem impossible to number the temptations, or to distinguish one from another. Maybe the worst crime was taking your personal life seriously, thinking it was a suitable area for acting out moral issues, considering what you did with yourself as emblematic. Maybe that was the temptation.

Now, it seems to me, the tyranny was youth, the sense of one's whole life in one's hands and on them, of one's obligation to dispose it well. Ideally, one would be Simone de Beauvoir, smoking with Sartre at the Deux Magots, making an eccentric domestic arrangement that was secondary to important things and in their service. One would be poised, brilliant, equipped with a past, above the fray, beyond it, foreign not domestic. (And ideally Sartre would look like Albert Camus.) But being sophisticated, one was realistic. Perhaps it was the case that life always involved a trade-off. Public performance, I had learned at home, was payment for private pleasures: I had to get married in exchange for being allowed to read. (Other girls, my mother pointed out, were made to dry the dishes.) Why not trade with the world as Creon suggested? Get married and in secret keep your soul? It was embarrassing to claim your soul loud and clear, like Antigone; she was embarrassed, you could tell. Why not do what everyone did, but for one's own reasons?

They all agreed: Creon, speaking for the state (and the ancient Greeks, and the cynical French); my mother, for the Jews and the family; and Peter Newman, I suppose, for the Dean's List. On the other side were massed the forces of Emily Brontë. Heathcliff, in 1956, was as he always had been, dark and indefinably dissolute, angry and sullen; he drank Scotch and smoked a little reefer, when he could get it, and hung out with Negroes and homosexuals in the West End Bar. Sexually, he meant business. He was a writer. What you would be was his woman. You would get up in the morning, after going to bed with him in his apartment, and you would be able to say, like Cathy, "I am Heathcliff." No; you would write it, and then everyone else would say, "She is Heathcliff." If there was paper in the house. If he let you get out of bed. If there was a bed.

Heathcliff's father was a doctor or a lawyer up in Thrushcross Grange, Westchester County, but he stood, himself, for Morningside Heights—not Peter Newman's Morningside Heights, that jewel set in a metropolitan sea, that little Oxford, but a place of dark streets to wander anonymous among the freaks. Sullen at your side, he would nod to drunks and junkies, wild-haired girls collecting for their abortions, spaced-out math majors who slept all day and ate hamburgers at Riker's at night. Heathcliff's ex-girlfriend was a tormented wraith who murmured incomplete sentences in a breathless voice and never got anything in on time; her parents were divorced. She had trouble ordering lunch, made you feel big and hungry and garishly clear in the mind, too definite and grammatical. You wanted to be able to say, "I am Heathcliff's girlfriend," that was it. Or maybe, "I am Heathcliff's ex-girlfriend," having got initiation all over with.

I had stories in my head long before I learned to read—a set of them, in fact, which together, like a novel, persuasively conveyed the sense of a whole lost world. It was radically different from the world of English novels, but like that world, it was very different from the America where I actually lived. The stories I heard as a child permanently colored my views, affected the way I came to read and to be. Like the novels I would read later on, they were all about the differences between fact and fantasy, and men and women. My mother's stories about her childhood were an important part of mine because they had the vivid details and the urgent, obscure moral burden of a novel, and because of their haunting frontispiece. A portrait of the central figure in the stories, my mother's grandmother, hung in our living room, presiding over my growing up.

She had to cross the border from Poland to Austria, or perhaps that year it was from Austria to Poland, in order to nurse a sick sister or daughter in a town twenty miles away. That was how it happened that my great-grandmother Brucha, in spite of the orthodox Jewish law against images, had her picture taken for a passport. A copy, enlarged and blue-tinted, hung like an icon over the couch. I say like an icon because when I first saw Russian icons the hooded Virgins reminded me of the photograph, and also because my mother's devotion to her grandmother's memory was religious. My great-grandmother Brucha haunted my childhood: sometimes the piercing light eyes seemed to follow me around the room, even into the next room, penetrating and knowing and measuring and judging. The face in the photograph is square, stern, and thin-lipped, wrapped in a babushka just far enough back on the head to show a slice of the satin she wore in place of her hair. Early on, of course, I thought it *was* her hair, perfectly smooth and gleaming, and its perfection scared me; the loose large knot of the kerchief under the chin was another place that some days throbbed with sinister power. I used to look through my lashes into the light, and imagine the shadow-circled motes of dust drifting down were the spirits of the dead. I would fear that my great-grandmother's might be one of them and that, happening by chance to fall here and not in China, recognizing a great-grandchild, she would assume her earthly form, the face in the photograph. This transformation of the vaguely ovoid dead soul into a human shape was the scariest thing I could imagine. I imagined it frequently. My great-grandmother had been a famously good woman; not only my mother but second cousins and family friends talked of her with reverence and respect. But I imagined her as a chastening visitant, and I was terrified, not joyous, as my mother would have been, by the idea of her coming back.

My mother spoke of her grandmother—still speaks of her—at least five times a day: "As my grandmother used to say, . . ." It is usually a maxim, occasionally a trenchant bit of philosophic realism. She says that three times in her adult life, when she was in serious trouble, her grandmother appeared to her in a vision. Her grandmother brought my mother up, took her in as a child of two; she slept with her grandmother, in one bed. Her grandmother was a wise woman, whom people would wake in the night and take to save a choking baby: she would touch her fingers to two places on its throat and it would breathe easily again. She was a charitable woman: on Friday afternoons she filled her apron with challahs she had baked, and she walked out, my mother running at her side, to distribute them to the needy.

The bakery she operated was worked by her sons-in-law, whose wives and children lived in her house, but she made the decisions. She did everything but keep the books, for she could only figure on her fingers, having never gone to school.

Moishidle kept the books: it was the only practical thing he did, his only connection with ordinary life. Only in the abstract, only in books, could getting and spending touch him. There is of course no extant picture of my great-grandfather Moishidle: no conceivable earthly obligation could have persuaded him to set aside scriptural injunction. But I can imagine him from my mother's stories, small, gray-bearded, shrill-voiced, and irascible, perched on a stool before his lectern, studying the Talmud and screaming, should he happen to scratch himself, for water and a towel to cleanse the profaned hand that turned the holy pages. As a child, I conjured up Moishidle as I imagine him now, only so as to entertain myself with the idea of him. I can see him: with his stick he smacks out at a passing child who is running too fast or whistling. His hand on the stick is soft and white. The only fork in the household was his; he ate alone, choice morsels, meat when there was none for other people, and was served only and always by his wife.

Moishidle's white hands were evidence that he was a learned man and therefore, for all his spidery physical being, a real man. Moishidle had been made in God's image as my mother's beefy baker uncles and her dandified father, who owned a fancy grocery store, had not been. Through my mother I got the message— Brucha's—that the fancy grocery store was evidence of spiritual mediocrity. Ahzha, my grandfather, was passion's slave and later his wives' (he had three). In his house the woman was the boss. But in my great-grandmother's correct establishment Moishidle reigned supreme, sole domestic tyrant, in one hand his stick and in the other his book. That he had enslaved the best woman in the world, who worked long hours to support and protect his scholar's leisure, was proof of Moishidle's godly, God-like manhood.

Years and years later, in America, when one of my mother's brothers or cousins showed signs of temper, eyebrows would move up and heads would nod in recognition, and someone was sure to say out loud, "*Uh-huh, Moishidle's ahn einickel,*" Moishidle's grandchild. It was understood that the tantrum in question was ridiculous, as Moishidle's own had been. The myth of Moishidle's superiority was something they had rebelled against, in childhood, because he had oppressed them. Little and shrill and excitable, demanding deference and getting it from the most powerful of the grownups, Moishidle was a false god, absurd. But the other image of him—the one my great-grandmother insisted on—also stuck in their memories, where even the unphotographed dead live on. What Moishidle claimed to be, the myth his wife had made of him, made my mother's notion of manliness. So for more than forty years she indulged my father's blessed ignorance of the mysteries of can openers and snow shovels, and soon after I married, when I told her my husband had packed a suitcase, she gave me a look that said, Yes, I had certainly got me a bargain, but at what price?

It was my mother, therefore, who worried about my going on to graduate school: my father was too pleased to be realistic. When I tell my feminist friends about it I say she was afraid I'd get more education than most men, that too few would be sufficiently my superior to marry me. This is partly true. The other part of the truth is harder to explain: it has to do with the incompatibility of reading and real life, and the importance of the practical. Moishidle's family was not poor—the bakery, in my mother's childhood, was big and flourishing—but once it had been. Comfort had come after a terrible time of poverty, which had driven my great-grandfather to ask help of a wonder rabbi. "Bake bread, and you'll have bread," the wonder rabbi had counseled with stunning simplicity. It was, of course, Brucha who had baked, and saved her scholar husband and five little children from starving. And although it was the ethereal, gnomic wonder rabbi who had given them the truth, the truth itself was earthy: that they had to rely on their own hands, to start with and stick to what was basic. The bread and the business of baking so as to have it were both symbolic of the importance of simple, real things.

To move too far from the kitchen was risky, my mother feared. Too many books and ideas interfered with the ability to manage. And while a scholarly melancholy, a moodiness, a fuzziness about reality, was attractive in men, it was not only unappetizing but downright dangerous in a woman. For who would take care of feeding and clothing and housing her, as Brucha had taken care of Moishidle? Looking around her in America my mother saw many men like Ahzha, her father, but these pawns and playthings of worldly wives were not worth much, and were no more capable of taking care of themselves, or of anyone else, than that rare breed of true men, the scholars, were. A woman had to keep her feet on the ground, my mother reasoned, because somebody had to and no one else would—or could.

My father would not have argued the point (of course, it was never quite made). My parents agreed that the domestic life is most real, and that it is woman's realm. At the same time they considered it bound to materiality, commonplace, and low. My hard-working mother's daughter was raised to rise above it, to read books and play the piano. Still, there was no question about it, I had to get married. Among other things, it would prove I was special.

At the time I got married, I wasn't thinking much about heroines or even novels. Although a middle-aged male colleague tried to say something clever and suggestive about my having written a dissertation about Byron, I prided myself on going about my business of teaching, reading, and writing as if I had been—well, not a man, but not particularly a woman, either. And being married and having children—my private life—seemed to have nothing to do with my profession.

Then in my thirties, as I sat in the park with the stroller or helped load the dishwasher at the dirty end of a dinner party, I found myself having more gossipy literary chats than I had had since college, talks that were nothing like what went on in the faculty dining room. Women who had majored in psychology or physics or music talked to me about English novels because that was something logical to talk to *me* about, but with peculiar urgency, the way they talked about joining consciousness-raising groups or going back to work. Exhausted young mothers desperately treading the soapy waters of family life were reading all of George Eliot, all of Thackeray, evening after evening, good read after good read. (I even knew an exception to prove my rule: my children's busy doctor, a man, was going through Trollope.) They were reading to improve themselves (the classics); they were reading to escape (but why not trash?); mostly, they were reading serious fiction because they needed to believe in the seriousness of the ordinary domestic life that seemed impossible to get beyond, or out of, or over. The New Feminism, meanwhile, was finding expression in novels about women going crazy in suburbia, women having sexual fantasies at their typewriters, women who wanted to break out of their roles and assert their identities. (As a writing woman I knew said then, "Well, you can't stand to live it, so you write about it.") The old novels and the new ones were very different from one another, but the reasons for reading the one and writing the other seemed to me to be related. To write a novel about how you are going nuts raising children makes it worth doing. If someone else writes a novel about how she is going nuts raising children and you are silently doing the same, you are somehow redeemed by her novel. Your life becomes as aboveboard and clear as going nuts working for the post office or an advertising agency or a corporation. You can hate it or laugh at it out loud, see its illusory nature—that it is not as real as it feels. Reading an old-fashioned novel about another kind of heroine also makes a woman's secret life public, valid, as more and less real as everything else. Recognizing the problems and the conventions of a woman-centered novel, the reader feels part of a community and a tradition of women who talk well about their lives and link them, by language, to larger subjects. Looking up from a novel about a girl's settling on a husband and a destiny so as to assert higher moral and aesthetic laws and her own alliance with them, the reader can feel the weight of her woman's life as serious, can see her own self as shapely and significant.

Domestic life is dull and disorderly. Consider Elizabeth Gaskell at her dining-room table, with her daughters and tradesmen and her husband's parishioners milling through, as she copes with one hand and, with the other, keeps stirring her novel. Mothers bake cakes, sort closets: they measure and establish order, making or remaking it continually. The lives of housewives are sequences of disillusioned days in which order is established, then lost, then established and lost again. Even the depressed ones live according to comic, not tragic, plot lines; what is threatened is not the possibility of a supreme meaning, which life proves, Monday to Monday, absurd, but the possibility of effective human artifice. A novel, in which ordinary life is organized in an obviously provisional way, to be discarded at the end of the book, naturally attracts someone who spends her days temporarily, provisionally organizing diurnal chaos: her life suits her to read novels, even to write them. Women like long novels because they give the illusion of sequence and continuity. Seated with her papers at the dining-room table, interrupted every five minutes, how Elizabeth Gaskell must have enjoyed creating a world in which every interruption has a meaning, a cause, an effect.

Mrs. Gaskell and Jane Austen writing as family life swirled around them are images of women worth recalling: reading a novel, too, one is effectively isolated from ordinary life while appearing to be solidly, normally, appropriately in the thick of it. The reader of a novel steals time: she must get back to work, return the book to the library, take seriously once more the world she has banished to peripheral vision. Since the eighteenth-century "closet" set aside for reading and writing and praying has disappeared, the novel-reader has had to steal space, too. The big novels of Dickens and Thackeray were read aloud in big families in the nineteenth century. But less public fictions are best shared intimately: George Eliot and George Henry Lewes read *Emma* together under a tree. Curling up with a good book is the better for such props of coziness as a fire and rain on the roof, a quilt, an apple, the sound of traffic in the distance. Time stolen to focus on individual experience, the intensities of private life, is enhanced by half-awareness of the unlucky, the unaware generalized mass in the distance. Reading a novel, wise to the motives of characters less aware than oneself, anticipating their destinies and admiring the shapes of them, the reader can fancy that—like a novelist—she understands and can manage everything.

The most serious and ambitious feminist novel that appeared in English in the 1960s quite logically renounced the conspiratorial tone that implies novelist and reader share the common language that ensures a common, ironic view of the world, and women, and fiction, and how they are related. *The Golden Notebook* directs its heavy irony at the enterprise of writing a novel about a woman in a time when war and madness inundate the private life and threaten to obliterate the individual. By its tone as well as its content, Doris Lessing's novel separates itself from the tradition of woman-centered novels in English. Nevertheless, doing so, it comments, as novels traditionally have commented, on the connections of women with fiction.

One reason *The Golden Notebook* "left its mark upon the ideas and feelings of a whole generation of young women," in Elizabeth Hardwick's words, is that it articulates certain facts that had previously been unmentionable. The classical English novel about a woman's life does not, for example—but of course this is no example, it is the thing itself—describe menstruating. The famous passage in Lessing's novel that does is a section of the heroine's blue notebook, the record of her daily life. As an experiment in truth-telling, she tries to write down everything that has happened to her in the course of a single day. As she does this, Anna Wulf acknowledges that her own self-consciousness makes the words she writes down untruthful:

> I am worrying about this business of being conscious of everything so as to write it down, particularly in connection with my having a period. Because, whereas to me, the fact that I am having a period is no more than an entrance into an emotional state, recurring regularly, is of no particular

importance; I know that as soon as I write the word
"blood," it will be giving a wrong emphasis, and even to me
when I come to read what I've written.

Deliberately or not, the style of Anna's pained prose breaks with
the tradition of graceful novels about women whose menstrual
periods are unmentionable. Anna Wulf is a professional writer,
and writing is hard work for her; the author of one successful
novel, she is blocked at writing her new one. No beautiful,
spunky young lady on the threshold of life, but a middle-aged
divorcée with a child, Anna is a woman with a "free" (the word
is ironic) sex life, whose womanhood complicates instead of
oversimplifying her destiny. The various forms in which she
writes and is written reflect her multiple selves. She works on a
novel about a woman who, like her, is a writer. Reflecting on
Ella, her character, Anna describes her as burdened by the history of literary women: she "makes bitter jokes about Jane Austen hiding her novels under the blotting paper when people
come into the room; quotes Stendhal's dictum that any woman
under fifty who writes, should do so under a pseudonym."

At the end of *The Golden Notebook*, it becomes clear that what
appeared to be a novel about Anna is, in fact, a novel by her. The
first sentence, "The two women were alone in the London flat,"
turns out to have been the first sentence of what Lessing later
characterized as "a skeleton, or frame, called Free Women, . . . a
conventional short novel." The truth-to-life of this conventional
novel about Anna and her friend Molly is undermined in various
ways, primarily by the sections of Anna's several notebooks that
interleave it and implicitly set up the claims of "fact" against
simple fiction. The notebooks—a black, a red, a yellow, and a
blue one—are nonfictions, antifictions, parafictions, metafictions.
The black one describes the periphery of fiction, being about the
successful novel Anna has written, the financial transactions connected with it, its sources in personal experience, and the banal
fictions it generates in the minds of filmmakers and TV pro-
ducers interested in adapting (and misreading) it. In the red notebook, Anna records her activities as a member of the British

Communist Party. The yellow notebook is the manuscript of Anna's novel about Ella, who is both like Anna and unlike her: for instance, Ella's novel is about a young man who goes mad and commits suicide, while in "Free Women" the son of Anna's friend Molly tries to kill himself. In Anna's blue notebook, "fact" corrects fiction: Tommy thrives. In Anna's fifth, golden notebook, she herself goes mad, together with a man.

The structure of *The Golden Notebook* makes the point that traditional realistic narrative is inadequate to the truth about the lives of modern women, who are powerless in a threatening world, and implicated in complex fictions. A novel about a fragmented, unstable, ineffectual self can center on a heroine only ironically. But Lessing makes the conventional identification of woman and the inner life in her introspective protagonist: Anna is devoted to the literary form—the journal—that has been associated with novel heroines since Henry Tilney, in Jane Austen's *Northanger Abbey*, pretended to be shocked by the idea that a young lady might possibly *not* keep a journal. Anna Wulf's keeping several portrays the inner life as split and frangible: history, Lessing shows, has altered both concepts of identity and the reality of the self. The heroine's inmost being, revealed in the golden notebook she finally writes, is not the expression of a separate and integral self but the record of madness. Anna's virtuosity in writing down her life reflects her drive to see and to make sense of herself. Anna and her friend Molly, Anna and her shadow-creature Ella, as they seem to be identical and then distinct, suggest the difficulties in declaring and claiming a separate identity. In the end, when Anna collapses into madness and rises purged, and as the lover with whom she shares the experience equips her with the first sentence of her new novel, there is some promise that by writing about it she will remake her self. There is also doubt cast on the promise: the novel, "Free Women," being conventional, is incompletely the truth. The man Saul is a kind of double or second self of Anna, as Ella and Molly and the semifictional mad young man are: a male "self" is a part of the modern heroine. The multiple doubles in *The Golden Notebook*

28

suggest a self proliferating so as to teach itself the difficult lesson that it is not unique.

In *The Golden Notebook* Doris Lessing undermines the traditional connections between women and fiction, demystifying the heroine and stripping her of glamour. Anna Wulf is not the sort of heroine romantic women dream of becoming. As the four notebooks plus one, the golden notebook of madness and recovery, raise questions about the truth-to-life of "Free Women," Anna's reflective, and fictitious, and mad selves make us doubt her reality. Still, notebook-keeping Anna, like the traditional heroine, is identified with interiority, therefore with her book or books. Rejecting the well-modulated tones and the conservative implications of the traditional novel, *The Golden Notebook* maintains the novel's characteristic self-consciousness, and Anna has the heroine's crucial characteristic: the sense of herself as a character as if in a fiction, which shapes her life.


I expect that my thoughts about women and fiction will be interrupted by a visit to Doctor T., but it turns out I am wrong. Showing interest in the patient as a person, he asks me what I am up to. Writing a book, I tell him, about English novels. "Georgette Heyer?" he supposes with a very cute wink. When I ask him if he reads her, he says of course not, but Sarah (nodding toward the door to the outer office), Sarah does. He assumes that as a writer I also am in a position to look down at Sarah. Then to save his nurse's face he adds that he doesn't think she does so much, anymore.

I have not meant to write about Georgette Heyer, but with characteristic sauciness she seems to be intruding herself. I read Georgette Heyer when I was in college; I traded volumes with a friend who was a lawyer, a woman in her late twenties. We were obliged to stoop thus, we reasoned, because Jane Austen had gone and died after only six books, and the pleasures of rereading were limited. Georgette Heyer is not like Barbara Cartland or Victoria Holt or Rosemary Rogers. Her prose has pretensions to wit, her characters are respectful of artifice and irony, and she makes a show of scorn for sentimentality. Reading Georgette Heyer, my doctor's nurse does not, I bet, merely escape a hard world owned and operated by the likes of her condescending employer. Her fantasy is not simply of being young again, and beautiful and loved this time round, although that, of course, must figure in it. Georgette Heyer appeals to the reader who enjoys being reminded how well she knows the elegant manners of an era when women who used English well had power.

Part of the pleasure of reading Georgette Heyer (and other romance writers, too) is the pleasure of predictability: the exotic details of eighteenth-century card games and cosmetics with which the novels are salted are the only elements of the unknown they contain. The reader's foreknowledge, her recognition of this as a variation on a theme, is depended on: of course the beautiful, intelligent, spunky, hard-pressed young woman disdained by the corrupt matron will in the end marry the arrogant, wealthy man distinguished by a pair of good legs and a sneer whose vigorous, contemptuous curl hints at his capacity for passion and even true love. In the fantasy life such novels feed, dreams of adventure and being swept away are mixed with dreams, just as powerful, of knowing, controlling, and containing: the reader enjoys what feels like a novelist's sense of satisfaction when she matches up new characters to the various obligatory parts she anticipates, when the action turns out as it has to. The Georgette Heyer setting, the world of Regency high society as it has been portrayed in comedies of manners, is meant to be bracing, not lulling: wit is the heroine's most prized characteristic, and sometimes also the hero's and the villainess's. The reader is flattered to imagine that like those crisp-souled eighteenth-century types she, too, scorns the spinelessly sentimental, the simply romantic. The first sentence of *Faro's Daughter* dismisses the sort of novels a Georgette Heyer reader is proud to condescend to:

Upon her butler's announcing the arrival of Mr. Ravenscar, Lady Mablethorpe, who had been dozing over a novel from the Circulating Library, sat up with a jerk, and raised a hand to her dishevelled cap. "What's that you say? Mr. Ravenscar? Desire him to come upstairs at once."

Lady Mablethorpe is glad to be saved from fiction by real life—by sparring in her drawing room with an ominously named man; the reader is cheered by the promise that this fiction will be more exciting than a novel from the Circulating Library. Georgette Heyer is no Jane Austen. But the reader of Jane Austen will recognize in her romances not only eighteenth-century types and manners, and the marriage plot rewritten, and the familiar Cinderella figure, but also the reminder of superiority to other, falser, softer, more commonplace fictions, the kind, a heroine is aware, that most women read.

## ⫷ 2 ⫸

# An Exemplar to Her Sex

DUKE. For women are as roses, whose fair flow'r,
Being once display'd, doth fall that very hour.
VIOLA. And so they are; alas, that they are so!
To die, even when they to perfection grow!

— *Twelfth Night*

But in a country where no she-saints were worshipped by any authority from religion, 'twas as impertinent and senseless as it was profane to deify the sex, raise them to a capacity above what Nature had allowed, and treat them with a respect which in the natural way of love they themselves were the aptest to complain of.

— Lord Shaftesbury

"The life of every Woman is a Romance!" wrote Mme. de Genlis. The truth is it is only a novel. Although the French word *roman* means both, the distinction is essential.

In life as in novels, women read romances, and look up from the pages with their vision blurred. Real women, like realistic novels, are haunted by the shaping shadow of romance. A nineteenth-century American girl wrote on the last page of her maiden diary, "And now these pages must come to a close, for the romance ends when the heroine marries." This happy end is carefully prepared for by a would-be heroine, who follows a course of private reading and writing, private schooling of the self in a perfection that will be realized, finally, when she is acknowledged as a heroine of romance by a man. The novel of her life depends on that.

In English, too, the words "novel" and "romance" have been used interchangeably. When Lady Delacour, in Maria Edgeworth's *Belinda* (1801), refers to "the novel" of her young friend's life, she means what the anonymous American diarist means by "the romance" of hers: "If you would only open your eyes, which heroines make it a principle never to do—or else there would be an end of the novel—if you would only open your eyes, you would see that this man is in love with you." A heroine's primary allegiance is to her romance: she cannot allow her intelligence to compromise the potential power of the ending. Life, like a novel, tends to remind her every now and then of this irony. Lady Delacour's irony reminds us *Belinda* is a piece of realism rather than a mere romance, and also that, on the other hand, it is not real life but only a novel.

From the beginning, the realistic English novel self-consciously countered the fantasies, fabrications, and falsifications of romance by making its own fantasies, fabrications, and falsifications very obvious. So Defoe's Moll Flanders, for instance, is emphatically a common London thief, whose "true" story is told in her "own" words—but not exactly, as they have been cleaned up a little by an editor. "He" says he is publishing her story partly to teach honest men how to protect themselves from the tricks of thieves, and partly to show that crime does not pay. Moll also insists on the moral burden of "her" tale. But her story proves that vice, not virtue, is rewarded: at the end of a life of crime she is rich and happy, with a fortune and a loving family. Although she claims to confess the whole truth about her past, crafty Moll keeps her "real" name a secret; and her "confessions" seem like vindications of herself sometimes, as she blames the devil for her sins. Some readers have found that parts of Moll's story are utterly implausible; others have observed Defoe's indebtedness to various literary conventions; yet others insist on the circular path of Moll's destiny and read the fact-obsessed story of her life as myth. I am suggesting only a few of the ambiguities of realism, the ambiguous "opposite" of romance.

The realistic novel rose in England alongside the newly leisured wives and daughters of the new middle class, who were rising to the economic occasion of the mid-eighteenth century and making themselves into ladies. In an era of new fortunes, when it was no longer absolutely necessary to be born to privilege, the newly literate eagerly read up. Richardson's *Pamela* (1740), a story about a servant girl's first parrying and then marrying her rich master, is said to have inspired the maids of England with fantasies of upward mobility. One legacy of romance was luxury: the bourgeois novel, perhaps a product of increased leisure time and certainly one product consumed in it, imitated aristocratic romance in its preoccupation with the privileged. In *Sir Charles Grandison* (1753–54), Richardson wrote about grander people than he knew; Fanny Burney loved a lord as a subject. The women who were inspired by novels to aspire toward the upper classes dreamed, like readers of romance, of having the perquisites of privilege, more nice dresses and gentlemanly lovers and more real power, too, than they had.

Defoe's two novels about women who are obliged to sell their bodies to save their lives, *Moll Flanders* (1722) and *Roxana* (1724), may be read as proleptic distortions of what was to become the domestic novel's dominant theme. In the Richardsonian tradition of novels about girls, body and soul are obliged to stick together, and therefore to become problematically confused. The heroine of the bourgeois novel, symbolic of perfection, is pure in mind and body. And although vulnerable, she is a stern, strong guardian of her own perfection. That is the premise of the plot. The question of whether a delicate girl could escape being brutalized by a brutal world was posed by Richardson, in *Clarissa* (1747–48), in such a way as to broach questions about how and whether the spirit could find accommodation on earth. The heroine-centered domestic novel defines the heroine's self (her integrity and her honesty) as real and rare. That the world is ruled by rival values proves the world is fallen and needs her to save it. The paradox of the central/peripheral, strong/vulnerable young woman is crucial to the novel. The heroine in the "realistic" tradition may say or even think she is of no importance; people may try to use her as a pawn, a mere means to their ends; but the novel focused on her implicitly argues that she is as important as a heroine in romance, and as perfect, a creature of a better world than this.


A beautiful virgin walled off from an imperfect real world is the central figure in romance. In Guillaume de Lorris's *Le Roman de la Rose* (ca. 1237), which was translated into English by Chaucer, the Rose is seen and sought by the Lover in a dream—his dream. She is a creature of his fantasy. Enclosed in her garden, she is an aesthetic-erotic-moral-semireligious ideal: the good and the beautiful, spiritual perfection in palpable form. By being, she inspires ennobling, enabling love. Her whole business is to be. The story of the *Roman de la Rose* is the Lover's story; the Rose is his objective. It is her nature to guard herself; by being what she is she tests his mettle; her glory is that she is unattainable, his glory that he desires to attain her. Guillaume died before finishing the *Roman.* When it was completed some forty years later by Jean de Meun, the poem was radically changed. Jean's portion is much longer and less dreamy; it continues the story of courtship through marriage, and includes children and money and the names of quantities of ordinary things. It is a sort of catalogue of the ingredients of commonplace domestic life, and as such it anticipates an important element of the convention of "realism" in fiction. (It is "realistic," too, in its insistence on the physical and the gross, in satirizing, not idealizing, women, and in insisting all women are whores.) Jean's is one way of rewriting romance; he puts it in its place as a part of life by tracing its connections with "reality." Another option involves tinkering with narrative point of view. Love or life, from the Rose's point of view, can hardly seem a perilous quest to be validated and ended by the capture of a reward. What is it, then? A confinement terminated by release? an ordeal of solitary waiting? a spectator sport? a pain or a luxury?

Everything that can happen to the Rose while the Lover struggles to reach her happens inside. She cannot but be self-preoccupied (which is not to say self-aware); unlike the Lover, she has no Rose outside of herself to draw her out or up. Her life must be passed in staring at the bare insides of garden walls. Eternal vigilance is her lot; if she lets herself be distracted it may be dangerous. No serious action is available to her, rooted as she is, effectively prevented from moving; the sole significant movement that so much concerns her is something over which she has no control. One suspects that from the Rose's point of view the greatest peril posed by romance is boredom. Discrimination is the only faculty the plot allows her to exercise, and she will have only one chance to use it. For the rest, she must look to her petals (her complexion, of course, and what people in Jane Austen call her "accomplishments," her pencils and her piano), and try to keep cool and out of trouble. This is not too much of a problem for a Rose of the right temperament.

The Lover's victory asserts the value of the single dedicated spirit; the Rose's story, on the other hand, is about the predicament of the individual who is consciously superior but unhappily, for that reason, alone. It is about whether the individual can join society without giving up identity, or those satisfactions of the separate self that are intrinsic to separateness. Marriage, which means joining society and active participation in biological, sexual life, cannot be sought outright by the Rose: her passivity, like her virginity, is essential to her being; without either she ceases to be a Rose. But nevertheless marriage is what she must have in mind, as soon as she has a mind. The ideal end of the story, from the Rose's point of view, is less a victory than a compromise. Its emblem is a symbolic celebration of community in the couple and the couple in the community. Marriage will ensure the Rose protection from the distortions and deprivations attendant on isolation, and also ensure that the self will not be overwhelmed by uncontrollable larger forces. It is a practical arrangement, as Jean de Meun insists. It promises orderly life will go on.

The Rose of romance is beautiful and exalted and beloved,

simple not complex, coherent not diffuse, perfect not faulty, finished not in process, signifying and not seeking, imaginary not imagining. She is the center of all action and its reward, the hub of meaning. In the seventeenth-century French heroic romances, political and seismic catastrophes exist primarily as occasions and metaphors for the sexual desire that dominates life: an earthquake, a deployment of ships to besiege a port, are important only insofar as they express or impede love. The heroine herself is passive, being perfect; the Rose has nothing to do but stay planted, waiting to reward the Lover (and Reader) for grasping her and all she means. If, like the heroine of Mlle. de Scudéry's ten-volume *Clélie* (1654–61), she goes so far as to swim the Tiber, she does so to preserve herself, not in order to get somewhere she wants to go. The heroine of romance is beyond change; she does not alter or reflect. The Lover's objective is more object than person. The flower image is telling: a Rose lacks psychological density. When the heroine has awakened into self-awareness, the Rose becomes Rosalind, uprooted, able to assume doublet and hose, actively a lover, even a philosopher of love.

Seventeenth-century French heroic romance has many of the characteristics of pornography: abstractness, implausibility, repetitiousness, narrowness of focus, titillating narrow escapes. Plot in both is characterized by a lack of subordination: every episode is more or less as significant as every other. Distinctions between sexual acts, in pornography, and tender emotions, in romance, are gross rather than fine, being limited to only body or only spirit; but what energizes both is a distinctively erotic force directed toward making such distinctions. Both romance and pornography reject body-and-soul reality and instead render one half sufficiently complex to pretend to mime the whole. Both identify the solitary language-using consciousness as the locus of desire. Both acknowledge language as desire's creator.

Pornography is written for men, romance "for the ladies," both for solitary pleasure. A passion intensified by being deferred, a lover concerned only with loving and ennobled by enslavement to his beloved, a heroine incomparably high-souled, beautiful, and good—these are the elements of the romance universe. In Scudéry's *Clélie* there is a map, the Carte du Tendre, of a world made entirely of emotions. The explorers and indeed the real proprietors of this world of unworldliness are women. Only men engage in action, in romance, but action in romance is only as important as its meaning; it is worth noting only as it involves some abstraction. Women, who make the distinctions among feelings as well as inspire them, give the meanings to desire. The fantasy that there exist intrinsic meaning, individual coherence, personal significance, is the basic fantasy of romance.

What is most remarkable about romance is its idealism, the lengths to which it goes in dismissing the physical world. In an incident in an English translation of a long romance attributed to Mlle. de Scudéry, a hero, finding himself in a burning town, pauses to apostrophize his mistress, who has been imprisoned in a threatened, distant castle. As he declaims his passion, women with their hair on fire pass by him, running, holding the hands of small children. The narrator takes pains to tell us that he would have helped them out, since they were good people and he was a sympathetic sort, if only he had not been otherwise engaged. Romance excludes the reality of the body as thoroughly as pornography excludes the soul; at the same time, of course, physical consummation is the unspoken obsession of the one, and extracting from the body some food for the imagination is the impulse of the other. Behind the logorrhea characteristic of both pornographers and romancers is often the profit motive; what they have to say about the erotic power of language and the inexhaustible nature of solitary sexual fantasy is nevertheless serious. The talky disembodied love of the French heroic romances, like the version of *amour courtois* popular in the salon of Mlle. de Scudéry, is all aspiration, all sublimation. Its pleasures are the pleasures of the erotic imagination reaching climax on its own, insisting on its own power.

The heroine of romance is unattainable woman, the symbol of invulnerable, immanent selfhood. The signifier is married to what it signifies; the Lover affirms *his* selfhood when he interposes his body between them, when he grasps the Rose for himself.

That others seek to attain her or destroy her is the Rose's condition: her being is defined by the forces directed toward not letting her be. She is a pole in a polarized world, crucial to its structure. The Lover exists during courtship so as to serve and protect her. The rhythm of Spenser's long line captures the music of her eternity:

> For he me seemes most fit the faire to serve,
> That can her best defend from villenie;
> And she most fit his service doth deserve,
> That fairest is, and from her faith will never swerve.

When the convention of romance is no longer asserted but debated—when it becomes problematic, in the heroine-centered novel—the heroine's getting enshrined once for all as fairest and most faithful occasions the plot. Her beauty and fidelity become both the givens and the goals: the heroine, no longer a still point in her garden-world, moves toward them. The conscious heroine of a novel measures the distance between romance and reality; her mind is a measure of that fluctuating space. To have read about the Rose makes it impossible to be a heroine of romance: consciousness consigns a girl to the novel, a different story.

"A Man's life of any worth is a continual allegory," Keats wrote. From her point of view, for all that men see her as a symbol, for all that she cannot help but do so too, so is a woman's.

In a novel about courtship, the parade of suitors subjected to a heroine's scrutiny tempts her to succumb to sloth, to greed, to worldliness, and so on. She is threatened by bad counselors, by flattery, by illusions. Her journey may be only through elegant drawing rooms, but it is as perilous and solitary as Christian's in *The Pilgrim's Progress*; her own sense of who she is and who she wants to be must pilot her to the safe haven of the house where she will be finally, safely, voluntarily immured, her own mistress.

The parents of a heroine in a novel of courtship are often absent, unfeeling, or incompetent; relying on her inner lights, she must make something of herself. She must make herself, by herself, in truth what the artful speeches of flattering suitors call her so as to deceive her. To escape the toils of the artful, she must make herself a transcendent work of art. She must fashion her character and her story into expressions of the truth.

There is a significant relationship between the novelist's enterprise and that of a young woman in a novel who is charged with the task of making herself a heroine. Heroine-centered novels about a girl's decisively fixing her character and fate "realistically" show how ideas and cultural and aesthetic constraints determine her choices. The novel that focuses on her charts the links between form and matter, truth and lies, imagination and conditions, identity and event, by giving a "life story" the shape of art. The real lesson the early novels teach has less to do with those they aver—the correct relations between parents and children and whether or not crime pays—than with the influence of concepts of character and career on characters and careers. The heroine in a novel about a young woman who must marry engages in a quest to achieve the perfection and signifying force that the Rose by definition has. The plot of her story chronicles her movement toward completing the ideal of herself.

Richardson's *Clarissa* is an exhaustive examination of the problems of defining and maintaining the integral self. The self is imagined as female; a female destiny is the image of its struggle. As Clarissa Harlowe struggles to be her ideal self, and to be loved and understood, and to understand her own meaning, she must struggle with her antagonist Lovelace, a seducer committed to a career of improvising selves. Clarissa aims to attain absolute identity with the perfect truth, goodness, and beauty for which she is famous, to realize what the vulgar can only dream of and admire; she imagines she is doing this for others and for God. She achieves utter, final perfection only when she translates herself into her tomb, her letters, her story. Dying, she makes herself an artifact, an inhabitant of another world; she realizes the self, makes manifest the inner life that has been determined by the idea of herself as a paragon, by achieving her own end. So she becomes an impossible person, a logical contradiction, a virgin who has been raped, a dead person who lives on—a heroine.

## Clarissa

We have fallen on an evil generation who would not read 'Clarissa' even in an abridged form.

—George Eliot to Mrs. Charles Bray,
21 December 1876

Reading *Clarissa* is like being trapped in a nightmare of trying to escape and knowing the exits will be sealed up before you get to them, probably because you're the one in charge of sealing up exits. It is too long a book to want to read, and it is often easy to put down, being painful and sometimes tedious, but one must go back to it, really one must (for all abridgments falsify it) read it all. Reading, there is simultaneously suspense, absolutely certain knowledge, and a perverse satisfaction in knowing knowledge is powerlessness. Everything that happens feels like a replay, in agonizing slow motion, of something that happened before, *déjà lu*. The narrative of the events of a year strains against movement, hoards moments. The protagonist runs off with a man who rapes her, and then she dies, yet while one is gripped by the drama of these events they seem only the shadows of happenings. Like events in dreams they are precise in their every detail, but the most urgent thing is the sense that what happens has a will to happen. The characters who besiege and torment Clarissa Harlowe have clear motives, coherent natures, identifiable voices; they are differentiated, well drawn, the creations of a fine novelist; yet they have the lurid common coloration of figures in a delusion. One feels the people in the novel are compelled to be what they are, that they do not choose to be themselves. Both events and character seem to be determined, half-willingly undertaken or assumed, confining. The heroine's character and her destiny are on the one hand remarkable, chosen by a strong, tenacious will, and on the other hand inevitable, helplessly submitted to.

*Clarissa* has occasioned fascinating critical commentary. Some of it disparages Richardson's politics and morality while acknowledging the greatness of his art. His professed aims imply another dichotomy: he meant to be true both to actual life and to the moral law that he thought life imperfectly followed. Clarissa is a young woman, and also she is a symbol, an exemplar. Her story is about her wrestling with an ideal image. Richardson's old chestnut of a novelist's claim—that *Clarissa* is both more realistic and more dedicated to higher, moral truth than "mere romance"—is made in the spirit that informs the novel. *Clarissa* is about the complex relationships of art to the actual and the true, about the reflexive connections between the self and its idea of itself.

If, as Henry Fielding imagined, a novel is a feast of human nature in which all the characters are dishes, Clarissa is the spinach of heroines. She is served up for our own good, "proposed," Richardson explained in his 1759 Preface, "as an examplar to her sex." * Fielding, who laughed at Richardson for moralizing, also meant to be instructive, but what his great novel *Tom Jones* aimed to teach was the way of the world, as "it is much easier," Fielding argued, "to make good Men wise, than to make bad Men good." For Richardson the distinction between goodness and wisdom was not so clear, and the student-readers he had in mind were neither one kind of Men or another, but Women. The author of *Pamela* had been criticized for the moral of his story of a servant whose difficult struggle to stay *virgo intacta* ends triumphantly in marriage to the very master who sought to rape her. Surrender your fair white body only for a price, *Pamela* seems to say. Soon after its publication, Richardson expressed concern about its implicit message "that a reformed rake makes the best husband." It was partly in order to point out the falseness of that maxim, he

---

* I have used the modern spelling throughout.

explained, that he wrote *Clarissa*. In making his second heroine an Exemplar, Richardson attempted to clear himself perfectly and to make himself perfectly clear. He did neither, brilliantly.

What Richardson means by an Exemplar is the feminine ideal of his time. She is a young woman perfectly chaste, dutiful, obedient, religious, useful, orderly, charitable, thrifty, and kind. She acts and requires others to act according to a firm ethical standard. But her essence is aesthetic. In effect the bourgeois Christian Exemplar is an adaptation of the cliché that a woman is a goddess, a convention of courtship, literature, and polite society that, as Richardson knew and Mary Wollstonecraft was soon to say, has long served to enslave women. An Exemplar is too good for the real goods of the real world. She is not born but made; she is not growing but fixed; she is not human but perfect. That an actual woman can be an Exemplar is, for all its Protestant trappings, a Romantic idea; a girl can no more remain an Exemplar than Keats could stay married to the nightingale. Like the poet's ecstasy, the Exemplar's existence is by definition temporary and ideal, an imaginative construct. Inherent in the Exemplar is the anticipation of its dissolution. A desirable woman is marriageable; an obedient daughter must marry: the Exemplar is both those things. One of the fragments Clarissa writes during the mental breakdown that follows her rape—the sequence is suggestive—sketches the Exemplar best, as, appropriately, the main figure in a tableau. On her lost wedding day, Clarissa imagines, she would have been at the still center of orderly ritual, looking up at her parents, being looked up to by the husband. The wedding day is the ultimate, and final, point of the Exemplar's glory. After that the tableau dissipates: once a wife, the Exemplar is an Exemplar no longer. Her task is to be the curator of herself until the time when she will reward the man she finds most worthy by bestowing herself upon him; her secondary task is to be a didactic work of art, to exist in a form sufficiently clear and attractive so as to inspire other girls to be like her and thus keep the world pleasant and safe for its owners.

Clarissa is the ideal of a materialistic society based on the preservation of private property through monogamy, a relationship sanctified by its religion. By her specialness she has caused those around her to fall into supporting or gawking roles, and to talk of nobody else, as her friend Anna Howe puts it. In the first letter of this epistolary novel Anna apologizes for inquiring into the truth of rumors about the goings-on at Harlowe Place: "It is impossible," she explains, "but that whatever relates to a young lady, whose distinguished merits have made her the public care, should engage everybody's attention." She sounds, as if casually, a portentous note: "You see what you draw upon yourself by excelling all your sex." Clarissa's tragedy begins as she seems to those around her someone who exists for their good: "Every individual . . . who knows you, or has heard of you, seems to think you answerable to *her* for your conduct in points so very delicate and concerning" (Vol. I, Letter I).* She is by one syllable short of definition *clarissima*, most famous; so her private life cannot be altogether her own.

Part of the trouble is simply that she is a marriageable young woman and therefore the subject of gossip and a candidate for romance. Her age and sex, her beauty and class put her automatically in a potentially dramatic situation from which the seeker after the meanings of lives can draw conclusions about love, choice, and human nature. Clarissa says she does not choose to be a center of interest; more precisely, it is Anna Howe who recalls that her friend is "desirous, as you always said, of sliding through life to the end of it unnoted." Clarissa says she wants "the single life," but she is obliged to be singled out for attention and for trials because she is singular; because she aims at being unique, her life will be pregnant with suggestions about human life in general. She cannot choose not to be the protagonist of a life story; her nature and circumstances require that she be talked about, written about, that she write herself and ultimately that she assemble the letters that tell and are her story, artist and artifact at once. She is constrained to be the heroine of a novel—

---

* Samuel Richardson, *Clarissa*, 4 vols. (London and New York: Dent and Dutton, 1967). All references in parentheses are to volume and letter numbers in this most accessible complete edition of the novel.

just such a novel as this, recalcitrant, always turning back upon itself and reexamining what's past. Tennyson called *Clarissa* "still"; *stuck* might be more accurate. Jane Austen's world is spacious in comparison: the reader of *Clarissa* feels there is no way out, no world outside the family, the couple, the house, the head. The heroine sits, assuming the opposite of a heroic stance. At the beginning of the novel, there is nothing on earth she wants to get up and do. It is her undoing.

The forces insisting that "the divine Clarissa" engage with the business of ordinary life are both internal and external, and what is wonderful about Richardson is his vision of how these are joined. Clarissa's story is about her struggle to preserve that objectified creature she perceives as her self—her separateness, which to her and others is inherent in the physical fact of her chastity—from the world's incursions and oppressions. Since she is both for the world and of it (its Exemplar, its creature), the struggle to preserve herself from the world is difficult and ambiguous. She is obliged to struggle to maintain her identity against her own family, "those with whom she was inseparably connected." (Author's Preface). It is not merely what is outside Clarissa but her integral self and its image reflected in her "father's house," where her self has been formed and her singleness preserved, that force her to engage with the world. She is not tossed out of the house, as Tom Jones is, and obliged to test what qualities she has; instead the house is transformed, changed from a haven to an arena where her parents, turned monsters, force her to marry a man she loathes. When, at the end of the first volume, she flees Harlowe Place, the image of that house divided stays in her mind. Its connection with her mind, her mind having been born there, remains firm. Other houses where she seeks shelter and finds danger mimic and parody and reinterpret it. (*Clarissa* is a reiterant and excellent gloss on itself.) When she transcends the world and her sufferings, toward the novel's end, she designs the coffin she calls her "house"; we are reminded, when her body is enclosed in it, that the words "define" and "finish" have the same root.

Driven from home by her family, Clarissa is followed not only by memories but by an explicit curse. "A father's curse" on her ("so father-fond," as Lovelace muses, and so religious) seems more terrible than any physical affliction. Its origin is her origin, its object her immortal soul. Her most solemn and persistent hope through her trials is that this curse be lifted. While the plot of the extroverted *Tom Jones* hangs on facts about parentage, *Clarissa*, seeking to comprehend "the most important concerns of private life," insists on the relationship between parents and children. While Fielding asks whether what Tom Jones does defines him, Richardson's novel is about who Clarissa Harlowe thinks she is, what she makes of herself. When Clarissa's parents cease to be the loving parents she knew, their house, her foundation, totters. The letter form of the novel, which makes point of view more interesting than event, supports Richardson's investigation of the integrity of individuals, the connections between their relationships with others and their separate "real" selves.

Newly rich, the Harlowe family is committed to increasing its wealth and power. They have no doubts about Clarissa's obedience to their will, since she has always been a perfect child. She will marry, then, for their good. The perfect chastity for which she is celebrated ensures her value as a commodity: because she is unworldly, the Exemplar is desired by the world. Wealthy, young, and beautiful, Clarissa whets every appetite, mostly by her innocence. But the correct disposal of her chastity is crucial also for her own ends. Since she is an Exemplar, those are different from the Harlowes'. So long as she is committed to being Clarissa, she is obliged to believe that she will sanction the man she marries. By choosing a man, a woman sexually contains him; in a world where salvation is believed to follow good works, or restraint from bad ones, she may be said thus to reform him. Clarissa is in a position of dramatic self-consciousness: she is aware of herself as both the prize and the judge who will award it. She rejects her first suitor, Wyerley, because he is a free-thinker. Perhaps even then she has one other complication of her predicament in mind: marriage to a man who is not entirely pure may compromise an Exemplar, contaminate her, and ruin her chances for eternal life, which is her great objective. The "best self" of the Exemplar committed to unselfishness is served by marrying wisely. Nothing good, obviously, can come of such a flock of paradoxes, and it does.

Through her family—in the nature of bourgeois life, Clarissa is very casually but effectively held prisoner in her father's house from the beginning—she is introduced to Robert Lovelace, who has come to seek her. Her reputation has drawn him, for he is a rake, a sort of officer, as he sees it, in a grandly conceived-of sex war where every virgin is booty, most prized when most cold. Social forces larger than he move him toward plucking the flower that is the Harlowe pride. An aristocrat, he is their class enemy: their rising power threatens his own. The Harlowe style—vulgar, petty, rude, with hypocritical pretensions to piety—is antithetical to his natural, easy elegance. Talk of their daughter has inflamed him. He is a glutton for girls; he needs excitement and variety; he seeks revenge on women because once he was jilted, he says. He cannot live without intrigue, he explains further, and elsewhere (his ventriloquist is middle-class Samuel Richardson), "This it is to have leisure upon my hands!" (II, Letter XXXII). He is rich, healthy, egotistical, energetic, young, clever, mischievous, and he has nothing to do. Most interesting of the reasons Lovelace gives for his ardent siege of Clarissa Harlowe is his description of himself as a satanic litterateur of the bedroom, inspired by the poets to create goddesses. The impossible idea of a real woman who is ideal will wreck his life as well as Clarissa's. A literary person, he is aware of the effect literature has had on his life:

> those confounded poets, with their serenely-celestial descriptions, did as much with me as the lady: they fired my imagination, and set me upon a desire to become a goddess-maker. I must needs try my new-fledged pinions in sonnet, elegy, and madrigal. I must have a Cynthia, a Stella, a Sacharissa, as well as the best of them: darts, and flames, and the devil knows what, must I give to my Cupid. I must create beauty, and place it where nobody else could find it: and many a time have I been at a loss for a *subject*, when my

new-created goddess has been kinder than it was proper for
my plaintive sonnet that she should be. (I, Letter XXXI)

Like an Exemplar, the "goddess" of a man like Lovelace must
necessarily be "unkind," or cold. To make her up is a triumph of
the imagination of a man who would be a god; to make a goddess
and destroy her is to be more than God. Allusions to Satan vest
Lovelace's lust with Miltonic majesty. Suffering from confusion
of literature and life, "the man," as Clarissa calls him, wants the
impossible: both a goddess of his making who will prove herself a
goddess by rejecting him, and the glory of triumphing over goddesses. He says he is the enemy of hypocrites who concern themselves with reputation; he acknowledges his glittering badness,
resting some of his claim to superiority on his domination of a
gang of rakes nearly as wicked as he. All women can be seduced,
he believes, and "once subdued, always subdued." He presents
this maxim as a fact of nature; Richardson will show that society
makes it real when it damns "fallen" women to be prostitutes.

Seeking out "the divine Clarissa," Lovelace is offered instead
the overeager Arabella, her older sister, not at all to his exquisite
taste. He manages to hear her acquiescence in his proposals as
discouragement, and to tell her she has turned him down; having
thus injured and rendered inarticulate the elder sister, he turns
to pay his addresses to the younger. But from a distance, where
he has gone to look over estates he recently inherited, Clarissa's
only brother, James, writes to his father. He objects to Lovelace,
whom he knew and disliked at college, where the sons of the
aristocracy scorned new men like James. Since the gentleman
after his daughter is rich and heir to a title, greedy Mr. Harlowe
has accepted him as a suitor for Clarissa; but he maintains reser-
vations in deference to his son and heir. For her part, Clarissa
claims "indifference," and "therefore" she condescends to enter
into a correspondence with Lovelace; he has agreed to write a
series of descriptions of European countries he has visited for the
benefit of a ward of her uncle, but only on the condition that
Clarissa, who writes well, be his correspondent. This epistolary

relationship, continued after James Harlowe has returned home and provoked a duel with Lovelace, who wounds him, will finally entrap her. In the hope of preventing further violence and in order to apologize for her family's rude treatment, she continues to write; her terrified mother agrees that she do so; but as Miss Howe knows, there are other reasons.

Lovelace attracts Clarissa, who denies it, by his incomprehensible, foreign, terrifying passion and his wit and freedom, his fine personal and literary style and his gallantry, and also by his physical beauty. She is eighteen. The confusing sexual awakening he provokes is complicated by "the odious Solmes," the suitor of her parents' and her brother's choice. It is not simply that Clarissa disapproves of Solmes's illiteracy and his manners and his ungenerous attitude toward his relatives, which she does, and not merely that she has no interest in his conversation, which she hasn't; she experiences violent negative sensations in the neighborhood of his body. She is contemptuous of him, but not coolly:

> The man stalked in. His usual walk is by pauses, as if (from the same vacuity of thought which made Dryden's clown whistle) he was telling his steps: and first paid his clumsy respects to my mother; then to my sister; next to me, as if I were already his wife, and therefore to be last in his notice; and sitting down by me, told us in general what weather it was. Very cold he made it; but I was warm enough. (I, Letter XXI)

Richardson was wise about the sexual attractions and repulsions of intelligence and the lack of it. It is appropriate that revulsion pushes Clarissa to absolute self-confident clarity. She makes the flesh crawl, although the spirit is where she locates the source of her disgust:

> there was the odious Solmes sitting asquat between my mother and sister, with *so much* assurance in his looks! . . .
> Had the wretch kept his seat, it might have been well

49

enough: but the bent and broad-shouldered creature must needs rise and stalk towards a chair; which was just by that which was set for me.

I removed it to a distance, as if to make way to my own: And down I sat, abruptly I believe. . . .

But this was not enough to daunt him. The man is a very confident, he is a very bold, staring man! Indeed, my dear, the man is very confident!

He took the removed chair and drew it so near mine, squatting in it with his ugly weight, that he pressed upon my hoop. I was so offended . . . that I removed to another chair. I own I had too little command of myself. It gave my brother and sister too much advantage. I dare say they took it. But I did it involuntarily, I think. I could not help it. (I, Letter XVI)

That this Solmes sadistically anticipates the joys of her resistance in the nuptial bed is one of the early prophetic horrors of Clarissa's plight. The conflict between Clarissa and Lovelace is an image of the battle between all women and all men. Of the men in the novel, only Anna Howe's fiancé, Hickman, whom his beloved deplores as "a *passive*," so boring that he drives her to the harpsichord to drown him out, seems to want to give as well as get pleasure with a woman. Anna and Clarissa describe the unattractive marriages of their parents, and smaller black stories of relationships between the sexes pepper the novel's pages. As the Harlowes try to force their daughter to marry a man she hates, the horrors of a woman's life in marriage are precisely drawn: she must give up her name, her wealth, her body, her privacy, and for life. Married, she will no longer be a separate person; she will become a shadow like Mrs. Harlowe, overwhelmed in the power of her husband. One looks almost in vain for a loving marriage in the novel. Lovelace is wary of marriage because he reasonably fears it will bore him; Clarissa is reasonably terrified that it will annihilate her.

Men seem especially to blame for the horrors of family life, but on the other hand Miss Howe's relationship with her widowed mother is not comfortable either. *Clarissa* suggests that the root of human difficulty is a desire for power that is lodged in the flesh. For Lovelace the sexual relationship is more than anything else a way of asserting power. He tells how he restrained himself from seducing the daughter of an innkeeper, and even gave her lover money so that she could be honorably married. "Spare my Rosebud!" he begs his fellow rake Belford, and it is clear he enjoys the assumption that Rosebud is his to spare, and the gratitude of her grandmother and her lover, and the dependency of the young couple, and the anticipation of the maiden's being led to bed, and his own posture. Lovelace wants power more than he wants women; he wants acknowledgment, fame, more than actual domination. Solmes and the Harlowe men make it evident that his attitude is not idiosyncratic. All of them want to crush Clarissa because as an Exemplar she is of considerable personal significance.

As all of Clarissa's relatives but one (the Cousin Morden who is abroad and will return to England too late) join together "to force a free mind," not merely marriage but all relationships of blood and body come to seem terrible. There are two bachelor uncles (Clarissa has a surplus of fathers), a married aunt, the Harlowe parents themselves, and the two children in whom the parental viciousness and hostility to Clarissa are intensified. They are children who have been less loved than she and they hate her for it. James and Arabella work together closely: at one point Clarissa sees them holding hands, "lover-like"; they egg on the father, who respects his son for being likely to be richer than he and is infuriated by a mere daughter who opposes him. Her relatives' collusion makes Clarissa's waking life (she sleeps less and less) a nightmare. Sartre suggested that hell is other people; purgatory, Richardson implies, is one's near relations. The happenings at Harlowe Place are out of R. D. Laing.

Like all politics, the politics of the family involve economics. Anna Howe says that the Harlowes are "too rich to be happy," and the comment is echoed by Cousin Morden at the end of the novel. Clarissa is independently wealthy, having been left enough to live on by her grandfather's will. This legacy is what provokes the envy of her family as a whole, and especially her brother and sister. "This little siren is in a fair way to *out-uncle*, as she has already *out-grandfathered* us both!" James warns Arabella (I, Letter XIII). Because of Clarissa's extraordinary charm and virtue and the grandfather's consequent unusual provision, some of the Harlowe property will go out of the family when Clarissa marries. James Harlowe has cause to fear that if Clarissa marries an aristocrat (like Lovelace), the uncles will follow the grandfather's example and leave their money to her: she would be the one to connect the Harlowes well and therefore be acknowledged as representative of the family. James, who already has his godmother's estate and has hopes of his uncles' as well as his father's, plans to pay his sister off in cash if she marries not splendidly but merely well. Then he will "raise a family," or acquire knighthood, himself. He has arranged to trade his northern property for Solmes's estate in the county when Clarissa marries him, an extensive "seat" being the first step toward aristocracy. He has clear practical, materialistic reasons as well as ones he does not acknowledge for plotting against his sister.

Although Clarissa's grandfather has left her a house of her own—he allowed her to design it herself, we recall when she designs her coffin—and the wherewithal to live in it independently, she refuses both. Her private fortune is a source and a symbol of Clarissa's specialness: she is more than a commodity to be bartered with like an ordinary dependent daughter. Yet in her own divided mind Clarissa is chattel and free woman at once. The fidelity to higher spiritual law on which she prides herself makes her disdain material settlements and wills. She has refused to claim her inheritance and has given over the management of her estate to her father. Independent wealth is not something she can approve of in a woman; it is right, she thinks, to relinquish the legitimate claim. Virtue as she defines it is obliged to spurn material things, even if they are Virtue's own.

As an Exemplar Clarissa must not compromise with reality; she cannot even acknowledge it. Although her parents cease to behave as loving parents, Clarissa insists on continuing to be respectful, not of what they are but of what they ought to be. It is an instance of the credulous commitment to the ideas individuals represent that determines the course of her heroine's destiny. The family home becomes a prison as the Harlowes insist on "rich Solmes." (Harlowe Place, obviously, is made of money. When Lovelace describes it he uses the appropriate Freudian imagery, saying disdainfully that "like Versailles, it is sprung up from a dunghill" [I, Letter XXXIV].) Self-righteousness imprisons Clarissa as much as her parents; while it is her legal right to demand the estate her grandfather left her, it is not within her imaginative scope. Clarissa defines herself as an ideally dutiful daughter, and such an act of (as she conceives it) filial impiety would be a sort of self-destruction. She can only imagine being destroyed by others, which would not contradict her idea of herself as a paragon of virtue.

One of Clarissa's more fascinating relationships is with her mother: she is determined to be different from her mother and afraid she is like her. Mrs. Harlowe, as Clarissa sees her, has been bludgeoned by a tyrannical husband into becoming a tyrant herself; by nonresistance to evil, she has done evil, in a sense more than her husband has, because her collusion in the pressures on her daughter hurts Clarissa more than anyone else's. Clarissa has expected her father to behave like a tyrant; of her mother she expected more, and in her mother she is therefore more disappointed. (Later, the fact that women are instrumental in her ruin, "female figures flitting" while Lovelace rapes her, shocks and hurts her especially—over-censorious of men, she has equally exaggerated but opposite expectations of women.) The pressures the Harlowes bring to bear on her are telling: you will make everybody happy, says her Aunt Hervey, by marrying Solmes; one's chances of being happy in any marriage are small, so why not marry Solmes and satisfy your parents and brother and sister and uncles—so many people! Strong physical feelings—revulsion from Solmes, attraction to Lovelace—and other feelings, too—resentment of brother and sister, childlike belief in the love of her parents, conviction that she can manage as she always has before—all these enable Clarissa to remain adamant. But her Aunt Hervey moves her: she has been so used, as she keeps saying, to thinking of others and not herself. She says it is a "dangerous" way to be; she sees it is the way her mother is. Her mother wants nothing but the preservation of the status quo, not because it is good but because it is better, in all probability, than an unknown alternative. Like Clarissa, Mrs. Harlowe is mistrustful of events. For the sake of keeping things quiet, keeping a potentially violent husband in good humor, she has given up a worth (she is better-born) greater than her husband's. Clarissa's struggle is against becoming such a cipher. But it is in the name of peace, which her mother values above all else, that she runs off with Lovelace in the face of his threats to kill himself and/or rouse her father and brother to arms.

The Harlowes have locked her up in her room; they have threatened to isolate her further by taking her off to an uncle's moated house (her horror of the moat is extreme), where there is a chapel to marry her in. They watch her, they search her things, they take away her paper and pens (of course she hides a few away; they are her life's blood and the novel's). Ambassadors are sent up to her from below with threats and ultimata. Much of the Harlowes' activity, we know but she doesn't, is caused by the invisible predatory Lovelace, who boasts to his friend Belford that the family are puppets on his strings, scared into action by rumors he plants, doing precisely what he wants them to do, which is to push Clarissa into running off with him. He has bribed a servant, who informs him of everything that goes on inside Harlowe Place.

Lovelace is one of two people outside her father's house with whom Clarissa is in contact. Miss Howe has been forced by her mother to offer no help; in secret defiance, she suggests something Clarissa cannot accept, her personal involvement in her friend's elopement. The two girls would go off together, Anna plans, but Clarissa refuses: such an escapade would cast a shadow on Anna's own reputation. Can we believe that Clarissa is too fiercely protective of her friend's reputation to risk compromising it for the sake of her own future? I do; the abstraction Virtue seems to her at this point manifest in Reputation, so Miss Howe's fame means more than anyone's body. Lovelace offers Clarissa, who is surrounded by the enclosing walls of her own people's wills and the inhibiting ideology she has accepted with her role, the only escape. What he literally offers is the protection of his *house*: when he uses it the word has something other than the literal, bourgeois Harlowe meaning. The "house" of the heir of Lord M. is not even M. Hall but more grandly and abstractly his family, Lady Sarah and Lady Betty and the Misses Montague and all the ladies who have lived before them. Clarissa, dazzled, reports to Miss Howe that the ladies of his family hope Lovelace will marry her " 'for the honour of their *house*,' was the magnificent word" (II, Letter XXIII). Committed to elevated virtue and immutability, attracted to beauty and charm, Clarissa Harlowe is impressed by rank.

She agrees, finally, to go with him, but a haunting, prophetic statement of Miss Howe's—"Punctilio is out of doors the moment you are out of your father's house" (I, Letter LXXXVII)—and other reflections move Clarissa to change her mind. She leaves him a letter saying so, which in a brilliant passive maneuver he neglects to pick up from the place in the garden wall that serves as their mailbox. She suspects him of deliberately leaving it there—she is so conscious of his plotting that we flickeringly suspect her of wishing him to be precisely what he is—and she resolves to meet him and tell him she will not go. Later, she will say she cannot imagine why it seemed to her imperative to do that; at the time, she rationalizes that, after all, she promised to explain. (Yet she exonerates herself of the charge of breaking another promise, to go with him, on the ground that a daughter's promise unsanctioned by her father is invalid while she is in his house; this she supports, with Richardson's help in a footnote, by chapter and verse from the Bible. As Dr. Johnson remarked, there is always something she prefers to the truth.) It is evident that she has a real need to see Lovelace, based perhaps on her admiration of that graceful figure which, she tells Miss Howe, it is impossible for him to disguise (he can fool her by a disguise later, when she has come to hate him); more important is her desire to convince him that she is right in deciding against the elopement. It will not do for Clarissa Harlowe simply to do what is right; she must also convince everyone around her that it is.

She accepts the idea of herself as an Exemplar, therefore the doctrine that every act of hers must teach others. Another way to put it is to say that her own seemingly absolute standards of correctness are dependent on the approval of others: of her parents, of Miss Howe, who counsels against flight and then, after the flight, for immediate marriage, and even of Lovelace, whose moral standards she disparages. How unrealistic to want him to think her right, when she knows he wants to carry her off, and more, when she has insisted that his standards of right and wrong are altogether faulty and must be changed! As unrealistic as an insistence that she remain the dutiful daughter of a loving father no longer in existence!

Her bizarre idea—all her ideas of human relationships are unrealistic—is that Lovelace will help her to go off and be somewhere from which she will begin to make peace with her family. She experiences enmity in her father's house; she wants the opposite of that, love. No mixture, nothing in between, seems to her possible; as the divine Clarissa she was beloved of all, and in order to remain Clarissa she must continue to be beloved. You could say that she conceives of herself as existing only in the eyes of others; or you could say that the outside world is barely outside her at all. Her mother's passivity, her sister's resentment, are aspects of herself; even her father's pride reflects something of her. She experiences her own importance and indeed her individuality through their appraisals of her: her self is the sum of their appraisals. At one point she admits to Miss Howe that what she used to think was concern for others was actually concern for what others think of her. Lovelace assures her that he'll fix things up so everyone will love her again, and he comes to let her out the garden door. When she says she will not go, he pretends (he has concocted the scenario with his agent, the servant, in advance) that people from the house are coming, and that he will fight them. Clarissa is terrified and he hustles her off into the waiting carriage.

Before that, there is an elaborate play with the key to the garden door. That he comes to her with a bared sword under his arm is lesser sexual imagery: the fumbling with lock and key and the escape out the garden door are brilliant bits of a novel that is about claustrophobia as much as it is about sex. With the loving perversity that characterizes Richardson at his most marvelous and "oozy," as Coleridge put it, *Clarissa* lingers over the terrors of being enclosed, isolated, unable to get out, hopelessly separated and walled in with death. (Variations on the theme proliferate as all its implications are investigated: Clarissa, still at Harlowe Place, presses herself desperately against a door and it is opened by malicious relatives, causing her to fall on her face; Solmes, with lumpish awkwardness, backs into a door; James Harlowe blocks Lovelace's way through the doorway; expatiating on his skill at corrupting servants, Lovelace says one must look to the "back door." Commonplaces and clichés—"darken my door," "death's door," etc.—swell to significance in the stagnant atmosphere.) Clarissa, whose father's house had seemed surety of safety before it became a fun house for the horrid Harlowes, its walls suddenly mirrors that distorted her image into ugliness, begs Lovelace to leave her to herself in a locked room. And he, of course, finds rooms suitable for his opposite purposes. (Floor plans map destinies.) The "vile house" of Mrs. Sinclair, a brothel, is his objective; there he plans to seduce Clarissa. Hidden behind another house which looks out on the London street, duplicitous by design, it will prove a caricature of her home, with "Mother" Sinclair abetting the plans of the rake, who likes to see himself as fatherly. He forges a letter, purportedly by a helpful friend, describing the apartments Clarissa may have there, which include a "light closet" where she can privately pursue her correspondence with Miss Howe, her only solace and the affirmation and source of her identity. Fooled, she goes, and after an escape Lovelace foils she is tricked into going back, and then raped there. From her father's house Clarissa travels only from jail to jail; once she is literally locked up by the law. Near the novel's end and hers, hounded by Lovelace, she spends a day abroad in a hired coach, and another afloat in a rowboat, so that he will be unable to find her. Public inns and drifting conveyances become, by a brilliant, persuasive trick of narrative logic, the only havens for the dying girl seeking a room of her own in which to define, by writing letters, her uniqueness and separateness. Finally, she ascends to a heaven she calls "my Father's house" in an effort to con Lovelace into expecting her at Harlowe Place; the phrase is also an honest description of the only vision she can possibly have of the site of everlasting life.


The house is the setting and the central image of the gothic novel. From its beginnings, in the dim stone vaults of the Castle of Otranto, that tradition has explored the hiding places of evil indoors. The castle, a monument to man's self-assertion, an indication that he can control his environment, a display of strength, wealth, and pride, because of its very size and magnificence is a place where sinister forces can secrete themselves, hide in the snug recesses of an attic or a room or a passage. The shelter from natural enemies—wild beasts, strangers, the weather—shelters unnatural ones, supernatural ones, ghosts and avengers the resident would prefer buried. The threatening recesses of the magnificent castle suggest the part of the mind denied by the daylight self. The castle of gothic is subversively a metaphor for the heroine, while the plot says it contains what threatens her; the suggestion that part of herself makes another part its victim, like the implication that a woman is unnatural, an artifact as a house is, makes the image more compelling. For Richardson, who exploits all its mythic significance, the house is associated with all imaginative constructs and concepts, works of art and artifice, that both define and confine the individual: the idea of an Exemplar, for instance.

Clothing is a related image: women's clothes, in the eighteenth century, were formidable enclosures. *Pamela* makes brilliant use of them: when the heroine stays on alone with Mr. B. after his mother, her mistress, dies, he gives her his mother's rich stays and fine stockings, and she endures his assaults on her chastity because she dutifully wants to finish "flowering him a waistcoat"; she plants her bonnet and skirts near a lake to trick him into believing she has drowned herself; she pads her pockets with letters that foil his roaming hands the way Bibles stop bullets in old war movies. Clarissa Harlowe, we are told, was regarded by her neighbors as a fashion plate and a style setter, but Anna Howe insists she dressed with merely natural simplicity and grace, which only *seemed* artful to others, and only became fashionable because it was *her* style and reflected her innate elegance. In his introduction to an abridged edition of the novel, George Sherburn points out that Clarissa's clothes—we are told how much they cost—are extraordinarily expensive for a middle-class young girl living quietly in the country. Richardson dressed her up for multiple contradictory reasons: to signify that she is "too rich to be happy," to manifest her pride, to declare her real spiritual gorgeousness, to indicate the solidity and the material nature of the wall between men and her virginity, the world and her. He was literal-minded: he saw that clothes do not make the woman but seem to, and that they can prevent her from being made. Her clothing is Clarissa's armor: Lovelace's early attempts, once she is in his power, are simply, as a first step, to glimpse her in dishabille. But she is vigilant. To his dismay and awe, she is fully dressed as early as four in the morning, not merely covered but correctly arrayed, a rebuke to the mere thought of impropriety, nakedness, physical desire. Richardson knew clothes affect the wearer as well as the beholder: when Lovelace sets a fire and manages to rouse her from sleep and get a peek at her breasts, Clarissa is reduced to cries and collapses. When formally clothed, she rebukes her tormentor with dignity.

Clothing gives Clarissa actual power as well as the useful illusion of it. Toward the end of her life, when she is alone and poor, she sells her clothes and lives on what they bring her. Before that comes her escape from the whorehouse where she has been raped: she manages to get away by promising one of her enviable dresses to a maid, arranging to have a seamstress come and alter it, and slipping into the maid's clothes herself. That she dons humble dress neatly symbolizes Clarissa's having been reduced in worldly status; there is also a suggestion that she has been more seriously, *i.e.*, morally, compromised. For it is Lovelace's way, and not Clarissa's, to masquerade: did she put on his manner in his power? By pretenses he managed to carry Clarissa off, and by pretending again he captured her when she escaped to Hampstead. Repeatedly, in the course of the novel, he changes lying into truth and vice versa: after he has first brought Clarissa to Mrs. Sinclair's, for instance, he takes a drug to make himself sick and then, sick in fact, moves Clarissa to show the real feeling for him that she had refused to reveal. The lie is his characteristic test for truth; lying is his truth; he confuses show and substance. But he does not win, finally, by his deceit: his plot has failed, so he can only rape and not seduce her, drugging her first, depriving her of will and himself of the victory he could gain only with her consent. Winning, he loses her. And, losing, Clarissa wins. When she goes to the uncharacteristic length of disguising herself in order to escape Mrs. Sinclair's house, Clarissa begins the process of translating the enclosures that have oppressed her into artifacts that express her. She learns to use first clothes and finally rooms, which had seemed to protect but in fact falsified and restricted her self, as she wishes to use them. She learns, even, to lie, or to clothe meaning in metaphor. Letters, like rooms and dresses, protect and present and enclose the self. They are used so brilliantly in this novel that one suspects the epistolary tradition did not endure because Richardson exhausted it in its infancy.

A middle-aged printer with a family of daughters, Richardson liked writing letters to members of his family in different rooms of the same house. As a boy, he recollected, he had made himself useful by writing love letters for the illiterate young women of his neighborhood. In his fifties, he wrote a book of "model letters"; he proceeded logically to write an epistolary novel, *Pamela*, because of his inclination to "instruct them how they should think and act in common cases, as well as indite." It was business sense that made Samuel Richardson give the new reading public what it wanted and thought (he agreed) it needed; and also he was deeply interested in letters as intermediaries between people and as both shapes and shapers of the soul. When his oldest daughter seemed eager to marry a surgeon from Bath after a very short acquaintance, he was in favor of the young man's returning home for a period of time so that the couple might correspond and discover each other's heart by letter. He seems to have had doubts about his future son-in-law, who was sponsored by Mrs. Richardson, and surely he also meant what he implied: that Polly and Mr. Ditcher would learn more about each other through letters than through meetings. Did he think the young people would be distracted from the truth by their bodies? inhibited by looks? by conventions? liberated by writing in solitude? Did he, who prescribed "correct" ways of expressing intimate thoughts and feelings, believe it was possible or even desirable that people correspond with complete sincerity? One can only conjecture. Richardson himself wrote voluminously to people he knew, and got to know people (the most important to him was a Lady Bradshaigh) by writing letters. In correspondence with his female admirers he gently disputed questions of right conduct posed by life and his novels. Only Wordsworth among English men of letters can be compared to him in need and ability to attract a company of female satellites. Richardson's wife and daughters were silent among the bluestockings who visited him. He was surrounded by women at home; more women came to visit from outside; he wrote about women. In one of the letters to Belford, in which Lovelace compares his "bashful" soul to a woman's, rakish put-on and cynicism barely conceal the accents of a short, shy, plump London printer:

> I have had abundant cause, when I have looked into *myself*, by way of comparison with the *other* sex, to conclude that a bashful man has a good deal of the soul of a woman; and so, like Tiresias, can tell what they think, and what they drive at, as well as themselves.
>
> The modest ones and I, particularly, are pretty much upon a par. The difference between us is only, what they *think*, I *act*. (II, Letter XVI)

Dr. Johnson said that the "soul lies naked" in letters; he also said that "there is . . . no transaction which offers stronger temptations to fallacy and sophistication than epistolary intercourse." People who try to bare their souls in a letter grapple with the fact that revealing comes quickly to its opposite. By being put into words, feelings are inadequately represented, even misrepresented; the act of putting them into words, and the fact of having put them, changes feelings. As she struggles against her parents and Solmes and Lovelace, Clarissa means to write all she feels to Miss Howe, who loves her; but it is important to remember that Miss Howe is in awe of her friend the Exemplar, and is a very quick-witted girl. Are you sure, she keeps asking Clarissa, are you quite, quite sure you aren't in love with this Lovelace? Of course Clarissa is; and of course it isn't quite love; and she is also afraid of whatever it is, and ignorant of what it might be; and even if she knew she couldn't admit it to Miss Howe without confusing her friend and jeopardizing the adulation that nourishes her. So she writes, before she leaves home, like this:

> I should be very blameable to endeavour to hide any the least bias upon my mind, from you: and I cannot but say that this man—this Lovelace—is a man that might be liked well enough, if he bore such a character as Mr. Hickman bears; and even if there were hopes of reclaiming him. And further still, I will acknowledge that I believe it possible that one might be driven, by violent measures, step by step as it were, into something that might be called—I don't know what to call it—a *conditional kind of liking*, or so. But as to the word LOVE justifiable and charming as it is in some cases (that is to say, in all the *relative*, in all the *social*, and, what is still beyond *both*, in all our *superior* duties, in which it may be properly called *divine*); it has, methinks, in the narrow, circumscribed, selfish, peculiar sense in which you apply it to me (the man, too, so little to be approved of for his morals, if all that report says of him be true) no pretty sound with it. (I, Letter XXVIII)

The contorted sentences reflect a mind examining itself, nearly flirting with the titillations of violence and the ambition to reform an ungodly man. It is oversimplification to call Clarissa a hypocrite—to read *Clarissa* as a novel about repressed sexuality is to reduce it to banality. But to dwell as Clarissa does on all these contradictions of feeling—is that not to overcomplicate life and make it unwieldy? By this novel of disproportionate, exhausting length, Richardson does just that; sanity requires that we stop short of seeing so many complexities in order to function in the real world. Yet in the real world such madness repeatedly intrudes: it is not idiosyncratically Richardson but the mind that overcomplicates. Not lusts and hatreds but self-doubts and deluding self-images are the dark side of us to which Richardson, as Diderot observed, carries a torch.

Lovelace arouses himself by writing letters that linger on the details of his victim's delectable discomfort: "I am—I am—*very* unhappy—tears trickling down her crimson cheeks, and her sweet face, as my arms still encircled the finest waist in the world, sinking upon my shoulder; the dear creature so absent that she knew not the honour she permitted me" (II, Letter XXXIX). Partly because of necessity (he knows it will take a long time to break her down) and partly because he has a real passion for foreplay, he is obsessed not merely with enjoying Clarissa, as they used to call it, but with the ways and means of managing to do so. One hesitates to go so far as to suggest that he collects sexual experience in order to write about it, but it is evident that detailed letters heighten his pleasure and perhaps draw out the pursuit. By taking up the rake's tone he thinks himself obliged to continue even after Belford's tune changes, he gives stronger outline to that persona which is behaving cruelly to Clarissa. The Exemplar's antagonist, the Rake, is an impossibly literary self-image, as the Exemplar is, an artifact. The word confines and distorts the living self. One wonders: might he have softened if he had ceased reaffirming the Rake in letters? Might she have?

Very few letters between hero and heroine are included in the novel: the two fail to make real contact. The bulk of the correspondence is from woman to woman and man to man, and in it there is a lot of generalization on the nature of the opposite sex. Lovelace writes and behaves as a recognized delegate from the party of men against the party of women, and Clarissa holds herself rigid with the consciousness that what she does will not only be widely spoken of but will be important to the rest of her sex. After she has run off from her father's house, Clarissa wonders if her fate is not a punishment for pride, and still pridefully but now with an increase of consciousness she sees this punishment as didactic: "How am I punished, as I frequently think, for my vanity in hoping to be an *example* to young persons of my sex! Let me be but a *warning* and I will now be contented" (II, Letter XXI). When the two are together their reports back to the hostile camps of their allegiance exacerbate their opposition. Egotism is magnified by sexual allegiance; he is not merely Lovelace but "a Lovelace," and she "a Clarissa," their punning names turned emblems. One might dismiss a passage like this one as Richardson's attempt to seize an epic dimension his novel does not warrant, but it is dramatically valid. Lovelace is magnifying his sex life to gigantic proportions, for that it is magnified is an aspect of his sex life. He has carried her off, and claims to be testing so as to prove her:

> And now, if I have not found a virtue that cannot be corrupted, I will swear that there is not one such in the whole sex. Is not then the whole sex concerned that this trial should be made? And who is it that knows this lady, that would not stake upon her head the honour of the whole? Let her who would refuse it come forth, and desire to stand in her place. (II, Letter XI)

The note of the trumpet is characteristic of Lovelace, who likes to think of himself as a public figure. Not only must he describe to his friend Belford every move he makes, and have witnesses present when he finally rapes Clarissa; but his language indicates that he fancies himself of even greater social importance than he is. His is an "imperial will"; he compares himself to popes and potentates. Lovelace was created at the beginning of a long tradition of English novels about love between ladies and gentlemen who do not work. The nephew of Lord M. will sit in Parliament and have some influence on the affairs of the nation, though. When Miss Howe plans to save Clarissa with the help of smugglers, Lovelace intercepts her letters and writes righteously to his factotum, "McDonald," that "private vices are less blamable than public," calling smuggling "a national evil" (III, Letter LXI). He really seems to think himself identified with the interest of the nation, and therefore more virtuous than Miss Howe. (It is interesting that Miss Howe, whose whole life, since she is a woman, is private, has nothing against smugglers.) But until Lord M. dies Lovelace can do nothing but manage his estates. He can have only fantasies of ruling, and whether they mingle with sexual fantasies because sex is the only arena available to him or because all such fantasies are deeply sexual is for the reader to decide. This is from a letter to Belford, written from Hampstead, while Lovelace is delightedly planning the trick that will enable him to recapture his victim, who is hiding in a house there:

> Upper Flask, Hampstead, Friday morn.
> 7 o'clock (June 9)

> I am now here, and here have been this hour and half. What an industrious spirit have I! Nobody can say that I eat the bread of idleness. I take true pains for all the pleasure I enjoy. I cannot but admire myself strangely; for certainly, with this active soul, I should have made a very great figure in whatever station I had filled. But had I been a prince!—To be sure I should have made a most *noble* prince! I should have led up a military dance equal to that of the great Macedonian. I should have added kingdom to kingdom, and despoiled all my neighbour sovereigns, in order to have obtained the name of *Robert the Great*. And I would have gone to war with the Great Turk, and the Persian, and Mogul, for their seraglios; for not one of those Eastern monarchs should have had a pretty woman to bless himself with till I had done with her. (III, Letter IV)

Self-consciousness and a sneaking sense of his own ridiculousness make him admit that as Robert the Great he would have been after women still, women first of all, and the military metaphor dissolves.

Lovelace thinks of himself as a conquistador; he thinks of Clarissa, and she thinks of herself, as a fortress. For all that I have said about her sexual interest in her antagonist, it is absurd to say that *really* she wants to be raped. Like his, her deepest and most morally questionable desire is not for mutual sex; it is for power. She wants to reform the rake. It is characteristic of her to translate desire into duty, to conceive of what she wants as a burden, a part of her burdensome self. Wholly dedicated to the care and maintenance of their separate identities, therefore inevitably dependent on other people in whom their selves are reflected, Clarissa and Lovelace are opposing principles: ultimate self-assertion for each of them involves denial of the other. Clarissa, famous for chastity, cannot say yes to Lovelace, who wants her acknowledgment that he is the only man in the world who can change her mind; Lovelace, famous as a sexual conqueror, cannot be reformed by Clarissa, who would assert her power by changing the man dedicated to destroying it. He can no more be Lovelace and a husband than she can be Clarissa his wife or mistress. From the road Clarissa writes to Anna Howe, "We are both great watchers of each other's eyes; and indeed seem to be more than half afraid of each other" (II, Letter XXVI). Although or because both are fluent writers to their friends of their own gender, words do not work well during their interviews. Appearances govern them; once, overcome by passion, he falls on his knees and proposes marriage, but her helpless fascination with watching herself from another's point of view prevents her from taking him, all vulnerable, at his word: "What *could* I say? I paused, I looked silly—I am *sure* I looked very silly. He suffered me to pause and look silly, *waiting for* me *to say something . . .*" (II, Letter XXXVIII). They can make neither head nor tail of one another. Lovelace is the more obviously guilty of blindness to another's humanity, but Clarissa, who runs off with him and then keeps haughtily lecturing him on his sinfulness, may be— and is—accused of something like his inability to perceive someone else as real. Each of them wants what Chaucer (he said love would not be constrained by it) called "maistrye." And more, each of them wants the other to be the impossible, simultaneously what he is and what he is not.

Their own appearances keep deceiving; the imagery that describes them is inadequate. She seems to be an angel in white, all spirit, a bird, sometimes a bird in a cage like a soul in a body; and he seems the very Devil, all body, an animal. "Like a restive horse . . . ," Clarissa says, "he pains one's hands, and half disjoints one's arms to rein him in" (I, Letter XXVI). He is less like an animal than a literary man as he describes a barnyard scene in an ingenious pursuit of the metaphor of the bird as spirit, converting the divine Clarissa into a hen:

> A strutting rascal of a cock have I beheld chuck, chuck, chuck, chucking his mistress to him, when he has found a single barley-corn, taking it up with his bill, and letting it drop five or six times, still repeating his chucking invitation; and when two or three of his feathered ladies strive who shall be the first for it [O *Jack! a cock is a grand signor of a bird!*] he directs the bill of the foremost to it; and, when she has got the dirty pearl, he struts over her with an erected crest, and with an exulting chuck-a chuck-aw-aw-w, circling round her with dropped wings, sweeping the dust in humble courtship; while the obliged she, half-shy, half-willing, by her cowering tail, prepared wings, yet seemingly affrighted eyes, and contracted neck, lets one see that she knows the barley-corn was not all he called her for. (II, Letter XIX)

Such a writer is "a man of sense," as Miss Howe grudgingly admits. Lies and disguises are to him what punctilio or adherence to a code of formal behavior is to Clarissa; she is no more all diaphanous spirit than he is all uncivilized animal. Both are human, which to Richardson means that both are deeply, uncomfortably committed to illusory and inadequate forms. Writers, both are kinds of artists.

His cleverness with words and imaginative aliveness to metaphor distinguish Lovelace from plain, blunt fools like Solmes and all the Harlowe men, platitudinous bores like his uncle, Lord M., and pedantic clods like Elias Brand. By keeping us waiting so long for Lovelace's first letter, and then by interleaving his letters with Clarissa's painstaking examinations of her conscience so they occur as relieving bursts of confident energy, Richardson plays Pandarus between the rake and his readers. A complex and

talented man, Lovelace is an attractive creature. He is persuasive
even when Richardson's compulsion to complicate turns him
into an analyst of texts: as he probes between the lines of the
dying Clarissa's meditations to find in her imagery evidence that
she is pregnant, we are convinced of the reality of an unlikely
man indeed, the rake as literary critic. Because Lovelace is artful,
good at managing appearances, he seems to us worthwhile, worth
saving. Lovelace the Romantic hero, a man of satanic drives, real
sensibility, and creative egotism, is in a way validated by a novel
that takes his obsessions seriously. This man, and not a mere
Restoration rake, attracts the fascinated virgin Clarissa.

Creating goddesses in order to destroy them, Lovelace is an
artist. Clarissa is his equal and his opposite: self-preservation is
her work because her self is the medium she works in. Like
Lovelace, Clarissa is attractive and physically desirable, and like
Lovelace she is artful, as her brother disparagingly says. The
novel plays constantly with questions about the morality of illusions. Clarissa is good at writing letters, although, being a girl,
she never went to school: like her lover's, her talent for appearing well is innate, natural. The differences between them as artists can be phrased variously: in moral terms, or in social terms
(she works for the good of society, while he is antisocial), or best
of all in terms of their objectives. Both of them seek to make art
out of the materials of life by identifying real women with an
ideal: the difference between them is that Clarissa is herself a
woman. The Romantic identification of the artist, the art object,
and the process of making art is made in her. That is why the
novel is Clarissa's—why Clarissa is the novel. The dialectic between Clarissa and Lovelace accounts for much of its brilliance
and for its comprehensiveness; the tension within Clarissa herself is the heart of its complexity and its wisdom.


Multiple ironies inhere in the fact that the central action of this
slow novel about psychological stresses is a rape. The rape points
to the sexual dimension of that idea of personal integrity and
autonomy which is Richardson's and Lovelace's and Clarissa's

concern. Rape dramatizes self-assertion linked to violation of another as it is linked in Mr. Harlowe's mind and Lovelace's. And it reifies as it violates the objectified Clarissa. By his attitude and intention and manner, a rapist changes the act of love into an act of hate: in a sense rape therefore is, perversely, an assertion of the imagination. Lovelace, dedicated to being acknowledged as a great lover, performs unimpressively upon an unconscious victim, for Clarissa has been drugged. Clarissa, famous for chastity, is not only not consenting but unaware. Is that the real reason she remains chaste in mind? The rape illustrates the fact that both Clarissa's and Lovelace's social roles, as virgin and rake, depend on the alienation of self from sex: he thinks of sex as destruction, and she thinks of it as a dying. (The social manifestation of this alienation on the part of both the upper class [Lovelace] and the bourgeoisie [Clarissa] is Mrs. Sinclair and her "nymphs," prostitutes whose *clear sin* represents the evil of fleshly indulgence to ladies and gentlemen devoted to continence and its brother, callous sex.) Lovelace the writer does not describe the rape: "The affair is over. Clarissa lives," he writes to Belford with stupid wit (III, Letter XXIX). Later on, the formerly analytic Clarissa records her vague recollections. This novel swelled to unnatural length by loving attention to detail converts the pivotal point in its plot into a blur. This is another telling irony: Clarissa is not violated by her violator, which makes the rape a dramatic form without content. What happened did not matter. One reason you cannot read Richardson for the story without hanging yourself is that story, action, becomes in his hands mere form, finite and therefore inadequately expressive. Like the possibility that Clarissa might be pregnant, the physical rape is an effect of questionable reality.

The rupture of Clarissa's consciousness interests Richardson more than the tear in the hymen invested with so much meaning. (Lovelace calls the physical one "a mere *notional violation* [III, Letter XL], a tortuous attempt to defend himself that has some truth to it, as we are tempted to agree that since she did not *know* Lovelace, she is a virgin still.) The victim is afterward "raving mad," Lovelace reports, and subject to blackouts. He fears, he says, that the damage to the mind may be permanent, and Clarissa laments her bewilderment and loss:

> What you, or Mrs. Sinclair, or somebody (I cannot tell who) have done to my poor head, you best know: but I shall never be what I was. My head is gone. I have wept away all my brain, I believe; for I can weep no more. Indeed I have had my full share; so it is no matter. (III, Letter XXXIII)

Lovelace alone raped her, but through Clarissa's letters Richardson makes it clear that that is just a technicality. And other technicalities compromise it: Mrs. Sinclair administered the drug, she and the whores witnessed the rape. To Clarissa it seems the culmination of the elaborate conspiracy against her that began at Harlowe Place, and although Lovelace says Clarissa is mad, to read the novel is to know that she is absolutely right. The attempt all along was to overpower Clarissa's will, as the drug did. Clarissa upbraids Lovelace: "My heart rises against thee, O thou *cruel implement of my brother's causeless vengeance*. All I beg of thee is, that thou wilt remit me the *future* part of my father's dreadful curse! The *temporary* part, base and ungrateful as thou art! thou hast completed!" (III, Letter XLVIII). The rapist is the Harlowe men's agent.

Mad or sane, Clarissa is haunted by other people and what they have the power to do to her. Clarissa exists only in relationships: it is why she exists only in letters. Mad, she tears up what she writes, and the servant brings Lovelace the pieces; "eloquent nonsense," he calls them, "which rather shows a raised, than a quenched imagination." His appraisal is characteristic, akin to his sadistic enjoyment of the pretty postures she assumes in agony. Neither original nor disorganized, Clarissa mad is no Ophelia. (Nor is she, as one of Richardson's effusive contemporaries called her, a Lear.) It is hard to feel the fragments reveal a more basic or true or real young woman than we have seen before. They make it clear that if there is a "real" Clarissa, she cannot find words. There are only the Clarissas we can see: the letters by a ruminating, self-conscious young woman so concerned with the way she presents herself to others, and the bits by that young woman gone literally to pieces. Clarissa's mind has not been pulverized, but neatly shattered into fragments, each one complete and finished as it coherently works through a single literary idea. As in certain surrealist paintings, the sinister is inherent in the sharp outlines, the fact that each discordant part of the jumble is itself a whole—and also in the fact that there is after all a relationship among the parts. As if she were an entire classroom of writing students charged with that assignment, Clarissa attempts to see what happened to her from different points of view. Lovelace encloses the fragments in a letter (III, Letter XXXIII) to Belford.

After an unsuccessful attempt to write Miss Howe a description of the crowdedness and confusion of her mind, of all the things in it that have made it impossible for her to think of herself any longer as a single, coherent individual, Clarissa tries a letter to her father on one subject, his curse. But it is difficult for her to write to him, for the trouble between them is all in words—the curse, the names: "But your heavy curse, my papa— yes, I *will* call you papa, and help yourself as you can—for you are my own dear papa, whether you will or not—and though I am an unworthy child—yet I *am* your child—." The sequence of the first two Papers is dramatic: we see Clarissa first overwhelmed by an attempt to see herself whole, then writing in order to gather up her words, her forces, to pull herself together. Her father, her root and her would-be destroyer in the next world as well as this, occupies the first piece of her mind. In Paper III, she distances her own life by converting it to didactic fable: "A lady took a great fancy to a young lion, or a bear, I forget which—but a bear, or a tiger, I believe it was." This "great fancy"—Clarissa could never admit directly quite such positive feelings toward Lovelace—naturally resulted in the beast's tearing the lady to pieces. Clarissa's conclusion indicates her guilt and her contempt of Lovelace: "And who was most to blame, I pray? The brute, or the lady? The lady, surely! For what *she* did was *out* of nature, *out* of character, at least: what it did was *in* its own nature." The phrase "out of character," with its suggestions of the theatre, replaces "nature" because ladies are not natural, as beasts and men and women are. That they have character makes them human, from another point of view: are they to blame for *acting* out of or for remaining in character? Clarissa reminds us, without meaning to, that Lovelace, too, is no beast; language raises questions *she* does not mean to raise.

She flagellates herself more hotly in the two following fragments, first in direct address ("How art thou humbled in the dust, thou proud Clarissa Harlowe!"), and then in the dignified plea to her envious sister which takes the form of a biblical psalm begging her not to rejoice. Paper VI continues to echo the Bible and its idea of joy, as Clarissa mourns the lost tableau of marriage, "the solemn preparations" for "a happy life" mocked by Lovelace's desecration of the Exemplar. And then the ego pulls itself together by loosing a glorious stream of invective and prophecy:

> Thou pernicious caterpillar, that preyest upon the fair leaf of virgin fame, and poisonest those leaves which thou canst not devour!
>
> Thou fell blight, thou eastern blast, thou overspreading mildew, that destroyest the early promises of the shining year! that mockest the laborious toil, and blastest the joyful hopes, of the painful husbandman!
>
> Thou fretting moth, that corruptest the fairest garment!
>
> Thou eating canker-worm, that preyest upon the opening bud, and turnest the damask rose into livid yellowness!
>
> If, as religion teaches us, God will judge us, in a great measure, by our benevolent or evil actions to one another— O wretch! bethink thee, in time bethink thee, how great must be thy condemnation!

Clarissa is carried by her language beyond the confines of a social world where each person's self is defined by the ability to withstand the incursions of others. Lovelace is no longer, here, a man who behaves like an animal: an insect, a worm, a canker, a blight, he is a pestilence that does not profit from the destruction it causes. Clarissa's imagery is drawn from those natural forces that seem to mock life. The objects of destruction are associated with

Spring: destruction of the unborn, of the virgin, of Clarissa, is worse than anything else because it is destruction not merely of matter but of promise. The last line, which finishes and closes the fragment the way a couplet closes a sonnet, explicates the imagery: you are not, after all, a force of nature but a man, and therefore you are obliged to be good, not evil, to the creatures around you, Clarissa means; because you have been evil you will be condemned. With the mention of her religion Clarissa swings back to the Puritan world, where a greater power, God, will punish a lesser.

There are many voices in Clarissa's mind, many people, and among them are several Lovelaces. To one of them she talks, in her madness, with a frankness and simplicity and girlishness, an ordinariness, she never showed when lucid:

> At first, I saw something in your air and person that displeased me not. Your birth and fortunes were no small advantages to you. You acted not ignobly by my passionate brother. Everybody said you were brave: everybody said you were generous. A *brave* man, I thought, could not be a *base* man: a *generous* man could not, I believed, be *ungenerous*, where he acknowledged obligation. . . . You seemed frank as well as generous: frankness and generosity ever attracted me: whoever kept up those appearances, I judged of their hearts by my own; and whatever qualities *I wished* to find in them, I was *ready* to find; and, *when* found, I believed them to be natives of the soil. (III, Letter XXXIII)

All the interplay between self-delusion and credulousness, between influences and inferences, seems clear to her. For this moment, Clarissa sees herself and Lovelace both as people; the paragon and the monster are gone.

Clarissa is a very long time in dying, which is no longer to our taste. Her ordeal, reminiscent of the model deaths of innocent children that were subjects of popular literature in Richardson's time and long after, is there for the reader's instruction: the terrible deaths of the bad people—the unreformed rake Belton, Mrs. Sinclair, Lovelace—support the didactic point. Clarissa proves to be literally for the next world rather than this, just as Miss Howe had said. "I am upon a *better preparation* than for an earthly husband" (IV, Letter I), she writes, but it is wrong, I think, to read the accounts of her gradual, gracefully gowned collapse, her concern with her coffin and the proper disposition of her corpse, as evidence of necrophilia on her part or Richardson's. Death promises Clarissa no orgiastic ecstasy; if she is half in love with it, as she was half in love with Lovelace, it is by no means because death is easeful. On the contrary: the preparation is a taxing struggle of mind and body through which she will prove herself independent of the world, immune to being harmed by others, integral in herself. She imagines being joined with her bridegroom in a ceremony, not a bed. She no more wants to die than she wanted to be raped; but she wills her death, in order to assert the capacity to direct and dispose the self that the rape brutally mocked.

The dying Clarissa is finally in control, and so is Richardson, who at his leisure ties up every end of his novel, finishes off the lives of all of the characters, goes back to Harlowe Place for a last contemptuous look at the inmates, whose living space has been diminished by the remorse that forced them to wall off Clarissa's part of the house, the best part, and skulk for the rest of their lives up the back stairs, cowed by their possessions. Punishing evil and rewarding good, ending the novel, Richardson mimes a dream of order, control, and enclosure that resembles Clarissa's. Meanwhile, Clarissa herself, with the help of Belford, who has become her acolyte, collects the letters that are the story of her life. She does so to vindicate herself, to show she was not at fault, to teach the world, to endow herself with that fixed aesthetic form and public significance she had sought earlier in the image of the Exemplar. The motive of the heroine is made manifest as she translates herself into art. Sublimed to pure self-consciousness, Clarissa turns herself into a novel, *Clarissa*.

Clarissa's preparations for death include the writing of a

lengthy, detailed *will*. She uses the coffin, which she calls her "house" or "palace," as a desk while she writes herself (the doctors say writing exhausts her) to death. She designed the coffin herself, and paid for it by selling her expensive clothes. Belford reports that she is aware of the ambiguities inherent in so elaborate a monument:

> She discharged the undertaker's bill after I went away, with as much cheerfulness as she could ever have paid for the clothes she sold to purchase this her *palace*: for such she called it; reflecting upon herself for the expensiveness of it, saying that they might observe in *her* that pride left not poor mortals to the last: but indeed she did not know but her father would permit it, *when furnished*, to be carried down to be deposited with her ancestors; and, in that case, she ought not to discredit those ancestors in her *appearance amongst them*.

Pride in her own self-consciousness, which allows her to prize her limitations for being limits defining her, is what makes her Clarissa and must kill her. In the end it does define her.

The "half-broken-stalked lily" is one of the several decorations on the coffin. Belford reports her apology for including so many: "She excused herself . . . on the score of her youth, and being used to draw for her needleworks, for having shown more fancy than would perhaps be thought suitable on so solemn an occasion" (IV, Letter XC). But of course there is only, appropriately, an excess of the perfectly suitable. The "principal device" is a serpent with its tail in its mouth, the phallic symbol foiled, "the emblem of eternity," and the symbol of the "serpent pride" the lady shares with Lovelace. It finally encloses within its perfect circle three defining facts: her name, her age, and the date she left her father's house, in place of the date when she will in fact die. (Metaphor of necessity stands in for fact.) A winged hourglass and an urn accompany inscriptions from Job and the Psalms. In addition there is "the head of a white lily snapped short off, and just falling from the stalk." Like the other two, the symbol is conventional, and it illustrates the Psalmist's simile: "The days of man are but grass. For he flourisheth as a flower of the field. . . ." But surely it is also significant that the lily is Lovelace's metaphor for Clarissa. By the time she designs the coffin the adoring Belford has brought her all Lovelace's letters, including the one with his description of how she looked pleading for his pity just before she was drugged and then raped:

> At last, with a heart-breaking sob, I see, I see, Mr. Lovelace, in broken sentences she spoke, I see, I see—that at last—at last—I am ruined! Ruined, if *your* pity—let me implore your pity! And down on her bosom, like a half-broken-stalked lily, top-heavy with the overcharging dews of the morning, sunk her head, with a sigh that went to my heart. (III, Letter XXVIII)

Clarissa dying in white satin unstained by any evidence of the body's dissolution, merely growing paler and more still, is bound as ever to see herself as others see her.

Dying, Clarissa balances exquisitely between self-awareness and self-deceit. Working hard at turning herself into a novel, she is obliged to write a chapter, a new letter, in a new style. Lovelace is still pursuing her, eager to be forgiven for his soul's sake and still hoping to be accepted in the flesh, and Clarissa is sure she is about to die. Exhaustion has made her more resourceful than ever. She sends him this letter:

> Sir—I have good news to tell you. I am setting out with all diligence for my father's house. I am bid to hope that he will receive his poor penitent with a goodness peculiar to himself; for I am overjoyed with the assurance of a thorough reconciliation, through the interposition of a dear, blessed friend whom I always loved and honoured. I am so taken up with my preparation for this joyful and long-wished-for journey that I cannot spare one moment for any other business, having several matters of the last importance to settle first. So pray, sir, don't disturb or interrupt me—I beseech you, don't. You may possibly in time see me at my father's; at least, if it be not your own fault.

I will write a letter, which shall be sent you when I am got thither and received: till when, I am, etc.

CLARISSA HARLOWE (IV, Letter LX)

The comparison of God the Father to his wicked servant James Harlowe is made by Clarissa in order to further her last earthly desire, freedom from Lovelace's attendance on her dying. She admits to telling a lie (to being *"guilty of such an artifice"* [IV, Letter LXXIX]) but not to impiousness. For the God she dies for is made in Mr. Harlowe's image, and created that world where women dress themselves like so much meat for their devourers. That God, requiring of Clarissa that she be an Exemplar, inevitably required her to die. Clarissa does not admit this, nor does Richardson. But art is double-faced; the letter in which Clarissa finally, consciously, uses words as Lovelace does, so as to lie, is provocatively paradoxical.

Since Clarissa, like her antagonists, conceives of identity, power, and art as related, her ultimate definition of herself in her coffin and her collection of letters cannot but be ambiguous, being made in the terms of the world she seeks to transcend. After she rejects Lovelace's offer to marry her, and with it the world, she turns herself into a character in an epistolary novel. Her transcendence is limited, as the novel's is, by a commitment to a small world dead set on believing itself significant. Seeking its kind of significance, she cannot quite leave the world: she remains in her coffin, in her story in letters. Even as she dies, she seeks to prove she was not at fault, to teach the world by warning it, to endow herself with that separate identity, fixed form, and public significance she had ever sought in the image of the Exemplar. But what else could she have done, being what she was? Clarissa's destiny perfectly realizes her idea of herself—which is to say everyone else's idea of her—as a paragon. Coming to her end as she does, she endows her life and her self with the coherence, the satisfying integral form, that she aimed to represent. The story of her becoming a heroine ends happily; Clarissa herself dies. The limits of her transcendence are worth pondering.

# PART TWO

<br>

# Getting Married:
# Jane Austen

"I am for having every-body marry. Bachelors, cousin Everard, and maids, when long single, are looked upon as houses long empty, which no-body cares to take. As the house in time, by long disuse, will be thought by the vulgar haunted by evil spirits, so will the others, by the *many*, be thought possessed by no good ones."

—Samuel Richardson,
*Sir Charles Grandison*

The major difference between Austen's heroines and the young ladies of today is that the former had a somewhat more realistic sense, from an early age, of the permanent effect on a woman's life of any marriage she makes.

—Ellen Moers,
*Literary Women*

"My dear cousin, . . . you have a better right to be fastidious than almost any other woman I know; but will it answer? Will it make you happy?"

—Jane Austen,
*Persuasion*

A heroine moves toward her inevitable end, death or marriage, along lines her body generates: the domestic novel binds her over and over to the sexual plot. For her, for sure, anatomy is destiny. One of two courses of action is possible: she will either get virtue's earthly reward, a rich husband, or be seduced and die of it. The conscious heroine must work out a view of this absurdly simple pair of alternatives by which to transcend them. Clarissa Harlowe imagines the perfect marriage, death, transcendence that realizes her self. Trapped in the constraints of the heroine's story, she triumphs—paradoxically, ambiguously—by writing her own variation on it.

A number of factors account for the novel's long marriage to the marriage plot. Eighteenth- and nineteenth-century women had little chance of living comfortable or fulfilling lives outside of marriage, social historians explain. And, they add, middle-class women liked to dream in their increased leisure time over undemanding fiction, which was provided for them in increasingly large part by women like themselves, who made novels out of the usual stuff of women's gossip. Feminists argue that in patriarchal society woman is defined as simply a sexual creature, and that novels that show women's lives as gender-determined help to define her thus. Meanwhile, literary critics observe that the novel is peculiarly suited to weigh the relationships between character and plot, to show how they make one another problematic, and that therefore the case of a conscious being who feels too narrowly defined by what Moll Flanders called her "carcase" is a natural for a novelist. I think all these points are worth making.

There are exceptions to the rule that the heroine of an eighteenth- or nineteenth-century English novel can only marry or not. Defoe's pioneering Moll and Roxana start off seduced and abandoned, and go on to have busy long lives. Jeanie Deans, of Sir Walter Scott's *The Heart of Midlothian* (1817), is another kind of exception. Scott's friend Lady Louisa Stuart commended him for unconventionally casting Jeanie as the heroine rather than her sister Effie, who is the victim of a standard sexual plot. Jeanie's story, like Clarissa's, is intricately involved with language; she is quite as literal minded, as bound to the letter, as any conscious heroine. She refuses to tell a lie to save the life of her sister, who has been condemned to death for infanticide, because she takes her own word too seriously to lie; she gives her sister her word to help her; so she walks to London to seek the King's word of pardon for the criminal. Scott recalled the Old Testament doctrine Richardson cites in *Clarissa*, that the promise of an unmarried girl, given when she is in her father's house, doesn't really signify: Jeanie, in defiance of the maiden's privilege, insists her word has meaning. She does not see herself as a creature defined by her gender. Jeanie is no beauty, and she is Scottish, not English, and lower-class. The marriage that occurs at the end of it is beside the point of her story, which is about a journey and not a courtship, a long and arduous walk in the course of which she is explicitly compared—by a wandering madwoman—to Bunyan's Christiana. The small world of courtship novels is hermetically sealed off from a wider world like Jeanie's, where there are mountains and revolutions and cheeses and cows, pregnancies and prisons and wandering wild women. Jeanie is not a lady. She is heroic, but she is not a heroine as I have been using the term here. Partly this is because her story is too rare. The main thing about the heroine is that hers is always the same old story.

The paradigmatic hero is an overreacher; the heroine of the domestic novel, the descendant of the Rose, is overdetermined. The hero moves toward a goal; the heroine tries to be it. He makes a name for himself; she is concerned with keeping her good name. (But at the end of her story, when it's happy, she takes her husband's name.) A hero is extraordinary, exempt from the rules of society; a heroine must stick to the social code and then some. She is governed by constraints as rigid as the ones that make a sonnet. The instructive contrast is between Richardson's good girls and Fielding's bad boy, Tom Jones, who proves the neighbors were wrong when they said he was born to be hanged. What the neighbors say can ruin a girl's life, and run like water off a duck's back off a boy's. A heroine must be perfectly well-behaved, well-spoken and well-spoken-of. She must be just like other girls and also she must be better, to be singled out once for all by the best of men.

At the end of Richardson's third novel, *Sir Charles Grandison* (1753–54), a discussion of marrying leads to a discussion of the bad effects of romance. The venerable Mrs. Shirley, the heroine Harriet Byron's grandmother, says that the popular literature of her youth, the heroic romances of the seventeenth century, misled girls by celebrating the overwhelming importance of first and passionate love. A second love, Mrs. Shirley maintains, can be as true and powerful as a first; and a first love may turn out to have been not true love at all; and an arranged marriage, based on reason not passion, may prove a most successful one. Richardson's last novel argues that while love is best, self-restraint and courtesy are very, very important, and fatal passions are not the only ones there are. *Sir Charles Grandison* has two heroines instead of one, as if to amend the emphasis on the singular that is central to romance and also central in Richardson's first two novels. Jane Austen admired *Grandison*, remembered it often as she went about her daily domestic life and, no doubt, when she wrote her books. By Austen's time, to reflect as Mrs. Shirley had done on the effects of reading fiction was to consider a large body of literature. Jane Austen rewrote romance and Richardson when she described a young woman's struggle to define herself by reflecting on and revising, doubting and reaffirming, the truth of the heroine's old story.

Jane Austen's first novel was published in 1811 as the work of "A Lady." She never dropped the persona; it is as central to her enterprise as Richardson's mask of editor and hagiographer is to his. Like Elizabeth Bennet and all her heroines but one, Austen was "a gentleman's daughter," a lady by birth and breeding. But the woman who described Elizabeth's being visited by "the two elegant ladies who waited on" Mr. Bingley's sisters—that is, by their maids—knew that a lady is an artifact, a social construct. As well as her Emma, Jane Austen knew "just what a lady ought" to say. And also she knew rather more than that. From her letters we can tell that genteel country life as she observed it was considerably more coarse-grained than the world of her novels, and that her real-life reaction to it was very different from A Lady's:

> Mrs. Hall, of Sherborne, was brought to bed yesterday of a dead child, some weeks before she expected, owing to a fright. I suppose she happened unawares to look at her husband. (*Letters*, p. 24) *

> . . . I am proud to say that I have a very good eye at an Adultress, for tho' repeatedly assured that another in the same party was the *She*, I fixed upon the right one from the first. (*Letters*, p. 127)

> We plan having a steady Cook, & a young giddy Housemaid, with a sedate, middle aged Man, who is to undertake the double office of Husband to the former & sweetheart to the latter.—No Children of course to be allowed on either side. (*Letters*, pp. 99–100)

> I was shewn upstairs into a drawing-room, where she came to me, and the appearance of the room, so totally unschool-like, amused me very much; it was full of all the modern elegancies—& if it had not been for some naked Cupids over the Mantlepiece, which must be a fine study for Girls, one should never have smelt instruction. (*Letters*, pp. 308–309)

---

* *Jane Austen's Letters*, ed. R. W. Chapman, 2nd ed. (Oxford: Oxford University Press, 1979). Page numbers in parentheses following quotations refer to this edition.

It was not prudishness that made the novelist prune and purify and choreograph her love stories to what seemed to Charlotte Brontë unnatural coldness. Austen leaves it to other pens to dwell on such commonplace miseries as devolve from the banal sexual adventurings of Maria and Julia Bertram, the cousins of the heroine of *Mansfield Park*. The excitement of the love stories of her chaste protagonists derives from a growing anticipation of preordained joy. Restraint heightens the tension, enhances the excitement. The pleasure the novels provide comes out of that space between what contains and what is contained, between what covers and what is covered, where Roland Barthes located the source of the erotic. Moving toward marriage, the heroines play decorously in that space, demonstrating what Austen, in a letter, praised in her niece Fanny, the maidenly "delicious play of Mind" that implies other energies. Austen's heroines often fall decisively in love at a distance from their suitors: Elizabeth Bennet does when she stands admiring Darcy's portrait, and Emma does while she talks about Mr. Knightley with Harriet Smith. Separation sharpens desire. In *Northanger Abbey*, the coolest of the love stories, Henry Tilney comes to propose to Catherine Morland after some time away from her. In *Persuasion*, the warmest, her lover's eight-year absence has turned Anne Elliot into the most tender of the Austen heroines. Many readers have observed that we are never brought close enough to overhear the proposals and acceptances that conclude all the plots. The little distance is a result of the novelist's choice, not her incapacity, and it makes our pleasure.

A novel published as the work of A Lady, rather than an individual truly or falsely named, announces itself as a certain deliberately pleasing kind of novel, one that will insist on distinctions of gender and class, as ladies do by existing. Such a guarded announcement accords perfectly with the social conventions to which ladies subscribe. We expect a novel so published will play with the notion of character as self-preservation and observe the overriding of idiosyncrasy by convention, which will be conceived of as a power that organizes. But now I am talking not of A Lady, whose output nearly rivals Anon's, but of Jane Austen. The stories of her marriageable young heroines are told in a distinctly feminine and well-bred voice, the voice of a genteel maiden. Jane Austen did not reach with feminist intentions for that shapely sentence perfectly suited to her sex which Virginia Woolf praised as an achievement in the history of woman. Emma Woodhouse must be speaking her creator's not-quite-feminist mind when, suspecting Robert Martin's sisters helped him write his letter proposing to Harriet Smith, she reflects that, on the other hand, it "is not the style of a woman; no, certainly, it is too strong and concise; not diffuse enough for a woman." But we know from her letters that Austen read the women novelists of her time with competitive zeal. "A Lady" insists too much— therefore it is ironic—on a novelist's gender and class, what the Brontë pen names Currer and Ellis and Acton Bell deliberately made ambiguous, what George Sand's and George Eliot's names denied. It is a crucial bit of irony, like the passage in *Northanger Abbey* that deliberately confounds novelists and their heroines as Austen declares her solidarity with both:

> Alas! if the heroine of one novel be not patronized by the heroine of another, from whom can she expect protection and regard? I cannot approve of it. Let us leave it to the Reviewers to abuse such effusions of fancy at their leisure, and over every new novel to talk in threadbare strains of the trash with which the press now groans. Let us not desert one another; we are an injured body. (*NA* I, 5) *

Jane Austen was acutely conscious of the consequences for women of women's taking up the pen. In the eleventh chapter of

---

* *The Novels of Jane Austen*, ed. R. W. Chapman, 5 vols. (London: Oxford University Press, 1953). All quotations from the novels are from this standard edition; references in parentheses are to abbreviated titles and, for the convenience of the reader who might have another edition, to chapter rather than page numbers. I follow this practice when I quote from novels throughout. Readers wishing to refer to other editions of Austen novels will find that chapters are often not numbered in separate sequences per volume, as they were originally and are in Chapman. I regret this.

*Persuasion*—an elaborate proposal scene which was written after Austen rejected an earlier version—there is a discussion of what men and women are and what they are said to be in books, and a play with writing implements accompanies it so as subtly to make some nice points. Anne Elliot and Captain Harville are chatting about a mutual friend who has become engaged again too soon after his fiancée's death, while Captain Wentworth, the lover Anne had been persuaded to reject eight years before, sits writing a letter within earshot of them. There are also others present, ladies whose conversation is characterized as a re-urging of "admitted truths" about young people in love, and Anne and Harville do not pretend to say anything new either, as they pursue an old argument about whether men or women are more constant in love. Anne remarks mildly that women's greater constancy, "is, perhaps, our fate rather than our merit. We cannot help ourselves," she goes on. "We live at home, quiet, confined, and our feelings prey upon us. You are forced on exertion. You have always a profession, pursuits, business of some sort or other, to take you back into the world immediately, and continual occupation and change soon weaken impressions." Harville protests that Benwick, the no-longer-constant lover in question, had been living quietly in England since his fiancée's death, and cannot, therefore, be said to have forgotten his sorrows abroad. With a gay "What shall we say now, Captain Harville?" Anne offers an alternative theory. But what she says is about men's greater distractions, and it shows she is not thinking of Benwick at all, but of Wentworth, who has been an adventurer at sea during the years Anne has remained at home and missed him. Pretending to argue now that man's nature rather than his environment makes him less constant than woman, Anne continues to insist on the latter:

> "You have difficulties, and privations, and dangers enough to struggle with. You are always labouring and toiling, exposed to every risk and hardship. Your home, country, friends, all quitted. Neither time, nor health, nor life, to be called your own. It would be too hard indeed" (with a faltering voice) "if woman's feelings were to be added to all this."

As Harville begins to answer, it becomes evident that faltering and feeling is not only for women, for "a slight noise called their attention to Captain Wentworth's hitherto perfectly quiet division of the room. It was nothing more than that his pen had fallen down. . . ." Anne correctly suspects he dropped his pen because he was listening to them—to her—and Harville resumes the conversation. He threatens to cite songs and proverbs in men's behalf, attesting to women's fickleness, and then he adds, "Perhaps you will say, these were all written by men." Anne answers, refining the accents of Chaucer's Wife of Bath, who long ago traced misogynistic tales to the pens of men, "Perhaps I shall.—Yes, yes, if you please, no reference to examples in books. Men have had every advantage of us in telling their own story. Education has been theirs in so much higher a degree; the pen has been in their hands." But as Anne is aware, the pen has just fallen. (Wentworth was using it to write a letter proposing to her, "under the irresistible governance" of "those sentiments and those tones" that reached him while she talked with Captain Harville.) The ironies are elegant. Jane Austen took up the cause of women when she took up the pen to revise those important books, novels, which, she was aware, gave women all the education most of them got.

By enlarging what goes on in heads and houses to Brobdignagian proportions, the author of *Clarissa* presents the commonplace stuff of domestic life—the ties between children and parents, women and men—as curious, even monstrous, and enormously important. Turning his protagonists like white and black diamonds, showing facet after multiplied facet of their selves to imply that facets are all we know, Richardson persuades us also that people and language are most thoroughly and accurately examined in the circumstances that form character and in character-building private events: in families and family-making. Richardson's literary method was characteristic of his time—encyclopedic, like Defoe's and Boswell's and Diderot's. The eight volumes of *Clarissa* imply that the exhaustive compilation of details is the best way of finding and telling the truth, that truth is the strange sum of its commonplace parts.

In Jane Austen's novels domestic life is raised to significance differently: by being held at arm's length. Writing at the end of Richardson's century and the beginning of the next, she wrought novels distinguished from those of her predecessors—and her rivals, and indeed most of her successors—by a tight, precise structure, a stunningly controlled, even tone. They are elegant variations on a single theme, Richardson's, the courtship of a virtuous virgin living in a world of families, where marrying is a biological, social, and economic imperative, and also the act by which an individual makes a definitive moral choice. In Austen's world desire and will mask themselves in the rituals of social life so as to maneuver effectively. Young men and girls meet at evening parties, picnics, concerts, and dances, regulated by a strict code of behavior. In *Northanger Abbey* Henry Tilney compares marriage to a country dance: critics have applauded by pursuing his metaphor, and applying it to Austen's six novels about courtship. But life in Jane Austen's world is not an effortless and not always a graceful dance. People bump into one another all the time; usually the ladies outnumber the men; girls are brutally snubbed; and everything depends on such practical matters as the leasing of houses, the measurements of rooms, the direction of draughts, and the preparation of enough white soup.

The plot of Austen's novels is the rhetorical equivalent of the social conventions that govern her people's lives, which her novels characterize as shapes and shapers of human nature. The little problem the novelist sets herself—how to bring this girl to marry that man—echoes her heroine's problem of expressing the complexity of her moral and emotional life in a single, obligatory, altogether conventional act. A heroine is necessarily central in Austen's novels as in Richardson's. The peculiarly artificial and allegorical aspect of a young girl in middle-class society is crucial in the fictions of both because the novel's great subject, as both conceived it, was the play between consciousness and convention.

Implicit in Austen's novels are these truths no longer universally acknowledged: that women are interesting only in the brief time they are marriageable, that marrying is the most significant action a woman can undertake, and that after she marries her story is over. Her goal achieved, a lady may lounge out her life on a sofa, dote on her children or neglect them, even run off with a lover, and be equally unworthy of attention. A retired Jane Austen heroine will of course do none of those foolish things, being a valuable person who has learned in the strenuous course of courtship precisely what she is worth. Married, she will concern herself with her cows' pasturage, or entertain and educate deserving relatives, and love and manage her husband and her house, and fall on rainy days upon her "resources," her pencils and her instruments and her powers of reflection. But no matter what admirable things she does, she will never again be the focus of serious interest, a heroine. Married, she is finished. Austen wrote ominously to her niece Fanny as if the ceremony put an end to the character as well as to plot: "Oh! what a loss it will be when you are married. You are too agreable in your single state, too agreable as a Niece. I shall hate you when your delicious play of Mind is all settled down into conjugal & maternal affections" (*Letters*, pp. 478–79).

Her Emma may be the rose in the garden of Hartfield, and Fanny Price at Mansfield Park is a pearl among swine, but Austen's heroines are not, like Pamela and Clarissa, to be taken seriously as ideals or representatives of womankind. Emma's father, who thinks her a paragon, is a fool; if Fanny stands for virtue, she deflatingly demonstrates that it is not necessarily resplendent. Emma and Fanny, and Marianne and Elinor Dashwood, Catherine Morland, Elizabeth Bennet, and Anne Elliot are individuals on whom gender and the sexual plot exert an overwhelming determining force, but their sexual "virtue" is not at issue. Their minds are. The danger facing them is not that they will be acted upon against their wills, but that they will let the right man and the chance for action pass them by. They are worth our notice not because they are fragile and vulnerable females in an interesting position, but because they are more truthful and sensitive and substantive, more able to see and interpret life's complexity, than most of the people around them. For that reason they are more valuable; for that reason they deserve, they warrant, a novel. What qualifies a girl as our heroine and Austen's is not so much that she is inherently a heroine but that she knows, or very nearly knows, what a real heroine is. She is rewarded in the end for having this knowledge and rightly assessing its value, by marriage to an admirable, admiring man. His corrective presence will crown her knowledge and give her power, will complete and perfect her. The end of an Austen novel dramatizes every closet heroine's secret fantasy: to be found out a heroine. Yet although the climax rewards her passivity, the action that inspires the suspense is the woman's: she must seize, she must cling to, her main and only chance.

Boredom and banality threaten Austen heroines more seriously than wrack and ruin do; the reason a girl must keep her wits about her is that the world is a fearfully quiet place. Considerable powers conspire to make her life obscure and dull. But "a mind lively and at ease, can do with seeing nothing, and can see nothing that does not answer," as the narrator of *Emma* moralizes. A heroine, like a novelist, can convert the least promising of lives into art, by the way she looks at it. Jane Austen disdained the heroine of romance: "Pictures of perfection as you know make me sick and wicked," she wrote to her niece. Her nephew recalled that she once confided smugly that Emma Woodhouse would be "a heroine whom no one but myself will much like"; she began *Northanger Abbey* with the declaration that "no one who had ever seen Catherine Morland in her infancy, would have supposed her born to be an heroine." Her heroines are deliberate revisions.

It is instructive to contemplate the difference between Austen's juvenilia and Charlotte Brontë's. Brontë borrowed from romance tropes to figure forth her feelings; Austen's youthful *Love and Friendship* is *about* romantic fiction. She insisted language and literary conventions were forms, and implied that form, if one doesn't look out, makes content. She defined living well, consciously and morally, as a matter of looking out. Her novels insist that people who use language thoughtlessly or credulously, pompously or stupidly or incompetently, are inadequate and even immoral; and on the other side of error, Mary and Henry Crawford, in *Mansfield Park*, are too glib to be good. Her heroines and readers know that a man may be measured by his language: rakish Willoughby in *Sense and Sensibility*, for instance, strikes stern Elinor Dashwood as not altogether worthless when he demonstrates the keenness of his ear. Describing the pain he felt on reading the letters of her sister Marianne, whom he jilted, he says:

> "Every line, every word was—in the hackneyed metaphor which their dear writer, were she here, would forbid—a dagger to my heart. To know that Marianne was in town was—in the same language—a thunderbolt.—Thunderbolts and daggers!—what a reproof would she have given me!" (*S & S* II, 8)

Even Marianne, the most ingenuously romantic of Austen's heroines, eschews the language of romance; and her unreliable lover nearly seduces us, for all that we cannot at all approve of him, when he shows he is conscious of words. To recognize the power of language and to use it with care indicates true sense and sensibility, in the world as Austen conceived it.

Setting the tone of that world, Jane Austen's novels revise not only romance and Richardson but, repeatedly, themselves. Their ironic embrace of literary conventions is insistent. Austen began writing novels by satirizing them, not because she was interested in literary criticism but because she recognized the haunting shape of romance as a shaper of consciousness, a metaphor for the biological and social limits that mold a girl's life.

The heroine of *Northanger Abbey* (published in 1818, but dated by most critics as preceding *Sense and Sensibility*), is a healthy, ordinary girl: "There are a great many people like me, I dare say," she says guilelessly. Precisely because she is normal Catherine Morland has an appetite for romantic, sensational fiction. She is so eager to visit abbeys and castles like the spooky ones she likes to read about that she agrees to tour one on the arm of boring, boorish John Thorpe. In other words, she makes sacrifices in her actual life in the service of the imaginary world she prefers to live in, putting up with the pains of the one to get the pleasures of the other. Catherine is lucky to meet, at Bath, a very attractive young man, Henry Tilney, preferable on many counts to Thorpe. She likes the way he teases her, although she doesn't understand everything he says, and she admires his ladylike sister Eleanor, so different from John Thorpe's showy and shallow sister Isabella, who insists on being her intimate friend. Henry's and Eleanor's father, General Tilney, thinks Catherine is rich—he has been misinformed—and he invites her to visit their home, Northanger Abbey. Catherine is delighted. From the evidence of (gothic) atmosphere, she concludes that her host, a widower, once did terrible things to his wife there. She imagines shrieks coming from the ends of the corridor. During a stormy night, she finds in a cabinet a manuscript that, she is sure, is the key to the horrible crimes against women the abbey has been a theatre for. The light of day proves the manuscript to be a laundry list, and Catherine to be deluded. She is wrong: Mrs. Tilney died of natural causes. But it turns out that she is not wrong in suspecting that the General is no good. When he finds out she is not an heiress, he turns Catherine out of his abbey, obliging her to make her way home unannounced and alone. A selfish, materialistic, rude, inconsiderate man, General Tilney is prosaically rather than exotically evil. Catherine, not his dead wife, is his real victim. And Catherine, who imagined she was ready for anything, is surprised.

The reason her encounter with evil shocks Catherine is that she had expected everything dreadful to remain between the covers of novels, while she stayed cozily aloof from it. Because she had read so much, she was not prepared to be involved, herself, in a plot. Catherine takes in too placidly the sensational novels she loves. This is made clear in the exchange in which, "in rather a solemn tone of voice," she begins to talk about a novel and Eleanor Tilney thinks she is talking about real life:

> "I have heard that something very shocking indeed, will soon come out in London."
> Miss Tilney . . . was startled, and hastily replied, "Indeed!—and of what nature?"
> "That I do not know, nor who is the author. I have only heard that it is to be more horrible than any thing we have met with yet."
> "Good heaven!—Where could you hear of such a thing?"
> "A particular friend of mine had an account of it in a letter from London yesterday. It is to be uncommonly dreadful. I shall expect murder and every thing of the kind."
> "You speak with astonishing composure!" (NA I, 14)

"Oh! I am delighted with the book!" Catherine exclaims over Mrs. Radcliffe's *The Mysteries of Udolpho*. "I should like to spend my whole life in reading it" (NA I, 6). In the course of her story Catherine learns that one cannot spend one's life safely reading. By being thrown out of Northanger Abbey, she discovers the world is a shocking place. She has made too sharp a distinction between literature and life: she has to learn that sensational novels tell truths about reality (where innocent girls are victimized by powerful men, and a young lady like Isabella Thorpe fulsomely professes a friendship she does not in fact feel). Catherine has to learn that the safety from which one ventures into books for thrills and chills is itself an illusion. Her story suggests that gothic novels must not be dismissed as "mere" fantasies, for "unrealistic" fictions reflect psychosocial facts. That Catherine herself is the heroine of a love story, perfectly happy in the end with the man who perfectly suits her, proves she was not so very silly when she planned to be a heroine, and that fantastic romantic dreams like hers (and so many girls') determine, for good as well as ill, real lives.

---

In the world of Jane Austen's novels, rakes are irresolute and fathers impotent; girls are not liable to be locked up for any man's pleasure. A young woman is lost not by being taken or given, but by throwing herself away. She may allow herself to be made a fool of, or she may fool herself, or she may misjudge her man or miss her opportunity. It is almost entirely up to her to choose where she'll end up; her life is in her hands. "Maria had destroyed her own character," Austen observes of the older daughter of Sir Thomas Bertram of Mansfield Park, who married a fool and then ran off with a rake. Maria's losing her reputation, or character, is a function of her weakness of character; destroying her good name, Maria makes it evident that she has no character at all. *Mansfield Park* demonstrates that Sir Thomas is partly to blame for Maria's fall, and Maria's mother, who neglected her, and her aunt, who indulged her, and the neighbors who let her beauty and accomplishments go to her head, and her doltish husband and his mother, and the rakish man who seduces her, and even the unprincipled uncle by whom *he* was badly brought up. But her destiny is nevertheless her own responsibility, as her immortal soul is: her love story is the mirror of her soul. Spiritually, Austen's young ladies are as alone as a tough heroine of Defoe's. So to Maria the novelist metes out the harshest punishment: she ends up living in another country in a little cottage with her awful Aunt Norris.

Except for *Emma*, all Austen's novels are about girls who are in some sense homeless and in the end find homes.* The heroine's story is always, like Clarissa's, about defining and being defined by a space, about finding a space of one's own. Austen's novels are about attaining the external correlative (husband, social position, house) that makes inner potential real. The heroines are not orphans, as so many fictitious maidens were in the

---

* Partial exceptions increase the rule's resonance: Catherine Morland in *Northanger Abbey*, like Charlotte Heywood in Austen's unfinished *Sanditon*, is merely away from home visiting; Anne Elliot, marrying Captain Wentworth, gains true love and improves her social position, but, since she marries a sailor, she remains unsettled for life.

eighteenth century; one of the difficult tasks before Catherine, Elinor and Marianne, Elizabeth, Fanny, Emma, and Anne, is to separate themselves from their parents or surrogate parents, and come to judge their families correctly. (It is a large part of Clarissa Harlowe's problem, too.) Austen's good girls will be rewarded by having families of their own. Elinor and Marianne Dashwood in *Sense and Sensibility*, Elizabeth Bennet in *Pride and Prejudice*, and Anne Elliot in *Persuasion* are victims of the patriarchal law of entail, which prevents them from inheriting their fathers' houses, favoring selfish and obnoxious men like John Dashwood and Mr. Collins, and even scheming hypocrites like Mr. Elliot, over deserving young women. No wonder the heroines must find husbands. Young women of sensibility, they of course do not go pragmatically husband-hunting, but it is as clear to them as it is to us that for their comfort they must marry. The Dashwood estate is already settled on the sisters' half-brother John when their story begins, and Marianne is mourning the prospect of leaving the house where she grew up. One of the things Willoughby does to make her fall in love with him is to show her through the "charming" house he will inherit: from the point of view of even so romantic a girl as Marianne, a man's attractions include his real property. The heroine of *Pride and Prejudice* deflects the charge by making it herself, but to some degree she does, as she claims, fall in love with Darcy "upon first seeing his beautiful grounds at Pemberley." "To be mistress of Pemberley might be something!" she reflects when she first sees the great estate. To be Mr. Bennet's daughter, whose entailed home will go to Mr. Collins, is to be not very much. Elizabeth is some*one*: personal merit makes her that. But she must also become some*thing*. When she does she becomes the image of all a woman may hope to be.

*Mansfield Park* (1814), with its witty anti-heroine, Mary Crawford, and its enervated protagonist, Fanny Price, is a revision of *Pride and Prejudice* (1813), which Austen on second thought decided was too "light, and bright, and sparkling." It is determinedly sober. Fanny, most remarkable for her tenacity, is an adopted poor relation at grand Mansfield Park; fastidious and high-minded, she prefers to be away from her parents' small, disorderly house. (Fanny is a model of filial piety to *surrogate* parents, as Anne Elliot is to Lady Russell in *Persuasion*; like Anne but with less justification, she is disdainful of her own. The "family romance" fantasy Freud described, of choosing parents worthy of one's superior tastes, is proposed and quietly exploded as Fanny's aunt and uncle, the Bertrams, prove, like Lady Russell, to be also inadequate.) Fanny's image of Mansfield Park is purer than the actual place. When she triumphs in the end by marrying her cousin Edmund, she becomes mistress of its parsonage and of the spirit of Mansfield Park. The poor girl excels her rich uncle's daughters, in the end, not only in moral but also in material good. The bad elements are purged from Fanny's Mansfield; her ideal becomes the real estate.

Of Austen's protagonists only the heroine of *Emma* (1816) is a middle-class princess. "Handsome, clever, and rich," she is the flower of Hartfield, her father's house, and the first lady of the neighboring village of Highbury. Like Clarissa Harlowe, Emma Woodhouse suffers from "real evils" of a "situation" which imposes on her the idea that she is uniquely set on a pedestal. In the course of her story she must discover "the beauty of truth and sincerity in all our dealings with each other," as Mr. Knightley puts it, and move closer to the rest of the world. When she gives up her fantasies and embraces reality, Emma joins together her father's and Knightley's estates, *Hartfield* and *Donwell*, to unite desire with doing.

In *Persuasion* (1818) Austen raises the revisionary possibility that personal fulfillment cannot be translated into terms of real property. Twenty-seven-year-old Anne Elliot is the daughter of Sir Walter Elliot of Kellynch Hall, a vain and empty baronet whose extravagance has driven him to rent out to tenants the property which will eventually go to a male relation. In the course of the novel Anne thinks of marrying her cousin, very briefly, when she imagines herself taking her mother's place at Kellynch. But Mr. Elliot is repellently reserved and careful, and Anne loves another. Since she broke her engagement to Frederick Wentworth eight years before the novel's beginning, she has lived as a displaced person, either making long visits or being overlooked by her father and older sister at home. Supposing she will never marry and continuing to think of Wentworth, Anne is alone among relatives very unlike her, and reflects with melancholy on where her eventual place might be. She is miraculously saved by a second chance to revise her life's plot. Wentworth's worth is not embodied in a permanent, stable home, but earned via new goings, piratical, nautical adventures; in the world of Austen's last novel, a new economy is replacing the old land-based one. Anne will be happy ever after with a man national emergencies will call from time to time to his country's service on the seas: "She gloried in being a sailor's wife, but she must pay the tax of quick alarm for belonging to that profession which is, if possible, more distinguished in its domestic virtues than in its national importance" (*P* II, 12). Glory, importance, virtue, happiness—all these abstractions, as Anne has learned, are taxed. The economics of *Persuasion* are different from those of the earlier novels, where man and woman are seen as consumers and commodities: here both sexes struggle for rare and elusive immaterial goods in a changing world where people are very concerned with aging and altering.

The symptoms of Anne's intense love for Wentworth are rushes of dizzying feeling that come and go, which perhaps foreshadow the "quick alarm" of the sailor's wife. For Austen's younger, earlier heroines, sexual feeling takes the cooler, chaster, eighteenth-century forms of esteem, respect, and determination to marry. But their passion is also strong, being equal to the forms that contain it. When "it darted through her, with the speed of an arrow, that Mr. Knightley must marry no one but herself," Emma Woodhouse was pierced by sexual desire so thoroughly implicated in the desire for exclusive legal possession of a male property that it is impossible to say whether she wishes really to be pierced or really to do the piercing herself. Both Emma, through whom "it darted," and Mr. Knightley, who "must marry," are rendered passive by the syntax: what is revealed to Emma is that the grand design of marriage must join the two of them to one another. Desire is as forceful as what organizes it.

The paradoxical conclusion of the marriage plot, the comic resolution that symbolizes social coherence, requires that the heroine distinguish and separate herself from the social world she lives in. She learns in the course of her story that apparently charming young men are not necessarily the best ones; by marrying she puts herself out of their reach. She learns that well-intentioned women are often wrong about whom to marry; becoming a matron herself, she escapes matronly power. But before she can escape both men and matrons she must separate herself from her sisters: she must learn from the fate of another girl, who has fallen or allied herself stupidly or indecorously, and so choose correctly herself. There is a witty turn on this in *Persuasion*, where Louisa Musgrove falls literally from the Cob at Lyme Regis, and events devolving from the accident move Anne and Wentworth toward marrying. (Louisa's fall renders her unconscious; Anne's consciousness, in contrast, is exquisite.) The heroine's wise marriage is a rejoinder to another young woman's foolish engagement with a man. To the extent that they affirm feminine capacity and value and are radiant in their context of less special and successful girls, Jane Austen's heroines are in a way exemplars.

A Jane Austen heroine must separate from other women in order to realize her self, but on the other hand she must also learn that she is like her sisters and her mother. For the self-consciously superior heroines of *Pride and Prejudice* and *Emma*, this is especially difficult, because of the way their fathers have brought them up.

Elizabeth Bennet's relationship with her father is conspiratorial: both of them believe they are cleverer than anyone else. After Mr. Bennet reads aloud the pompous letter his cousin Collins sends to announce his visit, Elizabeth asks, "Can he be a sensible man, sir?" and Mr. Bennet says to the child he has raised to share his antisocial pleasure in society, "No, my dear; I think not. I have great hopes in finding him quite the reverse." Elizabeth's father looks at life around him as if he were reading a comic novel. "For what do we live, but to make sport for our neighbours, and laugh at them in our turn?" he asks, amiably inviting others to see him as a character, too. Most conspicuous among the people excluded by the league of sensibilities between Mr. Bennet and his favorite daughter are Elizabeth's younger sisters and her mother. Mr. Bennet's boon companion, attuned to spiritual not material values, is superior to their commonplace feminine business of husband-hunting. Enjoying her complicity with her father, Elizabeth can be in no hurry to leave his house. When Mr. Collins proposes to her and Elizabeth's mother vows she will never see her again if she does not accept him, Mr. Bennet intones solemnly, "An unhappy alternative is before you, Elizabeth. From this day you must be a stranger to one of your parents. —Your mother will never see you again if you do *not* marry Mr. Collins, and I will never see you again if you *do*" (*P&P* I, 20). The lines are drawn: as her father's daughter Elizabeth is obliged to have contempt for her mother's values, for women's things.

What makes a heroine a heroine is her difference from most women. "Nothing so true as what you once let fall,/'Most Women have no Characters at all,'" Alexander Pope began a poem entitled "To a Lady" (1735), making the point that his friend Martha Blount's superiority is evident from her having once dismissed most women as characterless. By making that pronouncement, Pope suggests, Martha proved that she herself did have character. "The many become pedestal to the few," Mary Wollstonecraft complained about the condition of women in patriarchy, where goddesses are enthroned while most women are oppressed. A woman who wants more than what is offered most women deliberately separates herself from her sisters; she dismisses women and women's things, heaping them into a pedestal for herself. The favorite parent of Margaret Hale, in Elizabeth Gaskell's *North and South* (1854–55), is her father; describing a party to him, she explains, "I was very much interested by what the gentlemen were talking about, although I did not understand half of it. I was quite sorry when Miss Thornton came to take me to the other end of the room, saying she was sure I should be uncomfortable at being the only lady among so many gentlemen. I had never thought about it, I was so busy listening; and the ladies were so dull, papa—oh, so dull!" Gwendolen Harleth of *Daniel Deronda* has no father to confide in, but she has the same trouble as Margaret Hale at parties. George Eliot's analysis of her problem is severe:

> In the ladies' dining-room it was evident that Gwendolen was not a general favourite with her own sex; there were no beginnings of intimacy between her and other girls, and in conversation they rather noticed what she said than spoke to her in free exchange. Perhaps it was that she was not much interested in them, and when left alone in their company had a sense of empty benches. Mrs. Vulcany once remarked that Miss Harleth was too fond of the gentlemen; but we know that she was not in the least fond of them—she was only fond of their homage—and women did not give her homage.

Gwendolen shuns her own sex, girls like her who reflect her own insignificance. To feel significant she must be out of their company, admired as the best of women, the only woman, by men.

Martha Blount is praised by an early eighteenth-century poet for sober virtue and good taste; in the mid–nineteenth century, Margaret Hale distinguishes herself from the tame and tedious ladies by being vital. In both cases, other women are disparaged as artificial, and at the same time commonplace, gender-bound, earth-bound. The contradiction is in the prevailing attitudes toward women; the heroine must transcend women generally, via paradox, by being herself a contradiction. If one is to be a heroine one must be on the side of truth and feeling, against silliness and frivolity and falseness, but also against the everyday preoccupations of most women. A heroine imagines herself superior to both the price of eggs and public opinion—which is, as George Eliot wrote, "always of the feminine gender—not the world but the world's wife." The received ideas of women who are entirely possessed by the world are the ideas a heroine most pointedly scorns. Pope ends his avuncular, paternalistic praise of Martha Blount by saying she was blessed by a God who "Kept Dross for Duchesses," and gave her "Sense, Good Humour, and A Poet." As she is the image of spiritual values, a heroine's province is not life but art.

But in a novel a heroine must make an accommodation to life. For all her superiority, gender ties Elizabeth Bennet to the heroine's plot. It will not do for her to spend her forever-after in Olympian chastity with her father, gossiping about the world and its wives; it would be inconclusive, insufficiently expressive, uninteresting, disappointing. Elizabeth can realize herself only by getting married: in other words, she must do with her life what her mother did with hers, and what her mother wishes her to do. So as to be more than her mother's daughter, so as to triumph over her mother, she must do the same thing in a different, a sublimed, spirit.

Disdain for her mother and what she represents must be in some part abated if Elizabeth is to be more than her father's daughter, and distaste for the collusion against her mother that her father had forced upon her is an important beginning of the process. In preparation for leaguing forever with the decorous Mr. Darcy, Elizabeth identifies in Mr. Bennet's behavior "that continued breach of conjugal obligation and decorum . . . in exposing his wife to the contempt of her own children." When his youngest daughter, Lydia, elopes, her father's inadequacy is underscored. Elizabeth's separation from Mr. Bennet is effected mostly by her growing admiration for another man. Like her father, Mr. Darcy admires her above all other women for the liveliness of her mind. He resembles Mr. Bennet also in being haughty and exigent. When he asks for Elizabeth's hand, Mr. Bennet quickly gives it him, explaining: "He is the kind of man, indeed, to whom I should never dare refuse any thing, which he condescended to ask." Richer, younger, better-born than Mr. Bennet, Darcy rather terrifies Elizabeth's parent. Mr. Bennet begins to seem to us littler than he had. He disappoints us by suspecting Elizabeth is only marrying so as to have "more fine clothes and fine carriages than [her sister] Jane." Painfully, Elizabeth explains to her father that she no longer hates Darcy but loves him, that he is not at all proud but perfectly amiable, that he has saved her sister Lydia and that he will make her, Elizabeth, absolutely happy. Her father should have known all that. Glad to be satisfied, Mr. Bennet repairs to his library, ruefully declaring himself at the disposal of those who might want his remaining unmarried daughters: "If any young men come for Mary or Kitty, send them in, for I am quite at leisure." He has been diminished.

Mr. Bennet will visit Elizabeth and Darcy at Pemberley, to be sure, but in their last interview he has effectively given up his favorite daughter by assuming she is like most women after all. Because she has decided to marry, Elizabeth seems to her father no longer the special creature she was when she was altogether his, altogether virgin, altogether different from her mother and other women. He suspects her now of being tainted by the preference for worldly, sensual pleasures that ruined his own happiness and focused his philosophic disposition on a lifetime of unbecoming irreverence. The story ends well for Mr. Bennet and his daughter, because their intimacy ends easily: obliged to give her up, he imagines she is more ordinary than he had thought; meanwhile, she has found him to be a less reliable moral authority than she had imagined. Elizabeth goes on to have her real merit realized by a better man, a man who takes women and domestic life more seriously than her father can.

Mr. Woodhouse, Emma's father, is fatuous and foolish, narrow-minded and hypochondriacal. Smugness, and concern for his own comfort, and lack of imagination, make him think nobody—including his Emma—should marry. He needs her at home to amuse him, and he truly believes that no other place is as comfortable as his home. Mr. Woodhouse was married unimportantly, and he cannot suppose marrying can matter much to everyone else. Emma, who can imagine a lot, agrees with her father that marriage cannot improve her condition. Only twenty, she is the first lady in her social circle and the lady of her father's house. She already has what many young women marry for, as she explains:

> "I have none of the usual inducements of women to marry. . . . Fortune I do not want: employment I do not want; consequence I do not want; I believe few married women are half as much mistress of their husband's house, as I am of Hartfield; and never, never could I expect to be so truly beloved and important; so always first and always right in any man's eyes as I am in my father's. (*E* I, 10)

Like Elizabeth Bennet, Emma has been persuaded by her father's preference to think she is other women's superior. Elizabeth has four variously conventional sisters, and by her liveliness she outshines even the beauty among them, Jane; Emma's sister, a cipher entirely absorbed in her husband, her children, and her physician, was never any competition. Mr. Bennet's daughter prides herself on a brightness like her father's; Emma, who must be objectively appraised as handsome, clever, and rich, has been thoroughly indulged by an undiscriminating dotard, and more dangerously imagines herself a splendid free young goddess whose connection to most people is an amused puppeteer's (or a novelist's). The other women around her seem to her of another species, predictable and lesser characters in simple fictions. An "imaginist," Emma makes up a scandalous romance about shy Jane Fairfax, and decides to give little Harriet Smith the stature she thinks Harriet deserves by plotting a sentimental love story around her. Sure she herself will not marry, and living in a world where marrying is the only action, she preoccupies herself entirely with fantasies about other people's marrying. It is important that she comes to the painful and penetrating realization that she loves Mr. Knightley when Harriet confesses she thinks he means to marry *her*. The desire Emma feels then comes in part out of jealousy: she had thought herself superior to both jealousy and desire. Emma's humiliation began when Mr. Elton proposed to her, putting her in the place she meant for Harriet; when she comes to her senses, she takes for herself the place Harriet has been led by her folly to expect *she* deserves. When she marries like Harriet and Jane, in the end, Emma turns out to be rather more like other women than she had thought she was. In the end she manages to have it both ways, living happily ever after with both her father and her husband, for Mr. Knightley obligingly moves to Hartfield from Donwell Abbey so as to protect his father-in-law's house from poultry thieves.

Having too early, too easily, won the adoration of the man of their house, Emma and Elizabeth are not eager to move to another man's. They are in the happy childish habit of enjoying unstinted love, and not disposed to settle for something more complex. Both must learn that their fathers are inadequate men, and learn that from tutelary lovers who court to correct them. Both must learn that, defined only as daughters, they are incomplete, and in their adorable cleverness partly blind. When Mr. Weston flatters Emma with the conundrum, "What two letters of the alphabet are there, that express perfection?" (the answer he has in mind is "M. and A."), Mr. Knightley gravely comments, "*Perfection* should not have come quite so soon." Mr. Woodhouse thinks his daughter perfect, and she marries the man who does not: Emma learns to value Mr. Knightley's corrective care for her moral nature above the silly paternal adoration that bloats her pride. Choosing to marry, she chooses to be no longer worshiped, no longer aloof from the sexual life and the lot of most women, no longer a goddess. Accepting Mr. Knightley, Emma accepts her own limitations, which is to say her humanity.

Two things abut Jane Austen's life are important, in addition to the fact that it was brutally short: she was a spinster, and a sister. Those who do not like the novels invoke the novelist's maidenhood; her best critics are likely to insist on the importance of the fact that she began writing to amuse her family. Her tone is that of a family member: it presumes complicity, revels in our being special together. She puts us on, puts us off, playful and at the same time uncompromising, deliberately different. Wondering why she never married, one speculates that she had thought too thoroughly about it, and became paralyzed by self-consciousness. It is hard to imagine her half a unit, so sufficient unto herself does she seem. Her houses of fiction are more her own than Pemberley will ever be Elizabeth's, or Mansfield Fanny's.

She seems to have played only intermittently at keeping house in the literal way: "Composition seems to me Impossible, with a head full of Joints of Mutton & doses of rhubarb" (*Letters*, p. 466), she wrote wisely, apropos of another woman novelist. But it seems right to think of her as a housekeeper. She wrote to her sister Cassandra when she was twenty-two,

> My mother desires me to tell you that I am a very good housekeeper, which I have no reluctance in doing, because I really think it my peculiar excellence, and for this reason—I always take care to provide such things as please my own appetite, which I consider as the chief merit in housekeeping. (*Letters*, p. 28)

Taken too far, by the wrong person, this "chief merit" leads logically to Mr. Woodhouse's serving gruel and half-glasses of wine to his hungry guests. But it is the chief merit in living, as the novels define it, and in writing novels, too. (If the reader objects that the cads and villains she included in her books did not entirely please Jane Austen, he should be reminded that she had a good deal in common with Mr. Bennet, who gleefully awaits the visit of fatuous Mr. Collins and insists that slick Wickham is his favorite son-in-law.) Domestic metaphors occurred to Austen when she wrote about her writing. Pretending fear of a niece's impending criticism of a novel, she wrote playfully to Cassandra,

> I begin already to weigh my words and sentences more than I did, and am looking about for a sentiment, an illustration or a metaphor in every corner of the room. Could my Ideas

flow as fast as the rain in the Store closet it would be charming. (*Letters*, p. 256)

The store closet had suffered water damage: in the face of Disorder, her formidable enemy, the housekeeper mobilizes to match its power. To the inundating trivia of reality in which some women sink and others tread water, Austen responded by sifting and discriminating, choosing, distinguishing herself by distinguishing what she preferred. She did not allow other people's appetites to blur her clear view of her own; it is hard to imagine her married, but the novels she pleased so many people by writing to please herself suggest that had she run a household, her rule would have made it a successful one.

A passage in her letters to Cassandra prevents us from dismissing Austen's relationship to her sister as a lovely but not very strenuous involvement between genteel ladies. "How do you do to-day?" Jane wrote in 1801. "I hope you improve in sleeping—I think you must, because *I* fall off; I have been awake ever since five and sooner" (*Letters*, p. 123). Austen's world, for all its considerable comforts, is too small: neither time nor space nor love nor goodness is abundant; the money is all carefully counted, and at balls there are often not enough men. The novelist views this pervasive scarcity with rueful irony, wondering if there can be enough sleep or happiness to go around, and whether one girl's gain is necessarily another's loss. The many fictitious sisters in Austen's novels are seldom portrayed as rivals, with one important exception. In *Mansfield Park*, Julia and Maria Bertram's unsavory contest for Henry Crawford's attentions proves how completely they have been corrupted by their mother's sloth, their aunt's indulgence, and their own vanity. The history chronicled in that novel begins ominously by hinting at sisterly competitiveness, as it details the variously fortunate marriages of three sisters, the consequences of which bring Fanny Price from her mother's house to her aunt's.

In the very first novel Austen published, two sisters are rivals for the reader's attention. As the admirer of *Grandison* knew, to double the heroine is to interrogate the heart of romance: the twinned love stories of Marianne and Elinor Dashwood mock the idealization of the singular. Romantic Marianne learns, when she is jilted by one man and persuaded to love another, that second attachments are possible. The two heroines both marry men who have loved other women before. Nevertheless, we are assured the Dashwoods will be happy ever after, Marianne with her second choice, Elinor with her first, and the sisters with one another:

> among the merits and the happiness of Elinor and Marianne, let it not be ranked as the least considerable, that though sisters, and living almost within sight of each other, they could live without disagreement between themselves, or producing coolness between their husbands. (*S & S* III, 14)

Her "though" indicates Austen's awareness that it is more uncommon than not for sisters to have what Marianne and Elinor share, a tolerant love between opposites who honor each other and refrain from asking embarrassing personal questions.

Like Elinor and Marianne Dashwood, Elizabeth and Jane Bennet define themselves by studying each other, comparing and contrasting. Elizabeth compares Jane's "candour" and refusal to think badly of others with the satirical bent that temporarily blocks her own happiness, and the comparison helps her to achieve self-knowledge. Conversations between the sisters sharpen the characters, by sharpening the awareness, of both: Austen believed with Richardson, perhaps learned from him, that conversation with an image of oneself forms the self. Like Anna Howe and Clarissa Harlowe, Elinor and Marianne, and Jane and Elizabeth, define themselves in sisterly dialogues.* The

---

* So do, for instance, D. H. Lawrence's Ursula and Gudrun, Charlotte Brontë's Caroline and Shirley, Elizabeth Gaskell's Molly and Cynthia, Doris Lessing's Anna and Molly. Caroline and Shirley, in Brontë's *Shirley*, are not sisters; Molly and Cynthia, in Gaskell's *Wives and Daughters*, are stepsisters; Lessing's Anna and Molly are friends whose men friends confuse them. Sisterhood is not strictly biological.

convention of twin heroines holds up an instructive mirror to the nature of reading unromantically about heroines, in which one experiences at once their being like and unlike oneself.

Secondary female characters in heroine-centered novels exist in terms of the heroine. Pretentious Mrs. Elton is to some degree created by Emma—by Emma's rejection of Mr. Elton, who marries the egregious Augusta as a result of it. And she is also like Emma: she exists to be compared with her. The reader who observes how Mrs. Elton reflects Emma's pride in place, Emma's smugness, has been led to the observation by the novel's structure, and influenced also by the fact that Emma habitually compares herself with other women. The literary-critical act is a reflex of the fictional rivalry. Fiction entangles itself in our lives by teaching us at the same time how to live and how to read novels.

Austen's heroines, who must acknowledge that they are like other women, must in the end leave the company of their sex: Emma must break off her foolish connection with simple Harriet Smith, and Catherine Morland must learn that Isabella Thorpe is false, and Fanny Price must keep herself scrupulously aloof from the fascinating Mary Crawford. Most deliciously of all, Anne Elliot must learn that Lady Russell, the friend who talked her out of marrying the man she loves, is a woman of limited vision. As Lady Russell is Anne's dead mother's friend, she makes a stronger claim on her than a contemporary would. When the two women are driving through Bath in a carriage, Anne, who is looking out the window, notices Wentworth on the street. Aware her friend, too, has been looking out, she waits to hear what Lady Russell will say. At length she speaks:

> "You will wonder," said she, "what has been fixing my eye so long; but I was looking after some window-curtains, which Lady Alicia and Mrs. Frankland were telling me of last night."

Whereupon "Anne sighed and blushed and smiled, in pity and disdain, either at her friend or herself" (*P* II, 7). The sentence structure ironically belies the fact that she is separating her friend and herself, disdaining her friend for caring about the curtains, herself for depending upon her friend. It is a necessary prelude to becoming Frederick Wentworth's wife, whose primary attachment is not to a woman but to a man.

Austen's attitude toward her heroines, Edmund Wilson suggested, was sisterly, growing out of the most important relationship in her life. Of her development from *Sense and Sensibility* to the later novels, he writes, "The solicitude of the sober Elinor Dashwood watching her giddy sister Marianne becomes in time the detached interest of the author looking on at the adventures of her heroines." Wilson deplored the women readers who dislike *Mansfield Park* and its unprepossessing heroine:

> I believe that, in respect to Jane Austen's heroines, the point of view of men readers is somewhat different from that of women ones. The woman reader wants to identify herself with the heroine, and she rebels at the idea of being Fanny. The male reader neither puts himself in Fanny's place nor imagines himself marrying Fanny. . . .

It is not the first time the lax or poor reader has been identified, by a man, as female. I think readers are not meant either to identify with Fanny or to assess her in Wilson's male reader's manner, as a believable and available "kind of woman"; I think Austen made a heroine of Fanny Price in order to force her (female) readers, pointedly, not to identify with a heroine. What Austen would have us do in regard to Fanny is not see her as either another self or a possible bride, but regard her, in all her lack of brilliance, as a sister. To underscore the point, Fanny has a brother who adores her, and a lover who feels toward her as a brother. She lives in a world terribly darkened by sisterly rivalries: between Julia and Maria Bertram, and before that, between her mother and aunts. But Fanny's triumph is to save her own sister. "My Fanny," Austen famously calls her. The endearment

is intruded at a crucial moment, the point where we might fault
Fanny for experiencing her absolute selfish happiness in the
wrecked bosom of the Bertram family, which had sheltered her.
The uncharacteristic possessiveness has been explained by critics
as an irrepressible effusion on Austen's part, or a defensive one.
But I think we are being pointedly told that Fanny's own personal happiness comes first in her own mind, and first also in the
narrator's (and ideally also in the reader's), because Fanny is the
narrator's chosen heroine, the reader's sister. All the comforts of
a happy ending exist for her in a world where others end tragically because she is the heroine, whose happiness matters more
than the tragedies of others. Other pens would make other heroines; defiantly, Austen's makes one of Fanny.

In *Much Ado About Nothing*, when Beatrice insists all men are her
brothers, she does so to argue against marrying one:

> Would it not grieve a woman to be overmaster'd with a
> piece of valiant dust? to make an account of her life to a clod
> of wayward marl? No, uncle, I'll none. Adam's sons are my
> brethren, and truly I hold a sin to match in my kindred.

Jane Austen, the sister of several brothers as well as of Cassandra, effectively deflated the rake by imagining him, sister-like,
as one of Adam's sons. But being a good sister she stopped short
of desexing him. Like Beatrice, she invokes men's brotherhood
with women to claim the sexes are equal, which is to say well
matched. When Mr. Knightley, who is the brother-in-law of
Emma's sister, first presents himself to Emma as a suitor, he
shoulders aside the incest taboo at a dance, in a decidedly attractive gesture:

> "Will you?" said he, offering his hand.
> "Indeed I will. You have shown that you can dance, and
> you know we are not really so much brother and sister as to
> make it at all improper."
> "Brother and sister! no, indeed." (*E* III, 2)

The thought—Emma brings it up for him to dismiss—charges the space between them. Jane Austen comments on the ambiguities of the brother-and-sister connection while considering men and women as complements, in the course of revising romance.

*Mansfield Park* is of all Austen's novels the one most overtly concerned with brother-and-sister love. Fanny adores her brother William, and she loves and tenaciously hopes to marry her cousin Edmund, with whom she has lived since childhood. (Edmund, who has formed her mind, is a sort of father as well as nearly a brother.) In a world full of siblings, Fanny is courted by Henry Crawford, with whose sister Edmund is in love. But when Edmund's sister Maria scandalously elopes with Mary's brother Henry, Edmund gives Mary up and marries his cousin Fanny. They will continue to live where they have grown up. Many readers have noted that the marriage at the end of *Mansfield Park* is incestuous, being a turning inward toward the family rather than that embrace of new connections which traditionally comes at the affirmative end of comedies. Many have also observed that the unromantic relationship between Fanny and Edmund is also uninteresting. Beatrice's tone cannot be taken in *Mansfield Park*, as it is in Austen's earlier works.

In *Sense and Sensibility* and *Pride and Prejudice*, scenes in which a newly married ex-rake encounters the sister of his victim are parodistic versions of the conflict between the lady and the rake. The brother-and-sister relation is invoked there for two reasons: to deflate the rake and to generate a chaste but distinctly erotic excitement. In Chapter 7 of Volume 3 of *Sense and Sensibility*, Marianne Dashwood is recovering from a nearly fatal fever brought on by a combination of wet feet and the discovery that Willoughby, who had loved her, will marry another woman. Her sister Elinor sits alone late in the evening, in a strange house, as Marianne sleeps upstairs. There is no one else awake. Elinor is waiting for their mother. Undemonstrative herself, she anticipates with some dread first the enduring, and then the relieving, of her mother's predictable excesses of anxiety. She is nervously exhausted from nursing Marianne. It is already dark, and cold and stormy outside. Rattled, Elinor thinks she has imagined hearing a carriage, then finds there is indeed a visitor at the door. She goes to greet her mother: "She rushed forwards towards the drawing-room,—she entered it,—and saw only Willoughby." She has been thinking of him as a monster, but "only Willoughby" is what the interview that follows proves him to be.

As Marianne's charming deceiver confesses his feelings and his whole history, he exposes himself as weak and confused, the victim of his passions, his past, his guardian, and now his new wife. The young woman who hears him out in unusual, potentially scandalous circumstances—unchaperoned in a strange house late in the evening—is initially hostile. She hates him for what he has done to Marianne. But by the time he finishes talking she feels different. At the end she gives him her hand:

> He held out his hand. She could not refuse to give him her's;—he pressed it with affection.
> "And you *do* think something better of me than you did?"—said he, letting it fall, and leaning against the mantlepiece as if forgetting he was to go. (S & S III, 8)

The narrator is unusually attentive to bodies and gestures: prudent Elinor is being charmed by an attractive man. After he leaves she reflects on him and on the interview, and her forgiveness, she notes, is compromised by another kind of feeling:

> Willoughby, he, whom only half an hour ago she had abhorred as the most worthless of men, Willoughby, in spite of all his faults, excited a degree of commiseration for the sufferings produced by them, which made her think of him as now separated for ever from her family with a tenderness, a regret, rather in proportion, as she soon acknowledged within herself—to his wishes than to his merits. She felt that his influence over her mind was heightened by circumstances which ought not in reason to have weight; by that person of uncommon attraction, that open, affectionate, and lively manner which it was no merit to possess; and by that still ardent love for Marianne, which it was not even innocent to indulge. But she felt that it was so, long, long before she could feel his influence less. (S & S III, 9)

Willoughby blundered into her evening and stole for himself some of the feelings with which she had been nurturing Marianne, which she had been waiting to lavish on her mother. They have talked intimately and frankly. The warmth of his passions, frankly revealed, has made her like and respond to him. And his good looks ("that person of uncommon attraction") have not hindered his case.

In the encounter between Elizabeth Bennet and Mr. Wickham, late in *Pride and Prejudice*, the conscious, clever heroine herself points out a brother-and-sister tie like the one that might have existed between Elinor and Willoughby. But between Wickham and Elizabeth, something else also might have existed: once, she liked him. The newly (and forcibly) married Wickham comes to visit the Bennet home and chats with his sister-in-law there. Irrepressibly shameless, he continues to insist that the lies he told her long ago, about his relationship to the Darcy family, are true. Elizabeth knows better now, and insists that he acknowledge the truth: that he, and not Darcy, was at fault. As he fends off her increasingly difficult questions, Wickham refers to what he had told her when they had first met, when she had been thinking he was charming. By now she finds him quite the opposite, but for politeness' sake and perhaps for her sister's she smothers annoyance and lets him off easily with a good-humored smile. She says, "Come, Mr. Wickham, we are brother and sister, you know. Do not let us quarrel about the past. In future, I hope we shall always be of one mind." She holds out her hand and Wickham, defeated, kisses it "with affectionate gallantry, though he hardly knew how to look" (*P & P* III, 10). It is an oddly intimate moment, mixing irony and feeling in a manner characteristic of this novel. By insisting on the brother-and-sister relation, Elizabeth strips the rake of menace, seeing the vile seducer as a brother to be indulged and forgiven, even liked, for his weakness. Elizabeth thoroughly confounds Wickham by her deflationary wit; Elinor merely witnessed Willoughby's diminishing into honesty. Both retired rakes, both in the awkward position of being newly and uncomfortably married, extort and receive from the older sisters of their victims an indulgence that in effect dismisses them as possible threats. They are not made utterly charmless, and not rendered altogether impotent, but merely demystified by being taken firmly in hand. In both these scenes the woman is the more rational and competent person, the one in charge. In both, the couple that is not quite brother and sister, and not quite managing a meeting of minds, come to a kind of mutual understanding. Their sudden, fleeting intimacy, which depends on a difference of gender, is poignant. The heroine's awareness of kinship with her "brother" is erotic in a context where mutual consciousness is always highly charged. For the self-conscious heroine, a second self—a sister or a brother—mirrors her own dividedness, the pleasurable/painful fact of her self-awareness.

It is a mistake to believe that Lovelace attracts Clarissa by promising violence or tempting her to the luxury of submission. The reason she is drawn to him is that he seems to know about, to care about, all of her. His Plot, which involves sending a spy to her house to discover all that goes on there so he can make his plans to suit, is the expression in action of his kind of charm; and so is his epistolary style, which insinuates his expectation of a responsive reader. Unlike Clarissa's parents, who seem to her to be acting strangely, to be treating her as if she were a stranger, this strange man seems to have precisely the awareness she herself has of how horrible it would be to give herself to the odious Solmes. The familiar, Freud wrote, is uncanny when it looks like the unknown; the unknown is perhaps most attractive when it is almost familiar. Lovelace is Clarissa's brother James's enemy, but he might be her own brother, leaguing with her against the parents, sharing her estimate of her worth, being as concerned for her fate as she is. His charming her suggests he knows her deepest secret—which is that she is susceptible to masculine charm. The secret is something Clarissa keeps even from herself and Anna Howe, who suspects it. As he puts his plot into action, Lovelace seems to Clarissa to know both her desires and fears and to know how she is trying to control them. She is magnetized by his mirroring awareness of her, by his desire—it reflects her own—to control her.

The rake is exciting to the heroine because he is attentive, tuned in. That he studies his victims in order to seduce them is flattering; they find it seductive to be objects of study to a man, as they are objects of study to themselves. Under the pressure of passion Lovelace turns crude, supposes Clarissa Harlowe might be subdued by the idea of a fire in the house and the convenience of being half-dressed. But in the beginning, as he professes to worship her, sympathizes with her anguish, signals his sense of her desire, and promises her the protection of the ladies of his great house, he seems to be already her intimate. Richardson's good man, Sir Charles Grandison, is nearly as subtle and sensitive. Critics have grouped him with the "men of feeling" who began to be written about in novels of his time, but he is a heroine's hero not for being overemotional, but because of his capacity for responsiveness. The heroine's hero must be responsive first of all: he must treat her as if she were important, a heroine. If Darcy ever seems less than Elizabeth Bennet deserves, it is when he misreads women: when he misinterprets Jane Bennet's smile and tells Bingley Jane does not especially like him, and when he addresses his own first proposal not to Elizabeth Bennet but to any girl who has a vulgar mother. He is in need of being made more subtle and supple, and he will be made all that by the knowing laughter Elizabeth learned at her father's knee.

Darcy is the only one of Jane Austen's heroes who is not only entirely devoted to private life but also has nothing else on his mind. Neither a clergyman like Henry Tilney and Edward Ferrars and Edmund Bertram, nor a sailor like Frederick Wentworth, he is, at twenty-seven, not retired, either, like Colonel Brandon in *Sense and Sensibility*. While Mr. Knightley is, like Darcy, a landed gentleman, he is concerned in the affairs of the village where he is chief resident, and presiding over Donwell Abbey requires him to have frequent conferences with its manager, William Larkins. Darcy's Pemberley, in contrast, stands aloof in Derbyshire and seems gracefully to run itself. More than a substantial estate, it is a tourist attraction, one of the great places in England. When he comes there Pemberley welcomes its master bountifully, with "a variety of all the finest fruits in season . . . beautiful pyramids of grapes, nectarines, and peaches," more sophisticated fare than the strawberries of Knightley's Donwell Abbey; but Darcy is often away taking care of the affairs of his friends, whose business is all the business he has. The Bingley sisters rely on his example in the project of settling their brother on an estate, and Darcy takes complete charge of his friend's love life, "saving" the compliant man from Jane Bennet because he thinks Bingley's love for her is misplaced and unrequited. Wealth and skill and sensitivity to his own responsibility for other people's lives, as well as passion for Elizabeth, lead to his settling the affair of Lydia and Wickham. Married to Elizabeth, finally, he will help in educating her remaining marriageable sister, as well as his own, at Pemberley.

Darcy recalls the traditional nemesis of traditional heroines when he first appears, tall, dark, and distant, aristocratic, hard to please, suspected of trifling with the life of a dependent. But appearances prove deceptive: Wickham, who claims Darcy mistreated him, turns out to be a liar. The Austen hero of whom Darcy is a rewriting is Willoughby; his prototype is Grandison. A young man of wealth and family, a devoted, protective, paternal brother, the scourge of rakes, salvager of reputations, and maker of other people's marriages, Grandison is the acknowledged sun of his world. He knows that the most important thing in life is the domain of women, the creation of families and communities; he cares most, therefore, about what goes on between young men and women. The rake is committed to violating and exploiting women's emotions; Grandison honors and studies them. In Grandison virtue is imagined as male without being violent or personally ambitious —without, in other words, having the characteristics usually imagined as masculine.

Unlike Richardson's virtuous heroines, who have many fictional "daughters," Sir Charles Grandison has only a few stepsons. Men something like him appear in later novels, but usually they are rejected by a heroine who wants someone more complicated. Lord Warburton, in *The Portrait of a Lady*, is conspicuous among those. James's rich middle-aged Americans, who are exhausted by business and yearn toward a finer life, concentrate as Grandison does on domestic values and domestic matters, but Christopher Newman in *The American* and Lambert Strether in *The Ambassadors* both blunder as they too strenuously seek an alternative they have too late chosen. Mr. Wilcox in E. M. Forster's *Howards End* is perhaps a related figure. But men of sensibility in fiction, as in life, at least since the eighteenth century, are more often ambitious, egotistic artists than feudal lords of the earth. Like Grandison, Darcy has no personal ambition, no business but personal relationships, and no aim to use personal relationships for self-aggrandizement. From being refused, the first time, by Elizabeth Bennet, he learns what he not only needs but also wants to learn: to attune himself better to women. The "unfeminine" (or more than feminine) heroine of *Pride and Prejudice*—her father's daughter and a strong walker over muddy fields—marries in the end a more than masculine man, his sister's protector and his wife's straight man, a deeply domestic creature who has learned by loving a witty woman to alter his standards of womanly excellence, and to attune himself more finely and fraternally to women's feelings.

As if to emphasize the importance of her extraction, and the difficulties involved in her being extracted from obscurity and made a heroine, Elizabeth Bennet is approached as if from a great distance, distinguished from very far away. She is not introduced to us straight off like "Emma Woodhouse, handsome, clever, and rich"; we are not given her family history, either, but instead faced by an abstract formulation about life in general. "It is a truth universally acknowledged, that a single man in possession of a good fortune, must be in want of a wife." The famous first sentence of *Pride and Prejudice* invites us to contemplate with cool philosophical amusement a dubious truth about a distant humanity. The narrator pans in on Elizabeth Bennet first from the universe, then from what passes for it locally—the neighborhood—and then from the family, in which she is the inconspicuous second of five daughters. When she is described, at the end of Chapter 1, it is in negatives and comparatives. She is "silly and ignorant" like most girls, Mr. Bennet says, but "has something more of quickness than her sisters"; she is the best of a mediocre lot. Since Mr. Bennet's wit in short order seduces us into taking his side against his wife, we are inclined to believe him and think Elizabeth superior: praise from him is clearly hard to earn. Elizabeth's skeptical distance from the commonplace worldly business of husband-hunting echoes our own distance from the world she lives in, and makes us feel that we, like Mr. Bennet, have exercised discrimination by choosing her as our heroine, and believing that she above all women deserves our attention and the remarkably happy end to which a heroine is destined. In choosing Elizabeth above all women, we prove our superior taste; we discriminate with the strenuousness her rare excellence will demand of a lover.

After a glimpse of Elizabeth sewing in the bosom of her boring family we see her, in Chapter 3, being pointed out at a ball where there is, as there was in the Bennet parlor, a "scarcity of gentlemen," a superfluity of ladies. Urged to dance with her, the haughty Darcy rejects her as "tolerable; but not handsome enough to tempt *me*"—undistinguished, and therefore unworthy of the distinction of his choice. She overhears the snub and repeats it "with great spirit among her friends," having what she supposes is the last word and the last laugh; when she does that, Elizabeth begins to link herself to Darcy, and at the same time to wrest acknowledgment of her personal significance from her society. By telling the story on him, she insists (too much) that she is impervious to the temptation to become sexually or emotionally involved, and asserts a prerogative to look over others from a distance, to objectify them in order to define her own standards, her own self. Darcy's gender and class grant him such rights; Elizabeth becomes his equal by seizing it, like her father, or like a satirical novelist.

Satire is traditionally the weapon of the party out of power, which questions by mockery things as they have been established. The social position of woman, confining her and making her subordinate, has all but forced her to be satirical. As Lord Shaftesbury wrote in 1709,

> the natural free spirits of ingenious men, if imprisoned and controlled, will find out other ways of motion to relieve themselves in their constraint; and whether it be in burlesque, mimicry, or buffoonery, they will be glad at any rate to vent themselves, and be revenged on their constrainers.

Some degree of satirical spirit in a heroine is, if not inevitable, very plausible; Clarissa is cleverly critical of men, and her best friend is sharp Miss Howe. A virgin governed by a rigorous code of behavior, obliged to repress her energies and to accept some man or other in marriage, eventually, to save her own life, comes naturally by some bitterness, some scorn. Scrutinizing the world's available men, she acquires a degree of disillusionment and detachment. The courtship plot is a logical vehicle for satire. The men who present themselves as candidates for the heroine's hand are—all save one—in a position to embody the values she rejects. A satirical stance, finally, may be attractive in a woman: although too much sparkle will raise the eyebrows of dowagers, detachment, in a virgin, is a nicely metaphorical mode, and those men who see the sexual relation as a tussle may be attracted by a combative posture. The intelligent young woman whose "little body," as Shakespeare's Portia calls hers, is attached to a mind both broad and deep may stir erotic imaginings. Portia herself is obedient to her father's will, a docile daughter, and also she solves all the problems in *The Merchant of Venice* by her wit and wisdom: feminine dependence and extraordinary power coexist in her, inexplicably equal and linked. Henry James called Portia, admiringly, "the very type and model of the young person intelligent and presumptuous," thinking of her as he thought about Isabel Archer. The heroine who proves her spirit and superiority by the wit that enables her to transcend her body's limits draws attention to her little body. George Henry Lewes, that connoisseur of mind in women who would have married George Eliot if he could have, declared himself ready to go down on his knees to

Elizabeth Bennet. Her "quickness" is an indication of her vitality, her satiric spirit a sign of her readiness for love.

By the story Elizabeth tells on him she makes the point that Darcy's words reveal more about him than they do about her. The first words Elizabeth speaks, in the novel, are also a comment on another person's language—here, her sister Jane's. Elizabeth's cool, decisive style corrects Jane's muddled, maidenly exclamations over the perfections of the desirable Mr. Bingley:

> "He is just what a young man ought to be," said [Jane], "sensible, good humoured, lively; and I never saw such happy manners!—so much ease, with such perfect good breeding!"
>
> "He is also handsome," replied Elizabeth, "which a young man ought likewise to be, if he possibly can. His character is thereby complete." (I, 4)

"Ought to be" means different things to Jane, who means what's acceptable, and to Elizabeth. What Elizabeth means is gently to mock conventional standards and conventional outbursts by echoing Jane's phrase. Jane *really* admires Bingley because he is handsome; and of course he is handsome by accident, not because he obliged himself to be so. Jane's language is gently criticized by her sister as inadequate to what it aims to express and to suppress. What Jane says, like what Darcy says, insists on the conventions for gentlemen and ladies; both imply that the best appearances are reliable. Jane's and Darcy's feelings (female sexual interest and male sexual apathy, or arrogance, or both), which Elizabeth sees through their words, are not what ladies and gentlemen aim to reveal. Elizabeth is alive to the ways the unspeakable truth is curiously implicated in the formulations ("truths") that seek to conceal or deny it.

Like sincere Jane, who believes she can express her feelings in language, Darcy takes himself and language seriously. His "tolerable; but not handsome enough to tempt *me*" is telling: he moves characteristically from the general to the particular statement, from an even to an emphatic tone, in the belief that truth can be precisely told by narrowing things down. It seems to him that words can sometimes utterly conceal meanings and that meaning may stand solidly behind words; he is a man who thinks a mind improved by extensive reading should back up the standard accomplishments in the ideal woman. Elizabeth, on the other hand, is wary of language and conscious of its inadequacies, and also of how much it tells. The two fall in love because for all their difference they share a moral seriousness about language, which *Pride and Prejudice* equates with moral seriousness about life. The sexual tension between them, which the novel conveys without describing, is generated by dialogues in which, insisting on their opposition to one another, the protagonists provoke one another to respond. Lovelace and Clarissa are similarly matched, but tragically unable to talk as equals.

Darcy and Elizabeth are convincing characters in the fiction *Pride and Prejudice* because we are made sensitive to the gap between all they are and the fictions they present to the world and also believe about themselves—in the way we are sensitive to people we love, whose masks seem touching. Our complicity with the storyteller, who knows they are more than what they seem—who makes us suspect that Darcy *was* probably tempted against his better judgment, or his judgment of himself as better, and that Elizabeth was hurt by what she overheard, and told her story in self-defense as well as in play—reflects their complicity within the fictional world where their mutual understanding grows in spite of their conversational armor and because of it, beneath what they say in roomsful of chatter. Elizabeth comes to an understanding with Darcy the way Austen comes to an understanding with the reader, by using language so as to invite an awareness of how it imposes itself on reality. Austen draws our attention to the constraints of both fiction and social life in order to make the point that feeling and movement and meaning and understanding exist in an area that is defined only in the sense that it strains against boundaries and at the same time strives to attain them. It is the great theme of the heroine-centered novel.

The understanding between Elizabeth and Darcy develops mostly in the presence of third persons and is involved with an awareness of what third persons would think and say. The universal tendency to confound what is acknowledged with the truth is the foil to their intimacy and also the structure that makes it possible. The relationship between the two proceeds from the point where they talk publicly about each other with assumed objectivity to the point where they understand each other by reading between one another's lines, and finally to mutual exegesis.

For a gentleman's daughter living in the eighteenth century, Elizabeth spends a remarkable amount of time out of doors. When her sister Jane falls ill, just as their crafty mother hoped, at Mr. Bingley's house, Elizabeth walks the three miles to Netherfield Park to see her, "alone, crossing field after field at a quick pace, jumping over stiles and springing over puddles with impatient activity," and arrives "with weary ancles, dirty stockings, and a face glowing with the warmth of exercise" (I, 7). She enjoys moving, body as well as mind. Her rival, Miss Bingley, whose idea of exercise is a turn around the parlor with the gentlemen looking on, points out to Darcy the mud on Elizabeth's petticoat; toward the end of the novel, in a last attempt to snare him, she remarks that Elizabeth, who has been traveling, has grown "brown and coarse." An impressive number of the critical encounters in Elizabeth's story take place outside: Darcy hands her the letter justifying his proposal in the lane between Hunsford Parsonage and Rosings, and after studying it she wanders around for two hours. She meets Darcy again in his grounds while touring Derbyshire; later, she triumphs over the imperious Lady Catherine de Bourgh in the shrubbery; finally, Darcy proposes and she accepts him while they are taking a walk. The open spaces where she wanders are defined by the houses they are between or adjacent to. When she responds to her aunt's invitation to tour the Lakes with a rapturous, romantic "What are men to rocks and mountains?" we are not to take her altogether seriously, for she is only voicing transitory disgust for the social life that is the only one she can, the only one she wants to, live. The path of her destiny is a trajectory between the house she must leave and the house she must enter as a bride. The small spaces she walks, runs, or rambles in are analogues to the short time she has in which to accomplish this.

The difference between Elizabeth and a heroine of romance is reflected by her position without the walls. Her little distance from convention is what distinguishes her. The "quickness" that her father loves and her mother dislikes her for separates her from what's dead and enables her to be intellectual mistress of it. She scrutinizes the world so as to assess it and to keep herself at a distance from it. Satire, for Elizabeth, is self-defense; she says to Charlotte Lucas of Darcy that "he has a very satirical eye, and if I do not begin by being impertinent myself, I shall soon grow afraid of him" (I, 6). In a world where women are assessed by their appearances, she seizes power by taking the observer's role; she frees herself of judgments by making them. Her ultimate realization that she has accepted a false version of Darcy, the one framed by Wickham, is a realization of her own limitations that takes her outside herself and sets her free. (The true picture of Darcy hangs at Pemberley.)

Elizabeth keeps her head above the pompous, the platitudinous, and the merely vague by using words precisely. When she welcomes her aunt's invitation to tour the Lakes she imagines excelling other tourists by her language:

> Oh! what hours of transport we shall spend! And when we *do* return, it shall not be like other travellers, without being able to give one accurate idea of any thing. We *will* know where we have gone—we *will* recollect what we have seen. Lakes, mountains, and rivers, shall not be jumbled together in our imaginations; nor, when we attempt to describe any particular scene, will we begin quarrelling about its relative situation. Let *our* first effusions be less insupportable than those of the generality of travellers. (II, 4)

By being precise and particular about what she has seen, she will escape the offensive jumble of social life as effectively as by leaving society and going off to a rugged part of the country. In society Elizabeth imagines herself as an observer of framed scenes. During her visit to Netherfield Park early in the novel, when Darcy invites her to join him and the Bingley sisters on a wider path, she says, "No, no; stay where you are. —You are charmingly group'd, and appear to uncommon advantage. The picturesque would be spoilt by admitting a fourth" (I, 10). Seeing a scene in her life as if it were a picture, she takes charge by talking as a critic. When, at the end of the novel, she wants to say she is happy, she can only say how happy by saying she does not mean what others mean by the word, by separating herself from their conventional expressions. She writes to her aunt, "I am the happiest creature in the world. Perhaps other people have said so before, but not one with such justice. I am happier even than Jane; she only smiles, I laugh" (III, 18). Elizabeth's value is defined as something that cannot be contained and therefore cannot be expressed; it is in her liveliness, in her eyes. It can only be generated by the force of comparison. She is at her best, most herself, played off against someone else, and so of course—it is the most romantic of ironies—she must marry. Inevitably, the courtship of Elizabeth Bennet is a series of dialogues.

The first conversation takes place when Elizabeth is an uninvited guest at the house in her neighborhood that Darcy's friend Bingley has rented; it is on one level about Elizabeth's right to join Darcy's party, which is what she will do for good in the end. As the conversation begins she sits apart from the group, reading, but as she hears in Bingley's sister Caroline's small talk an undercurrent that aims to sweep Darcy off his feet she is "so much caught . . . as to leave her very little attention for her book." Darcy is saying he is uncommonly exigent about ladies who are called accomplished and language that calls them that. Elizabeth begins to differ, and Miss Bingley backs Darcy up by parroting a litany of particulars; she aims to claim him by spelling out what he means:

> "A woman must have a thorough knowledge of music, singing, drawing, dancing, and the modern languages, to deserve the word; and besides all this, she must possess a certain something in her air and manner of walking, the tone of her

voice, her address and expressions, or the word will be but half deserved."

She hopes she is describing herself by detailing this picture of the exemplary female, but evidently Darcy does not think so. A truly accomplished young lady, he intones, "must yet add something more substantial, in the improvement of her mind by extensive reading." Miss Bingley does not read; Elizabeth, although she has already rejected her rival's description of her as a great reader, is at that very moment holding her book. Darcy's definition of ideal woman as the sum of ladylike, describable perfections irritates Elizabeth, who rejects, along with it, his implicit invitation that she assume the exemplary position Miss Bingley has presumed to merit: "*I* never saw such a woman. *I* never saw such capacity, and taste, and application, and elegance, as you describe, united" (I, 8). She vanquishes Miss Bingley on the conversational field by opposing Darcy instead of agreeing with him. She seems Caroline's superior because she is talking about substantive matters rather than formal ones, because she uses superior language (words of four syllables, the kind Darcy likes) to organize matters less susceptible to order, as well as less obvious, than the ones Miss Bingley lists. She speaks for herself and she speaks from experience, insisting on the personal pronoun. A man who cares for language cannot but be impressed by the way she handles repetition and balance and rhythm, by the logic of her sequence and the force of the final, delayed participle. Nor can the reader, who must recognize her style, as well as her insistence that young women fall short of describable perfection, as very nearly Jane Austen's.

Everyone in *Pride and Prejudice* is aware that when form is imposed on the feelings and facts of life it alters them: the cover-up wedding clothes Lydia buys after her scandalous elopement are the clearest evidence that this is the way of the world. Darcy and Elizabeth alone focus on this problem with intensity; they alone know their lives depend on grappling with it. Their deepest emotions are generated in the gap between formula and meaning. When she finds herself constrained by politeness to dance with him at the Netherfield ball, Elizabeth archly strikes up a conversation about conversation itself—so as to punish him, she fancies: "It is *your* turn to say something now, Mr. Darcy. —I talked about the dance, and *you* ought to make some kind of remark on the size of the room, or the number of couples." Her assumption that he is quite as uneasy as she is with their obligation to exchange banalities is an implicit, inviting presumption of likeness between them—that there is indeed "a great similarity in the turn of [their] minds," a kinship like Benedick's to Beatrice. Although Darcy is not witty, we are convinced by Elizabeth's conviction. Later on, Darcy will make a feeling remark on the similarity between himself and Elizabeth ("We neither of us perform to strangers"), which echoes Elizabeth's last word in their first exchange during the dance at Netherfield: "I must not decide on my own performance." When Elizabeth challenges Darcy with the claim that she is trying to "make out" his character, he begs her not to "sketch" it, "as there is reason to fear that the performance would reflect no credit on either" (I, 18). To have such conversations about mutual connections and about the implication of the external with the internal is, as surely as a love of dancing is, "a certain step toward falling in love."

Darcy is first "bewitched" by Elizabeth when he is briefly resident in her neighborhood; in the end she will claim, laughing, that her love for him began when she visited his, "from my first seeing his beautiful grounds at Pemberley" (III, 17). But the crucial stage of their relationship takes place on neutral ground. When Elizabeth visits her friend Charlotte she is surprised to encounter Darcy in the neighborhood, and forced to accept his company at the social gatherings where the two resume their word game. Darcy boldly presumes intimacy when he says, in the presence of a stranger, "I have had the pleasure of your acquaintance long enough to know, that you find great enjoyment in occasionally professing opinions which in fact are not your own." Elizabeth counters by saying that she knows things about him that he wouldn't want to reveal (she thinks she does). Darcy maintains he is too honest to give a false impression of friendliness; Elizabeth accuses him of disingenuousness, with a metaphor. She is seated at the piano, and the conversation is a variation on the earlier one about feminine accomplishments:

> "My fingers," said Elizabeth, "do not move over this instrument in the masterly manner which I see so many women's do. They have not the same force or rapidity, and do not produce the same expression. But then I have always supposed it to be my own fault—because I would not take the trouble of practising. It is not that I do not believe *my* fingers as capable as any other woman's of superior execution."

Darcy is charmed by her power to drop a subject in such a way as to vex it. He says: "You are perfectly right. You have employed your time much better. No one admitted to the privilege of hearing you, can think any thing wanting. We neither of us perform to strangers" (II, 8). He appreciates her talk as performance; therefore he appreciates her. He is beginning to acknowledge that he and she are not strangers; to acknowledge that, and to receive her metaphor as a metaphor, is to claim and make intimacy. What passes for a merely witty rejoinder is in fact profoundly responsive, in part because it leaves a listening stranger, Darcy's cousin Fitzwilliam, out of a relationship that is by definition exclusive. Elizabeth's and Darcy's awareness of each other's self-consciousness is the force that draws them together.

When they are tête-à-tête, in Charlotte Collins's parlor, the two can think of nothing to say. Unable to perform without an audience, they are tongue-tied. So they talk of third persons—of Charlotte, who has moved so far from her family. It turns out that small talk is big: a chat about geography alters the geography in the room as Darcy is propelled by his own words to draw his chair closer to Elizabeth's. Catching himself, he reverts to a more careful chitchat. After that visit, silence signals the coming of an emotional storm. He comes to call again and almost immediately bursts out with a blundering proposal: "In vain have I struggled. It will not do. My feelings will not be repressed. You must allow me to tell you how ardently I admire and love you" (II, 11). His heartfelt declaration has the perverse effect of driving the two apart (as it logically must, in a context that defines mannered wit and not effusions as the food of love). Darcy explains he is proposing against his will, in spite of his feelings about her family. Elizabeth rejects not only him and his manner but the "established mode" of rejecting a man courteously. All veils stripped, they accuse one another of not veiling their motives well enough. Darcy insists once more on his sincerity ("disguise of every sort is my abhorrence"); his objections to her family are "natural and just." Elizabeth counters by claiming that the *mode* of his proposal, however rude, is not what she objects to: what she loathes is the inner man it reveals. The total alienation caused by this terrible attempt at self-expression and direct penetration to another's depths is suggested by the long, formal, confessional, unanswerable letter Darcy writes. Reading it over, Elizabeth exclaims, "Till this moment, I never knew myself" (II, 13). There is a promise of the end in the fact that she sees *her*self in the mirror he meant to show her *him*self in.

During the long separation that ensues, Elizabeth travels with her aunt and uncle, and on their holiday journey they visit Pemberley. She admires the estate; she has "never seen a place for which nature had done more, or where natural beauty had been so little counteracted by an awkward taste" (III, 1). Darcy's nature now appears entirely admirable. The housekeeper praises her master's character. Elizabeth visits the portrait gallery—the very one Caroline Bingley had in mind when she teased Darcy about his interest in Elizabeth and imagined pictures of her vulgar relatives there alongside his distinguished ones.

> In the gallery there were many family portraits, but they could have little to fix the attention of a stranger. Elizabeth walked on in quest of the only face whose features would be known to her. At last it arrested her—and she beheld a striking resemblance of Mr. Darcy, with such a smile over the face, as she remembered to have sometimes seen, when he looked at her. She stood several minutes before the picture in earnest contemplation, and returned to it again before they quitted the gallery. . . .
>
> There was certainly at this moment, in Elizabeth's mind, a

more gentle sensation towards the original, than she had felt in the height of their acquaintance. . . . [A]s she stood before the canvas, on which he was represented, and fixed his eyes upon herself, she thought of his regard with a deeper sentiment of gratitude than it had ever raised before; she remembered its warmth, and softened its impropriety of expression. (III, 1)

She finds his face among strange faces because his portrait *arrests* her, not by its resemblance to Darcy's features (it is an old painting, done before his father died) but by its expression. Looking at his portrait, Elizabeth can study a fixed manifestation of her lover as she studied it in his letter, which she read and reread as now she contemplates and returns to the portrait. She ponders the meanings of his image like a critic. Seeing him look the way he looked when he looked at her, Elizabeth sees a shadow of herself in his image, as she did when she knew herself by reading his letter.

The critic becomes partial creator, directing the gaze of the painted eyes, when Elizabeth stands before the portrait in such a way as to fix "his eyes upon herself." Being looked at by his picture, Elizabeth is moved by the "expression," which makes her forget the "impropriety of expression" in his proposal. One hesitates to call this a pun: Austen is pointing out that the evanescent, "natural" alteration of the features by feeling is described by the same word used to signify the deliberately composed words of a speech. Here the "expression" of the features is clear to the observer of a portrait. It is as if no one but Elizabeth, on whom that look was directed in life, could see the Darcy she sees in the picture; and it is important that she finds the picture's gaze by calibrating her gaze to the image's. What she loves, and sees, is what goes on between them. Not the real Darcy but his painted image makes her fall finally and decisively in love; she responds to it by thinking of his "regard with a deeper sentiment of gratitude than it had ever raised before." "Regard" is certainly a pun. Between the picture's eyes and Elizabeth's hangs what will be given shape when the marriage of the lovers is formalized.

When the master of Pemberley appears, Elizabeth and Darcy behave with the perfect civility of acquaintances. Like their earlier sparring, this is an indirect expression of feeling, which nourishes while masking it. A consciousness of the past loads some of their exchanges with private meanings, but both deliberately overlook those. To be one's best self involves concealing feeling: the presence of her aunt and uncle imposes on Elizabeth "the necessity of appearing more like herself," in other words, of not showing the confusion she feels, and in that way quieting it.

News of her sister Lydia's elopement comes to upset all decorum: shaken, Elizabeth blurts out the shameful truth and asks Darcy what he had once asked her, to keep a sister's secret. The reserved Darcy exclaims "Good God!" A separation is necessary; in the resultant silence each of the lovers puzzles over what the other feels, with no words and therefore no clues. Their union is finally made possible by a combination of language that falsifies and silence that reveals: a rumor that Elizabeth is to marry Darcy brings his aunt, the haughty Lady Catherine de Bourgh, to Longbourn to demand a denial, which Elizabeth refuses to give; her refusal, reported to Darcy, makes him suspect her true feelings for him. He recalls, "I knew enough of your disposition to be certain, that, had you been absolutely, irrevocably decided against me, you would have acknowledged it to Lady Catherine, frankly and openly" (III, 16).

What brings them to the stage of intimacy in which they can talk together about the distance between what they said and what they meant, between their present position and their past language, is Elizabeth's openly thanking Darcy for the help to Lydia he meant to keep a secret. Just as Darcy did in Charlotte's parlor, Elizabeth is articulating strong feelings she cannot contain. But hers is a courteous and generous rather than a selfish and rude outburst; and it is couched in language that, by apologizing for itself, shows an awareness of the other's sincere need for reserve. "You are too generous to trifle with me," Darcy says;

mutual open acknowledgments of generosity mark their coming together. They offer tributes to each other in formal but feeling language, then degenerate into inarticulate, halting professions of love. These the narrator charitably passes over. In the end, we are told, Darcy "expressed himself . . . as sensibly and as warmly as a man violently in love can be supposed to do," *i.e.*, not very sensibly and quite warmly. Elizabeth was unable to meet his eye; Jane Austen averts hers. *Pride and Prejudice* has defined this feeling as the function of the language it cannot find.

United, Elizabeth and Darcy enjoy talking over the talks that brought them together. They discuss the contradictions between what they showed and what they "really" felt. The novel has already proved that what they showed *made* what they felt. But they have an illusion of superiority to themselves and talk as if they were not the actors of their story but its readers: they look it over and quibble, even about "the moral." The novelist only implies their happiness by telling us of its social consequences, of the justice and benevolence and usefulness that will derive from their private understanding. The truth cannot be told outright. Austen's last sentence is about not the Darcys but the Gardiners, who were the means of "uniting them." All the other people with whom their relationship was less intimate have also been variously responsible for bringing about the arrangement, the marriage, that makes possible an exclusive relationship, a small circle whose perimeter is drawn by all it keeps out. Elizabeth's marriage will be the happiest ever, because it is the joining of two people who understand and complement and correct one another to perfection. Neither will be passive; neither will be worshiped; neither will give anything up; marriage will rid them of all the people—Miss Bingley and Lady Catherine, Mrs. Bennet and the Wickhams—who annoy by imposing on them, by thinking and pretending they know them. The Gardiners will come to Pemberley and trace its boundaries by riding around it; Georgiana Darcy and Kitty Bennet will be cultivated there; Mr. Bennet will visit often, evidently without his wife. The social ramifications of the Darcys' marriage are all we will see of it: they will be thirty miles even from Bingley and Jane. When we do get one glimpse of the couple, from the unexpected angle of Darcy's sister, it reassures us that when Elizabeth swallowed a satirical remark and reflected that Darcy "had yet to learn to be laught at, and it was rather too early to begin" (III, 16), she was not giving up laughing for good.

> Georgiana had the highest opinion in the world of Elizabeth; though at first she often listened, with an astonishment bordering on alarm at her lively, sportive, manner of talking to her brother. He, who had always inspired in herself a respect which almost overcame her affection, she now saw the object of open pleasantry. Her mind received knowledge which had never before fallen in her way. By Elizabeth's instructions she began to comprehend that a woman may take liberties with her husband, which a brother will not always allow in a sister more than ten years younger than himself. (III, 19)

In the end, in her way, Elizabeth is an exemplar.

"Happiness in marriage is entirely a matter of chance," Charlotte Lucas says in Chapter 6 of *Pride and Prejudice.* "If the dispositions of the parties are ever so well known to each other, or ever so similar before-hand, it does not advance their felicity in the least. They always continue to grow sufficiently unlike afterwards to have their share of vexation; and it is better to know as little as possible of the defects of the person with whom you are to pass your life." It is on the strength of this philosophy that Charlotte marries the insufferable Mr. Collins and manages to suffer him rather well, busying herself first with her poultry and later, probably, with her babies, keeping for herself a little back parlor away from the side of the house where her husband sits hoping for Lady Catherine to pass by. Elizabeth says Charlotte makes her laugh, and she protests that her doctrine "is not sound. You know it is not sound, and that you would never act in this way yourself," she says, and on rereading the novel we note her characteristic errors in judging character and predicting the future.

But it is harder to know if we are meant to perceive her notion that Charlotte's view "is not sound" as an error. Jane Austen clearly puts stock in knowing people's defects, and Charlotte's cynical counsel that ignorance may lead to bliss is the opposite of what *Pride and Prejudice* would seem to be preaching. Elizabeth attains perfect happiness by coming to know Mr. Darcy and thus learning to know herself. And the process by which she attains happiness does not seem a matter of chance, as it unfolds, but rather the logical, inevitable expression of her character in an action. In other words, *Pride and Prejudice* is not a picture of real life but a plausible fiction.

Charlotte does not believe that life is logical, or that we get what we deserve. Her "realistic" maxim is one of the many anti-romantic elements in this novel, which mocks as it exploits the conventions of romance. Elizabeth Bennet, who attains perfect happiness, is, for all her defiance of the ideal of woman, a novel heroine after all: her love story figures forth the novel's fantasies, that character determines fate, that virtue is rewarded, that to know oneself is to know and control one's destiny. A heroine, unlike other women, controls her life, shapes her self, makes her happiness; for other, real women, happiness is a matter of chance quite as Charlotte says. It is significant that of all the weddings in *Pride and Prejudice*, only Charlotte's will certainly produce what Mr. Bennet refers to with gingerly distaste, alluding to Mr. Collins's platitude about peace-making, as "a young olive-branch"; Elizabeth's marriage is the long-promised end to a perfectly made story, art not life. *Pride and Prejudice II* is unimaginable. Elizabeth is framed in the end.

# PART THREE

## Thinking It Over

"What tale do you like best to hear?"

"Oh, I have not much choice! They generally run on the same theme—courtship; and promise to end in the same catastrophe—marriage."

"And do you like that monotonous theme?"

"Positively, I don't care about it: it is nothing to me."

—Charlotte Brontë,
*Jane Eyre*

The constant sensitiveness of characters for each other—even in writers called robust like Fielding—is remarkable, and has no parallel in life, except among people who have plenty of leisure. Passion, intensity at moments—yes, but not this constant awareness, this endless readjusting, this ceaseless hunger. I believe that these are the reflections of the novelist's own state of mind while he composes, and that the predominance of love in novels is partly because of this.

—E. M. Forster,
*Aspects of the Novel*

There is no happiness in love, except at the end of an English novel.

—Anthony Trollope,
*Barchester Towers*

# ⤜ 1 ⤛

# Life as Literature, Revision as Romance

What fine weather this is! Not very becoming perhaps early in the morning, but very pleasant out of doors at noon, and very wholesome—at least everybody fancies so, and imagination is everything.

—Jane Austen to Cassandra Austen, 17 November 1798

Gloria has read *Wuthering Heights* sixteen times. She told me this not boastfully or confessionally but supportively, conspiratorially, to let me know she thinks I was right in assigning the book for the course. It was the first thing she ever said to me without first raising her hand, a low abrupt confidence she rushed up to deposit just after class. She blushed when I made some answer; she was not interested in further discussion, just in giving me this secret because I liked *Wuthering Heights* too.

Gloria is serene, complacent. She is majoring in home economics, and sixteen readings of *Wuthering Heights*, and nineteen years of living in Brooklyn, have not given her language. She argues in a class discussion of *Emma* that there are lots of guys like Mr. Knightley, good solid men who make a good living, like her fiancé, a pharmacist, and his friends. Mr. Darcy, now, that's

137

another story. You don't find a lot of guys like him, Gloria says.
He's, well, like, made up.

When I ask her if she doesn't mean that Mr. Darcy is more a
romantic hero like Heathcliff she says, "Yeah, that's it," without
conviction. Who is like Heathcliff to a girl who has read *Wuthering Heights* sixteen times, and seen the movie three? How can
Gloria, taking all this so personally as she does, find a textbook
phrase like "romantic hero" at all resonant? And how can
Gloria, who knows lots of guys like her fiancé, seriously intend
to get married to him? She is nineteen and he's nine years short
of Mr. Knightley's thirty-six (he's Darcy's age); for her he's an
older man. She can see why an older man might be just the ticket
for Emma, she says with an air of wisdom she must have borrowed from her mother.

For her term paper Gloria decides she will write on Jane Austen and Marriage. As she is not a good student, I take some time
to spell certain things out while we walk from the classroom.
Since the men Jane Austen's heroines marry are all different, I
point out, Gloria should be sure not to suggest that Jane Austen
is saying a girl should get married to such-and-such a kind of
man. Aware that she already knows this much, and conscious
that she doesn't know enough to write the paper she has in
mind, I add in a rhetorical flourish, limiting myself to the two
novels by Jane Austen I know Gloria has read, that Austen readers divide into two camps, those who like Mr. Darcy and those
who like Mr. Knightley. Right away, Gloria confesses she prefers
Mr. Darcy—"but I think I told you," she adds in her mild, smiling way, "that I'm engaged to someone just like Mr. Knightley." I
do not point out to her that neither Darcy nor Knightley can be
described as making a good living, or that it is Darcy whose
income is the larger, ten thousand pounds a year. I do point out
that she should remember as she writes her paper that Jane Austen, herself, never married.

"Oh, I know that," Gloria calls cheerfully (we are moving in
opposite directions across the campus by now). "How could she?
There was nobody good enough!"

It does seem to be possible to read novels passionately and

keep in mind the difference between literature and life. For some people.

For herself Jane Austen made the choice she put out of the question for her heroines. She was aware, clearly, that the single, logical, ideal resolution of a young woman's destiny, the one she six times portrayed as inevitable, is in fact highly unlikely. Writing to her niece after Fanny had turned down a suitor, she reflected wittily on the problem of identifying and locating the right man:

> There *are* such beings in the World perhaps, one in a Thousand, as the Creature You and I should think perfection, Where Grace & Spirit are united to Worth, where the Manners are equal to the Heart & Understanding, but such a person may not come in your way, or if he does, he may not be the eldest son of a Man of Fortune, the Brother of your particular friend, & belonging to your own County. (*Letters*, pp. 409–10)

And it is not only a matter of perfection's being easier to conceive of than to come by, she adds in a letter she sent Fanny the next week; another problem is that it might suit one imperfectly: "It is very true that you never may attach another Man, his equal altogether, but if that other Man has the power of attaching you *more*, he will be in your eyes the most perfect" (*Letters*, pp. 417–418).* So a girl might marry the wrong man, or she might not marry at all. Her own point of view, or consciousness, or imagination, as Jane Austen would call it, complicates the turns of a heroine's story, can even materially alter it.

Jane Austen promises that precisely the right husband, carefully chosen, will amend what faults or flaws or lacks a potentially perfect heroine has. He will restrain by sober good sense

---

* But see the view from another angle that Henry Crawford presents to Fanny Price in *Mansfield Park*: "It is not by equality of merit that you can be won. That is out of the question. It is he who sees and worships your merit the strongest, who loves you most devotedly, that has the best right to a return. There I build my confidence. By that right I do and will deserve you" (III, 3). The novel proves he does not deserve her.

her extravagant liveliness or fancy, and with his worldly goods and masculine power make her honesty, sincerity, and truth, which he admires and shares, effectively real in the world. Aiming at perfection, believing herself wanting, a girl marries in a triumphant effort at self-correction that proves she is a heroine.

Contemporary women are trying to discourage girlish dreams of being perfect, along with nightmares of inadequacy. We are soberingly aware of the connections between the two. The idea of finding oneself by finding one husband is also widely disbelieved in. But the subtler fantasy the English novelists nourish is harder to repudiate or to shake: the inclination to see oneself as a heroine. Thinking one's story over and seeing its pattern, discerning in that the meaning of one's integral self, is an exquisitely self-defeating mode of claiming mixed literary and moral distinctiveness—of becoming a heroine—that continues to be tempting. The traditional heroine-centered novel can be faulted, I suppose, for persuading susceptible readers to look at their own lives as if they were novels, and see themselves as unseen, unsung heroines, heroines by virtue of their keen eyes and ears and understandings.

The novel's trick of affirming as it seems to call in question the ideal of a perfected, integral female self appeals especially to people of a certain temperament—egotists disposed to irony, to thinking that what's special about them is the way they look at things. Their excessive self-regarding is perhaps intensified in unstable times, when the private life is a solacing focus, and romantic nostalgia for a bolder, more well-defined silhouette is contagious. The ideal of the heroine is singularly suited to survive re-evaluation and revision. Debunking perfection soon comes to redefining it: the realistic heroine-centered novel makes that clear as it critically revises romance only to create the romantic ideal of literary self-awareness.

In his book about his childhood, Jean-Paul Sartre recalls "poisoning" himself with stories written for children about the loaded, prophetic childhoods of great men: little Miguel, who came home and amused his family by telling of the strange knight he had seen on a broken-down horse, and little Raphael, who had begged to be taken to see the Pope, and told them all afterward he had seen nothing but colors. Little Jean-Paul meant to be a great man himself, and accordingly he lived his childhood for his unborn biographers and their readers. When his mother would find him working at his desk in the dark, and cry out that he was ruining his eyes, he would endow the encounter with the significance it warranted:

It was an opportunity to reply in all innocence: "I could write even in the dark." She would laugh, would call me her little silly, would put on the light; the trick was done; we were both unaware that I had just informed the year 3,000 of my future infirmity. Yes, toward the end of my life, more blind than Beethoven was deaf, I would work gropingly on my last book. People would say, with disappointment: "But it's illegible!" There would even be talk of throwing it into the garbage. Finally, the Aurillac Municipal Library would ask for it out of pure piety. It would lie there for a hundred years, forgotten. And then, one day, out of love for me, young scholars would try to decipher it; their entire lifetime would not be enough to restore what would, of course, be my masterpiece. My mother had left the room, I was alone, I repeated to myself, slowly, above all without thinking about it: "In the dark!" There was a sharp crack: my great-grand-nephew, out there, had shut his book; he was dreaming about the childhood of his great-grand-uncle, and tears were rolling down his cheeks. "Nevertheless, it's true," he would sigh, "he wrote in the dark!"

Sartre's point in recalling this is that it is an indulged, bourgeois child's fancy, a god-fearing, grandiose fool's dream, to think life is continuous and coherent and to the point, and that the ends of destinies are implicit in their beginnings. The passage fairly glitters with scorn, and its gaiety is only enhanced by a further irony that when he wrote it Sartre was in fact about to become blind.

The child Jean-Paul admires himself as the bud of all he will become; he waits to become great without trying to, persuaded greatness is his destiny. Assuming an ironic perspective transforms a child like Jean-Paul into destiny's secret ally: he becomes powerful by association. He imagines he has a better kind of power that is even greater than a great man's. Detached, reading the book of his life—Jean-Paul imagines what will happen to him years after his death—he is in a position to savor nuances not available to a mere hero of a life story. How can he resist, therefore, underlining or italicizing? The pleasures of seeing oneself as a character are voluptuous. The child tells himself his own story, because he knows from reading that how a story is told is what really matters most, and he knows from living that he can't trust anyone else to tell his right. Child ironists, like other children, think they know better than those who are supposed to know better; they find those others comically unaware of their limitations, pathetically blind to what's important ("It's so dark! My little darling is ruining his eyes," cries Jean-Paul's mother). The child who sees his own childhood dots the *i*'s and crosses the *t*'s in his life story by himself because he believes no one else is competent to do it right. One of the main things that make one's life story seem a story is the sense of reading it precisely as one might in a book, that is, surrounded by well-intentioned uncomprehending others who foolishly imagine one is really with them there in the living room. That close relatives don't understand the real meaning of one's life, fail to recognize statements and moments as premonitory, symbolic, definitive, consequential, is very nearly assurance that someday someone will. The gap between the way one appears and the way one is seems to a literary child analogous to the gap between the shelf it comes from and the world inside the book. That gap draws the eyes irresistibly: it is as if the meaning of life is just about to show itself right there.

I did not expect, as a child, what little Jean-Paul did, to be great or famous. But not only those who believe themselves destined to be named in histories suffer from self-aggrandizing childhood irony. The heroine of an unwritten fiction is the counterpart of the boy waiting to be recognized by the world as a hero, to have streets and squares called after him. The girl's concerns are ahistorical, almost entirely formal. Instead of biographers and admirers in distant times to come, she imagines invisible readers on her wavelength, endowed with a complexity of vision and an objectivity her parents lack, who can see her in the light of her being a heroine. For them she edits and annotates and rephrases her childhood as she lives it. I was haunted as a child by the sense that potentially telling, dramatic moments were passing by unnoticed, badly lighted, directed by nobody at all, lost too quickly to be savored and evaluated. The discrepancy between the real significance of events and the way my mother took things seemed to me full of irony. As my mother's sensible view of life was so plausible and persuasive, elaborate posturings on my part were from time to time necessary if it was to stay clear to me that my version and not hers was the one that was really happening, or perhaps in order that my version might happen.

Having read, then, in *Jo's Boys*, about a mother who puts her hands on her daughter's shoulders and looks tenderly into her eyes at the beginning of an intimate exchange, I marched into the kitchen one day and awkwardly maneuvered my mother into dropping her wooden spoon. So bewildered as to be willing, she submitted to her position in the tableau I had in mind, looking dubiously at each of my hands as they dropped down hard on her house dress, and then at her own floury ones. She stood still but impatient. The announcement I had to make that afternoon in the faded winter light, which might have passed unnoticed had I failed to take it and my mother into my own hands, was that I happened to know the Facts of Life. From a book (not by Louisa May Alcott) I had learned that the exchange of this information customarily took place in an important moment shared by mother and daughter. By one of the mistakes that seemed to occur too often in my life, I had learned what I knew in my mother's absence; I was trying to have the scene after the fact. It was a poor attempt, I knew, but who if not I was to give my life the resonance lives in fiction had? My mother was interested in baking; resonance was not her style. I must have been nine or ten: I remember having to reach for her shoulders. I was slightly embarrassed for her—she would regret having not yet got around to telling me the Facts of Life herself—but mostly I felt good about saving her from the embarrassing moment in which, when she finally got up courage to tell, I would have had to deflate her by admitting I already knew them. Did it occur to me that I was reversing the *Jo's Boys* posture by putting *my* hands on my *mother's* shoulders? Did I do it on purpose to signify I was reversing roles? Consciously or not, I not only borrowed a solemn gesture to make a weighty moment, but adapted it, perverted it, really, to suit a moment between mother and daughter that was altogether fabricated and false.

My mother was relieved by my confession. She said something on the order of "Is that all?" She showed me a huge drawer full of sanitary napkins. Why did she keep them in a drawer? Why did she have so many? Am I remembering it right? What I recall is thinking then, There she goes, eager to get on to some awful ordinary materialist's show-and-tell that makes the big difference between us.

A story I wrote in college was called "Virginity and Other Implications." Chances are it was set at Columbia University and the characters had some connection with a literary magazine, and one of them, probably a boy, was a lot smarter than the rest, who made him pay for it. And certainly sex, in the story, had the portentously, circumlocutiously, polysyllabically metaphorical significance it had in my life.

My friends and I felt ourselves chained by a heavy weight of metaphor: by all that our virginities implied, by all the ways we were implicated by virginity in falsehoods. Being a virgin posed some problems but on the whole it was a comfort. But the implications were intolerable, hilarious, pondered in hours of intense talk late at night over packs of cigarettes and cups of coffee. We set deadlines for ourselves and one another: If I don't lose mine by January, L. would declare, I'm dropping out of school. We colluded in plans: Why not bring a container of coffee to Professor G.'s office, and then he won't be able to throw you out, not before he drinks it; and one thing *has* to lead to another, and if it doesn't, well, after class you can go up and ask him about the assignment and then invite *him* out for coffee. (It probably matters that coffee was the aphrodisiac of choice.) Virginity, with all its implications, was an embarrassment because one did not, after all, feel like a virgin, worldly-wise as one was, all dressed in sophisticated black. A Virgin!!!! Me, a Virgin!!! It was a riot; we were all virgins, who would believe it!

Actually we weren't virgins. When, much later, we confessed, we explained that we had lied because, for one reason or another, we had each believed ourselves to be technically, or spiritually, virgin; because we hadn't known, or hadn't felt, or both, that "it" had actually happened to us. (We expected to know and to feel a very great deal.) One or two fumbly sexual experiences didn't count, were so unimportant that it seemed one could quite scrupulously ignore them.

The important thing was the irony: that we, persons of inordinate sophistication, were "technically" more or less innocent. We savored it uncomfortably. Appearance was at it again, misrepresenting Reality—and apropos of us, people so familiar with the ins and outs of the intricate relationship those two had. Virginity implied acceptance of monogamy and marriage, and romance, perhaps even God; virginity implied one didn't want sex; virginity implied one was committed to certain conventions and traditions and codes. Our virginities implied we were other than what we were; our bodies were at odds with us. That much we wearily, readily, accepted: girls learn to at puberty. The boast implicit in our cozy self-analyses was that we were not like all the thoughtless virgins in our class who were yearning for engagement rings; by those late-night talks we declared ourselves wilder, hotter. And also different from the wild hot girls, who had no need to talk, no trouble finding real life adequate to their needs.

It is egotistic and romantic to think one is different from one's classmates and expect fulfillment of a kind transcending theirs. It is not unusual, either. What was perhaps peculiar to us in our peculiar time was that we required a distinguishing fantasy to come along complete with its *apparatus criticus*. We demanded meaningful deflorations. (And having once, accidentally, misplaced one's virginity made one's commitment to losing it intelligibly even greater.) In our fantasy fulfillments bells rang out in choral exegesis; at the Moment the Moral was written in the sky.

One by no means meant to marry the carefully chosen instrument of one's transcendence; one was much too sophisticated for that. But the choice of man and time and place were as crucial as choosing a husband for life. English novels imply the fiction that only one husband can ever be chosen. But it is no fiction (we, who so casually lied about ours, argued) that virginity can be lost only once. We were superrealists, hanging a novel's worth of meaning on our hymens, but substituting the fact of sexual intercourse for the fiction of marriage. By the sex act we would define ourselves. The reason we did not require a prince apiece was that the resolution of choice was the ironic one. To bestow one's virginity on a man to whom it was not quite welcome, or on a man who did not at all deserve it, or on one who was not aware of its significance, or on one who misinterpreted that—each of these was a possible delicious climax. The ironic solution to an ironic predicament seemed to us, watching our lives instead of living them, an aesthetic obligation.


Today I chat on the phone with M., who tells me she's spending her vacation in the city. "I swim at the club," she confides, "up and down silently like a swan, with the dowagers." Now one might just mistake M., an imposing woman in late middle age, for a dowager; one might just argue that what really saves her from being one is just this remark, this ironic apprehension of how she appears and how different it is from who she is.

"Your fat Jewish mother turned up at the pool in her fancy bathing suit," I am told in my next telephone talk about swimming, by Guess Who. My mother is not so fat as she says, and she wishes insisting on it would make her not so fat as she is; she has always basked in the stereotype of the Jewish Mother, for whom one might easily take her.

One of my own favorite personae is the Girl from Queens. "What are you doing, identifying with all these heroines of English novels?" my old college friend asks. "A nice girl from Queens like you." In fact, since I went to high school in Manhattan, I had no friends in Queens, and never felt like a native there. I invented the genus I claimed to belong to when I was in college, to amuse my cosmopolitan friends from Manhattan who scorned their cousins from the boroughs with a vehemence unknown in older aristocracies. The private point, of course, being that I was different from what I seemed to be, as well as different from them—that I was in fact an original for whom there was no phrase, therefore an ironic parodist of phrases.

I told my friend I was writing about precisely that, about how a Girl from Queens could come to think her life had anything to do with an English novel. We mumbled the obligatory cant about upward mobility and role models, all of it, I think, rather beside the point. There are two points: that English novels flatter a self-consciously élite community of responsive readers into existence, and that these are among the people for whom "irony" is writ large, in ink, in the margins of life. Novels about those rare young women who know what a real heroine is address themselves to closet heroines; they assume and thus they encourage ironic self-consciousness. Seeing oneself as a character in a novel, one has the advantage, or so it seems, of seeing oneself objectively and clearly—whole. The disadvantages of being marginal are obvious.

The facts of life in Victorian England, where Perfect Woman was officially idealized as the Angel in the House and subversive feminism gathered its forces, intensified the novel's preoccupation with women's lives, and the self-reflexiveness with which it was inclined to pursue the subject. Becoming a heroine seemed more than ever fraught with ironies, in fiction as in real life.

That real-life heroine Florence Nightingale, in a book deploring the condition of women which her friends (including John Stuart Mill) persuaded her not to publish, drew a connection between the shape of middle-class women's lives and the desire for fantasy lives that led them to read romantic novels:

> What are novels? What is the secret of the charm of every romance that ever was written? The first thing in a good novel is to place the persons together in circumstances which naturally call out the high feelings and thoughts of the character, which afford food for sympathy between them on these points—romantic events they are called. The second is that the heroine has *generally* no family ties (almost *invariably* no mother), or, if she has, these do not interfere with her entire independence.
>
> These two things constitute the main charm of reading novels. Now, in as far as these are good and not spurious interests, let us see what we have to correspond with them in real life. Can high sympathies be fed upon the opera, the exhibitions, the gossip of the House of Commons, and the political caricature? If, together, man and woman approach any of the high questions of social, political, or religious life, they are said (and justly—under our present disqualifications) to be going "too far."

The real young lady really lived only when she was reading about a fictitious life, Nightingale suggests, because her real life was fantastically false; lavishly romantic novels reflected the desires nineteenth-century middle-class life's deprivations inflamed. Therefore romance continued to be written and read in the nineteenth century. Therefore, too, it continued to be rewritten, by "realists" committed to telling the truth about women in Victorian society.

Society assumed there were two kinds of women. A passage in a poem written toward the end of the nineteenth century suggests how the polarization of the sexes, and of "good" and "bad" women, and of "pure" and "impure" language, intensified the popular apprehension of a woman as a metaphor in the great age of the realistic novel. The speaker of Dante Gabriel Rossetti's "Jenny" (1870) is a young man in the company of a prostitute who has fallen asleep before doing business with him. Her golden hair lies across his lap, and he thinks of the gold in his pockets, and resolves to pay her off before she awakens. His self-congratulatory meditations over her sleeping face climax in this passage, a decadent rewriting of the metaphor of women as roses that links women and books, as well. (The connection between the two was fortuitously made in actual life by the Victorian habit of pressing flowers in heavy volumes.)

> Like a rose shut in a book
> In which pure women may not look,
> For its base pages claim control
> To crush the flower within the soul;
> Where through each dead rose-leaf that clings,
> Pale as transparent psyche-wings,
> To the vile text, are traced such things
> As might make lady's cheek indeed
> More than a living rose to read;
> So nought save foolish foulness may
> Watch with hard eyes the sure decay;
> And so the life-blood of this rose,
> Puddled with shameful knowledge, flows
> Through leaves no chaste hand may unclose:
> Yet still it keeps such faded show
> Of when 'twas gathered long ago,
> That the crushed petals' lovely grain,
> The sweetness of the sanguine stain,
> Seen of a woman's eyes, must make
> Her pitiful heart, so prone to ache,
> Love roses better for its sake:—
> Only that this can never be:—
> Even so unto her sex is she.

The lesson this lost, faded rose teaches can only be taught to a man, for a woman would be contaminated by looking at her and blush as she would blush over a "vile text." Jenny is the opposite of an exemplar; she is a warning, who automatically brings to mind the perfect, exalted, virtuous lady who is her opposite. Asleep and insensate, an object of study for a reflective man,

Rossetti's Jenny is the opposite also of the conscious heroine of fiction who examines her own aspect.

As the nineteenth century progressed, the courtship plot seemed to serious novelists increasingly thin. The heroine of moral, realistic fiction remained virtuous—English novelists only flirted with the idea of adultery—but perfect, perfecting marriage à la Austen was a less and less likely fulfillment of a novel heroine's increasingly inchoate yearnings. As women revised their expectations, novelists reassessed the constraints of woman-centered fiction, and in a variety of ways redefined the heroine as different from what the reader might expect. As the courtship plot was rewritten, the hero's character and his place in the heroine's life changed. In 1847, Mr. Rochester excited Jane Eyre by his ominous scowl; by the time he rewarded her virtue with marriage, the scowl had become a scar. In 1872, George Eliot described how Dorothea Brooke turned down polite and plausible Sir James Chettam, whose extensive lands lay just outside Middlemarch, because she wanted more than a pleasant, proper-tied baronet of her own county. In 1881, a slim American girl from Albany, Isabel Archer, refused a conventional great match, an important, handsome, generous, and rich British peer, giving the reason that she liked him too well to marry him. As it continued to ask whether and how virtue can be rewarded, the English novel disclosed more and more irreconcilable differences between moral and material good. The self-conscious heroine examined herself and anticipated her destiny in a sardonic, even cynical spirit. Continuing to seek her complement, and a connoisseur of her value, and her *semblable*, her brother, she found it harder to find all three in a single man. The likes of Grandison and Darcy were dying out with the passing of the old, land-based order. The post-Austen heroine has a choice of suitors, and it is clear that for her, second attachments are possible. She often forms several. Her troubles in fixing on a hero dramatize the heroine's besetting problem of choosing a character of her own. Elaine Showalter has argued that semisatanic lovers like Mr. Rochester and his descendants are projections of nineteenth-century women writers' ambition for spiritually satisfying rebellion against conventional feminine behavior; maimed heroes, she says, are evidence of the women novelists' desire for vengeance on real, repressive men, and also of the growing sense that a man must be feminized to be a whole person. The novel changed with changing ideas about the nature and relationship of the sexes.

Imagined often by women who themselves sought satisfaction in work as well as marriage, in recognition as well as work, nineteenth-century heroines do not conceive of satisfaction as love only, or as love alone. The yearning for useful work marks the stories of Charlotte Brontë's Frances Henri and Lucy Snowe, who end up more and less happily in schoolrooms of their own; a less specific yearning charges the lives of George Eliot's heroines. The heroine of Elizabeth Barrett Browning's novel in verse, the best-selling *Aurora Leigh* (1857), is a writer. Virginia Woolf wrote of her that "again and again . . . Aurora the fictitious seems to be throwing light upon Elizabeth the actual." She observes that "the idea of the poem . . . came to [Browning] in the early [eighteen-] forties when the connexion between a woman's art and a woman's life was unnaturally close." For the Victorians, the woman artist was a fascinating, ambivalent figure: women and art seemed problematically related both to one another and to society. When the heroine who yearns for the absolute like a Romantic artist is placed in a paragon's position in a woman-centered fiction, the reader is inclined to look past the text to the novelist. So Virginia Woolf writes of Elizabeth the actual in Aurora the fictitious, and of Charlotte Brontë as "Jane Eyre." Of George Eliot's heroines, Woolf wrote that they

bring out the worst of her, lead her into difficult places, make her self-conscious, didactic, and occasionally vulgar. . . . Her self-consciousness is always marked when her heroines say what she herself would have said. She disguised them in every possible way. She granted them beauty and wealth into the bargain: she invented, more improbably, a taste for brandy. But the disconcerting and stimulating fact remained that she was compelled by the very power of her genius to step forth in person upon the quiet bucolic scene.

The idea that "the very power of her genius" makes George Eliot fail as a creator of fictitious heroines, the idea that this is both disconcerting and stimulating, are reflections in a sensitive critic's mind of an ambivalence in Eliot's novels that is the most compelling thing about them.

Virginia Woolf is thinking of Gwendolen and Janet and perhaps Dinah and Maggie, but the George Eliot heroine most on her mind is Dorothea Brooke of *Middlemarch*. "Ardent" Dorothea, the would-be Saint Theresa denied a glorious ideal by a world that has fallen too far into the ordinary, ends up happily married to Will Ladislaw at the end. George Eliot moralizes:

> Many who knew her, thought it a pity that so substantive and rare a creature should have been absorbed into the life of another, and be only known in a certain circle as a wife and mother. But no one stated exactly what else that was in her power she ought rather to have done. . . .

It is a consciously revisionary passage, defying the tradition that confines a heroine to a beautifully patterned, finished life that realizes her integral self in all its moral and aesthetic perfection. Dorothea is described as dwindling out of art into nature, as diminishing into reality, dispersing and dissolving into space and time:

> Her full nature, like that river of which Cyrus broke the strength, spent itself in channels which had no great name on the earth. But the effect of her being on those around her was incalculably diffusive: for the growing good of the world is partly dependent on unhistoric acts; and that things are not so ill with you and me as they might have been, is half owing to the number who lived faithfully a hidden life, and rest in unvisited tombs.

This conclusion which defiantly (if defensively) refuses to entomb the heroine as Clarissa was entombed has been criticized by modern feminists, who protest that Dorothea's desires could not be satisfied by a conventional career as Mrs. Ladislaw. To be sure, the happiness in self-sacrificing obscurity of a girl who would have been Saint Theresa is hard to believe in: either George Eliot is remonstrating with her for wanting too much, or Dorothea had disappointingly declined with age. What seems to me more worth noting than this is the imagery describing Dorothea's end, which suggests the release of the heroine from the text. Dorothea slips away from the novel of her life. George Eliot, intruding to anticipate that "many" will judge her fate inadequate to her character, draws attention to the way her "heroine" aspect dogs Dorothea, but she lets Dorothea go. The usual conclusion to a heroine-centered fiction—even George Eliot's—leaves the protagonist bound to her self-consciousness, therefore to traditional ideas of character and how it is realized in plot. The ending of *Middlemarch* releases her from self-consciousness. Doing that, it rephrases the question of whether the romantic or literary or fantastic aspect of a woman's self is so deeply implicated in her consciousness that it must inevitably immure and entomb her. For readers struggling with their own attitudes toward illusions about the feminine, the various rewritings of the conscious heroine in the nineteenth-century novel are richly suggestive.

# ⫸ 2 ⫷

# Villette

"It's as the actress that the woman produces the most complete and satisfactory artistic results."

"And only as the actress?"

"Yes, there's another art in which she's not bad."

"Which one do you mean?" asked Biddy.

"That of being charming and good and indispensable to man."

"Oh, that isn't an art."

"Then you leave her only the stage."

—Henry James,
*The Tragic Muse*

When ideal woman is imagined as a painter's or a sculptor's creature, the feminine is defined as fixed, objectified, passive, unchanging, motionless, complete, framed, separate from warm life. When she styles herself a critic, standing outside the picture frame, Elizabeth Bennet mocks the idea of woman as a cold and finished artifact, asserting the alternative value of a vital womanly intelligence stimulated, not confined, by conventions of good taste and good form. In Charlotte Brontë's *Villette* (1853), Lucy Snowe scorns the paintings of "ideal" woman in a gallery, one a sensual "Cleopatra" and the others representing stages in a pious woman's life. The pictures fascinate her; the "Cleopatra" in particular sticks in her mind, to recur later. But Lucy is appalled by the paintings. Charlotte Brontë, just behind her, is dismissing the idea of woman-as-artifact by a derisive treatment of it. An alternative image is proposed in *Villette*: the image of the actress. For Brontë, it is an ambivalent image.

The theme of aesthetic form as psychological force, which runs through the woman-centered novel, is significantly altered as the actress takes the place of the painting, statue, or monument. For the actress is herself an artist, the creator of herself—of her selves, rather. These are, suggestively, assumed, several, and temporary. If the actress stands for doing and not simply being, she does so ambiguously, being dubiously truthful, sincere, virtuous, real. Like the beautiful portrait of a lady, the actress is an image of physical beauty, but she is problematically related to spiritual splendor. One might say—people have said—that in the actress, the female body (the locus of a heroine's identity) is prostituted, rented to house a soul not in fact its own. Is the actress metaphorically, if not actually, a whore? Even before the Puritans closed the London theatres in the seventeenth century, moralists associated the stage with sexual license. The middle-class novel, pretending as it does to morality, has traditionally looked askance—but very hard—at a sister art. In Austen's *Mansfield Park*, for instance, Sir Thomas Bertram objects to the private theatricals of his children and their friends, and his objections prove justified as the rehearsals encourage the carryings-on of his daughters. "True" essential selves are softened by playing roles, the argument goes; the integral ego and the sexual "virtue" that is so often an image of it are identified. In *Villette* the liberating or ecstatic abandonment of the self onstage is connected with both the confusing of genders and the mingling of the sexes; it is linked with passion, with the expense of spirit, waste, shame, death. Acting is most solemnly disapproved of—and true to the profound ambivalence of Brontë's last novel, it is at the same time exalted.

Charlotte Brontë's works are rewritings of the heroine-centered novel made in a spirit altogether different from Jane Austen's. Where Austen mocked the fictions that woman is passive, central, and ideally a perfect lady perfectly made for a man, showing they are false but also very telling, Brontë was enraged and attracted by "pictures of perfection." She projected fantasies of beautiful, beloved women into her early novelettes; in her later, realistic novels, she wrote about plain, scorned women whose bodies belied their fierce aspiring souls. Her involvement in the idea of the heroine was personal, intense, and her derisive attitude toward the conventional feminine ideal had paradoxical results. Charlotte Brontë's fictions about the lives of passionate young women were popular and influential, and so was she herself as the heroine of Elizabeth Gaskell's engrossing biography, and later of innumerable other versions of the romantic Brontë story.

*Jane Eyre*, published in 1847 as the work of an unknown "Currer Bell" of ambiguous gender, excited and infuriated readers by its convincing creation of a woman who was virtuous but passionate, ambitious, enterprising, flexible, and strong. Brontë's revolutionary heroine depends on adaptations of the formal features of the heroine-centered novel. By widening the period of time in which a girl is interesting, beginning Jane Eyre's story with the crucial events of her childhood, Brontë effectively argued—which is to say she won—the case for a heroine as a developing individual, not a creature made at puberty for a man.*
*Jane Eyre* ends in a marriage that defiantly affirms not the heroine's transformation but her remaining herself. (A white wedding, the conventional novel's and heroine's end, begins to take place in this novel's middle, but it fails to come off, and effects the heroine's separation from her lover, not her joining with him.) Instead of being objectified by a narrator, Jane tells her own story, an intimate confidence ("Reader, I married him"). It is about her refusals to make herself what others would have her be. Homeless to begin with, and forced from childhood into narrow constraining spaces, Jane in the end finds the garden behind the ruin that is her proper place, being, like her, both natural and scarred by all it has gone through. Before that she rejects a series

---

* "One does not care for girls till they are grown up," Jane Austen had written (*Letters*, p. 402).

of repressive enclosures, the terrifying Red Room she is locked in at Gateshead, the school where she suffers, the homes where she is not at home; she also endures a long period of wandering as if in a desert.

Read against the heroine's old story, the smallest details of *Jane Eyre* resonate with derisiveness: "Reader, I married him," for instance, emphasizes that Jane marries, in the active voice, the diminished, blinded and maimed Rochester, instead of being married, or a party to a marriage. Adrienne Rich has brilliantly and persuasively read *Jane Eyre* as a myth about womanhood independent of men, but the hundreds of girls who have read it as a love story also read it right. A rejection of the traditional concept of woman as man's opposite and complement may be traced throughout Brontë's novels; in each of them exclusive heterosexual passion nevertheless figures obsessively.

In *The Professor* (published in 1857), when the narrator, William Crimsworth, describes Yorke Hunsden bowing over Frances Henri's hand "absolutely like Sir Charles Grandison on that of Harriet Byron," the comment, like the gesture itself, is a travesty and a hint. Such bows as Grandison's, such novels as Richardson's and Austen's, were beside Charlotte Brontë's point: polite and gallant manners did not seem to her correct indices to morals. *Pride and Prejudice* she described as "a carefully fenced, highly cultivated garden, with neat borders and delicate flowers; but no glance of a bright, vivid physiognomy, no open country, no fresh air, no blue hill, no bonny beck." Austen herself seemed to her to have been unnatural, "a complete and most sensible lady, but a very incomplete and rather insensible (*not senseless*) woman." Brontë's heroes are often decidedly unmannerly; her heroines are abrupt, even abrasive; the love scenes between them are full of challenges, corrections, taunts, and gibes. Mr. Rochester is aloof, dark, and satirical, Byronic rather than Grandisonian, a sinner and a wanderer and a brooder and a cynic, with an error, not a history of good works, in his past. Although heroines are at their centers and they move toward marriages, Brontë's novels do not identify a girl's character with her sexual fate as Richardson's and Austen's novels do: whether to marry which hero is not the heroine's only problem, and marriage is not the final solution to her predicament.

In Brontë's early novelettes, glamorous heroines sit for their verbal portraits in the fixed and fashionable postures that characterized the illustrations in the annuals the novelist liked to look at as a girl. Charlotte Brontë wanted to be a painter; when she set herself deliberately to imagining, so as to escape bleak reality, in the solitude of her room, she delighted in conjuring up richly detailed visions of beautiful women. The heroine was the focal image of her fantasy life. In her early twenties she described one vision in her journal:

> What I imagined grew morbidly vivid. I remember I quite seemed to see with my bodily eyes a lady standing in the hall of a gentleman's house as if waiting for someone. It was dusk and there was the dim outline of antlers with a hat and rough great-coat upon them. She had a flat candle-stick in her hand and seemed coming from the kitchen or some such place. She was very handsome it is not often we can form from pure idea faces so individually fine she had black curls hanging rather low in her neck a very blooming skin and dark anxious looking eyes. I imagined it the sultry close of a summer's day and she was dressed in muslin not at all romantically a flimsy, printed fabric with large sleeves and a full skirt. As she waited I most distinctly heard the front door open. . . .

The abandonment of punctuation in the physical description of the lady—an *individual* expressive of *pure idea*—betrays the writer's excitement. The beautiful appearance of a heroine like this reveals her beautiful essence, and promises a happy congruence of outer and inner lives in fulfilling love. Brontë's own plain face made extreme the irony of her obsession with beauties: the men of her time who invidiously remarked on her hunger for love, Thackeray and Arnold among them, were not more aware than she that beauty was a prerequisite for feminine fulfillment. Her novels about women's search for love derive from her consciousness of the division between Miss Brontë, the provincial virgin, and the flaming creative spirit hidden behind the plain mask.

Yet the young woman whose fantasies were of fashionable beauties sternly believed that to look like a lady in a *Keepsake* volume was evidence of inherent cheapness of soul. Her friend Mary Taylor remembered a dream Charlotte once described, in which her revered dead older sisters appeared to her, lamentably changed:

> She used to speak of her two elder sisters, Maria and Elizabeth, who died at Cowan Bridge. I used to believe them to have been wonders of talent and kindness. She told me, early one morning, that she had just been dreaming; she had been told that she was wanted in the drawing-room, and it was Maria and Elizabeth. I was eager for her to go on, and when she said there was no more, I said, "but go on! *Make it out!* I know you can." She said she would not; she wished she had not dreamed, for it did not go on nicely; they were changed; they had forgotten what they used to care for. They were very fashionably dressed, and began criticising the room, &c.

To be fashionably dressed and fussy about the furniture was to be the kind of worldly woman Charlotte despised; that she had that dream about her dead sisters, and told it, reveals, as almost everything she wrote did, her obsession with the antagonism between the high soul and low matter. A complex rivalry with those who were literally and metaphorically her sisters was involved in her preoccupation with women's appearances. She wondered how she looked as she looked at other women; differences between women's appearances reminded her of differences between the way a woman looked and the way she felt herself to be. In the preface she wrote to *Wuthering Heights* she eulogized her sister Emily as a person whose exterior belied her depths:

> Under an unsophisticated culture, inartificial tastes, and an unpretending outside, lay a secret power and fire that might have informed the brain and kindled the veins of a hero; but she had no worldly wisdom; her powers were unadapted to

the practical business of life; she would fail to defend her most manifest rights, to consult her most legitimate advantage. An interpreter ought always to have stood between her and the world.

Brontë is famous for having explained to Robert Southey, in response to his advice that "literature cannot be the business of a woman's life, and it ought not to be," that she deliberately cultivated her own ordinary appearance, even strove to be as she seemed:

> I carefully avoid any appearance of preoccupation and eccentricity, which might lead those I live amongst to suspect the nature of my pursuits. Following my father's advice—who from my childhood had counselled me just in the wise and friendly tone of your letter—I have endeavoured not only attentively to observe all the duties a woman ought to fulfil, but to feel deeply interested in them. I don't always succeed, for sometimes when I'm teaching or sewing I would rather be reading or writing; but I try to deny myself; and my father's approbation amply rewarded me for the privation.

Usually cited as evidence of poor Charlotte's self-denial, the letter is evidence also of a certain smugness. To be divided between an exterior and an interior self seemed to her evidence of personal value. Brontë had contempt for those who aped the beauty that belonged legitimately only to the high-souled; she made a retaliatory equation of a plain face and the plain truth. She wrote, apropos of Caroline Vernon, a heroine of an early novelette:

> People who have been brought up in retirement don't soon get hackneyed to society. They often retain a notion that they are better than those about, that they are not of their sort, and that it would be letting down to them to give the slightest glimpse of their real natures and genuine feelings to the chance associates of a ball room.

The idea that caught her imagination when she was young and never quite let it go was Byron's idea of a person who is better than other people because he thinks he is worse—high because he is secretly low. The Byronic hero is different from Milton's Satan: Satan has sinned in fact, while the Byronic hero's sin is possibly only imaginary. It is not *simply* imaginary, as it may or may not be actual: it exists in some obscure, indeterminate realm between the actual and the imaginary. To have imagined sin seems sometimes to have been his sole sin; the imagination that allows him to be as guilty for imaginary sins as others are for real ones is his distinction. To preserve it, he keeps to himself, refusing to "let down." His hoarding of his "real" self proves his aristocracy of the spirit. Brontë wrote to her friend Ellen Nussey,

> I have some qualities that make me very miserable, some feelings that you can have no participation in—that few, very few, people in the world can at all understand. I don't pride myself on these peculiarities. I strive to conceal and suppress them as much as I can; but they burst out sometimes, and then those who see the explosion despise me, and I hate myself for days afterwards. . . .

If she was not vain of her peculiarities, she certainly was very proud of how hard it was to contain and deny them. To conceal her differences from others was on the one hand Charlotte's pious duty as a religious and modest young woman, and at the same time the very proof of her difference, her power, her heroism. The same demure appearance served both the docile wish to be unexceptionable and the strong will to be exceptional. A sense of strength was produced by the sense of irony. The posture is gender-determined: a Byron, a Wellington, a fantasized Zamorna, may engage in battles and politics, make arrogant speeches and conquests in love, but a woman can only express her passionate uniqueness by suppressing it; she can only express her uniqueness by giving it up.

Mrs. Gaskell's biography insists, as prescriptive writers on feminine virtue have traditionally insisted, on Charlotte Brontë's domestic virtue and filial piety. It glorifies her as the perfect Victorian woman; so it subordinates the story of her professional career, and insists on the exemplary quality of her personal life. Yet slyly, effectively, Gaskell lavishes pages on the weird wildness of the Yorkshire countryside, the harshness and peculiarity of the land and the people. And she quotes those extracts from the letters that reveal Brontë's pride in her repressed self. The heroine she creates by the interplay between what she says outright and what she leaves implicit is a woman of "unfeminine" eccentricity and passion. The heroine Charlotte herself presented—the gentle, dull little lady in mittens whom Thackeray's daughter remembered meeting—was the image of a heroic self-suppression that suggested a violent secret self.

Plain Jane Eyre is sharp-witted and satirical; Shirley Keeldar, in the second novel Brontë published, is high-handed, confident, and clever. A romantic hero expresses himself in sullenness or scorn, but antisocial behavior stands in the way of becoming a heroine. Not until she wrote Villette did Brontë allow the heroine to take the derisive accents of the narrator of the early novelettes. The language of Lucy Snowe, its sharply shifting tones and inexplicable intensities, is, like Hester Prynne's elaborately embroidered A in The Scarlet Letter, the language of the sensual self that has been denied expression and has acquired, in consequence, strange new energies that can transform conventional signs. Narrating Villette, Lucy transforms her woman's story and her woman's self. Lucy is unattractive, spiky, sardonic, full of smoldering violence. While Jane Eyre is plain, Lucy is faceless. Facelessness puts in question her bondage to a romantic heroine's body-bound fate.

Early in the English novel's history, the author of Tristram Shandy presented his reader with a blank page, instructing him to let his own mistress sit for the portrait of the Widow Wadman, the closest thing to a heroine his novel has. The joke is on both the reader and the Widow, and so on romance, which requires the heroine of a love story—the Widow is loved—to be beautiful.

A girl's face is commonly read as both an index to her character and the clue to her fortune. "The temper of a woman is generally formed from the turn of her features," the Vicar of Wakefield muses as he compares his daughters: in other words, blondes have more fun. "O, if I were only better looking!" the heroine of one of Charlotte Brontë's novelettes complains. "Adventures never happen to plain people." Her guardian does not contradict her: "No, not often," he replies. Perfect beauty distinguishes the heroine of romance; in novels that question romance's conventions, perfect beauty may very well signal perfect insipidity. A novel heroine's beauty is therefore often marked by some "natural" irregularity, a sweet disorder that hints perhaps at sexual vitality. Here is a representative example, the eponymous heroine of Charlotte Smith's *Emmeline* (1788):

> Perfectly unconscious of those attractions which now began to charm every other eye, Emmeline had entered her sixteenth year; and the progress of her understanding was equal to the improvement of her person; which, tho' she was not perfectly handsome, could not be beheld at first without pleasure, and which the more it was seen became more interesting and engaging.
>
> Her figure was elegant and graceful; somewhat exceeding the middling height. Her eyes were blue; and her hair brown. Her features not very regular; yet there was a sweetness in her countenance, when she smiled, more charming than the effect of the most regular features could have given. Her countenance, open and ingenuous, expressed every emotion of her mind. . . .
>
> The wind had blown her beautiful hair about her face, and the glow of her cheeks was heightened by exercise and apprehension.

Agitating winds and moods enhance an imperfect beauty that is more provocative, more stirring, for being almost debatable. To call it in question seems to many writers the appropriate way to express such beauty in language. George Eliot's *Daniel Deronda* (1876) begins with a question about Gwendolen Harleth: "Was she beautiful or not beautiful?" And *Gone with the Wind* (1936) begins as if with George Eliot's opening in mind, answering the question in the negative, then immediately negating that: "Scarlett O'Hara was not beautiful, but men seldom realized it when caught by her charm as the Tarleton twins were." Scarlett's most striking characteristics—green eyes and a seventeen-inch waist—are not every pretty girl's. Departing from the conventional standards of beauty, she promises to have more than conventional spirit. Dovelike Melanie, Scarlett's rival, is a variant of the heroine of romance, not, like Scarlett, a stimulating revision of her.

The trashier the novel, the more likely it is that the heroine's alleged "defect" will be charming: she may be cursed by an up-tilted nose, or hair not fair but dark and heavy like a gypsy's. This rule is not always reliable; a certain amount of authorial self-deception may affect the physiognomy of the heroine. George Eliot's Maggie Tulliver, for instance, has thick black unruly hair, and her height and queenly bearing are not to the taste of banal St. Oggs, which prefers kittenish blondes: the effect of this is to flatter the reader, who presumably has a nobler aesthetic. It is very hard to find a heroine with a cast in her eye, or heavy ankles, or coarse skin, even in novels of the twentieth century. Perhaps the most shocking oddity in the whole beautiful body of novel heroines is that of Sophia Western, whom Fielding mock-heroically hymns as the heroine of heroines in *Tom Jones*: her keenly observed flaw is a too-long chin. After Charlotte Brontë made Jane Eyre plain on purpose (she told her sisters it was immoral to make heroines beautiful) there was a positive vogue for unprepossessing protagonists. For just like a heroine's beauty, Jane's plainness is an index to her soul: her smallness and lightness make Mr. Rochester think her fairylike, and we admire her for her spiritual quality, which distinguishes her from her grossly physical rivals, Blanche Ingram (who is beautiful and big) and Bertha Rochester (who is big and loathsome). Like *The Mill on the Floss*, *Jane Eyre* suggests that there are modes of feminine beauty undreamt of in the philosophy of men and mistakenly undervalued, and it proposes that standards be revised.

It is another thing entirely to suggest that a heroine, made for love as she by definition is, may not look lovable at all. With ordinary-looking Catherine Morland and mouselike Fanny Price and faded Anne Elliot, Jane Austen three times broached that revolutionary possibility, but in the end she gave miraculous beautifying powers to time, in the first two cases, and to love, in the second. She did raise along the way several sharp questions about romance's habit of identifying perfect beauty with virtue. In *Persuasion*, the satirically presented Sir Walter Elliot is a vain man who surrounds himself with mirrors: Jane Austen observes that "few women could think more of their personal appearance than he did." Sir Walter prides himself on an unalterable appearance; his vain oldest daughter, Elizabeth, is an unchanging cold beauty, as attractive at twenty-nine as ever. But Anne, she of the unalterable constancy in love, fades and blooms. She has a responsive body rather than a fixed one: feeling makes her change color. While both the hero and heroine of *Persuasion* are conventionally good-looking, the expressiveness of their faces is what Austen stresses. *Persuasion* satirizes carefully tended, well-preserved good looks as tokens of hollowness and inhumanity.

When Emma Woodhouse is determined to make Harriet Smith the heroine of a real-life romance she wants to produce and direct, she misrepresents reality while painting Harriet's portrait. "You have made her too tall, Emma," sensible Mr. Knightley points out. Emma's romantic imagination requires Harriet to look like a heroine so that she may be one. Since beautiful women are imagined as made for love and the romances that love inspires, that inspire love, the beauties of the world look to readers like heroines. When the protagonist of Jane Austen's unfinished *Sanditon* sees a beauty on the street, she cannot but draw a responsive novel-reader's conclusions:

Elegantly tall, regularly handsome, with great delicacy of complexion & soft Blue eyes, a sweetly modest & yet naturally graceful Address, Charlotte could see in her only the most perfect representation of whatever Heroine might be most beautiful & bewitching, in all the numerous vol:s they had left behind them on Mrs Whitby's shelves.—Perhaps it might be partly oweing to her having just issued from a Circulating Library—but she cd not separate the idea of a complete Heroine from Clara Brereton.

The "realistic" novel insists that a true heroine is authentically, not artificially, beautiful. She is the girl who looks beautiful in any old thing she throws on, or in a deliberately assumed plain costume. The rivals who serve as her foils primp for vain hours before their mirrors, torment themselves by uncomfortable postures to display their figures. Waspish Caroline Bingley in *Pride and Prejudice* walks around the room to show off; frivolous Rosamond Vincy in *Middlemarch* keeps flexing and twisting her elegant neck. In a marvelous scene in *Roxana*, Defoe showed how men require their women's beauty to be natural, and then reward it, so as to stimulate themselves, by unnaturally adorning it—and how women, meanwhile, artfully use natural charms to get ornaments to enhance their beauty. The courtesan Roxana has been sent off by a rich lover to dress herself up elaborately, for his delectation, in an expensive costume he has bought her. She returns, dressed, and kneels to kiss his hand in gratitude; he lifts her up and discovers she is in tears. It is important that she insists her account of what happens next is truth and not fiction; her pride in the authenticity of a story that is not romance blends with her pride in a beauty that is "the mere work of nature," not art.

It wou'd look a little too much like a Romance here, to repeat all the kind things he said to me, on that Occasion; but I can't omit one Passage; as he saw the Tears drop down my Cheek, he pulls out a fine Cambrick Handkerchief, and was going to wipe the Tears off, but check'd his Hand, as if he was afraid to deface something; I say, he check'd his Hand, and toss'd the Handkerchief to me, to do it myself; I took the Hint immediately, and with a kind of pleasant Disdain, *How, my Lord!* said I, *Have you kiss'd me so often, and don't you know whether I am Painted, or not? Pray let your Highness satisfie yourself, that you have no Cheats put upon you; for once let me be vain enough to say, I have not deceiv'd you with false Colours:* With this, I put a Handkerchief into his Hand, and taking his Hand into mine, I made him wipe my Face so hard, that he was unwilling to do it, for fear of hurting me.

He appear'd surpriz'd, more than ever, and swore, which was the first time that I had heard him swear, from my first knowing him, that he cou'd not have believ'd there was any such Skin, without Paint, in the World: *Well, my Lord,* said I, *Your Highness shall have a farther Demonstration than this; as to that which you are pleas'd to accept for Beauty, that it is the meer Work of Nature*; and with that, I stept to the Door, and rung a little Bell, for my Woman, *Amy*, and bade her bring me a Cup-full of hot Water, which she did; and when it was come, I desir'd *his Highness* to feel if it was warm; which he did, and I immediately wash'd my Face all over with it, before him; this was, indeed, more than Satisfaction, that is to say, than Believing; for it was an undeniable Demonstration, and he kiss'd my Cheeks and Breasts a thousand times, with Expressions of the greatest Surprize imaginable.

Her lover adores her for being beautiful, but assumes her beauty, like her fine clothes, is unnatural, assumed. In order to delight the man who dressed her as a princess, she proves (with great art and vigor) that she is naturally a beauty. This makes him believe that she is the true image of all that is desirable—and therefore worth not only kisses but praise and, of course, more rich clothes and jewels, which will make her look nothing like the whore she really is. The pure heroine of a novel about courtship must also prove by artifice—manners, tasteful clothes—that she is naturally beautiful, and therefore good. She is as insistent as Roxana on the fact that she makes no effort to look as beautiful as she does.

A woman's body is a complex sign. Beauty fades; virginity, that physical token of a heroine's purity, the seal ensuring her value on the marriage market, can be surrendered only once. Her gender determines the plot which obliges a heroine to seize a very brief day, and covertly. To take a dim view of the heroine's body, as Charlotte Brontë did in *Villette*, is to begin to imagine a radically new kind of novel.

To begin at the beginning, the title, *Villette*, is a city's name, not a girl's, but a city's name that looks a lot like a girl's. Brontë's friend Elizabeth Gaskell was persuaded by her publishers to change her first novel's title from *John Barton* to *Mary Barton* so as to increase sales among a reading public that was pleased, just like the public of today, to read novels about women, to identify women and novels. Brontë's title faces this fact about the book business as if with a sneer. The dearest assumptions of readers were tried further by the novelist's giving the heroine of her novel not one love story, not one lover, but two. Contemporary critics attacked Lucy Snowe for her immoral redundancy of lovers and *Villette* for unseemly split in its middle, at roughly the place where one lover succeeds the other, as if the structural fault were clear evidence of the moral one. Both Lucy's love affairs are intensely felt; most of what takes place in them happens in the heroine's mind. The narrative as a whole oddly obscures important details about what in fact happens, so even the careful reader is hard put, at first reading, to tell exactly when Lucy transfers her affections from one man to the other. While it high-handedly ignores such facts, *Villette* pays extremely careful attention, so as to underscore the odd unreality of Lucy's outward life, to the affairs of other women.

Like *The Professor*, the first novel Brontë wrote, her last book is set for the most part in a foreign city—identifiably Brussels, where she had studied and fallen in love with her married teacher, M. Héger. Brontë links evil with the Catholic Church, as English novelists before her who had set their stories outside England had done, but here unimaginative, materialistic, cloddish Belgians take the place of the overheated Mediterraneans of early gothics. (In *Villette* Belgium is called "Labassecour," or barnyard.) Brontë deliberately recalls the gothic novelists with a strange story of a ghostly nun (who turns out to be a living man). The subject of *Villette*, like the subject of gothic novels, is the experience of being different and alone in a hostile and invasive place, of feeling both locked out and imprisoned. But in this post-Romantic novel the whole world the heroine faces is alien. Lucy Snowe's problem is not, like Clarissa's or a Jane Austen heroine's, to fit her assigned place in life in such a way as to transform both it and herself; it is to find a place in a foreign world.

*Villette* remains "almost intolerably painful" to read, quite as Harriet Martineau said it was when it appeared. The fact that its heroine-narrator deliberately rebuffs the reader—by overt challenge and condescension, by concealing shifts in narrative direction, by using French words (even the title of the novel is not English)—has the perverse effect of intensifying the reader's identification with her. For the repellent Lucy has herself been rebuffed and repelled; one stands, rejected and baffled, alongside her outside the probably poisonous banquet of life, nose pressed flat against the cold glass. Lucy is obscure, ignored, repressed, yearning, self-obsessed, self-hating, self-tormenting. The grayness she hides behind causes her pain; her sharp-tongued acerbity turns against her. To faceless Lucy the faces around her seem masks, mysteriously rigid and concealing. The people wearing them lack depth and dimension because they lack her hallucinatory perception of emotional reality. Social relationships for Lucy are a dialogue between a skinless self and skins perceived as equally meretricious alternatives. The encounters of the heroine with other people are occasions for examining and rejecting tinny identities. The realistic novel's most basic assumptions are revised as Lucy, instead of developing relationships, and getting on, or not, with other people, tries them on instead.

One is inclined to credit any narrator who tells her own story with having a good grip on herself. Clarissa Harlowe reached for an overview and collected her own letters to give both herself and her story a coherent shape. But although Lucy's hair is white when she tells it, her story is incomplete: having read it all, we cannot be sure of the resolution, whether she married her true love in the end or not. In the beginning *Villette* seems to tell not Lucy's but another girl's story, Paulina Mary Home's. The novel begins with *her* childhood. Little Paulina arrives at the house where Lucy is living, "a shawled bundle" in the arms of a servant. Unwrapped, she turns out to be

> a neat, completely-fashioned little figure, light, slight, and straight. Seated on my godmother's ample lap, she looked a mere doll; her neck, delicate as wax, her head of silky curls, increased, I thought, the resemblance.

The child treats herself as an object, speaking of herself in the third person:

> "What is my little one's name?"
> "Missy."
> "But besides Missy?"
> "Polly, papa calls her." (Chapter 1) *

Paulina is satisfied to be what she is called. As Lucy Snowe refers to her as "it," "this being," rather than as a girl or a child, she manages to suggest that Paulina's self-sufficiency, her very tininess, are deliberately assumed characteristics, manipulative and self-serving and also weird. She implies that Paulina is somehow oversimplified as she, Lucy, is not, that she is in effect a travesty of the feminine ideal. Looking at Lucy looking at Paulina is an appropriate introduction to this heroine, a "looker-on" at life: the perverseness of Lucy the narrator is characteristic. The heroine of a novel is conventionally central; Lucy is centrifugal.

Brilliantly, Lucy-Brontë uses a direct gibe both to fill and to point at a gap in the chronicle, to taunt the reader for having conventional expectations of this story about a woman. After the account of Lucy's early adolescence comes this:

> I will permit the reader to picture me, for the next eight years, as a bark slumbering through halcyon weather, in a

---

* Charlotte Brontë, *Villette* (New York and Harmondsworth: Penguin Books, 1979). All quotations from the novel are from this edition; I give chapter rather than page numbers for the reader who might have another one.

harbour still as glass—the steersman stretched on the little deck, his face up to heaven, his eyes closed: buried, if you will, in a long prayer. A great many women and girls are supposed to pass their lives something in that fashion; why not I with the rest?

Picture me then idle, basking, plump, and happy, stretched on a cushioned deck, warmed with constant sunshine, rocked by breezes indolently soft. However, it cannot be concealed that, in that case, I must somehow have fallen over-board, or that there must have been wreck at last. (Chapter 4)

A reader who imagines a world of good weather and safe ships is anticipated by a heroine-narrator who despairs of being read right. Lucy's point is that her story is unlike other women's, and that therefore it is unsuitable for narrative, which is bound to conventional concepts of woman. Lucy can only be suggested as a negative of her acute perceptions of women who are unlike her: perceptions of Paulina Mary, the exquisitely finished child, of old Miss Marchmont, whose story of passionate love and tragic loss is finished, of gay flirtatious ordinary girls and of matrons of sinister complacency, nicely settled in a distant, impenetrable world. Lucy leaves England after the death of Miss Marchmont, with whom she lives for a time as a paid companion, and on the boat to the Continent she meets Ginevra Fanshawe, a conventionally pretty young girl, who suggests she look for work at the school of a Mme. Beck, in the city of Villette. Mme. Beck is an efficient school administrator. Her smooth face, her "trim compactness," like Polly's tininess, suggest she is finished. Lucy, feeling herself amorphous, looks hungrily to other women for a clue to the mystery of pulling herself together. She is at once envious and contemptuous of what she perceives as a commonplace skill, and of the luck it brings. Those other women are composed within their bodies; for Lucy enclosure is torment. Lucy's life as a teacher in Mme. Beck's school in Villette, where she is spied upon and friendless, comes to a crisis during a long vacation when she is left in the school alone except for a servant and a cretin. The *pensionnat*, abandoned, is more pointedly than ever not a home. Inside the school walls, Lucy cares for the cretin as if for some maimed and hideous version of her self. Then she breaks down and flees in panic to make confession to a Catholic priest, in a characteristic act of passionate ambivalence, before collapsing outdoors on the streets of Villette.

The flirt Ginevra Fanshawe is awkwardly involved in the plot: it is her chance word on the channel steamer that gets Lucy to go to Mme. Beck's establishment in the first place; John Graham Bretton (whom Lucy loves) briefly loves Ginevra: and she is responsible for the "ghostly nun" who terrifies Lucy as the image of both a foreign religion and her own nunlike self. (The nun is exposed as Ginevra's masquerading lover in the end.) While all the machinery for Ginevra's being in the novel creaks alarmingly, her presence in Lucy's story is entirely convincing, for Ginevra is the image of a heroine, a *jeune fille moyenne sensuelle*, the normal high-spirited pretty girl, everything Lucy is not. It is precisely Ginevra's shallowness that Lucy finds fascinating and repellent: the two-dimensional quality of all the women around her is most conspicuous in this one. Ginevra's bright quickness of mind and her easy freedom from resentment enable her to trade insults with the melancholy critic of her frivolities she lightly calls "Timon." Lucy says she cannot figure out why she should be so drawn to Ginevra. Her feeling for the girl is loverlike, focused on Ginevra's prettiness and flirtatiousness; the two drink milk (Lucy is conscious of the intimacy) out of one bowl. Long before Dr. John Graham Bretton falls in love with Ginevra, Lucy is mysteriously compelled to single her out from all the other girls at Mme. Beck's school; then, imagining a great love between her and Dr. John, Lucy explicitly conceives of Ginevra as "a sort of heroine" for her own hero, an envied usurper of her place, an acter-out of her own dreams, her surrogate. Ginevra is the heroine also of the play in which Lucy is forced to act, and she figures importantly in a scene in which she faces a mirror together with Lucy and gloatingly points out the difference between her beauty and the other's plainness. She is at once loved and hated by Lucy; she is both her sister and her lover; she is simultaneously the antithesis and the reflection of the narrator, a simpler, luckier, prettier, envied, scorned self.

There are several moments in *Villette* when Lucy must face her face in the mirror. When, after her collapse, she is rescued by John Graham Bretton and awakens in his mother's house outside Villette, she is confused to see around her in this foreign room "the ghosts of such articles" as had been in his mother's—her godmother's—home in England. Among them she sees a mirror: "In this mirror I saw myself laid, not in bed, but on a sofa. I looked spectral; my eyes larger and more hollow, my hair darker than was natural, by contrast with my thin and ashen face" (Chapter 16). Among spectral furnishings she sees her own ghost. On another occasion, Lucy sees herself by accident, not laid out but erect and attractive, walking into a theatre in unaccustomed finery. Glancing by chance into a glass there, Lucy is tricked into admiring herself. In his essay "The 'Uncanny,' " Freud recalls recognizing with a shock that the elderly, night-capped gentleman he saw in a mirror on a train was himself. To see one's own image as if it were someone else's is to be confronted with the familiar as unfamiliar, he writes. The uncanny, *das Unheimliche*, is epitomized in a vision of the self as not-known. The literal meaning of the German, not-like-home, is worth recalling as we consider the history of homeless Lucy Snowe, who is doomed to find only tormenting parodies of homes: Miss Marchmont's dark house, Mrs. Bretton's identical English and continental homes, where she is only a guest, the institutional *pensionnat* that deprives its inhabitants of privacy. At the end of the novel her lover, M. Paul, gives Lucy a clean little school of her own in which to dream of him, wait for him, and begin to live independently. It is a mixed blessing and makes for an ambiguous ending, leaving Lucy finally in a home of her own, but alone.

Early in *Villette*, in the loneliness of a hotel room, Lucy confronts herself and sees a stranger without using a mirror: ". . . as I sat down by the bed and rested my head and arms on the pillow, a terrible oppression overcame me. All at once my position rose on me like a ghost" (Chapter 5). It terrifies her to see herself, for she seems to herself a frightening and uncanny creature. It is to grasp her own reality that she describes, throughout *Villette*, the not-Lucys around her, the real women she perceives as if they were novel-heroines—as if they had clearer outlines, more specific significations, more reality than she has. One of the torments she undergoes at Mme. Beck's school is being watched by that lady, whose system of *surveillance* allows privacy to neither teacher nor student. Her sense of solitude, confusion, and amorphousness increases under the pressure of being assessed; to fight back, she assesses others.

Lucy is living outside Villette with the Brettons, recovering from her breakdown, when, to amuse her, Dr. John takes her to the picture gallery. He leaves her there alone, promising to pick her up later; but before he returns, Paul Emanuel, a teacher at Mme. Beck's establishment, turns up at the gallery. He is shocked to find Lucy, both because she is unaccompanied and because she is looking at a painting of a half-dressed sultry woman. Judging such a picture inappropriate for her to look at, he directs her to other paintings, of pious women. The scene contrasts the two men Lucy loves and their attitudes toward women, and two ideals of women as they are presented in works of art. The largeness of the first painting and the important place it has been given in the gallery suggest the metaphorical weight of woman considered as symbolic of sensuality. Lucy rejects the Cleopatra as too large and bright, and the woman it depicts as fat, lazy, and slovenly. The contrasting pictures of a pious woman's life strike her as colorless, formal, and dull. With the paintings she rejects both Dr. John's ideal of an ornamental sensually appealing woman, and M. Paul's Catholic ideal of sensory self-denial. Their commitment to these opposed ideals makes both her lovers unwilling to embrace Lucy, and makes them prefer incomplete or imaginary women to the living one whose vitality is attested by her comprehension and scorn of both conventional ideals.

But M. Paul, unlike Dr. John, is temperamentally attuned to

Lucy, for whom he eventually abandons his fidelity to his ideal of renunciation, a dead nun he once loved. Beneath his religion is a soul as desiring, violent, tormented, and conflicted as hers. It is revealed when he forces her, against her will, to act in a school play. He insists that she perform the part of a man, the heroine's (Ginevra Fanshawe's) lover. The brutal force he exerts on her persuades Lucy of his feeling (the reader perhaps sees the intensity of his commitment to a school play as an indication of a lack of mental balance). For the novel—which is intense and unbalanced like M. Paul—the play is vitally important. Both the drama enacted in it and the events leading up to the performance shed strange light on the repressed relationships among the people at Mme. Beck's school, and complicate them. First the "fiery" little teacher locks Lucy in a hot attic to learn her part: she is beset by black beetles, which threaten to climb up her skirts, and by the spectral nun. Finally let out of the attic and mollified with something sweet to eat, grateful Lucy makes only one demand: to keep her woman's clothes in the play, and wear only a symbolic cravat, a token to indicate her assumed gender is only assumed. The character Lucy plays is a fop: in Ginevra's life such a man is the rival of John Graham Bretton, the more substantial man who loves Ginevra and whom Lucy loves. Both Bretton and the fop Alfred de Hamal, whom Ginevra eventually will marry, watch the play from the audience. Lucy, onstage, is initially shy, but soon she warms to her part and eventually she enjoys it very much. Therefore she vows never to go onstage again and allow herself such pleasure. All the intense mutually intensifying complications of this sequence suggest the ironies of Lucy's life, her near-apprehension of them, and of course the greater irony that they are concentrated rather than concealed by the play.

When Lucy goes to the theatre in her "normal" character as a "looker-on at life" she finds herself, again, unusually and uncomfortably moved. The actress Vashti, a character modeled on the great French actress Rachel (Elisa Félix), whom Charlotte Brontë saw in London, inspires Lucy to recall, derisively, "the artist of the Cleopatra," and to pity his materialism and his narrow vision. Of Vashti's performance she writes:

> It was a marvelous sight: a mighty revelation.
> It was a spectacle low, horrible, immoral.

The contraries cannot be reconciled. There is none of the glib sarcasm that had marked the description of the paintings, no attempt to explain or apologize for a profound and simple ambivalence. Vashti is Lucy's antithesis, and also the mirror to the spirit hidden in her modest exterior; at the same time she manages to mirror Lucy's plainness:

> I had heard this woman termed "plain," and I expected bony harshness and grimness—something large, angular, sallow. What I saw was the shadow of a royal Vashti: a queen, fair as the day once, turned pale now like twilight, and wasted like wax in flame. (Chapter 23)

She is the shadowy Lucy's more vivid shadow. The performance of the actress resonates with questions about what it means to act, to be an individual, an artist, a woman. Lucy records that John Graham Bretton, who sees Vashti with her, "judged her as a woman, not an artist: it was a branding judgment." Lucy herself is seared because she sees her as both.

The historical Rachel was the embodiment of the Romantic aesthetic, a public demonstration of its truth. Her art was celebrated as artless, instinctive, personal, peculiar, original, self-consuming. Her energy and passion seemed to express the truth of the Noble Savage: she was a *gamine* from the streets, illiterate and ugly, who was transformed when great poetry possessed her. The violence of the performances in which she spent herself was legendary: once when a dog barked as she took a curtain call, she collapsed, unnerved, to the floor. The daughter of a poor Jewish peddler, she single-handedly revived classical French drama in an age that had ignored it. Rachel stood for free love and free expression, for intense and unladylike living, for the imagination. Like George Sand, the queen of the stage and high priestess of art defined woman-as-art as an actively creative being, freely sexual, an enemy of convention. The old metaphorical association was turned on its head as ideas about both art and women radically changed.

Yet in Rachel's achievement of bringing to thrilling life the balanced classical periods of Corneille and Racine there is a subdued echo of the older association. She was admired by those who saw her perform for a cold "marble" quality of brow, a pallor and a rigidity of posture that recalled classical statues. One of the paradoxes of Rachel's transformation of herself onstage was that she did it night after night, and in classical alexandrines written long before by men unknown to her, to express the feelings of women they had imagined. As she consumed herself passionately onstage, speaking the measured words of the dead, she seemed to Brontë to stand at once for life and death: she was physically frail, small and consumptive. Lucy describes Vashti as "wasted like wax in flame," as "white like alabaster—like silver: rather be it said, like Death." Charlotte's passionate sister Emily and her brother Branwell were dead, along with their milder sister Anne, when she wrote this last novel. The cold, artificial exterior Lucy Snowe assumes is a gray composure that seeks to fool death by miming it; Vashti, exposing and expressing the emotional life boldly, as Lucy cannot express hers, is challenging what would consume her, consuming herself, letting go of masks and risking her life by acting.

Early in *Villette* Lucy makes a point of denying that she has anything of the artist in her. Characteristically, this analysis of herself is made through a strange combination of real and hallucinatory objects that reveals hysterical ambivalence. As paintings of women challenge her as a woman, a dull landscape challenges her as an artist: it seems to demand some response. To that challenge she reacts with terror and anxiety, and more confused denials:

> Of an artistic temperament, I deny that I am; yet I must possess something of the artist's faculty of making the most of present pleasure: that is to say, when it is of the kind to

my taste; I enjoyed that day, though we travelled slowly, though it was cold, though it rained. Somewhat bare, flat, and treeless was the route along which our journey lay; and slimy canals crept, like half-torpid green snakes, beside the road; and formal pollard willows edged level fields, tilled like kitchen-garden beds. The sky too was monotonously gray; the atmosphere was stagnant and humid; yet amidst all these deadening influences, my fancy budded fresh and my heart basked in sunshine. These feelings, however, were well kept in check by the secret but ceaseless consciousness of anxiety lying in wait on enjoyment, like a tiger crouched in a jungle. The breathing of that beast of prey was in my ear always; his fierce heart panted close against mine; he never stirred in his lair but I felt him: I knew he waited only for sun-down to bound ravenous from his ambush. (Chapter 7)

Pleasure, for Lucy, is hidden, dangerous, denied, potentially devastating. Therefore she can take pleasure only when it seems there is no pleasure there, from an ugly scene; and just as pleasure begins to "bud" it turns from a harmless flower to a ravenous beast. Lucy protests she lacks the artist's imagination that would produce either the buds of pleasant fancy or the horrifying visions of vengeful beasts; choosing as an occasion for this protest a view of a landscape where, she says, most people would see nothing of either sunshine or the jungle is of course a way of proving that she does have an artist's imagination. Lucy, denying, simultaneously, that she is a woman and that she is an artist, is identifying the one with the other. The painter's eye and the actress's talent that she says she does not have are metaphors for her writer's art: *Villette* is Lucy's effort at self-expression. It reveals most about her by its insistent denials.

Lucy is no actress: that is, she is not demonstrative of her feelings, and there is no action that will express her. She is too timid, too divided, too self-conscious and self-doubting, and for all her intensity she is too unfocused. Therefore she can have no self-expressive destiny; therefore this strange, inward, inconclusive novel sidesteps story. *Villette* is about how a destiny evades a girl, about how she watches it pass her by. Lucy Snowe yearns for love and love is denied her. From the beginning, when she watches her godmother, Mrs. Bretton, adoring her son, John Graham, and the extravagantly, cozily named Paulina Mary Home being adored by her father, it is clear that love is what Lucy cannot have. She has no mother, no father, no home. The two beautiful and loved children move toward one another and leave her out, for love breeds love, and lovelessness is worse in love's vicinity. When Lucy goes to live in the dark as a paid companion to Miss Marchmont, that woman's tragic story of love and loss underscores both love's all-importance and its remoteness from Lucy; it also prefigures her own final loss. On the packet boat that takes her to Belgium, Lucy observes and hears about arranged marriages, and reflects that they are abhorrent crimes against the holiness of feeling. To make a marriage that will achieve her capacity for love is her unvoiced, implicit goal. When she gets to the dark foreign port a handsome, shadowy stranger helps her with her luggage; he will turn out to have been the elusive John Graham Bretton, he will once again rebuff her, and in the end he will marry Polly, but Lucy tells us only that he was a tall handsome man whom she followed, blind and dependent, through the dark foreign streets. Her distance from the objectively desirable hero is the significant thing in their relationship.

In Brussels Lucy finds the professor instead of the doctor, the foreigner instead of the Englishman, a spiritual brother instead of her godmother's son, the irascible, hissing, scolding, secretive, peculiar little man instead of the blond Grandisonian ideal. "Currer Bell has found life not a home, but a school," a reviewer wrote in 1853. The difference of setting makes Brontë's difference from the other novelists whose subject, like hers, is private life. In all Brontë's novels teaching and being taught have erotic implications. Mr. Rochester is Jane Eyre's "master," who employs her as a teacher for his ward; he is her instructor in the ways of the world. Robert Moore in *Shirley*, a powerful mill-owner, is associated with instruction through his sister, who teaches French to Caroline Helstone in his house; and his brother, Louis Moore, is a poor tutor who wins the heiress Shirley Keeldar by instructing her. In *The Professor*, as in *Villette*, love blooms in à Belgian school, the way Charlotte Brontë's love for M. Héger did; and Frances Henri, although she is his equal, insists on calling her husband "*maître*" all her life. In *Villette* M. Paul is exciting to Lucy for criticizing and tormenting her, for seeming not to love her as he masters her. In the end, after he declares himself her lover and proves to be her benefactor, he goes away, and probably he drowns. Love is painful throughout, and lost in the bitter end. One is not born loved, or loved in childhood, if one is a Brontë heroine; therefore one must learn love at school, by being mastered there.

Although Lucy is in fact his colleague, M. Paul's inexplicable, absolute power over her is the power of a teacher over a schoolgirl. From their very first encounter he can see clear into her soul. Their relationship is a struggle in which Lucy's aim is to survive, and perform well, in spite of enormous, quixotic demands, and to be approved of by him for that. In the school, the good girl student is both open to unexpected attack and equipped (by her intellectual strength) to fight authority. The sexual implications are heightened by multiple displacements. A nightmarish vision of sex in the schoolroom is suggested in the surrealistic scene in *Villette* when two visiting inspectors force M. Paul to force Lucy to write a composition on "Human Justice." The authorities turn out to be the "loungers" who had seemed threatening when she first arrived, at night, in the deserted foreign streets of Villette. The reader experiences the reappearance, the recollection, the demand, and the names of MM. Boissec and Rochemorte (Drywood and Deadrock) as implausible and obviously contrived; the irony is heavy. This weird event, which gives one a sense of how Lucy experiences the world, rather than a "realistic" picture of it, is a broad hint as to how to read *Villette*.

M. Paul comes to an understanding with Lucy at the end, and gives her the school of her own—with a home attached—that she has longed for. Homeless Lucy finds a home at last, and success in her career. But love is still denied her. Paul is obliged to go away before they can marry. He is evidently lost at sea, but only oblique lyrical hymns tell us so: the reader is deliberately invited to believe that he lives to return, and to marry Lucy. The story goes that it was Patrick Brontë, surfeited with tragedy, who protested against the logical end to his surviving daughter's novel. The bone Lucy throws him—us—is, like her earlier passage about seas and shipwrecks, a covert expression of disdain for the convention-bound. She describes, in heightened language, a distant and terrible seven-day storm on the Atlantic, and this is how the description ends:

> Peace, be still! Oh! a thousand weepers, praying in agony on waiting shores, listened for that voice, but it was not uttered—not uttered till, when the hush came, some could not feel it: till, when the sun returned, his light was night to some!
>
> Here pause: pause at once. There is enough said. Trouble no quiet, kind heart; leave sunny imaginations hope. Let it be theirs to conceive the delight of joy born again fresh out of great terror, the rapture of rescue from peril, the wondrous reprieve from dread, the fruition of return. Let them picture union and a happy succeeding life.

Them—but not Lucy Snowe. She puts the period to *Villette* with grim, ironic simplicity, detailing the triumph of her enemies: "Madame Beck prospered all the days of her life; so did Père Silas; Madame Walravens fulfilled her ninetieth year before she died. Farewell" (Chapter 42). They whose hearts are dry as summer's dust succeed on earth, and therefore their characters find destinies, their stories find closure. Lucy insists on their stories to imply how surely her own eludes chronicling; she can no more express herself once for all in a narrative than in an action such as narratives chronicle.

# 3

# *The Egoist*

Thackeray can only have been teazing when he called *Vanity Fair* "a novel without a hero," as though that were a contradiction in terms. It is the heroine who is indispensable.

—Mary Lascelles

George Meredith kept it a secret that his grandfather and his father had been tailors. But the protagonist of his early novel, *Evan Harrington*, has a tailor grandfather conspicuously named Melchizedec and called "The Great Mel," just like Meredith's. The nature of the skeleton in his closet, and the fact that he half-closed the door to it and later pretended he hadn't, are suggestive details about Meredith. He was a snob ashamed of his humble Welsh origins, but he took pride in them, on the side—pride in being a Celt more witty and passionate than Englishmen, being George Meredith, the grandson of Mel. He lied about his grandfather in life, but told the truth in literature; it was like him to do such a thing, like him to use for fiction, at no matter what cost, the preposterous and ironic, therefore irresistible, revealing fact. The tailor as heroic patriarch is, like the best things in Meredith, a little bit too good, but true.

The tailors in the novelist's background are material beautifully cut out for the Comic Spirit, the goddess Meredith invented to worship. Her celebrated silvery laughter insists on them. No connection of hers was ever touched by a hint of vulgar trade! She is to be imagined by the reader as surrounded by irreverent gamboling naked imps, but calm and poised herself, well-dressed, high-nosed, absolutely *comme il faut*. Her domain is the drawing room of high comedy, her laughter a clear celestial-aristocratic tinkle. She stands aloof to mock the multitude, and shows the deserving few the high road from the seething caldron of the world to a level Meredith called civilization. There, men and women spar with bright, honed wits; they are equals and complements, freed from the hot narrowings of getting and spending, blood relatives, need, and desire.

The Comic Spirit is an apotheosis of the English lady: she is graceful and accomplished, aloof from the world in the high style of the upper classes, impeccable. She is a made-up, semiclassical deity, a Diana with impish children, a virgin mother nurturing with disdain, female yet sexless. The goddess of fortuitously fastidious grandsons of tailors is the corrective to God the funless father. It is her pleasure and her special pride to distinguish high bright spirits in the mass; she is never fooled by the mere garments of greatness, or, for that matter, the deceptive plain broadcloth of tailors' descendants. Her realm is the lofty, snowy Alps: at the end of Meredith's *The Egoist* she appears there and looks down at the world, compressing her lips as she gracefully and generously abstains from further mockery of men.

The Alps by themselves are not quite the whole picture of the Meredithian heights. Another image softens and complicates, the double-blossomed cherry tree of *The Egoist*. Meredith marries the images when Clara, the heroine, first sees the tree:

> the load of virginal blossom, whiter than summer-cloud on the sky, showered and drooped and clustered so thick as to claim colour and seem, like higher Alpine snows in noon-sunlight, a flush of white. From deep to deeper heavens of white, her eyes perched and soared. Wonder lived in her . . . wonder so divine, so unbounded, was like soaring into homes of angel-crowded space, sweeping through folded and

on to folded white fountain-bow of wings, in innumerable columns. (Chapter 11) *

As the Alps are, the tree is an astonishing, exhilarating, awesome natural wonder: the sight of it helps liberate Clara from her oppressive personal situation. In their softness and abundance the blossoms epitomize sensual beauty, and yet their whiteness, which recalls flushed Alpine snows, is cold and chaste. The tree is the creature of a gardener, not of nature, beautiful but fruitless. "Call this the Vestal of civilization," Clara's classicist father declares. Like the Comic Spirit, the cherry tree is feminine but not female, the image of a lady.

Meredith imagined himself a champion of women. His feminism was romantic, involving a passion for personal distinction more than one for equality. The heads of the fiercely sexual wag sadly over his revealing sort of hankering after a paradise furnished with silver sugar-tongs and fresh table linens; and his personal history of not having been able to live with his first, clever wife, Thomas Love Peacock's daughter Mary, would seem to bear out their suspicions. When Sir Willoughby Patterne, at the end of The Egoist, tries to assure himself that the marital booby prize he gets is the best bride after all, the narrator's inflection is ominous: "But he had the lady with brains! He had: and he was to learn the nature of that possession in the woman who is our wife" (Chapter 49). Meredith wrote a sequence of poems, Modern Love, about the break-up of his marriage. Like The Angel in the House, Coventry Patmore's celebration of Victorian family life and the ideal domestic female at its center, this long poem written in the great age of the long novel is about life after the wedding. Meredith's poem is the antithesis of Patmore's: it is analytic and meditative rather than simply narrative. And the marriage it analyzes is bad. The ordinary life of a couple has become a monstrous mockery that masks the truth of mistrust and despair. The writer of lyrical, lapidary prose made this pain-

---

* George Meredith, The Egoist (New York: W. W. Norton & Co., 1979). All quotations from the novel are from this edition; I give chapter rather than page numbers for the reader who might have another one.

ful story out of plain verse. *Modern Love* clings tenaciously to a
variation on the sonnet form as the couple whose story it chronicles hold on to the form of their marriage:

> At dinner, she is hostess, I am host.
> Went the feast ever cheerfuller? She keeps
> The Topic over intellectual deeps
> In buoyancy afloat. They see no ghost.
> With sparkling surface-eyes we ply the ball:
> It is in truth a most contagious game:
> HIDING THE SKELETON, shall be its name.
> Such play as this, the devils might appal!
> But here's the greater wonder; in that we
> Enamoured of an acting nought can tire,
> Each other, like true hypocrites, admire;
> Warm-lighted looks, Love's ephemerioe,
> Shoot gaily o'er the dishes and the wine.
> We waken envy of our happy lot.
> Fast, sweet, and golden, shows the marriage-knot.
> Dear guests, you now have seen Love's corpse-light shine.

*Modern Love* concludes that "Passions spin the plot," and that we
are "betrayed by what is false within." Meredith's is a novelist's
vision of the fatal implication of appearances in feelings. The self-
consciousness that marks his style is his subject.


There is no defending *The Egoist* against the charge of extreme
artificiality and linguistic denseness: that high-handed pyrotech-
nique is there to enjoy or reject, a matter of taste. But against the
common charge that the novel is cold and heartless, or the nearly
opposite accusation that it lets its victim off too lightly in the
end, defending is in order. Sir Willoughby Patterne, the eponymous Egoist, is a man-membrane, whose self-regard is inordi-
nately, inextricably involved with the regard others have or
pretend to have for him. He is a poseur; he is his appearance. The
membrane is elaborately wrought and very fragile—and it is all
there is to poor Willoughby. As a satirical portrait, he is not

unfamiliar: for centuries writers have pilloried persons overly dependent on others and on artifice, and celebrated the strong man who remains himself, come what or who may. The heroine, in contrast, has been described sympathetically as by nature implicated in artifice, and involved with others and what they think of her. The heroine-centered novel since *Clarissa* defines extreme susceptibility to the estimate of others, and an inextricable connection with artifice, as the feminine and also the quintessentially human condition. Read as a development of this tradition, *The Egoist* is something more than a satirical portrait of a monster. Willoughby Patterne stands very specifically for the upper-class Englishman of the nineteenth century, and Meredith satirizes in him the fatuousness and smugness, the callousness and heartlessness, of the type. But as a beautiful creature dependent on appearances and destined only for marriage, he is a version—a travesty—of the heroine. *The Egoist* is a sort of transvestite novel, the tailor's grandson's brilliant alteration of a genre to fit a radical critique of its assumptions. Liberating the heroine from the center of the courtship plot for feminist purposes, it puts in her place a "hero" who is her mirror-image. Like Clarissa, Sir Willoughby is the pride of his world and its creature, profoundly committed to what Lovelace might call a "mere notional" self—which is to say, a notion that has little connection with an emotional center of identity. But unlike Clarissa or any heroine, Willoughby also has real power in the world. Therefore he is seriously dangerous. Meredith exposes him, with glee but not without sympathy.

*The Egoist* turns the heroine's story on its head. It is both a send-up of the heroine-centered novel and a variation on it. It is about the breaking, not the making, of an engagement. This is the story: a beautiful virgin—well-born, intelligent, charming, wealthy, and eighteen, by objective standards the most desirable young woman in England, unaffected, lively, and witty—is being forced to marry a man she finds physically, spiritually, and morally repellent. There has been a formal engagement; preparations for the wedding are proceeding; time is on the man's side, and space, for the girl is virtually imprisoned in a house in the country. She feels, painfully, her littleness and weakness. Meanwhile the man's awareness of her reluctance to marry him whets his sexual appetite; her own feelings are turned, like her beauty, against her. Locked in a situation she has unwittingly produced, she feels guilty, constrained, claustrophobic; she wants freedom, she fights for air. She sees herself in horror as a heroine: "Dreadful to think of! she was one of the creatures who are written about!" (Chapter 15). She thinks of herself with a heroine's doubleness of mind, as someone who must stand for her whole sex and at the same time distinguish herself from it: "for her sex's sake, and also to appear an exception to her sex, this reasoning creature desired to be thought consistent" (Chapter 19). Along with her reputation and her fate, her identity, or idea of herself, is at risk.

Nobody will understand or indeed hear her objections to a marriage objectively grand, thoroughly approved by custom and convention. All the people around her suppose it will make her happy. Her father, her natural protector, is for his own reasons on her suitor's side. Seeking help, she makes several confidants. Her mind seems to her unreliable; she has doubts about the accuracy of her perceptions of a world grown hostile and flat; raised to submit, she condemns herself for feeling rebellious, and is nearly ready to give in. She is a lady and therefore she has been brought up to be a coward: the blunt assessment is Meredith's. But her woman's nature asserts itself. By stealth she escapes from the place where she is immured, intending to seek the protection of a female friend. A very charming young man offers to help her escape, but it turns out he wants to have her in the other man's place. It becomes clear to her (and us) that Woman's natural adversary is Man, whose lust is as unnatural as the civilized ploys he uses to entrap her. It becomes clear that civilization is the tool of lust. As she is civilization's creature, she seems destined to be lust's victim. It becomes evident that she must stoop to the world's ways in order to save herself, to make other people understand how she feels, who she is, to articulate that self the whole world conspires to ignore and destroy, and meanwhile not to be compromised in the world's eyes.

I have nearly exhausted the parallels. *The Egoist* is a comedy; Clara's story only recalls Clarissa's. A single sentence suggests how faintly:

> In a dream somehow she had committed herself to a life-long imprisonment; and, oh terror! not in a quiet dungeon; the barren walls closed round her, *talked*, called for ardour, expected admiration. (Chapter 10)

The italics are mine: "talked" contains Meredith's insight and emphasis.

Meredith is vague about what led Clara Middleton to engage herself to Sir Willoughby Patterne, and to make an extended prenuptial visit to his house with her father.* We are expected to take it for granted that an inexperienced girl would be dazzled by an offer from the handsome and wealthy scion of a great English family, a matrimonial prize, apparently charming—charming, that is, in public. Clara discovers the private man after the engagement. This is entirely logical, as the worst thing about Willoughby is the difference between his public and private selves. There is a screaming, greedy baby inside the gentleman's skin. In the privacy of Patterne Hall, he drops his plausible manner and expects his beloved to admire what he conceals from the world. Clara thinks, "How must a man despise women, who can expose himself as he does to me!" When he confides in her and says, "This is not a language I talk to the world," she begs, "But do, do talk to me as you talk to the world, Willoughby; give me some relief!" (Chapter 10). The private Willoughby is a primitive, a brute; marrying him, a girl must encounter the odious inner man.

---

* His name suggests he is the very pattern of a Willoughby—the name *par excellence* of a romantic gentleman, as the author of *Sense and Sensibility* thought early on. Like the heroine's name—Clara is not Clarissa, she is the inhabitant of the middle not the highest realm of being—the "hero's" deliberately reminds us of other novels. It is reminiscent of the popular Willow Pattern of china, and a story connected with that, as well. The heroine is also linked with china, underscoring the feminine connotations of the association and connecting the couple that will eventually break up.

In the intimate sexual relation, the Egoist is exposed. Clara experiences the question "Can a woman have an inner life apart from him she is yoked to?" as "a sharp physical thought" (Chapter 21). Mind and body, language and love, are confounded; therefore marriage is a situation like no other.

The conceit basic to *The Egoist* is that a man may be considered as women commonly are, as generic. Commenting on one of Willoughby's fatuous pronouncements about the nature of women, the intelligent Laetitia Dale observes tartly, "The generic woman appears to have an extraordinary faculty for swallowing the individual" (Chapter 14). Blind and deaf to all but the most superficial and measurable distinctions among women, Willoughby has sought a perfect bride. The dashing Constantia Durham has already jilted him when he meets Clara; Clara soon plans to do so, too, and eventually even Laetitia Dale decides not to marry him before (not because she wants to) she does. For the Egoist, for generic man, that is, "there is no individual woman. He grants her a characteristic only to enroll her in a class. He is our immortal dunce at learning to distinguish her as a personal variety, of a separate growth" (Chapter 19). Like a heroine, Willoughby is representative, part person, part pattern. He is an anti-exemplar, an anti-Grandison. Like Sir Charles he is described as sunlike, most hilariously when his adoring female relatives recall his standing on the chair as a child, crying, "I am the sun of the house!" (Chapter 44). He surrounds himself with women: faded, thirty-year-old Laetitia Dale, who has waited years to marry him; the dowagers Mrs. Mountstuart Jenkinson, Lady Culmer, and Lady Busshe, who delight in competing as prophets of his glorious fate; his slavish maiden aunts, Eleanor and Isabel. The Egoist is wedded to the social world as the conscious heroine is: like her he depends on reflection and on reputation to be sure of his value and to keep his grip on his valuable self.

Willoughby Patterne is partly exonerated by Meredith as not himself responsible for what he is. He is "a gentleman nurtured in idolatry," the product of hereditary aristocracy and primogeniture, of generations of Patternes. Centuries of ruthless egoism have produced him; he is owned by his House. All England encourages its idle gentlemen to pursue only their own pleasure on their own extensive lands the way Willoughby does, and it admires them for feeling no responsibility to the rest of the world, for thinking nothing of those who think so much of them. The social system that places Willoughby apart from the world in his artificial Eden at Patterne Hall makes him inhuman; and partly because he thinks *of* little else, he is unable to think *for* himself. He is the centerpiece, the result, of a corrupt social structure. His relationship to women epitomizes his society's; to analyze women's importance to him is to illustrate the importance of feminism for England. The story of Sir Willoughby Patterne's marrying is based on the condition of England as it is described in John Stuart Mill's *On the Subjection of Women* (1869), which Meredith had read with interest.

The novel turns on the illogical premise that an engagement must be unmade the way it is made, through a mutual understanding. Unlike Clarissa, Clara has engaged herself all by herself. The genteel world she lives in is like Jane Austen's world: there are clearly defined courtship customs, and a definable group of eligible men to choose from, and some very bad bets among them, and no one at all to save a girl from falling for one of those. Her fate is in her hands. Only Clara's word binds her to Willoughby. Her widower father, scholarly, polysyllabic, and bibulous, has amiably gone along with her decision to marry this unexceptionable if stupid young man, and he is enjoying the pleasures of a visit to palatial Patterne Hall, where there is a well-stocked library and a magnificent wine cellar, and the company of Willoughby's intellectual cousin and secretary, Vernon Whitford. Dr. Middleton is an accessory to the Egoist, as he is an egoist himself. Meredith's argument that Willoughby is a monstrously enlarged part of all of us is made as he shows a plurality, a conspiracy, of egoists.

Dr. Middleton very casually thinks little of women, tossing off classical references to support his stock ideas. Among the formulas and accepted ideas that bind Clara to Willoughby, therefore, are the misogynistic lines of Roman poets. It is part of the wall of words between them that prevents them from separating. Clara, for instance, is bound by a lady's language:

> She could not, as in a dear melodrama, from the aim of a pointed finger denounce him, on the testimony of her instincts, false of speech, false in deed. She could not even declare that she doubted his truthfulness. The refuge of a sullen fit, the refuge of tears, the pretext of a mood, were denied her now by the rigour of those laws of decency which are a garment to ladies of pure breeding. (Chapter 43)

She is too corseted with customs to tell the truth, so she cannot break her engagement. Meanwhile Sir Willoughby, in secret, recalls the plots of pulp fiction to salve his pride. He imagines "romances" in which Clara is ruined and comes back to him on her knees. In her company, he uses conventional polite formulas to feign incomprehension and fuddle his antagonist—another use of language in the service of misunderstanding. Stock phrases and standard images of women throng to his aid and make him almost clever. For instance, when she is bored with him Clara yawns and then feebly explains,

> "I am sleepier here than anywhere."
> "Ours, my Clara, is the finest air of the kingdom. It has the effect of sea-air."
> "But if I am always asleep here?"
> "We shall have to make a public exhibition of the Beauty." (Chapter 10)

Meredith keeps us mindful of the power of language by using it flamboyantly. Willoughby is perverse: he has, it is said, a "burning wish to strain her in his arms to a flatness provoking his compassion" (Chapter 23). *The Egoist* begins with a slow essay-chapter that ends with an epitaph for the hero, a line that kills him off before his story begins: "Through very love of self himself he slew." Its backfiring movement is the novel's: Sir Willoughby gets himself into his pickle of a plot by getting down on his knees once too often, and so, in the end, he is forced back down where he began, forced to marry the woman he jilted after being jilted himself.

Remembering *Modern Love*, and invoking Victorian euphemism, some readers have argued that *The Egoist* only pretends to be about the breaking of an engagement, and is really the veiled story of a divorce. This is not the case. Sir Willoughby himself makes the distinction:

> "You know, to me, Clara, plighted faith, the affiancing of two lovers, is a piece of religion. I rank it as holy as marriage; nay, to me it is holier; I really cannot tell you how; I can only appeal to you in your bosom to understand me. We read of divorces with comparative indifference. They occur between couples who have rubbed off all romance." (Chapter 15)

*The Egoist* is about the undoing of a romance; therefore it mirrors the courtship plot. What has placed Clara in Willoughby's house and hands is only her word—Yes—and she is constrained by logic to extricate herself by another word—No—which she cannot say and he cannot hear. The relationship of the couple is purely verbal; they are bound only by a promise.

Yet Willoughby wants Clara for her body. She is qualified to be the mother of the sons (not daughters) of Patterne because she has health, wealth, and beauty, and is a virgin. When Richardson identified woman's adversary as the rake, a rebel and an outlaw, he spoke on behalf of both women and society; an attack on the Egoist satirizes the establishment, and identifies woman with the outsider and the satirist with her cause. Willoughby's fetish for feminine chastity is implicated in the selfishness of his lust: to maintain himself and propagate his kind, he must possess the natural world's finest creature, a "quick nature," and assert his overlordship of the earth. Clara is saved in the end by the health that enables her to fight back with energy, and the beauty that finds her an alternative lover. He is Vernon Whitford, Willoughby's cousin. Vernon is a scholar and an accomplished pedestrian (like Meredith himself and Leslie Stephen, the literary Alpinist who was a model for Vernon, who became the father of

Virginia Woolf). Where Sir Willoughby's favorite posture, on horseback, bespeaks the man who aims to be master, his cousin Vernon's prowess as a walker suggests his doggedness and simplicity, his closeness to the earth. Sacrificing realism to romantic fantasy, Meredith idealizes the rational and perfect love between the young scholar and an older scholar's daughter. Clara and the charming, half-Irish Horace de Craye are delightfully witty together, but the novelist arranges for the quieter man—not the Celt—to get the heroine in the end. Vernon is a humanist and a human being; his devotion to flowering trees and to the Alps prove he is worthy of a heroine who can race a twelve-year-old boy without getting winded, a girl who, like Elizabeth Bennet, is impervious to mud and English weather. De Craye, like Willoughby, has a history of casually exploiting women of the lower classes; Vernon, in contrast, once went so far as to marry one (she is conveniently dead). The fact shadows him, ever so lightly, with the glamour of sexual experience; in contrast, the shadow on Willoughby, who has once been jilted, is impotence. Vernon is poor, and scholarly, and tactful, and modest—the literary man as a perfect Perseus, "Phoebus Apollo as fasting friar," as Mrs. Mountstuart Jenkinson has it.

In Mrs. Mountstuart, the reigning matron of the Egoist's universe, the powers of the word, the world, and woman are imagined as one. She is the icing on the cake of this epigrammatic novel. Her specialty is the devastating one-liner. Of Laetitia Dale she says, for instance, "Here she comes, with a romantic tale on her eyelashes." Her epigrams, like caricatures, depend on the tiniest bit too emphatic a focus on a single feature, often a good one the epigram calls into question by attending to it. Vernon is too thin and ascetic, but basically, we are meant to think, he is perfect, has the soul of a saint and is made like a pagan god. Laetitia, who writes poems and romances to support herself and her father, has long eyelashes—what can that mean? Is she batting off a romantic tale? Trembling on the brink of tears? Of Sir Willoughby himself Mrs. Mountstuart says heart-stoppingly little:

"*You see he has a leg.*" Not two legs but one. It "will walk straight into the hearts of women." Is it a phallus or the leg made in bowing, made for dancing attendance? Does it suggest his deep subservience to women, and to conventions? Far commoner synechdoches for the whole man are "a head," "a heart." Is "leg" to suggest that Sir Willoughby has neither? He is physically a perfect specimen; nonetheless, "leg" mystifies. The observation is repeated; Mrs. Mountstuart, who relishes her phrases, cracks that one like a whip. There is no way to ask what it might mean. Sir Willoughby, terrorized, interprets her *mot* as a flattery. Much depends on tone: "*You see,*" is how she puts it, "*he has a leg.*" ("You *see* it; or, you see, *he* has it. Miss Isabel and Miss Eleanor disputed the incidence of the emphasis, but surely, though a slight difference of meaning may be heard, either will do: many, with a good show of reason, throw the accent upon *leg*" [Chapter 2].) We are supposed to see, and we pretend to, or think we do. Or do we?

About Mrs. Mountstuart's epigram for Clara, Willoughby very circumlocutiously attempts to inquire, delicately concealing distress: what *does* dear Mrs. Mountstuart mean by "a dainty rogue in porcelain"? Why rogue? he wants to know, complacently accepting the rest of it, his fiancée hit off as an ornamental figurine. The lady does not say, chary like any sybil of talking too much, waiting like her rival Lady Busshe for the event to prove her a prophet. Questions proliferate about whether Clara (her heart? her hymen?) or the engagement will break, and then the brittle wedding presents begin to arrive. One is a broken vase; the other, a dinner service, comes legitimately in several pieces. The matter of patterns on porcelain is loaded with significances. Is the point only that Clara will not accept her woman's place? Or is Mrs. Mountstuart merely putting some people on by seeming to send others up?

Mrs. Mountstuart is a worldly widow—she has lived in British India. The savage point is delicately made that, being British, she has handily escaped suttee. Her only amusement is to be amusing. She aims to defeat better-born and better-married rivals by her native wit. As Sir Willoughby is the chief young man in her world, she defines herself as his chief supporter, chronicler, chorus: she depends on him to provide plot and characters on which to base her *bons mots*, to lend his importance to her statements by being their subject. To keep him at her side she must seem to be on his but also she must keep him awed, and afraid that she will lose the respect she pretends to have for him, or that she will stop feigning it. The Egoist's dominance depends on the egoism, or at least on the selfishness, of others. Willoughby has more than Mrs. Mountstuart to lose. She explains him to Clara, explaining herself:

> The secret of him is, that he is one of those excessively civilized creatures who aim at perfection: and I think he ought to be supported in his conceit of having attained it; for the more men of that class, the greater our influence. . . . We must be moderately slavish to keep our place; which is given us in appearance; but appearances make up a remarkably large part of life, and far the most comfortable. . . . (Chapter 35)

It is in the interest of ladies like Mrs. Mountstuart that men be artificial creatures like Willoughby. The high place of women in drawing rooms, Mrs. Mountstuart knows, is only "given us in appearance," and therefore she values appearances, which not only make up a large part of life but also affect the disposition of realities. In reality, Sir Willoughby is a slave to the sex he would enslave; aware of this, Mrs. Mountstuart can manipulate him. The acknowledged mistress of ceremonies, she is, in a ceremonious world, mistress of considerable power. Willoughby's terror of her tongue is critical in the process by which he is outmaneuvered and forced to save face by letting Clara go. For the women band together against him, Mrs. Mountstuart and Laetitia on Clara's side, in a sisterhood to be reckoned with. The glutton who aimed to eat up the world's fairest flower and fruit finds himself "in the jaws of the world, on the world's teeth," brought to sacrifice himself "for the favourable looks and tongues of those women whose looks and tongues he detested" (Chapter 46), Mrs. Mountstuart and her friends. The consumer is consumed. Clara is allowed to disengage herself for the reason she would have been married—for his appearance's sake. And Sir Willoughby, jilted a second time, is obliged to marry Laetitia, whom he has jilted twice. The romances Mrs. Mountstuart observed trembling on her eyelashes have fallen like scales from Laetitia's eyes in the course of Sir Willoughby's courtship of Clara; she agrees to marry him because she is poor, so as to be able to stanch the flow from her pen. By marrying him as she does, reluctantly, she reduces the grandiose Sir Willoughby to his goods and chattels; because she includes them in her mind, those will not include her. All the victorious women in the novel defeat the Egoist by the way they think of and look at him.

The first time Clara Middleton feels the impulse to laugh at Willoughby Patterne she has to stifle it. The giggle swells in her when, after her father praises the rod as an instrument of education, Miss Eleanor and Miss Isabel murmur to each other that Willoughby in his youth "would not have suffered it!" Clara sighs and Meredith interprets her silence:

> She sighed and put a tooth on her underlip. The gift of humourous fancy is in women fenced round with forbidding placards; they have to choke it; if they perceive a piece of humour, for instance, the young Willoughby grasped by his master, and his horrified relatives rigid at the sight of preparations for the deed of sacrilege, they have to blindfold the mind's eye. They are society's hard-drilled soldiery, Prussians that must both march and think in step. It is for the advantage of the civilized world, if you like, since men have decreed it, or matrons have so read the decree; but here and there a younger woman, haply an uncorrected insurgent of the sex matured here and there, feels that her lot was cast with her head in a narrower pit than her limbs.
>
> Clara . . . asked for some little, only some little, free play of mind in a house that seemed to wear, as it were, a cap of iron. (Chapter 9)

The repression of the maiden's mind is analogous to the physical punishment administered to boys, which little Willoughby escaped. It is as formative. The Egoist's iron cap is made to match that other uncomfortable garment for girls, the iron maiden: armored uncomfortably in invisible versions of both, well-bred English girls are preserved for their possessors, and impressed as the foot soldiers of their repressive society. At Patterne Clara is made to stifle her physical self—her desire, her impulse to run swiftly, her laughter—by an enclosure of her mind. But as it turns out in the end, "Miss Middleton owed it to Sir Willoughby Patterne that she ceased to think like a girl" (Chapter 10). Accurately perceived, the Egoist cures the ills he causes. Tickled by his absurdity, infuriated by his presumptions, terrified by suffocating in his caresses, and seeing that her whole life is at stake, Clara begins to think no longer like a girl but like a woman—but not one of those servile women of whom Meredith writes that "a shadow of the male Egoist is in the chamber of their brains overawing them" (Chapter 11). To begin to laugh at the Egoist is to banish his shadow, burst the iron cap. One need not laugh out loud, Meredith cautions timorously; one can retain good manners, decent dress, aristocratic attitudes. Clara breaks free, gracefully, allowing Sir Willoughby what shreds of his dignity remain. The novel's final image is of the cool Comic Spirit. Vernon and Clara, who have married, have gone to the Alps; the Spirit sits beside them there, and looks from her eminence down and across Europe to Patterne, to Willoughby. She says nothing; instead "she compresses her lips," like Elizabeth Bennet when just before her marriage she swallows a sharp remark and reflects that Darcy "had yet to learn to be laught at." Willoughby lacks the capacity to learn; the Spirit is simply through with him. Gracefully, she restrains herself. Her silence is not imposed by an iron cap, but freely chosen.

As the last volleys of silvery laughter echo and die away in the Alps, it is a little hard to say who laughs last. *The Egoist* ends conventionally, with marriages. There is some obvious irony: one is meant to doubt that Laetitia and Willoughby will be happy ever after. But in the face of Clara Middleton's happiness with Vernon Whitford, we seem to be meant to be misty-eyed. Yet Clara, for all of Meredith's assertions that she has begun to think, never quite breaks free enough of the novelist's hovering analytic intelligence to acquire a mind recognizably her own; she is too well supervised and well monitored to be a convincing character. The indispensable Whitford, too, is a shadowy figure, as hard to picture as Mrs. Mountstuart's impossible image, Phoebus Apollo as fasting friar. So far as one can see him he looks gray. Meredith praises the scholar in him, and the Alpinist, and the modest, helpful man. Are we meant to observe the hypocrisy and passivity that enable him to coexist with Willoughby, or to find his remoteness and lack of sparkle unattractive? I suspect not. Vernon and Clara are idealized as a perfect couple for the top of the obligatory wedding cake at the novel's end. Having put Willoughby in a heroine's place, and satirized his pretensions to perfect selfhood, Meredith gives himself room to idealize Clara— to have the heroine both ways, as the novel form is calculated to have her, as a subject and an ideal object, a person and a metaphor, at once. The Comic Spirit finds nothing to laugh at in the happy couple in the Alps. But why does she haunt their honeymoon?

Meredith was both critical of the prevailing sexual myths of his time and embroiled in them. From the story of *Diana of the Crossways* (1897)—the story in the novel and some stories that hang around it—we can gather some illustrations of this, and of related matters I have been discussing.

Meredith was a prolific but not a popular novelist until his beautiful, brilliant Diana captured the imagination of English readers. "There is a large and beautiful conception of womanhood in Diana rather than a single woman," Virginia Woolf wrote astutely of this heroine, in whom the generic and the particular urgently combine and clash, as they do in Sir Willoughby, but not to satiric effect. A delicate "portrait" of Diana was featured in a book of sketches of chaste and lovely heroines of popular fiction, drawn as if they were so many actual society belles, which was published as a coffee-table folio around the turn of the century. *Diana of the Crossways* got attention partly because it revived a scandal about a real woman, the Hon. Caroline Norton, who had been dead some twenty years when the novel appeared, but who was still well enough remembered to be recognized as Meredith's model. (The novelist had once met her.) Rather like Byron, whom she physically resembled, Mrs. Norton had lived a myth, and therefore was susceptible to fictionalization. One of three beautiful granddaughters of the playwright Richard Brinsley Sheridan, she was brilliant as well, dashing. As her 1909 biographer put it, "the lyric touch, too often wanting in her verses, is never lacking in her life; her story, told in her own dramatic words, is her real contribution to the literature of her century." Caroline Norton wrote poems and novels and tracts, and she was a witty and charming conversationalist. The stories told about her by envious enemies contributed to her notoriety: in the elaborately periphrastic introductory chapter of *Diana*, Meredith analyzes, with sympathy, a talking woman's special vulnerability to talk.

A lawsuit brought by Mrs. Norton's estranged husband made her the victim of serious slander as well as mere envious insinuations. Separated from his wife, Norton sued the Prime Minister, Lord Melbourne, for enjoying her favors. In that time women were so little recognized as persons that Caroline figured in the lawsuit as a piece of property. The case was dismissed; Mr. Norton had no evidence. But the suit intensified Caroline Norton's sense of the wrongs that had been done her under sanction of law. When her husband had left her he had taken the children. Under England's law, they belonged entirely to him, and for years he prevented her from seeing them. Mrs. Norton wrote tracts and attempted to charm powerful politicians in an effort to alter the laws regulating the property of married women and the custody of children.

Meredith's Diana is, like Caroline Norton, the sort of woman women envy; a society belle, well born and well placed, she is beautiful, witty, and spirited, and furthermore a published writer. Diana is also an unhappy wife, a (chaste) intimate of great politicians, and the subject of gossip, again like Mrs. Norton. But there are inevitable differences between life and novels: while the fictitious Diana's husband dies and she marries again, happily, while she is still young, Caroline Norton was not free to marry until shortly before her death, when she was in her sixties. And Diana is not a mother. Literary convention made Meredith strip Mrs. Norton of her three children quite as the laws of England had allowed Mr. Norton to do the same thing. Finally, Diana writes romances, not tracts. I suppose a childless Diana could not convincingly be shown as passionately directing her mind's best efforts toward reforming the laws of child custody. Obvious other reasons too made Meredith soften her from a pamphleteer to the most acceptable type of literary lady, a popular novelist.

The plot of *Diana of the Crossways* turns on an episode in which the heroine sells to a newspaper editor a political secret that has been told her by Percy Dacier, the young politician she loves. More than enough motive is provided for Diana's act: in dramatic scenes we see her out of money and blocked at writing a novel that is to release her from debt, and horror-struck by a sudden attempt Percy has made on her chastity. At an earlier crisis in her life she had also reacted like the chaste goddess Diana to a man's sexual assault: then maidenly flight had led to the disaster of her first marriage. If we grant that she has been badly scarred by that earlier overture of her best friend's husband, and grant also that her long relationship with Percy Dacier has been intimate yet "pure," we must believe in her terror. But Meredith wants us to believe in addition that she would go on from terror to utter intellectual confusion—that a sophisticated woman, an accomplished hostess wise in the ways of political life, would not know it was wrong to sell a political secret to the newspapers. Meredith asks us to believe that Diana has no idea she is engaged in a serious act of betrayal. Committed to idealizing his heroine, he is unable to let us think she knowingly performed a base act: so instead he suggests she is unimaginably naïve. A "real" Diana, we suspect, would have known what she was doing; Mrs. Norton, for example, would certainly have known.

But as it turns out, Mrs. Norton was accused of doing precisely what Diana does in the novel. When *Diana of the Crossways* appeared, Meredith was accused of reviving false rumors about her. (All subsequent editions of the novel were prefaced by a note insisting the story was a fiction.) Faithful to gossip, the novel is false to historical truth and psychological plausibility, and so it founders. What is the moral? Is there a moral?

The heroine of *Diana of the Crossways* is adorably a sexual being because she is a literary woman: her wit, her being a novelist, make her attractive. Meredith insists on his brilliant writer-heroine's difference from the docile and dull blond heroines of romance, but he writes, nevertheless, with the worshipful delight of a dreamer adoring a Rose. The point of the novel about her is Diana's deliciousness. If, on rereading, she proves not quite so wonderfully witty as Meredith says she is, we must still believe in her brilliance if we would give ourselves at all to the fiction. Diana is the fantasy of a man who adored witty women. She is a novelist. But when she sells the truth to the newspapers, she uses language as witty women novelists never use it. She uses the language of politics and newspapers, the language of men's world. Diana breaks the rule that separates domestic or private language (bedroom, drawing-room, novel language) from public language. In effect she claims for her own purposes a language women are barred from using. But the feminist point is obscured in *Diana of the Crossways* because selling the secret is by any standards wrong and even contemptible, and because Meredith's argument that Diana knew not what she did is unconvincing. What Meredith pretends to present as evidence of his heroine's bold spirit identifies radical action with treason and moral cowardice, with hysteria, selfishness, and even stupidity. Meanwhile the fabric of the fiction is rent because the novelist blindly and sentimentally protects his heroine.

Tracts like the ones Caroline Norton wrote aim to change the world by language; novels like George Meredith's aim to delight and to civilize. Two different kinds of change, two different languages, are involved. A novelist's playful language is, like Diana's wit, an agent of Eros. Meredith shows us his heroine intoxicating herself, writing alone in her room, as she transmutes facts into fictions. She pleasurably changes herself into her lover when she writes a novel about a Young Minister of State (Percy Dacier). We can imagine George Meredith in a similar frame of mind as by language he transformed a dead Caroline Norton (and a male wit named Meredith) into a vivid, female, fictitious Diana, romantically Celtic like himself. The novel changes reality into fictions, makes lies into effective truths, and perilously calls attention to its own processes, and reverses them. But it avoids the function of language Caroline Norton's tracts reached for: it lacks the ability to effect real social change, the aim that statements and secrets of statesmen have. Affirming the mythical character of a heroine named for a mythical goddess, Meredith reaffirms the conservative message the bourgeois novel has usually transmitted, identifying the traditional conflation of the domestic, the private, the separate, the individual, the unique, and the conventionally feminine, as an ideal. Because he cared more for myth than for history, he changed Caroline Norton's story; he used gossip as the basis of a fiction. Is there a lesson in the fact that, so doing, he flawed his novel? Is there another in the fact that *Diana of the Crossways* deliberately raises the issues that undermine it?

Ironies compound themselves outside the fiction, too. Biographies of Mrs. Norton have since *Diana* included a chapter on Meredith's novel; a heroine of feminism, who did good work for her sex, is best remembered as the prototype of a glamorous character in fiction. On the other hand, the historical Mrs. Norton, Mary Shelley's friend, a novelist and a wit, was in fact glamorous in precisely the old, high way Meredith adored, and celebrated in making Diana. The question of what in fact is fair, not to mention what is fact, is dizzying.

## —◆ 4 ◆—

# Daniel Deronda

By your Discourse, Miss, replied *Arabella*, one would imagine, you knew as little in what the good Reputation of a Lady
consists, as the Safety of a Man; for certainly the one depends
intirely upon his Sword, and the other upon the Noise and
Bustle she makes in the World.

—Charlotte Lennox,
*The Female Quixote*

From George Eliot's letters we gather that the first scene of
*Daniel Deronda*, in which the hero sees a pale young English
beauty at play in a continental gambling hall, was based on an
incident in the novelist's life. On a visit to a German casino,
George Eliot was much struck by the sight of a Miss Leigh, said
to be Lord Byron's grandniece and reputed also to be his grand-
daughter, gambling. It was a spectacle calculated to stir this particular novelist's imagination: an intellectual and a moralist,
middle-aged, middle-class, and personally unprepossessing,
George Eliot stared with complex compassion at another,
younger woman, an English lady in the heroine style, a cool
beauty unnaturally excited, a symbol of aristocracy fallen into the
mob: she was perhaps reminded, too, of the rumored scandalous
connection between Byron and his half-sister, as she saw the

fabulous Noble Poet's descendant visibly afflicted with inherited sin.

A Victorian shadow of the Romantic theme of incest haunts many of George Eliot's works. Her early sonnet sequence called "Brother and Sister" is about the childhood of a girl afflicted by the love she attributes to Maggie Tulliver in her autobiographical novel, *The Mill on the Floss.* Maggie longs to be always with, exactly like, the same as, a loving and sensitive brother slightly older than she, an imaginary person she confounds with her brother Tom, who rejects her with casual brutality. Maggie attracts Tom's opposite, a delicate and bookish surrogate brother whose spirit reaches toward and meets her own. Philip Wakem falls in love with her, but he does not awaken her sexually: he is physically inadequate, deformed. The man who later on does arouse her, Stephen Guest, is nearly as simple and unimaginative as Tom Tulliver. Maggie cannot have Stephen, who is her cousin Lucy's lover. Bewildered by a life that seems designed to thwart her, she is doomed to die. During a flood, she goes in a little boat to save Tom, and brother and sister drown locked in one another's arms. "In their death they were not divided," the epigraph to the novel reads.

From her own brother, Isaac Evans, George Eliot was divided—first, like Maggie, by gender and sensibility, then by geography, education, and achievement, and finally by what he considered her sin. Isaac repudiated his sister Marian, who was not yet the novelist George Eliot, when she went to live with another woman's husband, George Henry Lewes. Her brother's conventional standards were not Marian's, but neither was she entirely free of those standards. She insisted always on her love's respectability and her household's, and she refused to dispute the social code that denied her invitations to dinner because she was a fallen woman. As George Eliot, she seemed to many the sanctified embodiment of domestic morality, but Isaac Evans forgave his sister only after she married John W. Cross, after Lewes died. She herself died soon after that; Isaac followed her to her grave. Ruby V. Redinger, whose emphasis on the brother-and-sister theme in George Eliot's life and works has influenced my reading, concludes her biography of the novelist by describing Isaac in the funeral procession, the last salient scene in George Eliot's life.

In *Middlemarch*, the brother-and-sister theme is not articulated, but it is intimated by the structure. The parallel plots, one for a hero and one for a heroine, suggest both the fact that the two are equally important beings with analogous quests, and that hero and heroine are a pair forbidden to couple. Lydgate and Dorothea also resemble each other as a brother and sister might, being young, idealistic, and ambitious. Both make bad choices of mates who are very unlike them, but although they experience at least one fleeting moment of spiritual intimacy, there never is a question that they might choose one another. Lydgate is not interested in Dorothea; he is doomed by his faulty character to prefer false and frivolous women. Dorothea does not think of him, because he is not of her class, and spiritually, too, he is different. In *Daniel Deronda* the differences of class and soul between the hero and heroine in the parallel plots become a charged issue. The relationship of Daniel and Gwendolen is vastly more substantial and problematic than the acquaintanceship of Lydgate and Dorothea, who like and help one another in a comradely (brotherly/sisterly) way. From the first scene of *Daniel Deronda*, the protagonists of the parallel plots are strongly and mysteriously linked by a complex fellow-feeling that turns each back upon himself and herself. There is something in the connection reminiscent of Marian and Isaac Evans, and something of George Eliot watching Miss Leigh. The heroine and her inevitable love story are given new significance in *Daniel Deronda* by a vision of multiple forms of love.

Daniel Deronda is first seen having a vision of Gwendolen Harleth. Like a donor kneeling in the corner of a religious painting, he assumes a posture that, presumably, those of us outside the work of art will imitate. It is not the conventional worshipful attitude, but instead an odd interrogative one:

Was she beautiful or not beautiful? and what was the secret of form or expression which gave the dynamic quality to her glance? Was the good or the evil genius dominant in those beams? Probably the evil; else why was the effect that of unrest rather than of undisturbed charm? Why was the wish to look again felt as coercion and not as a longing in which the whole being consents? *

In place of the pretty little flaw that saves the heroine of fiction from perfectly boring beauty, Gwendolen has this question cast like a flattering shadow on her face. As a mole (or a balanced pair of moles) might, the question of whether she is beautiful (or not beautiful) points up her beauty.

It is fitting that the first we see of Gwendolen is her effect on a man. Deronda finds her attractive, confusing, distressing, divisive of his "whole being." He cannot understand it, and his proliferating questions convey both his excitement and his efforts to rise above sex to philosophy. He attempts to judge the girl but instead he wonders at her; meaning to decide about *her*, he grows increasingly aware of himself. The distinctions that he tries to make between "form" and "expression," between what's apparent and what's "secret," or hidden, begin to blur. So does the boundary between him and the object of his attention, whose subjectivity, glimpsed in her "dynamic" glance, generates the questions inside him, imposes some "coercion" on him, involves him.

The first paragraph of *Daniel Deronda* is in both senses of the word overwrought. This is perhaps acknowledged by the epigraph to Chapter I, which begins, "Men can do nothing without the make-believe of a beginning." Is it men like George Eliot the novelist means? Is she drawing attention to the fact that the novel begins *in medias res*, or the fact that the relationship between Daniel Deronda and an unknown girl is a fantasy? The silent questions in Deronda's mind raise, by their position, larger

---

* George Eliot, *Daniel Deronda* (New York and Harmondsworth: Penguin Books, 1967). All quotations from the novel are from this edition, which has a helpful introduction and notes by Barbara Hardy; I give chapter rather than page numbers in parentheses for the reader who may have another edition.

questions: why should such questions about a girl so clamorously pretend to matter? why should a serious novelist, as late as 1876, in the face of a wide, complex world, interest herself in the likes of a Gwendolen Harleth? As it turns out, only part of *Daniel Deronda* will have to do with Gwendolen and the consequences of her being beautiful or not beautiful; but by connecting Gwendolen with Deronda, and thus with the whole nation of the Jews, George Eliot gives her heroine startling importance. And simultaneously diminishes her.

Well before the Jewish plot begins, as Gwendolen is reflecting with characteristic self-centeredness about the man she will marry, that "the chief question was, how far his character and ways might answer her wishes," Eliot in her most sonorous and public voice interrupts to phrase the question she begged by putting Deronda's questions first:

> Could there be a slenderer, more insignificant thread in human history than this consciousness of a girl, busy with her small inferences of the way in which she could make her life pleasant?—in a time, too, when ideas were with fresh vigour making armies of themselves, and the universal kinship was declaring itself fiercely: when women on the other side of the world would not mourn for the husbands and sons who died bravely in a common cause, and men stinted of bread on our side of the world heard of that willing loss and were patient: a time when the soul of man was waking to pulses which had for centuries been beating in him unheard, until their full sum made a new life of terror or of joy.
>
> What in the midst of that mighty drama are girls and their blind visions? They are the Yea or Nay of that good for which men are enduring and fighting. In these delicate vessels is borne onward through the ages the treasure of human affections. (Chapter 11)

The too-resounding "answer" to the question of the relative importance of history and what Henry James called "the mere young thing" is inadequate, vague, sentimental. In fact *Daniel*

*Deronda* vindicates its choice of Gwendolen as its heroine by its vision of her consciousness, and not because it identifies her with higher things important to masses of people. The historical phenomenon the novel is most closely concerned with is a small movement; the actual public event it heralds, the establishment of a Jewish state in Palestine, was not yet history, since it was to occur years after George Eliot died.

Zionism emerged in the 1860s from the debate between assimilationist and traditionalist European Jews. George Eliot was interested in its argument for "separateness with communication." Both the prejudice against the Jews and the Zionist solution dramatized her preoccupations—the social, moral, and psychological effects of links between people. She aimed to write a novel that would help English readers by teaching them to know and love a race they despised. To that end she wanted to create Jewish characters they would find sympathetic: so Deronda is first presented, cleverly, as a noble type of young Englishman, and later revealed to be a Jew. The publisher as well as the author of *Deronda* anticipated that the conversion of the English would be difficult: in an effort to offset possible suspicions of its foreign-sounding title, John Blackwood advertised the novel as a story of English life. The early chapters bear him out, as they focus on Gwendolen. Quite like Gwendolen, they lead one on. Eliot did not acknowledge this: she was irritated by readers who "talk of nothing in it but Gwendolen," and insisted that she "meant everything in the book to be related to everything else there." F. R. Leavis complained that the novel splits into two parts, but the complementarity of these parts is palpable and strange and interesting, like Daniel's and Gwendolen's.

Deronda is struck by the cool, aristocratic young girl he notices in the murky continental gambling "hell" because she is spectacularly winning, widely admired, and, clearly, playing a part while she plays her game. The xenophobia Charlotte Brontë challenged by having Lucy Snowe fall in love with Paul Emanuel is ironically involved in the dark young Jew's horror at the sight of a classic English beauty, pale, self-controlled, and nearly marmoreal, a version of the national goddess of love, being elbowed and jostled in a heterogeneous foreign crowd. The English heroine is traditionally idealized as an island separated from others by her cool boundaries, aloof in her fastidious chastity; and the continent, in English novels, is often suggestive of sin. When we move from inside Daniel's head to inside Gwendolen's we find that she is entertaining "visions of being followed by a *cortège* who would worship her as a goddess of luck and watch her play as a directing augury." She reflects as she basks in admiration that "such things had been known of male gamblers; why should not a woman have a like supremacy?" Her silly question is oddly like Deronda's serious ones: it shows a similar dividedness of mind. They are equally self-conscious persons: that is why she both provokes and responds to the stare that reveals the division in his "whole being."

Her own secret visions are working together with the admiration of the onlookers to buoy up Gwendolen's pose as a woman unlike other women, more like a sylph, a spirit, a goddess, even a man. When Deronda's questions mysteriously imprint themselves on her consciousness they have the opposite effect: they sap her confidence and make her lose at the game the lies helped her win. Daniel is distressed by being attracted to a gambling woman he cannot approve of, and Gwendolen is discomfited by a solemn stare in which she sees her own self-critical feelings reflected; she loses faith in herself and can no longer act the goddess part. Yet neither her mind nor his controls the wheel: the goddess in Gwendolen's mind, and the devils at play with whom the playing gamblers are compared as Deronda surveys them, suggest that a supernatural force is exercising some "coercion" over both of them. Or is it simply sex, mystified, half-apprehended as sinful and forbidden, and therefore overbearing in its power?

Gwendolen wants to be a goddess; Daniel (who is not judged for a parallel temerity) wants to judge like a god. The exactly equal balance in them of strong desire and strong denial of desire is what links them from the first, makes their union at once nearly palpable and utterly impossible. The novel places them opposite one another as if to promise fulfillment of the reasonable expectation that their meeting of minds is a prelude to a meeting of bodies. But they never do come together; their destinies only intersect. They provoke in one another a negative apprehension of desire that places them in a permanent polarized relation. Deronda's awareness that Gwendolen has been shaken by his stare moves him to act to save her: secretly, later, he goes to redeem the necklace she has had to pawn to pay her gambling debt; he sends it to her anonymously, but she knows it is he who sends it. (Connections multiply: the necklace was her dead father's; the pawnbroker is a Jew; Deronda, who will discover he is a Jew, is taking a paternal or maternal part in her life. From another man, later, Gwendolen will receive another necklace, and that will damn, not save her.) The bond between Deronda and Gwendolen is a peculiarly intense and uncomfortable type of those connections between separate selves that George Eliot insists are the vital parts of human lives. But Daniel's and Gwendolen's feelings cannot lead to a sexual action, a marriage or a divorce. The novel leaves man and woman, Jew and Gentile, separate but connected: their spiritual union is affirmed, at the end, and they part forever.

*Daniel Deronda* sets out to counter prejudice and preach brotherhood, but it best expresses a tragic consciousness of the opposed compulsions to connect with another and to remain separate, a consciousness that is intrinsic to the heroine's story. This is related to other paradoxes. The novel tells of a merely titular hero's languid progress toward performing an only visionary, preordained action that will occur in another world (Palestine). A ghostly world of struggling good and evil, meanwhile, shadows the "real" one. Deronda's "discovery" that he is a Jew is simply a worldly explanation of a truth that the prophet Mordecai already knows. Things that do not happen are the most important events in *Daniel Deronda*: Gwendolen does not, for instance, murder her husband, or marry the man she loves. She is the heroine of this novel, which is about both the world we know and a world beyond it, because of her flashy "iridescent" consciousness, in which the true and the not true, the real and the not real, the beautiful and the not beautiful, the good and the not good, take turns at mutual suffusion, and become more and less real. It is very significant that *Daniel Deronda* begins by asking questions.


The assumptions that underlie the narrative are the assumptions of psychoanalysis (which was to emerge in the actual world even later than Zionism: George Eliot, like Mordecai in the novel, was prophetic). Deronda's story is about finding his true self, his identity and his vocation; he does so after discovering the truth about his origins in an encounter with his rejecting mother. To tell Gwendolen's story the narrator takes an opposite approach that implies the same theory. Anticipating popular novelists of a hundred years later, Eliot first exhibits her heroine frozen in a glamorous pose, and then proceeds to probe beneath appearances, and to move backward in time to account for them, so as to reduce to common humanity a creature who had seemed finished, remote, and extraordinary.* The first of the novel's eight books is called "The Spoiled Child"; from it we learn most of what a psychoanalyst would need to know, beginning with the facts that Gwendolen's father died when she was very young, and that her mother remarried, losing most of her money and acquiring four "superfluous" daughters. Vaguely guilty for having led her own life, and having bungled it and injured her oldest child, Mrs. Davilow dotes on Gwendolen. The spoiled child develops a strong sense of independence with the notion that she is unique among young women. † Used to being indulged, she is self-indulgent. As a little girl she found it too troublesome to get out of bed to fetch her mother's medicine, and once, in a murderous fit of irritation, she strangled her sister's canary. This weird violent detail is ominous. Gwendolen is high-strung, impulsive,

---

* For this technique see, for instance, the beginning of Judith Krantz's *Scruples* (1978).

† There is a daunting superfluity of women in *Daniel Deronda*: three Meyrick girls, three Mallinger girls, three illegitimate Grandcourt daughters, Gwendolen's sisters, and the three Mompert girls she is almost engaged to teach. Gwendolen's sense of distinction is understandably uncommon.

neurotic. She is terrified of a picture of a dead face and a figure fleeing from it. She is terrified of open spaces. Her fear of the world's wideness and her awareness of her own vulnerability are symptoms of her intelligence: the world that acknowledges her heroine's preeminence is indeed very small, secluded, false. Willed ignorance keeps her snug and smug in it most of the time: she orders that the picture be locked behind a panel. But it is her curse and her tragedy—and ultimately also her salvation—to be afflicted by sudden wild apprehensions of wider worlds and unknown modes of being. The sense of her labile consciousness was what led Deronda to stare and to ponder whether she was good or evil, and it commands Eliot's attention and ours. It has something to do with her being beautiful or not beautiful, and with its being hard to decide which.

Gwendolen wants to be a heroine: that is, she wants to be different, remarkable, important, admired, even weighed for her moral significance as Deronda weighs her. Seeing her dressed in her pale green and silver, like a sea serpent, in the casino at Leubronn, and hearing her bright talk among the dull people she knows, we are so persuaded of her superiority as almost to credit her pretensions. A mistress of appearances, she also can cut through them with the skill of a satirical novelist of manners: grandiose Gwendolen has something like a novelist's overview of social life. George Eliot, who assesses her with such acuteness, seems fascinated in spite of herself, rather like Deronda, as she admires a fellow creature doomed by her own self-image. We too cannot but admire the play of light on Gwendolen's iridescence, and enjoy the illusion of a play between surface and depths; we wonder, like Deronda, what she means, both what she signifies and what she has in mind, and like him we are aware that those two different things may melt together. Gwendolen wants "to be happy—not to go on muddling away my life as other people do, being and doing nothing remarkable." Therefore she wants, George Eliot observes sharply, to do "whatever she could do so as to strike others with admiration and get in that reflected way a more ardent sense of living." Others are important to Gwendolen only as negatives of what she would be, or as potential admirers; she has no role models, no plot in mind, because her grand aspirations are too vague. The narrator comments that "her thoughts never dwelt on marriage as the fulfilment of her ambition; the dramas in which she imagined herself a heroine were not wrought up to that close" (Chapter 4). When she becomes engaged her half-sisters, delighted, think that "real life was as interesting as 'Sir Charles Grandison' "; Gwendolen's more original imagination and fiercer desires make her want more than the love between ladies and gentlemen that is sketched in novels of manners. Her "uncontrolled reading," the narrator tells us sarcastically, consisted "chiefly in what are called pictures of life," but it has failed to enlighten her about such unpleasant facts of life as that men take and cast off mistresses, and then ask foolish virgins to be their wives. What George Eliot called "Silly Novels by Lady Novelists"—romances that lay claim to being realistic— have shaped Gwendolen's ideas about herself; or perhaps the point is that Gwendolen's ideas about herself can be most accurately described with reference to novels:

> She rejoiced to feel herself exceptional; but her horizon was that of the genteel romance where the heroine's soul poured out in her journal is full of vague power, originality, and general rebellion, while her life moves strictly in the sphere of fashion; and if she wanders into a swamp, the pathos lies partly, so to speak, in her having on her satin shoes. (Chapter 6)

Her aspirations are as incoherent as her preoccupations are trivial; indeed, they are fed by trivia, they are trivia's foil. She enjoys being the most brilliant and beautiful young woman in her set, for whom a splendid marriage is generally anticipated, and thrives on being treated like "a princess in exile" at home. Her feeling of being unique is a reflex of everything silly and false in her life and the lives of all society girls.

Yet there is something special and splendid about Gwendolen

in her bright energy, in a world where there is nothing for her to do with herself. She spends herself in games and play-acting, and deludes herself with illusions, because there is no work, no fair destiny, available. Part of Gwendolen's problem is the problem of every sensitive ambitious individual, man or woman, in England as George Eliot saw it toward the end of her life. Daniel Deronda, too, cannot find an occupation, and he drifts idly, going to Leubronn, sitting on the Thames in a little boat, until he is called to take on the Zionist mission and leave England and Europe for good. The effect of comparing the heroine's quest to his rare story is poignant: Deronda does not seek to pursue a vocation, like Lydgate in *Middlemarch*, but rather to find something worth doing. If it is true that Gwendolen Harleth is sillier than Dorothea Brooke, it is also important that she lacks Dorothea's independent income and therefore is more powerless. Like Clarissa's and Elizabeth Bennet's, Lucy Snowe's and Isabel Archer's, Gwendolen's destiny is involved with the need and the desire for money and social status. Like Deronda, she is a good-looking young person tenuously connected to aristocratic circles where people with money spend it on entertaining themselves; like him, she is perceived as decorative, and expected to do nothing serious. Gwendolen lacks the moral passion that leads Dorothea to make the dry scholar Casaubon her intellectual idol; she is also a victim of economic insecurity, and of diminished hope and opportunity in a post-Reform world past reforming. Rich Dorothea thinks of building cottages for the poor, and ends married well to a politician. But art, not social work, is the place to look to for changes in the world *Deronda* portrays. For a young woman who has enjoyed being prized as an artifact, this is especially interesting.

George Eliot had written of beautiful young women before: of childlike and ignorant Hetty Sorrel, in *Adam Bede*, and "infantine" Rosamond Vincy of Middlemarch, with her serpentine neck like Gwendolen's. Eliot's heroines, Romola and Dorothea and Dinah Morris and Maggie Tulliver, are, in contrast to them, creatures of noble mold and queenly bearing, with nothing of the fashion plate. Critics have studied photographs of George Eliot and passages like this one and concluded the harsh judgment of pretty girls was an expression of jealousy and spite:

> "Do you call yourself a raw country girl?" said Lydgate, looking at her with an involuntary emphasis of admiration, which made Rosamond blush with pleasure. But she remained simply serious, turned her long neck a little, and put up her hand to touch her wondrous hair-plaits—an habitual gesture with her as pretty as any movements of a kitten's paw. Not that Rosamond was in the least like a kitten: she was a sylph caught young and educated at Mrs. Lemon's.

Rosamond, *rosa mundi*, is worldly, a travesty of the Rose, an acidulous footnote to romance. In the quite-as-romantically named Gwendolen, Eliot rewrote Rosamond with sympathy. The increment of complexity is suggested by a comparison of the name "Vincy," with its hard hint of conquering (and also of Rosamond's plain father, the mayor of Middlemarch), to "Harleth," which reminds us both of Clarissa and of the fact that her surname sounded like "harlot." In *Daniel Deronda* George Eliot more thoroughly analyzes the delicate relationship between "the set of the head" and "the hunger of the inner self for supremacy." Gwendolen's beauty is both a clue to her moral nature and a factor in it. George Eliot's extension of her sympathies to embrace the conventionally beautiful (or not beautiful) Gwendolen irradiates *Daniel Deronda* with the sympathy for strangers the novel preaches.

Shortsighted Dorothea Brooke suffers because she cannot see as the world sees, but Gwendolen's "long sight," which makes her good at recognizing faces at parties, signifies the worldliness it serves. She sees her own beauty as a commodity to be treasured and profitably disposed of. She spends a lot of time looking at the mirror; she kisses her image in the glass. Since she delights in herself as she is, maidenly and separate, she is passionately a virgin: "she objected, with a sort of physical repulsion, to being directly made love to. With all her imaginative delight in being adored, there was a certain fierceness of maidenhood in her" (Chapter 7). For Gwendolen Harleth, as for Clarissa Harlowe, "the life of passion had begun negatively in her." After her handsome cousin Rex tried to take her hand, she ran, distressed, to her mother:

> Gwendolen gave way, and letting her head rest against her mother, cried out sobbingly, "Oh mamma, what can become of my life? there is nothing worth living for!"
>
> "Why, dear?" said Mrs. Davilow. Usually she herself had been rebuked by her daughter for involuntary signs of despair.
>
> "I shall never love anybody. I can't love people. I hate them."
>
> "The time will come, dear, the time will come."
>
> Gwendolen was more and more convulsed with sobbing; but putting her arms around her mother's neck with an almost painful clinging, she said brokenly, "I can't bear any one to be very near me but you." (Chapter 7)

The spoiled child, enclosed in her beauty, cut off from everybody but her mother by her own body, despairs of living. Her question, "What can become of my life?," occurs to her when it does because her girl's life depends on her marrying, or making a connection with others. She suspects—and the novel's omens lead us to suspect also—that such a connection will destroy her.

Mrs. Davilow vaguely depends on time to change her daughter's attitude. Unwilling to divulge the details of the marital unhappiness she herself has suffered twice, she has told her daughter nothing about sex, conspiring in her silence with novels and with the whole world that deludes girls. Gwendolen therefore has no idea of "unmanageable forces in the state of matrimony, but regarded it as altogether a matter of management, in which she would know how to act" (Chapter 28). She "had about as accurate a conception of marriage—that is to say, of the mutual influences, demands, duties of man and woman in the state of matrimony—as she had of magnetic currents and the law of storms" (Chapter 27). *Daniel Deronda* criticizes "civilized" society for concealing and lying about the strange invisible forces that in truth rule the lives of men and women. The "dynamic" quality Deronda felt in Gwendolen's glance and suspected to be of demonic origins is one piece of evidence of those forces. (It is worth noting that the "laws" governing magnetism and storms, the invisible forces of nature that are compared to the "mutual influences" of couples, explain them inadequately; preaching the saving power of knowledge, George Eliot repeatedly comes up against mystery. *Daniel Deronda* creditably depicts Jewish life, but its persuasively foreign "Jewish part" is less anthropological than mystical. The visionary Mordecai's prophetic passion, expressed in archaic exhortations, is the strange heart of the Deronda story.)

Gwendolen has been produced by a world that conceals the truth, and she has thrived in that world, so concealing the truth makes her feel good. She enjoys exchanging flirtatious innuendoes with the insinuating Grandcourt, a man of thirty-five who is very rich, cool, aloof, and in line to inherit the entailed property of Deronda's adoptive father, Sir Hugo Mallinger. Gwendolen's self-possessed, careless air attracts him. At the dizzying height of his courtship, Grandcourt's cast-off mistress seeks Gwendolen out to tell her her story and to demand, for the sake of her illegitimate son, that the younger woman refuse Grandcourt. Lydia Glasher is a terrifying, near-allegorical apparition for Gwendolen: "it was as if some ghastly vision had come to her in a dream and said, 'I am a woman's life' " (Chapter 14). The true "vision" contradicts the pretty, false "drama" of flirtation in a gay country house; the history Lydia recounts has the superior reality of truths unacknowledged by polite society. Mrs. Glasher abandoned her husband and child for Grandcourt, who is now about to abandon her. Neither frail nor delicate at thirty-five, she is "a lost vessel after whom nobody would send out an expedition of search," while Grandcourt is "seen in harbour with his colours flying, registered as seaworthy as ever" (Chapter 30).

After she first decides to meet Lydia, Gwendolen "turned back to rejoin the company, with that sense of having something to conceal which to her nature had a bracing quality and helped her to be mistress of herself" (Chapter 14). What she represses propels her into action. As a consequence of the interview she leaves England for the continent. While Deronda observes her losing at the tables at Leubronn, Grapnell & Co., in charge of her mother's money, are failing, too. It appears that organized capitalism is an ally of the economic system based on the inheritance of lands according to rules of legitimacy, primogeniture, and entail, which keeps power in the hands of the few, and women's hands away from power. The system that ensures that Grandcourt and not Sir Hugo Mallinger's daughters will inherit Sir Hugo's lands, and that Mrs. Glasher's illegitimate son will have nothing, conspires with chance and convention, too, to push Gwendolen into Grandcourt's arms.

Gwendolen returns from Leubronn to find her bewildered mother depending on her. Grandcourt's note requesting permission to call comes as a last chance: Gwendolen seems destined to be a governess. When she learns Grandcourt pursued her to the continent and missed her, she is flattered. She is too young and bold and eager for admiration to turn away from what she fears: "The young activity within her made a warm current through her terror and stirred towards something that would be an event—towards an opportunity in which she could look and speak with the former effectiveness" (Chapter 26). Those elements of Gwendolen's nature that Grandcourt's whole being opposes—her spontaneity, hopefulness, energy, warmth—are paradoxically activated to accept him. Circumstances speed the process: the servant who has brought his note waits for an answer; her mother wonders aloud if he has already heard of their poverty. Gwendolen has "a vision" of what a rich son-in-law might do for her mother. To write "No" in answer to the note, she reflects, is to cut off all possibility; to say "Yes" to just a visit, she tells herself, is not quite to make a commitment. Sending off "Miss Harleth's" compliments to "Mr. Grandcourt," Gwendolen enjoys the comforting illusion of having the upper hand that handling the amenities well always gives her. She has made the most of a dramatic moment; she has ensured the possibility of further drama. She has also, of course, rehearsed her consent to marry.

Grandcourt is fatally made for her. She is at her most brilliant and glittering, her most heroine-ish, in precisely the sort of mutually guarded, teasing encounters of leashed opponents that he invites. After reading "the wondrous scene where Gwendolen accepts Grandcourt," and thus escapes being interviewed for a job as governess to the daughters of a Mrs. Mompert, John Blackwood wrote to George Eliot:

> You kept me uncertain up to the last moment as to whether it was to be Yes or No. I had not the heart to tell her to say No and send the bright creature to be "looked over" by Mrs. Mompert and all the hopeless gloom she foresees so clearly. This feeling in my mind proves I think the surpassing skill of your workmanship.

Like the heroine, the reader is subjected to a pressure that runs counter to reason and good judgment. It is exerted by the compelling structure of romantic story, the literary analogue to the impulse that moves Gwendolen toward tragedy. The wisest of novelists can only make us ruefully conscious of how well it perversely possesses us.

An irrational, unspoken force beyond language accounts for Grandcourt's hold on Gwendolen. She finds his use of silence and innuendo erotically exciting: "his reticence gave her some inexplicable, delightful consciousness" (Chapter 29). His bored style of mingled platitudes and formalities provokes her to stir him to passion or originality. Inarticulate forces that move solid bodies together—sex, storms, and magnetism—escape laws and language; reticence, the withholding of language, may be powerful by suggesting the existence of hidden power. While "suitors must often be judged as words are, by the standing and the figure they make in polite society" (Chapter 28), George Eliot writes, the invisible interpersonal substance of a courtship escapes language: "the subtly-varied drama between man and woman is often such as can hardly be rendered in words put together like dominoes, according to obvious fixed marks" (Chapter 27). The novelist renders mutual tensions by concentrating on tiny movements, gestures, and pauses:

"But I am very unreasonable in my wishes," said Gwendolen, smiling.

"Yes, I expect that. Women always are."

"Then I will not be unreasonable," said Gwendolen, taking away her hand and tossing her head saucily. "I will not be told that I am what women always are."

"I did not say that," said Grandcourt, looking at her with his usual gravity. "You are what no other woman is."

"And what is that, pray?" said Gwendolen, moving to a distance with a little air of menace.

Grandcourt made his pause before he answered. "You are the woman I love."

"Oh what nice speeches!" said Gwendolen, laughing. The sense of that love which he must once have given to another woman under strange circumstances was getting familiar. (Chapter 28)

The spoiled child arrogantly contemptuous of her mother and sisters has been brought up to effect the betrayal of Lydia that is symbolic betrayal of her whole sex. Grandcourt's mistress is the ruling spirit of Gwendolen's eventual punishment. Lydia Glasher sends Gwendolen a curse along with her wedding gift of Grandcourt's mother's diamonds; like Clarissa Harlowe's father's curse, it is the potent formula that is on some level responsible for the crucial events that torment the heroine, a creature determined by literary conventions.

Gwendolen's and Grandcourt's mutual consciousness of "nice speeches" and unspoken ironies whets their matched opposing appetites for control. Early in the courtship there is a sinister little scene in which Gwendolen parries flatteries as she beats the (rhododendron) bushes with a gold-handled whip which she accidentally lets go of. (Rosamond Vincy, accepting Lydgate, dropped a chain she was crocheting.) Grandcourt is of course the real owner of the symbol of male and class authority; Gwendolen is playing a game according to his rules. Sexlessly bald like a baby, he is also bald like the men in front rows at burlesque houses, exhausted by a whole erotic lifetime with Lydia Glasher, needing the perverse for stimulation (therefore defining Gwendolen as perverse, and making her so). He is bald, too, like hairless creatures from alien phyla; he is a lizard, an alligator, a crab, a serpent to match Gwendolen's serpent aspect, a creature of the sea for all that he owns extensive tracts of the earth. (He is doomed inevitably to be lost at sea, in a novel where the relationship of destiny to character is ironic.) He is a shell, a relic: thoroughly bored and cold, "inert," passive, numb, in some sense he is already dead. He is perfectly conventional because there is nothing left of him but the exoskeleton of human life: he has been reamed out. His pleasures are refined: we first see him at characteristic play, inflicting mental torture on a whining female dog by deliberately caressing her rival. He does not exactly want to marry Gwendolen in order to torture Lydia Glasher or Lush, his hanger-on and Lydia's partisan, but their pain enhances his pleasure. He wants to marry Gwendolen because she is so perfect a specimen, and also because she is reluctant. He relishes knowing she knows about Lydia and does not dare to speak to him about it; her ladylike silence about sex makes her his partner in concealing his sexual history, makes him sexually her master. What they do not say loads their connection with a meaning that binds them together as if in a parody of silent sympathy.

In order to get the sense of self that Gwendolen gets from controlling unseen and unknown inner forces, Grandcourt inflicts himself on others. The punishments and silences he imposes on her after their marriage are terrible analogues of what she has always imposed on herself; their marriage grimly dramatizes her heroine's divided consciousness. Grandcourt is an ally of her conventional self. The novelist's Victorian reticence obliges us to speculate about the Grandcourts' sexual life, but there is a suggestion of what must come later in a moment during courtship. Complacently, Gwendolen had been reflecting:

Grandcourt's behavior as a lover had hardly at all passed the limit of an amorous homage which was inobtrusive as a wafted odour of roses, and spent all its effect in a gratified vanity. One day, indeed, he had kissed not her cheek but her neck a little below her ear; and Gwendolen, taken by surprise, had started up with a marked agitation which made him rise too and say, "I beg your pardon—did I annoy you?" "Oh, it was nothing," said Gwendolen, rather afraid of herself, "only I cannot bear—to be kissed under my ear." She sat down again with a little playful laugh, but all the while she felt her heart beating with a vague fear: she was no longer at liberty to flout him. . . . Her agitation seemed not uncomplimentary, and he had been contented not to transgress again. (Chapter 29)

The shift from Gwendolen's consciousness to Grandcourt's makes apparent the extent of their mutual embroilment: Grandcourt is, like Gwendolen, a prisoner of their power struggle. Before marriage, Gwendolen finds their interviews exciting because he allows her to think she is controlling him, and "Gwendolen had not considered that the desire to conquer is itself a sort of subjection" (Chapter 10). She is excited by controlling her own real "vague fear" of sex and him. Meanwhile, Grandcourt's prenuptial pleasure is served by fooling her and by watching her fool herself—and by fooling himself, too, thinking the sign of repugnance is "not uncomplimentary." They will thoroughly torment one another. George Eliot might argue that the specific bedroom tactics of Grandcourt's anger are unimportant. Marriage is the epitome of human interdependence; Gwendolen is constrained to see the world through her husband's consciousness, stained as if by a clouded glass.

The nature of their connection prevents Grandcourt and Gwendolen from presenting themselves to one another as other than composed and controlled. At passion's very extremity, they seem passionless. So, when near the end they appear in the harbor at Genoa to go out in the little boat that takes them to catastrophe, the crowd of poor Italians stands and admires them as *objets d'art*, creatures in a play, a mannequin and a statue:

And when they came down again at five o'clock, equipped for their boating, the scene was as good as a theatrical representation for all beholders. This handsome, fair-skinned English couple manifesting the usual eccentricity of their nation, both of them proud, pale, and calm, without a smile on their faces, moving like creatures who were fulfilling a supernatural destiny—it was a thing to go out and see, a thing to paint. The husband's chest, back, and arms, showed very well in his close-fitting dress, and the wife was declared to be like a statue. (Chapter 54)

As the narrator assumes the Italians' point of view, our sense of Gwendolen's hidden distress is heightened: here as in the first chapter of *Daniel Deronda* the heroine's inner life is suggested as she is marveled at for her appearance. Her striking attitude of self-control, as in the casino scene, masks powerlessness; artifice is the shelter and the manifestation of the demonic. Precisely when Gwendolen and Grandcourt seem most absolutely masters of themselves they are puppets, "creatures who were fulfilling a supernatural destiny," in the hands of dark forces beyond their control.

When they pretend to be superior creatures, *Daniel Deronda* insists, people are at their most human; and their "unnatural" behavior is evidence of "supernatural" forces. This argument is developed through an extended play on the words "acting" and "action." It is only the bluff baronet Sir Hugo Mallinger who says, "There is no action possible without a little acting" (Chapter 33), but his aphorism is taken seriously in this novel, which questions the possibility of sincere or effective action in the world, and of a conventional narrative "action" or plot in a novel. Plays, George Eliot writes, are, unlike novels, confined to "the clumsy necessities of action," and cannot show "the subtler possibilities of feeling" (Chapter 4); this novel takes pains to show it is hard to draw a line between feeling and pretending to feel, and also between real actions and visions of acts. As the unseen and unnamed move in minds and merge with reality to alter it, reality appears unreal, becomes so. As one character says, "events come upon us like evil enchantments: and thoughts, feel-

ings, apparitions in the darkness are events—are they not?"
(Chapter 51). The important emotions in *Daniel Deronda* are
those that defy expression in action or in language. Gwendolen
does not kill Grandcourt, but Grandcourt does die of her wanting him to die, of their hellish marriage, which he cannot handle
except by going out to sea with her in a little boat he can't handle
any better; she kills him by inaction, by taking the moment when
she might have thrown him a rope to recognize her desire for him
to drown, and to go into a shock of self-awareness that paralyzes
her.* "I saw my wish outside me" (Chapter 56), she says of the
moment when the dead face of her drowning husband appeared
to her eyes either not real or more than real, less like a man than
like the dead face in the picture hidden behind the panel, of
death and the fear of death. She confesses to Deronda and he
absolves her like a priest or a psychoanalyst; if she is not technically guilty of murder, still she suffers from imagining she has
sinned, or from committing a sin in imagination. She is purged
by suffering; she may be imagined even as learning from her sin
of omission to abandon whatever remaining credulousness she
has about the importance of what seems to be, of what comes to
pass in the world.


Gwendolen acts as if she were onstage in the "natural" course of
her life as a nineteenth-century society girl. The world in which
she is successful enjoys *tableaux vivants*, and she is good at them.
At Offendene, she plays Hermione in *A Winter's Tale*, a statue
who is to come to life at the sound of a chord struck on the
piano. The spectators are meant to be awed at first by her perfect
control of her body, its subjugation to an overall design, and
then amazed when Hermione moves. But as the faithful servant,
played by Mrs. Davilow, commands the music, and as the pianist

---

* Catherine Arrowpoint, the heiress who unlike Gwendolen defies convention
and marries the man she loves, is linked to the heroine's moment of paralysis
and truth by an anti-drowning image: " 'Why should I not marry the man who
loves me, if I love him?' said Catherine. To her the effort was something like the
leap of a woman from the deck into the lifeboat." (Chapter 22)

strikes "a thunderous chord," a terrible thing happens to Gwendolen. The noise makes a panel swing open and reveal the picture of the dead face and the figure in flight from it:

> Everyone was startled, but all eyes in the act of turning towards the opened panel were recalled by a piercing cry from Gwendolen, who stood without change of attitude, but with a change of expression that was terrifying in its terror. She looked like a statue into which a soul of Fear had entered: her pallid lips were parted; her eyes, usually narrowed under their long lashes, were dilated and fixed.

Genuine emotion freezes the pretend-statue pretending to come to life; the hidden picture of death interferes with the pretense of magical rebirth. The mother goes to the side of her stricken daughter and has the reviving effect she was meant to have in the performance: "the touch of her mother's arm had the effect of an electric charge; Gwendolen fell on her knees and put her hands before her face" (Chapter 6). Later, Gwendolen seizes a slender chance to save face by pretending she had been pretending all along: when the musician Klesmer, who struck the chord, politely suggests Gwendolen's scream of terror was deliberate, and praises it as well-acted, she chooses to believe he has indeed been fooled, so as to fool herself.

Being a woman seems to her to slide into being an actress; therefore it occurs to Gwendolen, when her mother loses her money, that instead of marrying Grandcourt or becoming a governess, she might be able to live independently by going onstage. Even before she was poor, "having been once or twice to the Théâtre Français, and also heard her mama speak of Rachel, her waking dreams and cogitations as to how she would manage her destiny sometimes turned on the question whether she would become an actress like Rachel, since she was more beautiful than that thin Jewess" (Chapter 6). Gwendolen's idea that beauty is all an actress needs is, like her casual contempt of Jews, a clue to her shallowness. Her notion that it is but a small step from managing well in drawing rooms to shining on the stage of Europe is a silly girl's. On the other hand, she is correct, or at least conventional, in seeing the actress's life as the aesthetic alternative to a governess's. Like a governess, an actress is a sort of professionalized lady, the epitome of her accomplishments and her appearance(s), a complete and successful creature of masks and pretenses. Like a governess, she trades on her gender while insisting on the preeminence of her spirit over her body. The actress who assumes different "characters" to make a career of her own, who expresses emotion by accepting constraint, who lives off entertaining and being admired, is the lady's shadow self. So is the governess, whose qualifications are a lady's appearance and accomplishments, and whose business it is to train up ladies. George Eliot, who admired *Villette* as a novel with "something almost preternatural in its power," surely remembered how the timid teacher Lucy Snowe saw Vashti-Rachel as a mirror image of herself. The actress is a powerful image in *Deronda* as in *Villette*. She belongs to a demimonde forbidden to proper young ladies, alien to repressed little governesses: she is un-English, and free, rich, famous, as a governess is not. But the actress and the governess are produced by the same society, one that makes acting and governessing a woman's only options outside marriage.

In James's *The Tragic Muse*, the half-Jewish Miriam Rooth, who also would be an actress like Rachel, must put art before life to succeed. Gwendolen cannot do this: she has been made for the "life" of an artificial English lady. The underside of her egotism is a low opinion of herself. Therefore, she believes that those who judge her harshly judge her correctly, and before she decides to risk her life onstage she seeks out the man who had once criticized her singing, to get his opinion of her talent. "Poor thing!" the narrator reflects,

she was at a higher crisis of her woman's fate than in her past experience with Grandcourt. The questioning then, was whether she should take a particular man as a husband. The inmost fold of her questioning now, was whether she need take a husband at all—whether she could not achieve substantiality for herself and know gratified ambition without bondage. (Chapter 23)

The language suggests the specifically female nature of Gwendolen's desire, and its being both gender-based and generic in women as the question of "a particular man" cannot be. The real issue for Gwendolen is not really creative self-expression, and not only subsistence; it is "substantiality," or the sense of solid being and "gratified ambition" for which most women trade their independence when they marry, and which the actress achieves onstage—at another cost.* Gwendolen seeks through acting to experience her own seriousness. Because she does not believe in herself, she accepts Klesmer's decision that she lacks genius, and then she accepts Grandcourt.† Gwendolen lacks the single-mindedness of the woman Daniel Deronda comes finally face to face with at the end of his quest: the professional actress who is his mother.

The Princess Halm-Eberstein appears only briefly in the novel, not to act but to narrate past actions. A spectral figure of a dying woman, she seems to be conjured up by coalescing themes that could not but crystallize in her, a mother, an artist, a Jew. It is significant that an actress is the mother of the paragon of authenticity who saves Gwendolen from her life of artifice: and his mother's being an actress makes ironic her recounting the "historical" facts that support the truth that Deronda is a Jew. The princess was once an imaginative, arrogant girl like Gwendolen, who wanted to achieve substantiality and know gratified ambition. Severely restrained by her Jewish father, she rebelled out-

---

* George Eliot used the word "substantive" in *Middlemarch*, writing of Dorothea as "so substantive and rare a creature."

† George Eliot means us to believe that Klesmer, a Jew and a genius, is absolutely right about Gwendolen, as Deronda is. I want to propose half-seriously that the relationship between realism and fantasy in *Daniel Deronda* may be illustrated by this: the novel is realistic in showing that serious Jewish men find frivolous pale girls mysteriously compelling, and fantastic when it suggests that these serious men find these frivolous girls absolutely transparent.

right, asked no one's advice, and went onstage. Altering the name of her father, Daniel Charisi, she called herself "Alcharisi"; she gave her father's first name to her son, the issue of her marriage to a cousin who died. Talent and hard work made her a success; she was widely celebrated, widely loved, à la Rachel. But, unlike Rachel, she did not love her child, and hated her father and all things Jewish. She chose to have Daniel raised, away from her, as an English gentleman. Sir Hugo Mallinger, an admirer, agreed to adopt him and to keep hidden from him the truth about his ancestry. When she explains all this to her son, the princess insists she is not like other women; women, she says, are imagined to be all alike, and so most of them pretend to be as they are said to be:

> "Every woman is supposed to have the same set of motives, or else to be a monster. I am not a monster, but I have not felt exactly what other women feel—or say they feel, for fear of being thought unlike others. When you reproach me in your heart for sending you away from me, you mean that I ought to say I felt about you as other women say they feel about their children. I did *not* feel that." (Chapter 51)

She insists on the truth of the particular, that all women are not "womanly" and therefore the same. A boldly conceived exception to one of the most cherished "rules" about women, she is portrayed with sympathy as an honest person who admits she does not feel mother-love.

In *Villette*, when Lucy Snowe sees Vashti perform, she is stunned by the sight of a woman transforming herself into art. In *Daniel Deronda* the actress is seen not onstage but in a scene from her private life which she has deliberately arranged as if it were a scene in a play; the heroine does not see her, but the guardian of her conscience does. The Princess Halm-Eberstein, dying, has summoned her son to give him an audience in the manner of a stage queen, with the lighting and the emotions carefully controlled. The control of her life she took for herself has worked in the end against her. Seemingly self-possessed, she is possessed by the antagonists of those spiritual forces which possess the noble prophet Mordecai, whom Daniel has adopted as a father. Seeing her for the first time, Deronda wonders what it is that gives him "a painful sense of aloofness": "her worn beauty had a strangeness in it as if she were not quite a human mother, but a Melusina, who had ties with some world which is independent of ours" (Chapter 51). The princess has been transformed by the world of appearances and play-acting. The world of casinos, where beautiful women dressed in pale green and silver mime Melusinas and appear to be serpents, is a related one. The masks such women assume become the agents of their dissolution.

Social life as *Daniel Deronda* portrays it is like a stage: it oversimplifies, and corrupts. Actions in the world only partially express the soul, but they permanently affect it. Because it is impossible to find anything in this world to which the whole being will consent, the noble Deronda must leave it for Palestine, another world. As for Gwendolen, her story ends in a nonaction: she does not throw a rope to her drowning husband. The self she has concealed leaps out before her eyes, and she sees her wish (for Grandcourt to die) outside her, reflected in the face of her antagonist. The frozen moment beautifully captures one aspect of the heroine's dividedness, and points up the parallel between the conflict inside her and her conflict with a man who would crush by mastering her. Gwendolen's evil part dies with Grandcourt; so does her vitality. With the help of her mother's and Deronda's love, she is just saved. In a world that is wanting, the bruised heroine has nowhere to go but back. In a movement equal and opposite to Deronda's visionary transit to the East, she "reverts" to being the unspoiled girl she never was. Like Blake's Thel, the virgin who runs back shrieking to the Vale of Har after she has seen the world of Generation, Gwendolen returns to a presexual Eden where there are no serpents, no disguises, and also no dangers of dissolving or of being transformed. No, she is not pregnant; so Grandcourt's estate and Sir Hugo's will go to Mrs. Glasher's son. At the end of the story Gwendolen stands stripped of her wealth and position, of her wit and selfpossession. She is become, herself, as a little child. She neither drowns like Maggie Tulliver nor dwindles into reality like Dorothea Brooke; she is translated into an impossible arrested time, where she shucks her heroine's skin to prove she is not the serpent she seemed:

> All that brief experience of a quiet home which had once seemed a dulness to be fled from, now came back to her as a restful escape, a station where she found the breath of morning and the unreproaching voice of birds, after following a lure through a long Satanic masquerade, which she had entered on with an intoxicated belief in its disguises, and had seen the end of in shrieking fear lest she herself had become one of the evil spirits who were dropping their human mummery and hissing around her with serpent tongues. (Chapter 64)

This extraordinary sentence, with a motion both birdlike and serpentine, contrasts the natural springtime world with an apocalyptic vision of terrifying tangled becomings and travestied satanic rebirths. The "artificial" world has terrible, real power: the natural world in its benign aspect is affirmed as "a restful escape," "a station" in a reality in terrible flux. Deronda escapes European society for Palestine; Gwendolen is so much a creature of the world that her only way out is to escape herself. Purged, she miraculously becomes the unspoiled child she never was; the novel comes full circle, to contradict itself.

After she has come to know him a little, Gwendolen coquettishly reminds Deronda of their first encounter, and she asks him what it was that so distressed him when he first saw her gambling. "Is it because I am a woman?" she wants to know. "Not altogether; but I regretted it the more because you were a woman," says Deronda. He explains that "we need that you should be better than we are." And she counters, " 'But suppose *we* need that men should be better than we are,' . . . with a little air of 'check'!" Deronda replies evenly, "That is rather a difficulty" (Chapter 29). And it is, I suppose—outside *Daniel Deronda*.

Deronda is famously a failure as a credible character in fiction. "And as for Deronda himself, I freely confess that I am consumed with a hopeless passion for him," says Theodora, one of the people Henry James invented to have "A Conversation" about *Daniel Deronda*. To which her friend Pulcheria answers shortly, "He is not a man at all." He is an idea of a man, unreal as the Rose, the idealized Other (*der andere*), unattainable, all spirit. One can no more imagine marrying him than his acquaintances the Meyrick sisters can:

"No woman ought to want to marry him," said Mab, with indignation. "*I* never should. Fancy finding out that he had a tailor's bill, and used boot-hooks. . . ." (Chapter 52)

When he goes off in the end to marry dovelike musical Jewish Mirah, who always sits with her hands and feet crossed, one is at a loss to imagine the marriage except as the flight of some Brancusi bird to the world to come, which will prove once for all the unreality of this world. He is, as Henry James in his own person put it, "too abstract by reason of the quantity of soul employed." But he is valid, nevertheless—valid in relation to Gwendolen. Her journey toward a purely ideal connection with a man of soul only is a logical culminating irony of her heroine's story. In Deronda, Gwendolen finds and fails to get what she needs, a man who is "better than we are," and therefore not available. It is the reverse of the story of the Rose. Persuasively, *Daniel Deronda* leads the reader to identify closure with nonfulfillment of the romantic plot, and with the marriage in mind only of the protagonists. That it is all so ingeniously conceived does not "save" Deronda as a character—one would not risk setting him up against, say, Lovelace or even Darcy—but it does mean that Gwendolen's story requires him, and that its dimension of meaning as an exploration of the relation between real women and heroines cannot properly exist without him.

Daniel Deronda is too good to be true: he is intelligent and perfectly handsome and polite and noble and gentle; he has beautiful manners, having been beautifully raised and educated. He is a Grandison of exotic blood, alienated and detached rather than, like Grandison, in the center of a web of family. In his detachment, and mostly in the intense and serious attention he gives to women, his "rare and massive power" of "receptiveness" (Chapter 40), he resembles not Grandison but the rake. For all his ideal quality Deronda is not without appeal to the female erotic imagination; indeed, I think he is, precisely, a figure of feminine fantasy. Sir Hugo Mallinger's jocular remark, which seems to Deronda "a tasteless joke," has its measure of truth: "You are a dangerous young fellow," declares the pleasant baronet, "—a kind of Lovelace who will make the Clarissas run after you instead of your running after them" (Chapter 32). He is attractive to women because of his capacity for understanding and sympathizing with their unhappiness—Gwendolen's, Mirah's, his mother's. As Gwendolen's rival for the reader's attention, Deronda is ineffectual. He is so alive to the nerves of others as to be nearly transparent. That he does not ask about his parentage for fear of giving Sir Hugo pain is as absurd as the fact that he does not, as Steven Marcus puts it, "look down" at himself and see he is a Jew. Listless and deracinated, he is too comfortable in his melancholy to capture a reader's imagination: the passionate dying Mordecai seems more desperate to discover Deronda's identity than he does himself. Daniel is most alive with Gwendolen, especially in the moment at the end of the novel when he realizes that "she was the victim of his happiness." But he is too good to be much with her, too much better than the real casinolike world in which one person's gain is another's loss. Therefore he is off to the mysterious East, so that, as he says, "I may awaken a movement in other minds, such as has been awakened in my own" (Chapter 69). His Zionist enterprise is fixed in the realm of the visionary: like Aeneas he aspires toward establishing a country for his people, but unlike the hero of more heroic times he will not perform but merely conceive the action.

Daniel touches Gwendolen's hand only once, with a "grasp [that] was an entirely new experience to Gwendolen, [who] had never before had from any man a sign of tenderness which her own being had needed" (Chapter 56). She melts. But his tenderness is reserved for Mirah, whom he uninterestingly loves. "Now we can perhaps never see each other again," he tells Gwendolen just before he marries. "But our minds may get nearer." She doesn't answer; what can one say? Instead she sends him a letter (signed "Gwendolen Grandcourt"). He receives it on his wedding day; it is the reverse of the curse she was sent by Mrs. Glasher, a benediction. Now the rejected lover asks the happy one not to grieve for her. She promises to work toward being "one of the best of women," and repeats what she said in her last interview with Deronda, that "it is better—it shall be better with me because I have known you." "I shall live. I shall be better," Gwendolen also assured her mother (Chapter 69). The merely comparative "better" and the future tense that implies process mark her difference from the would-be heroine who would be perfect. The relationship between her and Deronda—eternal, ideal, unconsummated—frees her from the fixed static self that imprisoned and almost destroyed her.

Surely Daniel takes her letter of forgiveness to the East with him, and surely he does not show it to Mirah. It is "more precious than gold and gems" (Chapter 70); presumably it will affect him as thoroughly as Lydia's curse and the diamonds affected Gwendolen. The bond between him and Gwendolen, and not Deronda's marriage, resolves the action of the novel. The mystic union of their minds is the end promised by their first conjunction in the casino.

Some talmudic explication of Mordecai's obliquely validates the novel's use of the courtship plot:

> " 'The Omnipresent,' said a Rabbi, 'is occupied in making marriages.' The levity of the saying lies in the ear of him who hears it; for by marriages the speaker meant all the wondrous combinations of the universe whose issue makes our good and evil." (Chapter 62)

It is the ultimate vindication of the "delicate vessels" idea. A young woman's fate is to be taken seriously because her enterprise, marrying, is the crucial connection, and the emblem of those connections which are at the heart of human life. The Omnipresent was producing evil when Gwendolen married Grandcourt, to whom the worst in her responded; the force of good George Eliot asserts by the "unrealistic" or visionary countermovement of this novel arranges the heroine's final connection with Deronda. Tragedy has liberated Gwendolen from the prison of her self: she has had a horrifying vision of her own subjectivity as the face of her loathed dying husband reflected her heart's desire. The vision of her inner ugliness effectively frees her from being beautiful. Since Leubronn, Deronda has watched and understood her: if Grandcourt's face has reflected her hard will to power and destructiveness, Deronda's has shown her her wonderful iridescent consciousness.

At the end of *Daniel Deronda* the twinned protagonists are spiritually joined in a union higher than Gwendolen's other, worldly marriage, and more significant and resonating than Deronda's. Two odder couples share with this uncoupled pair the place, at the end, that is usually accorded a bride and a groom. The last time we see Gwendolen she is waking in the morning to see the tender mother who has sat up all night with her; the last time we see Deronda he is allowing the soul of the dying Mordecai to pass into him, in a parallel scene of nurturing and rebirth. "Where thou goest, Daniel, I shall go," says Mordecai to his brother-in-law, echoing Ruth to her mother-in-law in the Bible. "Is it not begun? Have I not breathed my soul into you? We shall live together" (Chapter 70). Because he has absorbed Mordecai's spirit as Gwendolen has absorbed his, Deronda, like Gwendolen, shall live, shall be even better; poor, sickly, mystical Mordecai is to him, as he is to Gwendolen, a spiritual beacon, an almost palpable bond with the world beyond. It is a world of unselfish feeling, of nourishing sympathy. Sick Mordecai is Deronda's mother/child, as weak Mrs. Davilow is Gwendolen's; the echo of Ruth to Naomi draws attention to the fact that this novel ends not with a heroine's marriage but with multiple polymorphous pairings.

The name of George Eliot warns against taking hers as a woman's case: and perversely, her name insists that we consider her womanhood. In her life she used many names. As a young girl writing to her friends, she called them and herself, in play, by the names of flowers. More seriously, she was called, she called herself, Mary Ann and Marian Evans, Polly, familiarly, and Pollian. She was Miss Evans and M. E. Lewes and Mrs. Lewes, and finally Mrs. Cross. In private she was Madonna and Madre and Mutter and Mother. To make a name for oneself, "Defoe," say, instead of plain "Foe," or to give oneself a *nom de plume* or multiple names as George Eliot did, is to declare independence of what one has been named, and perhaps from the parents who did the naming. It is as if to claim to be one's own child, one's own parent.

Few successful women writers have been mothers; in *A Room of One's Own* Virginia Woolf mentioned the childlessness of the great novelists, and Tillie Olsen, more recently, has meditated on the conflicting claims of art and motherhood in *Silences*. George Eliot did not in fact have a child, any more than she in fact married G. H. Lewes; she could be defined by the usual criteria as neither a mother nor a wife. Yet she called herself Mrs. Lewes and she called herself Mother, just as she called herself George Eliot.

Sensibly, she did what any intelligent woman who writes would do if she could choose to, and made herself the mother of grown children, not babies. Experience as well as authority argues that it is hard for the mother of babies to write. But a mother left in a roomy nest, looking out from above to consider, benignly, the flight of the young, is in a different position. When she wrote *Daniel Deronda* George Eliot was fifty-six. The Lewes children, who called her "Mutter," were grown: two were married, and there were grandchildren the novelist and her companion considered "ours." Numerous other young people were financially and emotionally dependent on George Eliot. She was occasionally visited by her grown niece and nephew, and she adopted "nieces" and a "nephew," Emily and Mary Cross and their brother John, whom she later married. She had one correspondent, Mrs. Mark Pattison, whom she addressed as "Figliuolina" in letters she sometimes signed "Madre"; another friend, Elma Stuart, she invariably called "My dear daughter Elma," in letters signed "Mother" or the German "Mutter" the Lewes boys used. John Blackwood wrote often to the Leweses about his son, and through a letter from Lewes to Blackwood we can glimpse George Eliot in the act of being a parent:

> Mrs. Lewes begs me to say she thoroughly sympathizes with you there, and that we both think a deficiency of scholastic brilliancy the smallest possible defect where there is good honest heart and brain—*those* are the levers of this world! This is how we have felt about our own boys.

If Jane Austen may be imagined as seeing her heroines from a sister's point of view or an aunt's, George Eliot's view of Gwendolen Harleth is a good stepmother's. *Daniel Deronda* insists there are all kinds of mothers, ranging from the overindulgent to the unfeeling; there are good and bad biological mothers and there are foster mothers like Mrs. Meyrick, who adopts the waif Mirah into her family. In Gwendolen, George Eliot imagined a young woman utterly unlike herself, of the type that had once made her irritable and contemptuous. Gwendolen is conceived without the superiority her creator felt toward Rosamond, and she is judged—with care and grief—as Dorothea is not judged. It is probably presumptuous and fanciful to suggest that George Eliot created Gwendolen Harleth out of her own brain in order to overcome the obstacles in the way of her loving such an unlikely offspring, and even more presumptuous and fanciful to characterize this Olympian, figurative childbirth as evidence of maternal feeling, or as a maternal act. Perhaps I should stop at suggesting that George Eliot dealt at once with personal, intellectual, social, and aesthetic problems in *Daniel Deronda* in such a way as to make them convincingly a set, and that this novel about various forms of love seems to derive from deep fellow-feeling achieved strenuously, with difficulty. George Eliot's vision of the novel as an art form engaged in social action, and creative of human love, is clarified by her compassionate re-vision of the traditional heroine: the narrator's exemplary sympathy for Gwendolen illustrates her Zionist vision of separateness with communication, her novelist's ambition of making the reader feel for unlike persons.

At the time she wrote *Daniel Deronda*, George Eliot was not merely lionized but revered. Her books were selling well, among them a book of extracts called *Wise, Witty, and Tender Sayings in Prose and Verse Selected from the Works of George Eliot.* Admirers wrote to her of having drawn comfort from her words, of having learned how to live from them. A woman Lewes referred to as "an American worshipper" wrote this in a letter to her, which, Eliot decorously replied, she valued "very highly":

> I feel the most intense desire to know you, to actually look at, talk and clasp hands with you. . . . Do you ever receive people *just because they love* you? That is the only excuse for the boldness of this request. . . . I care for you as the embodyment of my highest principles, and after reading your books with me my husband shares my enthusiasm. If we may never see you, we have much true, married happiness to thank you for.

The unmarried instructor in married happiness took great pleasure in the evidence of her effect on the personal lives of her readers. Lewes wrote to one of her admirers:

> what you say about Mrs. Lewes's happiness in her work is true—the pain is there but it is delicious pain after all; and the deep feelings she creates in others react upon herself and make her prize her power.

George Eliot worried, as she wrote, about connecting with the readers she hoped to teach how to make and understand human connections. "The Jewish element seems to me likely to satisfy nobody," she observed nervously in her journal while *Daniel Deronda* was appearing in serial form. Her readers were meant to experience what she called elsewhere the "equivalent center of self" of another human being; the novels were intended to exert the "blessed influence of one true loving human soul on another." As an aging sybil living in semiseclusion, enjoying the domestic happiness with Lewes that she so oddly described as "unspeakable," giving audiences to the few on Sunday afternoons but refraining, in the main, from social life, George Eliot oversaw humanity from the vantage of a benign mother whose grown children are more actively engaged in life than she is. She was widely read; she was looked up to as a fecund creator, the repository of emotional strength. Sympathy and understanding, she preached, are the ties that bind. Dispensing and dispersing these, she connected with people who were not connected to her by blood, the readers who were in effect her children, as Lewes's children were. She made herself a mother in name, by naming.

# ⟨ 5 ⟩

# *The Portrait of a Lady*

> I am what is around me.
>
> Women understand this.
> One is not duchess
> A hundred yards from a carriage.
> —Wallace Stevens

Contemplating the fate of a character in *Adam Bede*, George Eliot explains that, "Hetty had never read a novel: if she had ever seen one, I think the words would have been too hard for her: how then could she find a shape for her expectations?" Poor Hetty, a dairymaid, is seduced and abandoned by the young squire Arthur Donnithorne, and made miserable and mad enough to kill her baby. How might reading a novel have saved her? What kind of novel? Surely George Eliot is not supposing Hetty might have read a novel by George Eliot. What Hetty needed to know was not what George Eliot taught, for one thing, and for another, novelists as a rule mean something other than the book in hand when they moralize about reading novels. Romantic novels—novels such as Hetty might conceivably have read—have more often been warned against than recommended. Stories in which, for instance, the rich young squire who falls in love with the pretty dairymaid marries her are famously dangerous to susceptible, ignorant virgins. Since the eighteenth century, men have complained that novels distort and raise readers' expectations, arouse and enervate women and render them unfit for their domestic duties; on the other side, feminists since Mary Wollstonecraft have condemned popular fiction for leading girls to think (as illiterate Hetty does) only, foolishly, of love. The silly romance-reading young lady is a familiar figure in fiction at least since *Gulliver's Travels* (1726), where the fire in the palace of the Lilliputian queen (the one extinguished by Gulliver's urinary prowess) is traced to the carelessness of a maid of honor who fell asleep reading a romance. The heroine of *The Female Quixote* (1752) by Charlotte Lennox believes every word she reads in seventeenth-century French heroic romances, and therefore imagines the real world is populated almost entirely by lovers prepared to die for her. Commending Lennox's novel as a useful warning for girls, Henry Fielding added that it was also more realistic than its Spanish model: for the idea of a sensible person's head being turned by reading, he wrote, is "more easy to be granted in the Case of a young Lady than of an old Gentleman." (In other words, told about a woman, the story of believing in a fantasy self is a story of everyday life.) Nonsatiric, romantic realism has traditionally been attacked as even more dangerous to credulous females than romance is: a speaker in *The Progress of Romance* (1785), a critical survey and discussion of novels and romances by the novelist Clara Reeve, makes the point that girls sensible enough to know real life cannot bring them an ideal hero will be moved to look on earth for "a fine gentleman in a novel"—to look too high, in other words, like Hetty. So how would reading novels have done anything but encourage the foolish ambitions and dreams of a girl like her?

The standard charge against fiction is that it is untrue, immoral, and therefore threatening to the purity of female readers. Not quite bearing it out, the stereotyped young woman *in* fiction who reads novels is pure, a girl like Charlotte Lennox's Arabella, bright and naïve, full of unfocused, unconscious sexual energy. The portrait of a heroine as a novel-reader is a sketch of an adorably silly creature, someone to be condescended to quite as George Eliot condescends to Hetty, who does not read at all. Lovely Lydia Languish, in Sheridan's 1775 comedy *The Rivals*, reads novels and books about love instead of uplifting, informative works. When she hears her elders coming she scolds her maid to rearrange the literature:

> Here, my dear Lucy, hide these books. Quick, quick!—Fling *Peregrine Pickle* under the toilet—throw *Roderick Random* into the closet—put *The Innocent Adultery* into *The Whole Duty of Man*—thrust *Lord Aimworth* under the sofa—cram *Ovid* behind the bolster—there—put *The Man of Feeling* into your pocket—so, so—now lay *Mrs. Chapone* in sight, and leave *Fordyce's Sermons* open on the table.

Lydia's addiction to the lending library is a coy metaphor for her sexual readiness; reading like hers is a type of sensual indulgence, a pretty girlish *faiblesse* that prepares a girl only for love.

Is it possible that the experience of fiction taught Lydia Languish a thing or two about concealing books, and about other kinds of deception? Can it be that those are the things George Eliot laments Hetty's not having known? In Hardy's *Tess of the D'Urbervilles*, published more than thirty years after *Adam Bede*, another peasant girl, also seduced and abandoned by a man of a higher class, suggests that she might have been saved from being deceived by reading novels. Tess accuses her mother of neglecting her education:

> "Why didn't you tell me there was danger in menfolk? Why didn't you warn me? Ladies know what to fend hands against, because they read novels that tell them of these tricks; but I never had the chance o' learning in that way, and you did not help me!"

From novels Tess and Hetty might have learned some facts: that girls arouse some men who hurt them, and that making love leads to babies. But as farm girls they must have had some idea of some of that, already. The most important things novels would have taught them are fictions, things a clever mother might teach a girl about playing and winning the games of love. Novels show girls how tricky men behave, Tess argues, and teach them the tricks of ladies; she could add, if she knew how, that novels instruct their readers in the sensibility appropriate to those who want to stay ladies, and teach the hypocritical moral lesson of *Pamela*, that chastity is all-important because chastity pays.

From novels Tess and Hetty would have developed a sense (exaggerated) of their own importance, possibilities, destiny, power. They might have learned to be more conscious and careful of themselves, and avoided giving themselves away. A girl who thinks of herself as a potential heroine aspires to strength and seriousness, and such an aspiration, although it leads to other kinds of trouble, corrects the inclination to give in. Hetty and Tess might have gathered from novels, although they might not have put it to themselves in these words, that character is fate, and that actions have consequences. The middle-class heroine is sure of that. Hetty's opposite, she is a girl preoccupied with the shape of her expectations. She is in fact shaped by such expectations as are formed by reading novels; what most engrosses her is the conflict between those expectations and her actual life. Her involvement in this conflict is central in the novel about her life. It is not so much that she anticipates a certain plot, or a particular kind of fine gentleman who will appear and love her; it is rather that she expects her destiny will have a shape and meaning, like a heroine's. That she anticipates becoming a heroine.

After Emma Bovary first makes love with Rodolphe, she is exalted by her recollections of novel-reading:

> She remembered the heroines of novels she had read, and the lyrical legion of those adulterous women began to sing in her memory with sisterly voices [*des voix de soeurs*] that enchanted her. It was as though she herself were becoming part of that imaginary world [*Elle devenait elle-même comme une partie véritable de ces imaginations*], as though she were making the long dream of her youth come true by placing herself in the category of those amorous women she had envied so much.

Stepping outside her bourgeois life into an adulterous relationship is for Emma effectively a step into an alternative world of romance. She sees herself as transformed, imaginary. She responds to her new, intense, unfamiliar experience by recollecting the intense foreign feelings she had as a girl reading, feelings of being transported to another world and of being other than herself. Her fictitious sisters, the other selves she had become then, seem to welcome her as adultery initiates her into a sorority of imaginary adulterous women. When she searched in life for the emotion that had been stirred in her by literature, she found Rodolphe. (The books she had read in her girlhood were as glib.) Her transports in his arms are attempts to replicate those feelings of being lifted outside "real" life which came to her when she secretly read the romances forbidden in the convent, and felt herself embraced not by imaginary lovers, but by the amorous women she wanted to be.

The respectable English novel in the nineteenth century was too chaste to tolerate a heroine as ready to abandon herself to love or to literature as Emma Bovary. The heroine in the English style, the young woman to the English taste, is apparently cold; she proves her passion by the strength with which she restrains a strong desire. A proper heroine must be literate, unlike Hetty, but her relationship with books is usually rather like her relationship with the lover she keeps at a distance until her story's end. Jane Austen's Emma, quite unlike Flaubert's, makes lists of improving books she means to read.

Catherine Morland is addicted to novels, and Anne Elliot reads poetry and Italian, but of Austen's heroines it is Elizabeth Bennet whose connection to literature is most interesting. When Lady Catherine de Bourgh questions her about her education and her sisters', Elizabeth says, "We were always encouraged to read" (*P & P* II, 6). Her pedantic sister Mary must have read improving works, and giddy Lydia probably leafed through sensational novels, but although Elizabeth is easily imagined seated with a book, it is not quite clear what she might read. She insists to the critical company at Netherfield Park that she is "*not* a great reader," but she evidently has a keen and catholic appetite for books. While we ought not overinterpret her being easily distracted from the one in her hands when she overhears a conversation between Caroline Bingley and Mr. Darcy, that picture of her holding but not exactly reading a book is both memorable and significant. It is the conscious heroine's characteristic posture.

When her aunt comes upon her in Albany, she finds Isabel Archer sitting with a book. And therefore, perhaps, Mrs. Touchett recognizes her as a heroine, and proposes to take her to Europe and romance. The heroine of *The Portrait of a Lady* is shown several times with her finger in a book; at one point we even find her self-consciously without one, thinking to herself that she should really be reading as she sits on a bench on her uncle's lawn. Isabel's connection with literature is at once important and rather vague, like those of Clarissa, whose brother suspects her of writing too well, and Elizabeth Bennet, and clever Gwendolen Harleth, whose "wide reading" taught her so little about real life. Like those other verbal girls, Isabel gives other people the impression that she is literary—especially people not literary themselves. Because she seems to have read more than they, they think of her in a muddled way as a girl in a book, or perhaps a girl who writes books. Isabel's hearty brother-in-law, Edmund Ludlow, says he prefers translations to "originals" like her. She is reputed to be a writer, and this rumor makes her seem both intimidating and erotic. Girls who spend their time reading about love are generally supposed to be in training for it; but the young woman who writes (presumably novels) is presumed even today to have some special knowledge of love, probably more than a nice girl should have, and an excessive interest in it that is the more dubious for being theoretical, or general, or abstract. The woman with many lovers is more easily forgiven: she is a victim, poor tainted thing. But the other, the writer, seems more obscurely and profoundly tainted. If the poets make goddesses of women, as Lovelace says, women who write are popularly suspected of compounded *hubris*, of making goddesses of themselves. Meredith's novelist-heroine, Diana, is a case in point. James writes of Isabel Archer that her "reputation of reading a great deal hung about her like the cloudy envelope of a goddess in an epic; it was supposed to engender difficult questions and to keep the conversation at a low temperature" (Chapter 4).* In *The Wings of the Dove* he uses a related image: marveling at a lie Kate Croy has invented to explain her relation to him, Merton Densher reflects that it "served her as the fine cloud that hangs about a goddess in an epic." The false fiction serves, that is, to protect and to halo Kate. A connection with fiction makes a heroine attractively unlike real women, desirable in the way imaginary girls and imaginary worlds are. Isabel's unearned reputation of being a literary woman, and Kate's reprehensible fabrication, surround them with a glamorous haze; and this false "envelope" in the end will determine the fate of each girl's flesh. Her literary inclination is a manifestation of the self-consciousness that determines a novel heroine's destiny.

About Isabel James makes the conventional protest that she is no unattractive bluestocking, not really bookish:

> she used to read in secret and, though her memory was excellent, to abstain from showy reference. She had a great desire for knowledge, but she really preferred almost any source of information to the printed page; she had an immense curiosity about life and was constantly staring and wondering. (Chapter 4)

Every heroine meant to be attractive to readers must prefer life to literature; and at the same time she must partake of fictitiousness, of the condition of art, of goddesshead. Without being laughably a professional "literary woman," like her friend Henrietta Stackpole, the journalist, or the dead poetess-mother

---

* Henry James, *The Portrait of a Lady*, ed. Robert D. Bamberg (New York: W. W. Norton & Co., 1975). I quote throughout from this Norton Critical Edition, a reprint of the 1908 New York Edition, which contains a list of the variants in the earlier, 1880-81, version of the novel, as well as other supplementary material. Chapter rather than page numbers are in parentheses.

of Gilbert Osmond, "the American Corinne," Isabel is literary. Her literary quality is not an accomplishment or a profession but a grace. She uses language wittily and well; she reads her life as if it were a novel. For instance, one of her suitors, Lord Warburton, strikes her as "a hero of romance," and she keeps his proposal a secret from her sister because it "was more romantic to say nothing, and, drinking deep, in secret, of romance, she was as little disposed to ask poor Lily's advice as she would have been to close that rare volume forever" (Chapter 31). Links between women and books are made often in *The Portrait of a Lady*: "I prefer women like books—very good and not too long," Gilbert Osmond observes; Isabel thinks his daughter Pansy is "like a sheet of blank paper—the ideal *jeune fille* of foreign fiction," and hopes "that so fair and smooth a page would be covered with an edifying text"; a woman who has had many lovers is described as "by no means a blank sheet; she had been written over in a variety of hands." And Isabel will conclude in the end of her husband, Osmond, that "she had not read him right." She aims to rewrite the heroine's story, and learns to reread it.

The chaste heroine's identification with the chaste novel is problematic, and, in the end, paradoxical. A talent rather than an accomplishment, innate and inexplicable, her literariness is linked to her sexuality. It is morally ambiguous. The chaste heroine is necessarily at odds with herself. She is at odds with the sexual plot—by definition at odds then with her book. She can triumph only when she and the novel come together in the end, when she takes her destiny in her hands by understanding it is justly her own. Doing that, she accepts the novel's myth that character is fate, and the novel's limiting mandate of closure. Becoming a heroine, realizing her most shapely self, she becomes her best reader, in thrall to her own self-consciousness.

From the first, Isabel Archer rebels against the plot prescribed for girls. "I don't want to begin life by marrying. There are other things a woman can do," she tells her cousin Ralph Touchett as her career begins. Ralph answers, "There's nothing she can do so well." Isabel is expected, determined, doomed to do well. As surely as Clarissa Harlowe has to die and Elizabeth Bennet has to marry Mr. Darcy, as surely as both those young women are the daughters of their parents, James's heroine is destined to be undone by becoming the heroine-victim of her own awareness. That was the idea of the whole thing from the beginning. James conceived Isabel's story as ironic first of all: "The idea of the whole thing," he wrote in his notebook as he planned the novel, "is that the poor girl, who has dreamed of freedom and nobleness, who has done, as she believes, a generous, natural, clear-sighted thing, finds herself in reality ground in the very mill of the conventional." Being who she was, Isabel could not but marry the man who described himself, lightly but rightly, as "convention itself," could not but be caught in the tawdry, banal, melodramatic plot of another woman, her *semblable*, her anti-mother, her nemesis. Her pain is exacerbated by that consciousness of hers, which feels acutely the ironies it finally recognizes as the truth in a heroic feat of vision.

The fact that Isabel's consciousness is where the novel's significant action takes place—James's point of pride—is emphasized by two conspicuous gaps in the story of what happens to her: the first years of her marriage are not shown, and her ultimate fate is not made clear. Like *Daniel Deronda*, which James read with respect, *The Portrait of a Lady* places that climax, the marriage ceremony, in the middle of the heroine's story rather than at its end, and gives it a wide berth—wider, indeed, than it gets in Eliot's novel. While we see Gwendolen and Grandcourt riding home together after their wedding, even going down to their first appalling intimate dinner, we witness neither the marriage of Isabel and Osmond nor any event in the three years that follow it. We are left more or less in the dark about the character of the man so well formed to destroy Isabel Archer, until she herself begins to understand it; the deliberate evil in Gilbert Osmond's nature is not given us straight off in a scene like one in *Deronda* where Grandcourt, before we see him with Gwendolen, torments his female dogs. It is, therefore, almost as if Isabel, by being who she is and seeing as she does, provokes Osmond to be what he might not have been without her—as if her nature has aroused him to kill what is antithetical to his. Like the high-handed handling of the marriage plot, this tactic conveys the enormous power of Isabel's point of view.

What the heroine makes of it and not her marrying is the real issue in *The Portrait of a Lady*. The ending is not merely inconclusive, but elaborately that, conspicuously a rewriting of romance. The novel ends in the classic manner of romantic comedy, with a kiss, but it is the least romantic, least comic of kisses. It takes place when the promising light of late afternoon that gilded the beginning of Isabel's story has turned into darkness, when the wheel of her destiny has brought her back to Gardencourt, to the lawn where her story began, and left her there alone. Caspar Goodwood, her American suitor, intrudes on her solitude, and the abrupt violence of his kiss and its specific sexuality are startling in a novel that presents life as a process of passionately discriminating among perceptions and shades of feeling. This kiss is no symbol of union: after it is over, Isabel decides, by herself, to return by herself to Rome, where her husband is. Yet the heroine must not be imagined as violated by the embrace. The physical part of her has always responded to Goodwood, who has always been intrusive; just before he extended them, she longed to "let him take her in his arms," and she "took" the kiss bestowed. The most important difference between the conventionally conclusive kisses of literary love in closure and this one has to do not so much with what it means (discord not harmony, separateness not union) as with the way it signifies. Caspar kisses in order to argue for love as well as to express or give it; Isabel privately converts the kiss into images, so as to know the meaning of her experience. On the pictures before her mind's eye she bases her ideas about how to dispose her life: the pictures and their meaning are more important than any actual, physical event. The kiss effects a resolution instead of expressing one, as literary kisses conventionally do at volumes' ends.

But the details of this resolution are famously unclear. Does Isabel really go back in the end to the constriction and falseness and pain of her life in Rome as Mrs. Gilbert Osmond? Does she return to Rome only so as to save Osmond's young daughter from being sacrificed to his ambition in a mercenary marriage like Isabel's own, only because she promised Pansy to return? Does she mean to divorce Osmond? Confront him? Avoid him? Does she mean then to come back to England? To go to America? To whom, and to what? Isabel's jolly journalist friend, Henrietta Stackpole, is the one who tells Caspar Goodwood of Isabel's having left for Rome, and in the last scene of the novel, she says what *she* makes of it: "Look here, Mr. Goodwood," she tells him, "just you wait!" In spite of the fact that poor Goodwood does not know where to look, in spite of the fact that Henrietta is no oracle, many readers have found it impossible not to grasp at the straw of her promise, and believe that the future will hold something more for Isabel than entombment in the dim palazzo in Rome. For they think along lines Isabel's own mind has traveled, which derive from the very idea of a heroine: "To live only to suffer—only to feel the injury of life repeated and enlarged—it seemed to her she was too valuable, too capable, for that" (Chapter 53). Valuable (as an object), and capable (as a subject), Isabel is trapped by her awareness of being both, as the reader is caught between wanting her to find happiness and wanting her career to express her character.

At the outset, having no parents, equipped with beauty and intelligence and spirit, she prepares herself deliberately to know the world "so as to choose," she says. Like Gwendolen Harleth, she seems to be capable of choosing and confident in her capacity to choose. The charmed aunt who brings her from Albany to Europe places the world all before her; the captivated cousin who arranges she be left a legacy equips her to move before the wind with absolute freedom. But a single predictable end is the only possible one: things turn upon themselves. The gifts of Europe and wealth prove to be snares, and Isabel's aunt and her cousin give way to a more sinister pair of schemers who take her fate in their hands. Limited by the dominating force of irony and the intransigence of the actual, Isabel is obliged to choose limits, and obliged in the end to seize the only possible mode of transcendence available to her: a clarified, completed vision of the truth that James calls "revision."

 

The account of Caspar Goodwood's kiss is the most celebrated among the passages James changed in revising the novel for the New York Edition of his complete works. The increased sexuality in the 1908 *Portrait* has been widely noted in audible post-Freudian accents of commendation. "If erotic feeling was absent in the earlier work, the Master now made amends," Leon Edel writes. And, "[Isabel's] fear of passion had been suggested; here it is made explicit—and in the language of Eros." Here is the first kiss:

> His kiss was like a flash of lightning; when it was dark again she was free.

And here is the second, much longer one:

> His kiss was like white lightning, a flash that spread, and spread again, and stayed; and it was extraordinarily as if, while she took it, she felt each thing in his hard manhood that had least pleased her, each aggressive fact of his face, his figure, his presence, justified of its intense identity and made one with this act of possession. So had she heard of those wrecked and under water following a train of images before they sink. But when darkness returned she was free.

It seems to me that there is an increment here less of "erotic feeling" than of the facts—his sexual part importantly among them—of Mr. Goodwood. The text is certainly more daring than the first edition; "she felt each thing in his hard manhood" is a marvel of tactful specificity. But Isabel cannot be said to experience either responsive passion or a reactive fear of passion. What she feels is plain Caspar Goodwood; she experiences his embrace as expressive of Goodwood, a justification and imposition of his very particular, very specific identity (he is, in Edel's phrase, "monotonously male"). At the same time she feels as if she were going under in the face of so much of him. As she anticipated his kiss in panic, she felt that the world

> seemed to open out, all round her, to take the form of a mighty sea, where she floated in fathomless waters. She had wanted help, and here was help; it had come in a rushing torrent. . . . [S]he believed just then that to let him take her in his arms would be the next best thing to her dying. This belief, for a moment, was a kind of rapture, in which she felt herself sink and sink. In the movement she seemed to beat with her feet, in order to catch herself, to feel something to rest on.

Goodwood's embrace signifies, to Isabel, obliteration of her consciousness and therefore of her being. Repeating the drowning image in the long description of the kiss, James allows Goodwood's real embrace all the force Isabel imagined it would have as she anticipated it—and no more. Spelling it out, he indicates its limits. To Isabel Osmond the sexual connection presents no surprises, and contains more disappointments than she imagined—particular ones, perhaps connected with that part of Mr. Goodwood that is always "rising before her" at crises in her life. In his "act of possession" Goodwood justifies his existence (which has always weighed on Isabel because she has always suspected it was justified). The kiss as described in the revised version emphasizes that the facts of Goodwood's "intense identity" obliterate Isabel and her history. For what one hears of the images seen by the drowning is that they are images of the drowner's own past; here as Isabel feels herself sinking she focuses on Goodwood instead of on her own life. His appropriation of her imaginative space is an imposition she cannot suffer. The "flash that spread, and spread again, and stayed" is lyrically described; the erotic is not repellent to her. But the lightning she experiences is blinding, and blindness is intolerable. In the end, she can find freedom only "when darkness returned." She moves from the garden to the lighted doorway of the house, seeking the authority of Euclidean form and firm structure: "There was a very straight path."

Revision was integral to the writing of *The Portrait of a Lady*. James remembered every part of the first draft written in 1880 being written twice; and when he revised it in 1908 he made very extensive revisions. "Although there is only one novel by Henry James called *The Portrait of a Lady*, we have what amounts to two separate 'Portraits,'" a recent editor writes, confounding the heroine, in the familiar way, with the novel about her. Isabel may be identified with the maker of *The Portrait*, whose Albany childhood in some details resembles hers; she is, as he was, an American excited by Europe, and her characteristic meditative, revisionary mode is markedly—there is no better word—Jamesian. The novelist, and many readers after him, have thought the best thing in the novel is the great Chapter 42, in which the heroine reviews a disturbing image her eyes have recently taken in, of her husband sitting and her friend Madame Merle standing, and then is led by her mind's eye through a gallery of images, of remembered pictures and of word-pictures through which she recalls feelings. As she sets herself to re-dream the nightmare of her married life so as to see its true meaning, sitting alone in the Roman palace by a dying fire, calling for candles to illuminate her private, internal re-viewing, she prefigures the Master preparing his works for the New York Edition, seeing the true images come clearer. To revise, James wrote, is not necessarily to change things; it is

to see, or to look over, again—which means in the case of a written thing neither more nor less than to reread it. . . . [T]he act of revision, the act of seeing it again, caused whatever I looked at on any page to flower before me as into the only terms that honourably expressed it; and the "revised" element in the present Edition is accordingly these terms, these rigid conditions of re-persual [*sic*], registered; so many close notes, as who should say, on the particular vision of the matter itself that experience had at last made the only possible one.

Revision for James is confrontation with the way of putting what one sees cannot be put otherwise—and thus with the truth, life converted to art. At the end of *The Portrait of a Lady* it is as if Isabel experiences such a confrontation, and as if she concludes, like James revising, that "to 'put' things is very exactly and responsibly and interminably to do them." It is—but it has always been—a question of the physical self she must put in relation to other people and the world, quite as James writing the novel had to "put" her. The history of the girl from Albany who comes to Europe to look about her and is last glimpsed after Goodwood's kiss, seeing the "rigid conditions" of her life before her—"There was a very straight path"—resolves itself by placing the heroine once for all, placing her, that is, in relation to parts of the actual world, houses and gardens and other people. James anticipated his critics, writing in the Notebooks:

> The obvious criticism of course will be that it is not finished—that I have not seen the heroine to the end of her situation—that I have left her *en l'air*.—This is both true and false. The *whole* of anything is never told; you can only take what groups together. What I have done has that unity—it groups together. It is complete in itself—and the rest may be taken up or not, later.

Isabel resolves her career as a heroine as the novelist does when she puts herself in the context that completes her. To see her way is fully to be herself; to see is in effect to "do," to act; therefore we observe her seeing the path before her, but not walking along it.

In revising, James added two rather elaborate images to characterize the eyes of the Misses Molyneux and Henrietta Stackpole, those very different, indeed contrasting, maidens her own age whom Isabel half-seriously refers to as her "ideals." The sisters of Lord Warburton, who in 1880 had merely "the kindest eyes in the world," give Isabel in 1908 the impression "of having, as she thought, eyes like the balanced basins, the circles of 'ornamental water,' set, in parterres, among the geraniums" (Chapter 9). The slow discriminating rhythm suggests both Isabel's inclination (intensified in the revised version) to find precisely the right phrases for everything she sees, and also the stately home where the Misses Molyneux so complacently reflect their stiff, prosaic flowers. These young ladies accept their dull domestic place in the world. In contrast to them, the American journalist Henrietta Stackpole has "clear-cut views on most subjects"—rather different ones from Lord Warburton's "new views," which bewilder his good sisters. Henrietta is impassioned by a will to see the "sights" of Europe, including "the inner life." She is equipped with a "peculiarly open, surprised-looking eye" to do her business. ("You do see through us, Miss Stackpole," Ralph says in a satirical tone she cannot hear.) While in the Preface to the revised *Portrait* James acknowledged that we have "indubitably too much" of Henrietta, he nevertheless chose to add to the New York Edition a little bit more, a startling modern image that contrasts with the staid "circles of 'ornamental water.'" When Isabel sees Henrietta again after some time, she notes that "Henrietta was as keen and quick and fresh as ever, and as neat and bright and fair. Her remarkably open eyes, lighted like great glazed railway-stations, had put up no shutters" (Chapter 47). The ugly industrial newness of the railway-stations is linked with Henrietta's too-open eyes to connect her lack of insight and vision, range and subtlety, with her utilitarian, very American distance from the complex shadowed beauty of the past. The Misses Molyneux, equally flat-eyed, are as far as Henrietta is from a capacity to see in life all the heroine sees.

Of Isabel James writes that her "light grey eyes, a little too firm perhaps in her graver moments, had an *enchanting range of concession*" (Chapter 5; italics mine): in the first edition the phrase reads simply, "softness when she smiled." "Concession" helps define her charm as a matter of promising to yield, and in stages—in other words, her seductiveness. Isabel is seductive, very obviously, to her creator, whose tenderness for her is nearly doting. He attempts to disarm us early by confiding that we, too, are to dote, that he knows "she would be an easy victim of scientific criticism if she were not intended to awaken on the reader's part an impulse more tender and more purely expectant" (Chapter 6). The link of tenderness and expectancy is ominous: knowing Isabel, knowing what must await her, we must, James says, be generous, not scientific but romantic. Expectancy is her attitude, and the attitude of those about her, and it is to be ours. It is the attitude a heroine inspires. James's indulgent attitude toward Isabel is romantic. George Eliot, as F. R. Leavis pointed out, was more sagacious, being more critical, in her treatment of Gwendolen Harleth, the vaguely aspiring, presumptuous, "delicate vessel" whom James rewrote. Noting that Gilbert Osmond is a more credible, sympathetic, and well-rounded character than the monster Grandcourt, one might speculate along Leavis's lines that it is a case of women knowing women better than men do, and vice versa. To support such a view, there are in *The Portrait of a Lady* a few awkward, pompous generalizations about women, which betray some discomfort and mistrust; for instance:

> It was not exactly that it would be base or insidious; for women as a general thing practise such manoeuvres with a perfectly good conscience, and Isabel was instinctively much more true than false to the common genius of her sex. (Chapter 41)

> Women find their religion sometimes in strange exercises. . . (Chapter 42)

> It hereupon became apparent that the resources of women are innumerable. Isabel devoted herself to Pansy's desecrated drapery; she fumbled for a pin. . . . (Chapter 43)

(The first of these quotations occurs just before Chapter 42, and the second comes at the end of Isabel's great meditation: James frames his most intimate picture of Isabel by trying or pretending to look at her objectively, critically, from a man's distance.) When Isabel dismisses Caspar Goodwood in Rome by partly covering her face with a fan, meeting his eyes, and telling him he may think of her with pity "every now and then," the female reader certainly cannot but feel some irritation, but the narrator makes no critical comment. Isabel leads Goodwood on, and also Lord Warburton and Ralph, without being even mildly rated for flirtatiousness.

But the tone James takes toward her is the only one that can create her. Contagiousness is the essence of Isabel's being. What makes her a heroine is that she makes others experience her as one. Isabel's slimness, her dark braids, her gray eyes and black dress—the physical details of the portrait—are memorable, but not essential. Isabel is idealized, to some extent, by both Osmond and James, who see her very differently but who both think she has "too many ideas." She is not quite an idealist; as James wrote of his cousin Mary Temple, she is "much too unliteral and too ironic" to be expressed "in the mere terms of her restless young mind." Yet Isabel's mind is what most impresses those around her, and what we know best of her. Of Mary Temple, James wrote that "she made it impossible to say whether she was just the most moving of maidens or a disengaged and dancing flame of thought"; he wrote of Isabel's "delicate, desultory, flame-like spirit," and its being combined with "the eager and personal creature of conditions," the physical maiden. Like the Mary who died young and then grew "legendary" in her cousin's memory, leaving behind her a nostalgia that touched the characters of his fictional American girls, Isabel is remarkable for being "moving"; she is interesting as she moves those about her, as she moves us, reading. Isabel cares very much about the impression she makes: she wants "to look very well and to be if possible even better." She is attuned to the subjectivity of those around her; the impression she makes there bears the same relation to her ideal self as Clarissa Harlowe's friends' idea of ideal woman does to hers. Her notion is that "her life should always be in harmony with the most pleasing impression she should produce; she would be what she appeared, and she would appear what she was" (Chapter 6). Meanwhile she contains the images of others: James wrote in the Preface to *The Princess Casamassima* of "the thickly-peopled imagination of Isabel Archer." She is endowed with a novelist's sensibility and condemned by her image of herself as a heroine to make her own life into a novel.

*The Portrait of a Lady* opens on the still scene of three men, one old, one ill, one bored, drinking tea on a beautiful English lawn. Soon after the old man, Daniel Touchett, observes that "the ladies will save us"—from lives without meaning, he means—Isabel suddenly appears, and all three fall in love with her. Their lives will be changed by her. Isabel is American, "quite independent," unused to confining codes of decorum for young ladies. Her surname suggests she will be the active agent of her destiny. Nevertheless her story, like the medieval Rose's, will be of being sought. Isabel Archer is shot like an arrow by the aunt who discovers her in obscurity, in ugly provincial Albany. Rather like Jane Austen, that avatar of aunts, Mrs. Touchett wants to allow Isabel to find her own plot, and a hero to make her a heroine. Her observant aunt's attitude toward Isabel is a hint that the girl's story will always depend on how she is appraised; the older woman comes upon her as Isabel is seated with a book, quiet and passive, a portrait of a lady.

Isabel is framed from her career's beginning and the novel's. We see her for the first time as she stands "in the ample doorway" of Gardencourt, her uncle's home in England. From where Ralph is on the lawn he sees "a tall girl in a black dress," pretty, bare-headed. Only later we learn how it is that Mrs. Touchett found her and brought her from America. The placid beauty of the grounds of Gardencourt, like the very different bleak shuttered house in Albany, serves as a foil to Isabel's liveliness, beauty, and energy. *The Portrait of a Lady*, with its interesting light and long vistas, its drives and views and courtyards and high-ceilinged palaces, its quick focusing on telling details in momentary closeups, often reads like a film script. The heroine strikes those who see her as a portrait trembling on the brink of animation.

Soon after she arrives at Gardencourt, Isabel goes with Ralph to the gallery, even though the light is insufficient, to look at the pictures. She is eager for culture and beauty. As she walks around holding her candle, Ralph finds her "better worth looking at than most works of art." Later, she visits Lord Warburton's Lockleigh, and again she walks with an admiring man in a picture gallery, looking at what is on the walls, or pretending to, and at the same time "showing him her charming back, her light slim figure, the length of her white neck as she bent her head, and the density of her dark braids." Again she is the preferred object for which other works of art are ignored: Ralph and Warburton admire her vitality as they have been used to admire things. In Ralph's case certainly this is no mere admiration of her physical appearance, but an aesthetic appreciation of her soul. Of all the men Isabel meets, her cousin is most capable of appreciating her, with a consciousness finely attuned to her own. But he is unluckily ill and sexually *hors de combat*: he proposes to give himself pleasure by watching Isabel, and takes an active hand in arranging the spectacle of her career when he persuades his father to leave her a fortune. By watching, then, Ralph affects his cousin's destiny, and perhaps his fine appreciation of her prepares her for that other expatriate aesthete, Osmond. But the connoisseur whose view of her has greatest effect on her destiny is Isabel herself.

When Isabel goes to Osmond's hilltop above Florence it is ostensibly in order to see his treasures. This time, as she looks at a man's possessions, we are conscious of her appraising the owner—this owner so much less considerable than the other two. Osmond is "a student of the exquisite," and Isabel has been introduced to him as a "rarity" to titillate his demanding taste. But what is most importantly in the air as they meet is *her* sense of *his* being a work of art. We are firmly in Isabel's consciousness:

His pictures, his medallions and tapestries were interesting; but after a while Isabel felt the owner much more so, and independently of them, thickly as they seemed to overhang him. . . . It was not so much what he said and did, but rather what he withheld, that marked him for her as by one of those signs of the highly curious that he was showing her on the underside of old plates and in the corner of sixteenth-century drawings: he indulged in no striking deflections from common usage, he was an original without being an eccentric. She had never met a person of so fine a grain. (Chapter 24)

(His withholding is an ominous sign.) Osmond is the finest thing in his possession; Isabel is caught first by her own good taste and then by the plot that puts her "framed in the gilded doorway" of the grim palace in Rome, "the picture of a gracious lady" (Chapter 37).

A collector as well as a commodity, Isabel sees Gilbert Osmond as a desirable object. In the 1908 *Portrait* James described him elaborately: "he suggested, fine gold coin as he was, no stamp nor emblem of the common mintage that provides for general circulation; he was the elegant complicated medal struck off for a special occasion" (Chapter 22). In the image wealth and art are brilliantly conflated. Osmond is cold, ornamental, and shallow, like a head on a medal, as well as elegant and complicated. His worth, like a special medal's, derives from no ordinary system of coining and exchange, which is commonly imagined to reward worth or even virtue. He seems to Isabel to represent and to live by the governing principles of art—he seems therefore perfectly equipped, as most are not, to appreciate a Portrait of a Lady, to see Isabel as she herself would be seen and not merely as any rich and attractive young woman. Courting her, he shows her his collection of medallions: he is what he has, one is invited to observe (she does not). When finally she leaves him he is engaged in fastidiously copying a drawing of an antique coin; his copying a copy underscores his critical distance from the real thing. To Isabel, when she meets him, this distance of his—his elevation on a hill above Florence, his walled garden and shuttered house—seems to be a sign of his purity. Osmond seems the better for being not a wealthy man; instead of the crude, common money amassed by crude and common Americans he has a few old and beautiful coins with a patina of age and beauty, European coins.

He has immense charm, immense taste. Dazzled by the glitter of these immaterial goods, Isabel cannot see that he really wants the fortune her uncle has left her. With terrible unconscious irony, she bestows herself on him to reward disinterestedness. Her aunt, who is opposed to Isabel's marrying a middle-aged widower with a child, observes sagely, before the engagement, "There's nothing in life to prevent her marrying Mr. Osmond if she only looks at him in a certain way" (Chapter 26). Isabel's angle on Osmond is "purely" aesthetic, which is to say that she sees him as if such an angle existed—what she sees in him depends on her point of view. As it happens, her point of view admiringly embraces his pretensions. For what he pretends to is a special consciousness, a special kind of vision. He invites Isabel to look forward with him to "a future at a high level of consciousness of the beautiful" (Chapter 35).

But as the image of the elegant complicated medal suggests, beautiful things are expensive; aesthetic values are related to monetary values, are even versions of them. Since Richardson, the heroine's story has shown how the concepts of virtue and reward manage in the end, like most couples, to compromise one another, how the effort to imagine the economic and sexual relationship of marriage in rarefied moral and aesthetic terms is inevitable and also doomed. Osmond attracts Isabel because she is newly rich, and feels burdened with her money, while he has, he is, nothing. As a poor man he is an opposite, potentially a complement, therefore romantic: that she chooses him over her other, rival, suitors betrays that Isabel's imagination has been caught by her wealth, that she has set her self-image comfortably upon it as on a pedestal. (She feels more her best self when she inherits her uncle's money. It is as if it flatters her like a lover.) She wants to lay the fortune she is charged with where its grossness will be sublimed, at the elegant feet of Osmond. She likes the idea of filling his emptiness; and also she is afraid of substantial men. When she assures her aunt that since Osmond is nothing he will not be able to hurt her, she implies a belief that men who are something will hurt her. Lord Warburton, he of the large and capable hands, and Caspar Goodwood, with his stiff urgency, frighten her. She finds the physical fact of sex, like the physical reality of money, very exciting and yet terrifying and distasteful: she is eager to divest herself of both her body and her fortune, to give them over to another, but she wants also to have them herself. She refuses her rich and vigorous suitors, whose substantiality might obliterate her, and chooses a man who is effete, languid, middle-aged, thinking he will appreciate both her and her money, refine them by his way of taking them. She turns away from the whole continent Goodwood offers her, and from Warburton's extensive lands and many houses, choosing instead an enclosed space. It is as if to join Osmond's collection of beautiful things is to translate herself out of the flesh into art, or to be translated.

A fastidiousness like Osmond's partly accounts for Isabel's tragic fate. Back in Albany, the businesslike Mrs. Touchett startled her niece by suggesting that she rent out her property: such a clear-headed attitude toward material things is not congenial to the young woman sentimentally attached to her gloomy ancestral home, disdainful of getting and spending. At Gardencourt, Isabel chats with her uncle, who has come to appreciate the beauty of his great English house only in old age and terminal illness, having been too busy for art before. As he looks at his property Mr. Touchett reflects, "I sometimes think I've paid too much for this," and adds to Isabel, "perhaps you also might have to pay too much" (Chapter 13). He does not have money in mind, but it is in fact because he leaves her money that his niece is put in the way of paying in metaphorical as well as real currency. Isabel had thought too little of the business of paying, had thought herself above all that, and she has to pay for *that*. On the other side of the coin with the goddess head on it and the old motto "Virtue Rewarded" is a legend to the effect that you pay for what you get. The woman-centered novel argues, traditionally, that the rate of exchange between different kinds of currency is constant, that the joys of the flesh may be traded for triumphs of the spirit, that if one suffers one gains insight. Isabel, like Clarissa, must pay, in the end, for wanting to avoid those tokens of the world and the flesh, for prizing elegant complicated medals above gold coins, and being blind to the resemblance of one to the other.


Doublings and repetitions throughout the novel underscore the heroine's doubleness, also reiterate that it is well to look twice at things. In the two volumes, there are two courtship plots: the main business of the first one is the marrying of Isabel Archer, the American Rose transplanted to Gardencourt; at issue in the second is the disposal for life of the little, more obscure, more elaborately painted flower, her husband's daughter, Pansy. Isabel has two pairs of suitors. The first two men are healthy and wealthy, and if not wise, perfectly presentable: the egregious American, Caspar Goodwood, and "the eminently amenable nobleman," the Grandisonian Warburton. Then there are two other men, both American expatriates, clever and charming connoisseurs imaginatively equipped—as the presentable suitors are not—to respond to Isabel. Both of them are defective: her cousin Ralph Touchett, who arranges that she be made an heiress, is mortally ill, and Osmond, who marries her for the money, is morally defective. There are also two surrogate mothers who figure in the life of the motherless young woman from Albany who returns to Rome in the end partly so as to mother another girl whose own mother has rejected her. Mrs. Touchett, Ralph's "paternal, and even . . . gubernatorial" mother, Isabel's "crazy Aunt Lydia," gives her birth as a heroine of a novel (James's third) about an American abroad, puts her in Daisy Miller's interesting position. The second surrogate mother in Isabel's life is Pansy Osmond's secret parent, the smooth white Madame Merle. She is "the great round world itself," Mother Earth, perverted. With the secret purpose of tying up the ends of her own life's plot, she involves Isabel in a marriage plot that is not what Isabel thinks it is. Isabel is caught up and made a minor character in another woman's love story: it is the worst thing that can befall a heroine, striking as it does at the heart of her specialness. Serena Merle is Osmond's former mistress. She has given up her illegitimate daughter to save her reputation, and she arranges that Isabel marry her former lover, who has kept the child, in the hope of making Pansy's fortune. Both Isabel's differently unnatural mothers are women imperturbably themselves, unapologetic, assured, and original, and Isabel, whom each in a manner adopts, aspires to be something like them. If she has in her nature some of her aunt's cold dryness, she admires the accomplishments of her aunt's elegant friend.

Isabel meets Madame Merle when she returns to Gardencourt from a visit to London. By this time she is fairly drunk with the sense of possibilities. She has rejected Lord Warburton—his houses, his tradition, his rank, his strong man's hands and heart. Then she has rejected his American counterpart, Mr. Goodwood, who offers her his stubborn energy and the future. She returns to Gardencourt because her uncle is dying; when Daniel Touchett's death occurs, men in general seem to have shrunk in power, in interest, in attractiveness, and women seem glorious. What will seize Isabel Archer to grind her "in the very mill of the conventional" is not the system of a man's world, the organization deriving from male power that overcomes Gwendolen Harleth. In James's novel the heroine is heartlessly seduced by a woman.

Before she sees Madame Merle, she hears her playing the piano; the music draws Isabel across the grand parlor at Gardencourt. She first sees her nemesis from behind: an eventful time will elapse before the final confrontation, when face to face she feels that "the light of this woman's eyes seemed only a darkness." Madame Merle makes it hard to see her directly. She sits at the grand piano and like a spider spinning out a filament she sends out beauty to trap her victim. Isabel admires her as the epitome of the cultured lady: in her connection to so many of the arts, in her beautiful devotion to beautiful things and to behaving beautifully, she seems to have rewritten a woman's daily life in a key to harmonize with eternal music. To a perfection he could not have imagined, Madame Merle embodies Mr. Darcy's idea of an "accomplished" lady: any grimness or crudeness or earnestness or eagerness of application has been beautifully polished away in forty years of self-cultivation. Art is Madame Merle's element: no, her genius is for adapting art to life, for making the one slide into the other. She had

> to Isabel's imagination a sort of greatness. To be so culti-
> vated and civilised, so wise and so easy, and still make so
> light of it—that was really to be a great lady, especially when
> one so carried and presented one's self. It was as if somehow
> she had all society under contribution, and all the arts and
> graces it practised—or was the effect rather that of charming
> uses found *for* her, even from a distance, subtle service ren-
> dered by her to a clamorous world wherever she might be?
> After breakfast she wrote a succession of letters, as those
> arriving for her appeared innumerable. . . . She knew more
> people, as she told Isabel, than she knew what to do with,
> and something was always turning up to be written about.
> Of painting she was devotedly fond, and made no more of
> brushing in a sketch than of pulling off her gloves. . . . That
> she was a brave musician we have already perceived, and it
> was evidence of the fact that when she seated herself at the
> piano, as she always did in the evening, her listeners re-
> signed themselves without a murmur to losing the grace of
> her talk. . . . When Madame Merle was neither writing, nor
> painting, nor touching the piano, she was usually employed
> upon wonderful tasks of rich embroidery, cushions, cur-
> tains, decorations for the chimney-piece; an art in which her
> bold, free invention was as noted as the agility of her needle.
> . . . She laid down her pastimes as easily as she took them
> up; she worked and talked at the same time, and appeared to
> impute scant worth to anything she did. She gave away her
> sketches and tapestries; she rose from the piano or remained
> there, according to the convenience of her auditors, which
> she always unerringly divined. (Chapter 19)

I have quoted this very long passage for all its delicious particulars, and also for the subtle attribution of calculation to the lady
described by so meticulous a catalogue of talents, activities, and
attitudes. (That "she knew more people . . . than she knew what
to do with" is sinister, if only on rereading.) Madame Merle is to

perfection the lady as self-made artifact: so artistic is she that she has many talents, humble feminine ones (an agile needle) along with a striking boldness of imagination. What is most marvelous about her is her disinclination to take herself seriously. She is willing to lay down anything, or give it away, at the request of one of her friends; she is entirely at the service of others. A perfectly social being, distinguished in her ability to accommodate people with alacrity and grace, she is skilled at telling what it is they want, in order that she may give it them. This subtlety of penetration that is Madame Merle's great talent is a social gift, a gift for being social; Isabel will come to discover that the lady can use it against others—against her—under cover of seeming to please them, that she is duplicitous, hypocritical, manipulative, pathetic, even tragic. But to begin with she strikes Isabel as a role model or exemplar, a perfect lady and a perfect guest. Madame Merle is welcome at Gardencourt while its master is dying as no other person would be, because she makes so few personal demands. Homeless, poor, counting on her ability to please, distinguished by intuitive gifts and the ability to use them artfully, Madame Merle is the paradigmatic powerless woman.

She seems to be drawn to Isabel even before the girl becomes an heiress, and useful. They are both guests in a gloomy house, Americans, women, subtle, self-conscious, watchful creatures. They have an extraordinary conversation about the relation of essence to appearance, and the nature of contingency and convention. Madame Merle's argument is for the necessity of a beautiful outer life, a conventional "envelope" that will suit the inner self. (She uses the word James had used for the reputation for being literary that had made Isabel seem a goddess in America. The envelope of convention Madame Merle has in mind is an envelope of art that will make a woman seem more than a woman.) Isabel argues that the inner life can flourish independent of its manifestations. It is on one level an argument of America against Europe, of the skeptical new world against the tradition-bound old one, of innocence against experience. It is also an argument of the Romantic conception of the self against a more complex modern one. Isabel in her black dress imagines she is freer than she is, unaware that a black dress makes its own statement. To dress at all is to be enveloped in convention, Madame Merle observes; why not then, in all knowledge of this, take pains to choose as well as one can, choose so as to express oneself? Is this cynicism, or aestheticism, or realism? Madame Merle's idea that one may express oneself by choosing the conventional is the idea Isabel will act on when she acts on Madame Merle's choice, and "chooses" Osmond.

Like Dorothea Brooke, Isabel Archer fancies herself original in choosing a man no one else would choose—a man her relatives disapprove of, a man twice her age. Like Dorothea's, Isabel's moral passion transfigures the appearance of its object in her eyes: she loves Gilbert Osmond as a beautiful embodiment of art the way Dorothea loves devotion to the truth, incarnate, in Mr. Casaubon. Both young women imagine in their egotism that they can choose in defiance of ordinary worldly realities, choose as if they were living purely literary, symbolic lives. Wealth and independence of parental control enable them to scorn what partly motivates most marriages; their "freedom" leads to marriages that are disastrous. If they triumph in the end it is because the novels about them proceed beyond marriage, to chronicle both an action and a revision. Mr. Casaubon is no hypocrite but a well-intentioned, very limited man, whose intellect is impeded by his fearfulness; Osmond is an aesthete in whom a passion for beauty is limited by his incapacity for passion. Their marriages to ardent young women bring to both men's minds an uncomfortable awareness of their own desiccation and poverty of spirit, and produce a petty, jealous hatred of the women who remind them of their own limits by refusing to be reduced to them. George Eliot's analysis of Dorothea is that she is shortsighted first of all, and secondly deprived of opportunity and guidance; James shows us Isabel choosing Gilbert Osmond because he stands for limits. He tells her before they marry that he is "convention itself," and this evidently does not displease her.* She chooses Osmond to be her envelope.

---

* "Mr. Darcy is all politeness," is how Elizabeth Bennet hypostasizes her man, with a smile (*P & P* I, 6).

It is not of course all Isabel's doing: we have to blame Mrs. Touchett for bringing her from America, and Ralph for falling in love with her and persuading his father to leave her the money that would "put wind in her sails" so he could watch her; we must blame Goodwood and Warburton for being importunate, for being who they are; and we must blame Osmond and Madame Merle for the sin of using another person for selfish ends. The issue is not really blame. It is not only moral, but also aesthetic. The outline of the life story in which Isabel Archer meant to express herself has been drawn by those around her—by "what grouped together," in James's phrase. She is the sum of her relations; she is those who are around her. Therefore the scene of Madame Merle and Osmond as she saw them framed in a doorway can be studied as if it were a work of art full of significance vital to an understanding of her own life. The fireside scene begins as Isabel sets about to think, as Osmond has charged her to, of why his artificial little daughter, Pansy, should not be married to Lord Warburton, married off, Isabel thinks, as one puts a letter in a box. The question of being boxed, dispatched, married, mailed (maled?) once for all is the question she meditates, but she, not Pansy, is the subject.

What Osmond has asked Isabel to do when she begins her meditation is in effect to sell herself: to encourage Lord Warburton, who still is devoted to her, to marry Pansy so as to be near Pansy's stepmother. Isabel is not meant to contract an explicit sordid arrangement but merely to be subtly encouraging, and deliberately exploitative; for the sake of Osmond's daughter, she is to adopt Osmond's values and his style. She stays by the fire to think about this, as her husband has asked her to, but she cannot, quite; all she can think of is the difference between her husband's values and her own, and what that has meant in her marriage. For the central fact is that she cannot think as he wishes her to think. Their difference is a difference of mind: Isabel's is ranging, flexible, and quick, while Osmond exerts his to limit it, muffle it, put it out. Chapter 42, which shows us how Isabel thinks by showing us Isabel thinking, is the real portrait of a lady, the gauntlet James throws down to painters. This portrait framed by the rest of the novel can only be painted in words. It is the concealed, more vivid aspect of the woman who seems to sit passive and impassive, alone through the night, by a dying fire in a room in a Roman palace.

As Isabel sits through the darkness into the dawn she gains insight into her past and her husband's character, into her life story, into the truth—what blind poets have been able to see because they have not been distracted. But her mind is full of images of darkness, enclosure, and constriction: a few, more fleeting, images remind us of oceans and shores and boats, of freedom and space. Isabel is locked in and yet her mind widely ranges. The fact that such a mind is forced to address a narrow subject—the business of marrying Pansy profitably—strikes the reader dramatically with pity and terror. What Isabel meditates on, ultimately, is precisely the character of her mind, and why it has inspired her husband to hate it, to hate her. We watch her taking that mind's measure, and while the effect is not precisely to show us Osmond's point of view, it nevertheless becomes clear to us why he hates her: what Osmond hates is dramatized as Isabel moves her mind. The question of Pansy distresses her because she is generous, and also because Pansy is related to her, by analogy and by marriage. Saving Pansy from a loveless marriage to Lord Warburton very like the one Lord Warburton once offered her, Isabel will spare herself Lord Warburton's loverlike overtures. Saving Pansy is saving herself. Isabel has been asked to do for Pansy what she had not done for herself; the question that had come up at the beginning is posed her again. The second deliberate sale for money and power would be morally worse than the first would have been; the pressures that urge it are greater. To do it she would have to give up her point of view—her self—for Osmond, which is what she cannot do. Hence the resurgence of her self as she thinks, and with that of all her objections to Osmond. What her husband has always asked is that she give herself up. In her meditation she in effect promises to refuse to, and by doing that, by clinging to her own truth, she comes close to seeing the truth outside herself—Osmond and Madame Merle, "unconsciously and familiarly associated."

Intelligent and presumptuous, Isabel Archer could not but "affront" her destiny, cannot but confront, in the end, the consequences of her effort to choose. By doing so, she expresses herself more completely than she can possibly do by an action. Dramatically in Chapter 42, and then again as incidents from her own life come "before her as the deed[s] of another person" toward the end of the novel, it is as if she is rereading her own story.* "One must accept one's deeds," she tells Henrietta when she is brought finally to confess the truth about her marriage. "I married him before all the world; I was perfectly free; it was impossible to do anything more deliberate. One can't change that way," Isabel says (Chapter 47). (Henrietta intelligently insists that she *has* changed, that she is corrupted, no longer the American girl she was.) Isabel's doctrine is the corollary of the idea that one can express one's unique self by one's life story, the idea of a simple relationship between character and event. It also sets that notion on its head, reversing the terms. When she makes that declaration to Henrietta, Isabel is still unaware of how Madame Merle functioned in her life, and believes she was "perfectly free," as in fact she was not. By the very end of the novel, full knowledge has shown her the limits of her freedom. Madame Merle's self-exile to America, Warburton's marriage, Mrs. Touchett's withdrawal, Ralph's death, Henrietta's forthcoming marriage, free her from all but a few links to her past. There is poor Pansy in the convent, denied her beloved Mr. Rosier by a father who would marry her off for money; there is Osmond; and there is the promise of oblivion in the arms of Mr. Goodwood. Isabel is constrained to accept the history that derived from her attempt to be herself. She must revise, to reread, to see more inescapably the significance of her story, to be the conscious heroine of a novel. Such virtue as hers can have no other reward. The passionate orgasm of insight Isabel shares with Ralph before he dies is fleet-

---

* When she sat alone in Albany before Mrs. Touchett appeared, "the years and hours of her life came back to her" similarly.

ing; his consoling assurance "that if you've been hated you've also been loved. Ah but, Isabel—*adored*!" is cold comfort. "Oh my brother!" she cries, recognizing her spiritual mate in the impotent man whose gift has led to her destruction, in an ending even more full of knifelike ironies than the bitter end of Gwendolen Harleth's story. George Eliot suggests that Gwendolen will find some manner of salvation as a bare, forked animal, having given heroinism and egoism over for good; James more exigently allows Isabel to divest herself of no shred of a heroine's regalia. She must look again at her palace, at her envelope, if she would clearly know herself. Gwendolen's "brother" is the religious, political, noble Deronda; Isabel's is the flawed, aesthetic Ralph. Eliot's vision is Utopian; James's is unregenerately literary.

His tragic vision of the heroine's fate is finely shaded by the story of Isabel's antithesis, Madame Merle. She, having been so very clever, having married her old friend Osmond to Isabel Archer, expects something for her pains: gratitude, acknowledgment, affection, vice's reward. But Pansy's father is cold and cranky. Alone with his former mistress, he examines one of the delicate objects on her mantel, an "attenuated coffee-cup," preferring, as usual, the *objet d'art* to the person. Peevishly, he fancies he sees "a wee bit of a tiny crack" in the thing. When he leaves her Madame Merle goes to look at the cup; she holds it in her hand, sees no crack, sees nothing. "Have I been so vile all for nothing?" she "vaguely" wails. She has got what she deserved.

# ~⟨ 6 ⟩~

# *Mrs. Dalloway*

So we are driven back to see what the other side means—the men in clubs and Cabinets—when they say that character-drawing is a frivolous fireside art, a matter of pins and needles, exquisite outlines enclosing vacancy, flourishes, and mere scrawls.

—Virginia Woolf,
*Jacob's Room*

*The Portrait of a Lady* was widely assigned at colleges in the 1950s, and much taken to heart; when Leon Edel says that Isabel Archer formed a whole generation of American women, either he means mine or he is making too modest a claim. Some evidence suggests her influence persists among girls of a certain temperament even today. Recently, in a high school yearbook, I found these lines, half-hidden by koans and rock lyrics, under one graduating senior's photograph:

"I always want to know the things one shouldn't do."
"So as to do them?" asked her aunt.
"So as to choose," said Isabel.

Isabel's story can be easily faulted by feminists: it encourages an overvaluation of fastidiousness, a preference of insight to plea-

271

sure, a desire for "pure" imaginative control rather than for power and happiness in the world as it is. It suggests that the noblest and finest young women deserve more than this world has to offer. But it is also true that the novel about Isabel powerfully portrays a woman's need to choose, to imagine her life for herself. James set about deliberately, he tells us in his Preface, to transform the ordinary "ado" about a "mere young thing" and her marrying into a work of art by the act of putting her point of view at the center of the novel about her. The source of Isabel's distinctiveness, of her being a heroine, is her power as a knower and interpreter of the sign that is her conventional heroine's self.

*The Portrait of a Lady* ends the heroine's story by coming round full circle to the novel. As Isabel, in the end, rejects this world for another, not "the next," which Clarissa Harlowe chooses, but a post-Christian Rome symbolic of art, a heroine's dilemma is presented starkly: Isabel is obliged to choose the past over the future, stasis over process, art over life because she sees herself as a heroine and her story as a story. The novel clearly forces her hand as she seems to take the action in hand herself: the direction in which she takes her solitary way is toward the Jamesian house of fiction. *The Portrait of a Lady* is in a sense the last word in the heroine's story: I might write here, like Lovelace, that now I can go no further. James's later heroines have a different relation to their sexual fates, which do not bear the whole moral burden of the novels they figure in. The "bad" ones, Kate Croy, in *The Wings of the Dove*, and Charlotte Stant, in *The Golden Bowl*, disturbingly combine a conscious heroine's intelligence, vitality, and imagination with greed and a talent for betrayal. Their ancestress, perhaps, is Mary Crawford of *Mansfield Park*, the brilliant product of an immoral household who can calmly expect Tom Bertram to die so his brother will inherit the estate and marry her. Kate Croy and Charlotte Stant are not rich like Mary Crawford, and they are more desperate and daring. As James, unlike Jane Austen, allows them to steal the reader's attention, as well as everything else they can get, from the "good" heroines, the story of a young woman's attempting to control her destiny becomes an occasion for exploring subtle dimensions of evil. The romantic dream of self-realization is no longer the primary theme.

Changes in society and history and thought shaped the development of the domestic novel after James. New ideas about women and their desires and capacities, about sex, about narrative, about morality, about the self, radically shifted the ground where the house of fiction stood. The relationship of inner to outer, private to public, imagined to real lives seemed different in the twentieth century; history changed people's ideas about controlling their destinies. The novel heroine altered accordingly. Possibly what happened was that along with its ideas about time and space and culture and language, "human character changed." The formulation is Virginia Woolf's. Novelists who believed that it had, or that it should, or that really it had been different all along from what people pretended it was, invented new kinds of characters and plots, new relations of character to plot—new forms.

The novel's inherent disposition to attend to its own conventions and play with them has always served the purpose of pointing up what's novel in a particular fiction. "Experimental" fiction, which questions accepted ideas about sequence and causality and relationship, has its roots in the very beginning of the novel's history: it was 1759 when Laurence Sterne attended at the birth of the English novel to describe Dr. Slop's equally eccentric attendance at the birth of Tristram Shandy. In the early twentieth century, novelists who rejected assumptions and therefore forms that seemed false in a changed world revitalized a tradition that had seemed lost in the great age of realism. The subject of the realistic novel, the idea of the heroine, changed utterly as it occurred to the modernist Virginia Woolf. When she organized a heroine-centered fiction—*Mrs. Dalloway* (1925)— along other lines than those which are plotted by the trajectory of a young woman's sexual destiny, Woolf wrote a brilliant coda to the heroine's story, which is suggestive about both the heroine's persistence in the literary/feminine imagination and some of the changes in her connections with it. As middle-aged Clarissa Dalloway confronts—retrospectively—her destiny, Virginia Woolf confronts and transforms the woman-centered novel.

To consider Virginia Woolf is to consider the conflation of the feminine and the literary—a favorite subject of hers. Pages have been written about Woolf by romantics interested in the beautiful lady writer who died, and other pages have been written by feminists, antiromantic in intention if not always in effect. The idea of the heroine is romantic, and Virginia Woolf has effectively become a heroine. Her personal life is more widely known of than her novels: the names of her friends and members of her family are viable tokens of literacy, in some circles; her face, her charm, her sex life, figure in a legend with a familiar structure that seems to be about Woman, or Modern Woman; and whether her suicide is interpreted as the act of a victim or a martyr or a madwoman, it is too often imagined as a self-realizing act, the story-of-her-life's validating goal. Her plainest-speaking biographers are obliged to note some extremely romantic facts. She was the daughter of a beauty and the niece of a famous woman photographer of beauties, and a beauty herself and the rival of a sister who was, as Leonard Woolf put it, "normally" more beautiful than she. She was connected through her father, Sir Leslie Stephen, to Thackeray by marriage, and by friendship to Meredith and James and the literary establishment of the nineteenth century. Like a lady in a tower she was educated in the Stephen library, steeped in literary tradition, proud of that but rather resentful, too, that learning had not been conveyed to her as it had been to her brothers, at a university. She was well-bred, not always comfortable but usually pleased in the company of aristocrats. She married a Jew. She had intimate friends who adored her, was delightful gossipy company, and suffered several mental breakdowns, and the fear of them. She drowned herself in 1941. In her lifetime she was archly referred to (by her friend E. M. Forster) as the Invalid Lady of Bloomsbury; she continues to seem a symbol of both pretentiousness and impish mockery of pretensions, of both serious feminism and clubby, campy, self-indulgent preciosity. She was the lover of another woman writer she wrote of, and to, in a novel, *Orlando*, which is partly about English literature and the matter of gender. As a devoted, famously frigid wife, a literary lady whose politics were socialist, a beautiful woman who worked very hard and was a notable novelist, critic, and biographer, Virginia Woolf in her own person presents a set of problematically related facts and images of the kind good novels dwell on, which put in doubt the truth-to-life of novels. Like a heroine who seems at once paradigmatic and unique, she both exemplified and examined the connections between women and fiction. And unlike a traditional heroine, she was not artistic but an artist.

Her observation in her journal in 1928 on the anniversary of her father's birth has been widely quoted:

He would have been 96, 96, yes, today; and could have been 96, like other people one has known: but mercifully was not. His life would have entirely ended mine. What would have happened? No writing, no books;—inconceivable.

On the other hand, had Sir Leslie Stephen not been who he was, the eminent editor of the *Dictionary of National Biography*, there would have been no such life, writing, or books, no such vision of a life of writing books. In 1923, considering with some amusement the psychological problems of her brother Adrian, Virginia Woolf wrote in her journal that

the D.N.B. crushed his life out before he was born. It gave me a twist of the head too. I shouldn't have been so clever, but I should have been more stable, without that contribution to the history of England.

The daughter of her father was the daughter of the book, a Victorian Peerage of accomplished persons. Her mother, who died when Virginia was thirteen, also haunted her, an Angel who had too soon left the house for heaven. Woolf had a twentieth-century consciousness of the importance of parents and early childhood that Charlotte Brontë, for instance, could not have had. She herself conjectured that by writing *To the Lighthouse*, about Mrs. Ramsay, the beautiful nurturing hostess-mother, and Mr. Ramsay, the abstracted gloomy philosopher spiritually bound to the letter, "I did for myself what psychoanalysts do for their patients. I expressed some very long felt and deeply felt emotion. And in expressing it I explained it and then laid it to rest." The central figure in the novel Woolf wrote just before *To the Lighthouse* (1927), *Mrs. Dalloway* (1925), is like Mrs. Ramsay linked by gender to domesticity, society, tradition, and the artistic temperament. If Virginia Woolf wrote as the daughter of the father, as some contemporary feminists suggest all women who write are bound to do, she also wrote as her mother's daughter. And this particular father's daughter was both more and less obedient than others when she chose literature. Woolf's personal situation directed her attention to the general subject of women and fiction, and equipped her to reassess their traditional connections, to question and in the end to reaffirm them.

Although she was aware of psychoanalytic theory, Woolf mistrusted psychiatrists (*Mrs. Dalloway* indicates how much) and the theory of psychoanalysis did not capture her creative imagination. The effects of parents on children are a more important subject in Richardson's and Jane Austen's more linear fictions than in hers. It does not interest her to account historically for the set of characteristics that make up individuals: her subjects are the emotional entanglements of contemporaries, and the moments and fragments in lives that belie their large, obvious outlines. In her most original novels Woolf traces the shifting kaleidoscopes of fluctuating consciousnesses. Like Clarissa Dalloway, she is pleased to be inconclusive, proud to be one who "would not say of Peter, . . . would not say of herself, I am this, I am that" (p. 11).* Choosing to write novels, she devoted herself to revising traditional modes of "character-drawing."

---

*Virginia Woolf, *Mrs. Dalloway* (New York: Harcourt, Brace and World, Inc., 1953). Page references in parentheses are to this edition.

"I'm puzzling, in my weak witted way, over some of your problems: about 'form' in literature," Virginia Woolf wrote too apologetically to Roger Fry in the period when she was working on Mrs. Dalloway. "I've been writing about Percy Lubbock's book, and trying to make out what I mean by form in fiction. I say it is emotion put into the right relations; and has nothing to do with form as used of painting." Elsewhere she wrote that Mrs. Dalloway was to have "the quality of a sketch in a finished & composed work." This statement reflects not false modesty but a deliberate aim. The subject of the "sketch" had begun her life in fiction with The Voyage Out (1915), Virginia Woolf's eerily conventional first novel, where Clarissa is perceived as "astonishingly like an eighteenth-century masterpiece—a Reynolds or a Romney." Later, the novel Mrs. Dalloway was conceived first as a sketch, then as a series of sketches; its being most remarkable for conveying a sense of life as elusive seems to me related to all this. The story of Clarissa, Judge Parry's daughter, who summered in the country as a girl, and was pursued by Peter Walsh, loved Sally Seton, married Richard Dalloway, had a daughter, Elizabeth, and feels herself precariously placed in her world at fifty-two, is told by tracing the consciousness of the protagonist as she goes about preparing to give the party that takes place at the novel's end. Interleaved with Clarissa's thoughts and perceptions and memories are those of Peter Walsh and others, most prominently Septimus Warren Smith, a young man Mrs. Dalloway doesn't know, who moves through London as she does, not to a party but to his death, the mention of which momentarily darkens her very different world. "For there she was," the novel ends triumphantly, but the line is ironic; to "catch" Clarissa as realistic novelists caught their characters, to make a portrait of a lady looking as if she were alive, is not this novel's aim. Mrs. Dalloway is about how time, connections, people, feelings, slip away.

Virginia Woolf's puzzling over the question of form in fiction as she read James's admirer Percy Lubbock and wrote Mrs. Dalloway involved puzzling over character, too. In a 1924 lecture she gave at Cambridge, published as "Mr. Bennett and Mrs. Brown," she declared that the traditional forms of fiction were outmoded because "in or about December, 1910, human character changed."* She described that change as a change in relation "between masters and servants, husbands and wives, parents and children." To imagine character as a function of relationships, especially of the relationships of authority and power that determine a person's place in society, is to see like a traditional novelist. And Woolf acknowledges that, just like the realist Arnold Bennett, she thinks character is the important thing in fiction. On the other hand, her vision is new. Her title, emphasizing the binary opposition between Mr. Bennett the novelist and the character he is obliged to "catch" if he can, Mrs. Brown, implies that the dichotomy is between masculine attempts to pin things down and feminine emotion and elusiveness—between the male author and female subject—but the distinction she develops is a historical one. Woolf spoke for her generation of post-Victorians when she insisted on the gulf between what Matthew Arnold had called "the buried life" and the world of appearances, events, and actions. "Realistic" fiction seemed to her and many of her contemporaries to falsify life as it feels, the inner life, and character as it is. For the sake of truth a new kind of fiction was necessary, she said, and in *Jacob's Room* (1922) and then *Mrs. Dalloway* she wrote it.

In traditional realistic narrative, characters are drawn in terms of the several fixed relationships they have with one another: their being husbands and wives, parents and children, masters and servants, makes them who they are. Plot, or the chain of events that ties them together, makes the "real" nature of their mutual connections clearer. *Mrs. Dalloway* hardly has a plot. The

---

* Quentin Bell writes, "Virginia once said that human nature changed in or about December 1910. She is seldom accurate in her use of dates but it is true that the world (or at least her bit of it) was at this time transformed; things were happening which would very much have astonished the maidenly Miss Stephen of 1907. As usual it was Vanessa who gave the lead; she proposed, I do not know how seriously, the creation of a libertarian society with sexual freedom for all. The world at large would not have been surprised to hear it; Vanessa and Virginia had gone to the Post-Impressionist Ball as bare-shouldered bare-legged Gauguin girls, almost—as it seemed to the indignant ladies who swept out in protest—almost naked" (*Virginia Woolf: A Biography*,

important connections between the characters are the inexplicable, fleeting ones. Woolf's vision contradicts the domestic novel's emphasis (through sequentially reported conversations and actions) on "solid" relationships and on a stable self that derives from those. Odd seconds, like bits of light, stay alive in the minds of her characters; these epitomize their selves. Occurrences inside consciousnesses, and connections between them, are the events the novel chronicles. These do not always involve the heroine: Clarissa Dalloway is not a privileged vessel of true feeling. Even the dullest, stuffiest people are portrayed in this novel as caught in delicate webs of relatedness, which (even if they fail to recognize it) make the fabric of their lives. So, as Hugh Whitbread and Richard Dalloway, stolid men, walk across London after lunching with Lady Bruton, and she falls asleep, the narrative records the attenuation of the links that had briefly bound the three together:

And they went further and further from her, being attached to her by a thin thread (since they had lunched with her) which would stretch and stretch, get thinner and thinner as they walked across London; as if one's friends were attached to one's body, after lunching with them, by a thin thread, which (as she dozed there) became hazy with the sound of bells, striking the hour or ringing to service, as a single spider's thread is blotted with rain-drops, and, burdened, sags down. So she slept. (p. 170)

The social relations that create such events as luncheons, and determine who comes and what happens (Lady Bruton asks the

---

p. 170). The change was not primarily in sexual mores. As Bell concedes, "the intellectual character of Bloomsbury was beginning to change" at that moment. "The doctrines of G. E. Moore no longer seemed quite so important when Cézanne was the chief topic of conversation, and Lytton Strachey might seem less pre-eminent when compared with Roger Fry" (p. 168). Woolf's date seems to be quite remarkably precise, in fact; December 1910 was one month after the Post-Impressionist exhibition, organized by Roger Fry, opened in London. By December the first impact would have been felt: the new ideas about form and perception that were exemplified in the show inform a novel such as *Jacob's Room*, and make it different from "realistic" narratives like Arnold Bennett's.

gentlemen, but not Clarissa, so they can help her write a letter to the *Times*), are important because they create emotional reality; but such respectable established relations also betray true and significant feeling. Clarissa Dalloway, a wife and mother, lives her most vivid life in her solitary imagination (which her being a wife and mother keeps protected and rich). The perceptions and memories and reflections that occur there are her real connections to other people. Events and relationships that might be described in a history or a realistic novel are subordinated in this novel to the consciousnesses that move around and through them. The main consciousness is that of the narrator, who draws our attention and also suggests it might be tactful to ignore her presence by the arch personal pronoun ("as if *one's* friends") through which she glides from one character's mind to another.

"A convention in writing is not much different from a convention in manners," Virginia Woolf wrote in "Mr. Bennett and Mrs. Brown."

> Both in life and in literature it is necessary to have some means of bridging the gulf between the hostess and her unknown guest on the one hand, the writer and his unknown reader on the other. The hostess bethinks her of the weather, for generations of hostesses have established the fact that this is a subject of universal interest in which we all believe. She begins by saying that we are having a wretched May, and, having thus got into touch with her unknown guest, proceeds to matters of greater interest. So it is in literature. The writer must get into touch with his reader by putting before him something which he recognizes, which therefore stimulates his imagination, and makes him willing to cooperate in the far more difficult business of intimacy.

When Fielding introduced himself in *Tom Jones* as an innkeeper, he projected the image of the publishing storyteller as a host—the hearty masculine keeper of "a public ordinary" who draws up a bill of fare to the feast of fiction. Virginia Woolf's emphasis is on the less material aspects of conviviality. Her novelist-hostess is an intermediary rather than a purveyor of fine provisions, a woman, not a man, who traffics in feelings, not things. Woolf imagined that the essential conventions of literature were not clues to content, like Fielding's "bill of fare," but instead both the subjects and the object of a social-literary occasion. To touch a reader's inner life she sought to find a form that would show the outer and the inner lives interacting. If she wrote about conventional people, it was to unsettle convention: she wrote to a friend that she wanted to "weight and sharpen dialogue till each sentence tears its way like a harpoon and grapples with the shingles at the bottom of the reader's soul." The wild mixed metaphor suggests despair, and suggests also that the ingredients of the domestic novel since Richardson—drawing rooms and dialogues—seemed to Woolf critically involved in those moments and phrases that make life seem suddenly there, awesome and terrible or wonderful, subversive of the conventional. The hostess-novelist sought to involve her readers through mere conventions in her fiction about a woman who gives a party.

Whereas Richardson's *Clarissa* is a chronicle of the events that occur in a year, *Mrs. Dalloway*, like *Ulysses*, which Woolf read (and disliked) while she wrote it, takes place on a single day. Although the heroine is told by an admirer "that she might be a girl of eighteen" (p. 8) and although vivid memories of being eighteen haunt her, the evocations of the age of Richardson's Clarissa are ironic. Virginia Woolf's is fifty-two; she has a daughter who is eighteen. Clarissa Dalloway is not at all on the verge of marrying but on the contrary solidly married, married first of all, as the title indicates. Although she sleeps alone now in a narrow, white-sheeted bed, and although her having married Richard Dalloway, not Peter Walsh, who too much pressed her, continues to weigh on her mind, she is happy to be married as she is. Being both married and celibate, she confronts no significant sexual dilemma as a heroine usually does: the only thing she is about to do is give a party. As her celibacy suggests (it began with her recovery from a serious illness), the serious fate her body faces is death. Anticipating dissolution, Clarissa pleasurably imagines herself already dissolved:

> ... somehow in the streets of London, on the ebb and flow of things, here, there, she survived, Peter survived, lived in each other, she being part, she was positive, of the trees at home; of the house there, ugly, rambling all to bits and pieces as it was; part of people she had never met; being laid out like a mist between the people she knew best, who lifted her on their branches as she had seen the trees lift the mist, but it spread ever so far, her life, herself. (p. 12)

Walking alone to fetch flowers for her party, she feels disembodied:

> She had the oddest sense of being herself invisible; unseen; unknown; there being no more marrying, no more having of children now, but only this astonishing and rather solemn progress with the rest of them, up Bond Street, this being Mrs. Dalloway; not even Clarissa any more; this being Mrs. Richard Dalloway. (p. 14)

As Mrs. Dalloway, she feels more purely a part of the human life that has gone on through history, free from those personal particulars that, like a too-fond lover, weight the spirit, encumber the soul. And yet she still puzzles over her self, therefore tries to bring her life into sharp focus. Images from the past recur to her as if to assert a protest that her life is a coherent, significant unit, or was meant to be:

> she was a child, throwing bread to the ducks, between her parents, and at the same time a grown woman coming to her parents who stood by the lake, holding her life in her arms which, as she neared them, grew larger and larger in her arms, until it became a whole life, a complete life, which she put down by them and said, "This is what I have made of it!

This!" And what had she made of it? What, indeed? (pp. 63-64)

By turns Clarissa pulls herself together and lets herself dissolve. By turns she seeks solitude and society. Nursing personal resentments, she feels narrowed, lowered, reduced; alone reading memoirs in bed, or walking alone in London, she can also feel liberated and light. People afflict her by making demands on her, but being charming to people makes her feel good. So she gives a party.

Virginia Woolf described what she called "party consciousness" in her diary as a state "where people secrete an envelope which connects them and protects them from others, like myself, who am outside the envelope, foreign bodies." The familiar metaphor of the envelope—Henry James's, Madame Merle's—is mixed with the image of the mollusc who secretes his shell to imply that the envelope-shell, which connects and protects, derives from the body it covers and is not just put on. The mixed metaphor also makes a neat analogy between the organic and the literary, the hidden self and the personal letter. If Virginia Woolf felt herself outside the shallow "fashion world" whose party consciousness she liked to study, she was also one who heard with great excitement the party sound of envelopes shuffling together, and the smaller undersound of subversive secretings. Her autobiographical writings indicate how much she felt drawn to convivial groups, and also driven from them.

The party at the end of *Mrs. Dalloway* is semisatirically presented. Like the marriage that concludes the courtship plot, a party is a ceremony symbolic of social coherence. But unlike a marriage, it is a temporary union of a group, not a couple, sanctioned by no gods, and it changes nothing by occurring. The hostess Clarissa's creation, her party, stands simultaneously for civilized warmth and beauty, and intimate connections among people, and for those false appearances that betray the soul. She gives her party to pull herself together; becoming a hostess, she flees her real self. Her party is an expression of Mrs. Dalloway the creator of beauty and the reflection of Clarissa as Peter Walsh always told her (to hurt her) she would end up, the perfect hostess. Virginia Woolf satirizes the party, where the Prime Minister is a guest, as frivolous and full of false feeling, and on the other hand regards it as an expression of the civilization that has created Britain and Bond Street where there were swamps, and raised man from beasts, and been the impulse behind all creative human endeavor.

Her party is a microcosm of the social world of which Mrs. Dalloway (no liminal heroine) is a keystone, or lynchpin. Lady Bruton and the Prime Minister, Peter Walsh from India and Sally Seton from Manchester, poor Ellie Henderson and too-grand Sir William Bradshaw, people from her childhood and people involved in her life as a Westminster hostess come together, in effect, to celebrate her determination to exist in spite of ominous threatening forces. Just as Clarissa has recovered from a debilitating illness that has left her hair white, her world is recovering from a shattering war. Neither will ever quite recover, and they are both being wonderfully brave. The party reaffirms life as opposed to war. But the shadows of war and of death and of violence fall on it: an invited guest, the psychiatrist Sir William Bradshaw, arrives late and explains he was detained by a patient's suicide. As Mrs. Dalloway shrinks from tragedy in anger because it spoils her party, the reader shrinks from the heartless, selfish society matron; we have followed Septimus's disintegration as she has not. The shell or envelope of Clarissa, which we have seen through from the novel's beginning, at the end ironically seems to be the real Clarissa after all. Clarissa, with whom we have been intimate, is last seen at a distance, from Peter Walsh's perspective: she has recovered from her anger and shock, has even drawn new vitality from her violent revulsion from death. She stands upright and charming in silk at the head of her stairs, the perfect hostess, just the thing he always satirically said she would end up as, and Peter admires her.

By chronicling the day Septimus Warren Smith disintegrates at the same time as the day Mrs. Dalloway prepares to give her party, Virginia Woolf draws an unnerving analogy between a lower-class man and an upper-class woman, between a mad and a sane person, between the unmaking and the making, the decomposing and composing, of the self. The sad contrasting story of Septimus points up the narrowness and self-centeredness and callousness, the frivolity and destructiveness of Mrs. Dalloway's world (which honors and embraces Sir William Bradshaw), and also its charm, its virtues of grace and coherence. At the same time, Septimus's parallel psychic world makes Mrs. Dalloway's more poignant. The frail links between Clarissa and Septimus are made by their passing one another in the busy streets of crowded London, and seeing some of the same things, and brushing up differently against some of the same people. As we watch both of their minds watching their own processes, we sense a kinship they could never perceive. The connection between Clarissa and Septimus, mysterious until the end and incomplete then, suggests that disconnectedness is a factor in the lives of people who live among others. Septimus, who knows no one and is married to a foreigner, is not moored like Mrs. Dalloway in a stable social world; his memories of war and death are terrible; his life was always unpleasant and hungry. He is driven to death by his sense of being different and alien, but also by a horror of others— Holmes and Bradshaw, the doctors—whom he experiences as invading him, forcing his soul. Losing his balance between solitude and society, he asserts the integrity of his self, kills himself.

In the diaries Virginia Woolf kept while she wrote *Mrs. Dalloway* she describes, often wryly, her alternating selves, "Virginia," and the "sensibility" she became when she wrote. Here, characteristically, she approaches the personal through the theoretical:

> It is a mistake to think that literature can be produced from the raw. One must get out of life—yes, thats why I disliked so much the irruption of Sydney—one must become externalised; very, very concentrated, all at one point, not having to draw upon the scattered parts of one's character, living in the brain. Sydney comes & I'm Virginia; when I write I'm

merely a sensibility. Sometimes I like being Virginia, but only when I'm scattered & various & gregarious. Now, so long as we are here, I'd like to be only a sensibility.

She believed the artist had to be free of distractions, simplified, therefore objective and able to work. Ideally, she wrote in her critical essays, the work of art testifies to the artist's having freed himself of personality.

The great novelist feels, sees, believes with such intensity of conviction that he hurls his belief outside himself and it flies off and lives an independent life of its own, becomes Natasha, Pierre, Levin, and is no longer Tolstoy.

This has the ring of familiar praise: to create a character that seems to live a life of its own has been the alleged goal of many writers, and many critics have evaluated characters in fiction as more or less independently alive. But her work makes one wonder if Woolf means her comment as praise. Can we say of Virginia Woolf, who quarreled with the realists' form, that when she wrote fiction, she hurled her belief outside herself and became no longer Virginia Woolf but Septimus Smith, Mrs. Dalloway? Do we ever meet, in our lives, a Septimus or a Clarissa, or someone who brings Septimus or Clarissa to mind, the way we meet people who remind us of Natasha or Pierre or Levin? I think not. Not that in Isa or Rhoda or Lady Bruton, or Jacob or Septimus or Clarissa, we are distracted by Virginia Woolf. But the best things in her novels—like the dissolving threads between the guests after Lady Bruton's luncheon—remind us that her characters figure in a vision, that the vision is what's important. His characters are in the service of Tolstoy's vision, too; as Woolf writes, every novelist's "fortunes colour and his oddities shape his vision until what we see is not the thing itself, but the thing seen and the seer inextricably mixed." She adds, "There are degrees, however." Mrs. Dalloway is not a memorable character like Natasha or Levin, an individual with clear outlines. She is of a recognizable type, and she is complicated as real people are; but she asks of us an odd mixed or double reaction, one that is a reflection of her. The long distance between seeing Mrs. Dalloway as she appears and as she feels herself to be is experienced by the reader, who by turns satirically judges and feels with her. Our double response to Mrs. Dalloway, and Mrs. Dalloway's alternately dissolving and assuming clear form, are related to one another, and perhaps related also to the fluctuating process of becoming now a concentrated and then a diffused self that Virginia Woolf observed in herself. The novelist's experience of escaping the self, which for Tolstoy ended in his being Natasha, Pierre, or Levin, evidently finished differently for the author of *Mrs. Dalloway.* That she does not have an independent existence is the most original quality of Clarissa Dalloway as a heroine.

Clarissa the shallow society matron reflects, when she sees her face in the glass with her lips pursed "to give her face point," that when there is "some call on her to be her self" she becomes "pointed; dartlike; definite." This defined self both conceals and helps her resist "all the other sides of her—faults, jealousies, vanities, suspicions, like this of Lady Bruton not asking her to lunch." The "call" to which Clarissa Dalloway responds is not like the call to Virginia Woolf: she is not an artist whose concentrated "living in the brain" is productive. On the contrary; precisely what Woolf experienced as the "irruption" of another person is the "call" which Mrs. Dalloway responds to by composing herself to become

> one woman who sat in her drawing-room and made a meeting-point, a radiancy no doubt in some dull lives, a refuge for the lonely to come to, perhaps; she had helped young people, who were grateful to her; had tried to be the same always. . . .(p. 55)

Yet Clarissa Dalloway is like Virginia Woolf when she hates feeling clogged by the merely personal, and shies away from invasive people who would force her soul, and shuttles between being a diffused and a concentrated self. She escapes the personal into flowers, memories, and perceptions of life's beauty, into London, movement, the creation of parties, not literature. She escapes her own ambiguity and complexity into the conventional "Mrs. Dalloway," a version of the self composed as if it were an artifact, tendered to others as if it were an object, which I have been calling "the heroine." Then she feels concentrated, as Virginia Woolf said she herself did when she wrote. In the light of the legend of Virginia Woolf, and her letters and journals and criticism, Clarissa Dalloway seems both a travesty and a projection of her creator, a semisatirical self-portrait of the novelist as hostess and heroine.

A little more than two months before she wrote the last words of *Mrs. Dalloway*, Virginia Woolf made some notes in her diary about plans for reading:

> It strikes me, I must now read Pilgrim's Progress: Mrs. Hutchinson. And should I demolish Richardson? whom I've never read. Yes, I'll run through the rain into the house & see if Clarissa is there. But thats a block out of my day, a long long novel.

She never wrote about *Clarissa*; but of course she had read about it before—most effectively, perhaps, by reading novels about heroines in the Richardsonian tradition. Her Clarissa is in many ways reminiscent of Richardson's.

Clarissa Dalloway like Clarissa Harlowe is first of all the protagonist of a struggle to be integral, coherent, defined, self-aware, self-controlling. This struggle is not dramatized in *Mrs. Dalloway* the way it is in the courtship plot; nevertheless, the tensions that dominate and unify Woolf's novel are generated between the traditional polarities of intimacy and identity, male and female, the social and the inner lives, which this novel both examines and relies on. Conceiving of herself as the creature of her relationships with others, and bound by her woman's fate to a life of relationships, the conscious heroine longs for solitude and separateness. That this is not a subversive desire—that she is admired precisely for being separate and unique—is the paradox in which she and her world are caught. The heroine's secret self inclines her to observe and assess her apparent self from a little distance: her actively self-scrutinizing consciousness is what distinguishes her as a heroine. Clarissa Harlowe's self-consciousness finds its literary form in letters, Clarissa Dalloway's in Woolf's stream-of-consciousness technique. The heroine is inevitably involved with romance: Mrs. Dalloway in middle age is haunted, through letters and memories and now, all the way from India, a visit, by Peter Walsh, the man who would have given her too little space had she married him. The heroine's traditional antagonist, the rake, is made a little absurd in Peter, a fiftyish failure still romantically adventuring, now arranging his new young fiancée's divorce. After so many years, Clarissa observes with maternal amusement, Peter is still playing with his pocket knife. She quite depends, though, on his staying attractive and in love with her, depends on the distance, too, between Westminster and India. By marrying Richard not Peter, Clarissa has kept herself free not to share, not to go into, everything. Her marrying Richard and her continued pleasure in being Mrs. Dalloway may be read as a little death analogous to Septimus's actual death. But to fault Clarissa Dalloway for being frigid is like criticizing Isabel Archer for not yielding to Goodwood: it is to remove the heroine from the novel. Clarissa's distance from mutual passion, like her self-conscious distance from herself, is what her story is about. The novel explores the heroine's struggle to be herself and yet be complementary to a man. Or—to put it another way—that is one of the givens from which the novel is generated. Her disembodied intimacy with a man imagined as her spiritual mate makes the romantic, antiromantic plot. Only by a strenuous effort of the comic imagination—Shakespeare's or Jane Austen's—can the conscious heroine be imagined as achieving intimacy and identity together. Her truest mating must be like Gwendolen's with Deronda, Isabel's with Ralph—or, most tenuously of all, like the one the narrator of *Mrs. Dalloway* fabricates, between Clarissa and Septimus Warren Smith, the total stranger who is her opposite, her shadowy nemesis, her brother in the vale of soul-making.

In drawing a heroine past the life of the body, and drawing a parallel between her continued struggle to conceptualize her self and the struggle of poor Septimus to stay sane, and mostly by emphasizing Clarissa Dalloway's fluidity, Virginia Woolf revises the concept of the novel heroine, and the reader's relationship to her. One is not moved by the exemplary image of Clarissa Dalloway as *she* was moved by Sally Seton, who kissed her, or as Emma Bovary was moved by the women she read about, or as readers are moved by Isabel Archer. Instead of creating a woman who seems more integral and sharply defined than one feels one-self to be, Virginia Woolf in *Mrs. Dalloway* conveys a sense of the self as evanescent, of people slipping away like moments. In an autumnal mood, *Mrs. Dalloway* looks back nostalgically and also satirically on a self-deluded society, and on the kind of novel that portrayed and sustained its attractive false values, and on the heroine of both, the central symbol of the separate self. In Woolf's evocations of the fleeting links between such ordinary individuals as Hugh Whitbread and Lady Bruton there is iron-ically imaged the truth that links and parallels between not par-ticularly special people are as important as unique individuality—and have the same doomed poignancy. *Mrs. Dalloway* shows death and madness and foreigners and the lower classes intruding on the heroine's world, and depression and dissolution threaten-ing her self, and her world and self asserting themselves in the only way they know.

Lytton Strachey's reading of *Mrs. Dalloway* as satirical seems to me fair. Virginia Woolf indicts the establishment that produced the war that kills Septimus Smith years after he survived combat: its pillars are Sir William Bradshaw, the rich psychiatrist who would force the soul, and Peter Walsh, the weak servant of impe-rialism, and stuffy Hugh Whitbread, carrying dispatches of an aloof government, and that inarticulate public man Richard Dalloway. By going about their business these conventional men repress and deny the poetry of living, the vital personal life. Woolf shows that Clarissa Dalloway and her strictly personal life flower out of that grim establishment. They appear—they pretend—to justify it. Clarissa's radiant memories and the delicious folds of her green silk dress and her upper-class housekeeping charm the novel-reader; the grace she represents is attractive. But at the end, her assertion of her integrity and separateness from the world calls our attention to her sinister connections with it, and makes us ponder how story-telling and character-drawing are related to her self-enclosure. As she stands poised precariously at the top of her stairs, Mrs. Dalloway promises her world's brief moment is passing.

# Afterword

On the road to Canterbury, the Wife of Bath tells two different stories, stories of two different kinds. One she tells deliberately and the other, we are meant to think, because she can't help herself. Both stories characterize her as a female. The "long preamble to a tale" which enumerates her husbands and troubles and triumphs is elaborately informal, being partly a parody of a medieval clerk's standard argument: the Wife claims to be the voice of experience as opposed to "auctoritee," that is, to be no pedantic scholar but Nature's own wise child. By its digressions and self-reflexive interruptions her Prologue claims truth to life, not literature. The other story, the Wife's contribution to the pilgrims' general undertaking of storytelling, is told in the third person, in an authoritative auctorial voice. It is about a knight who rapes a maiden and is condemned to death and then promised pardon by a queen and her court of women if, within a year, he discovers what he chose as a rapist to ignore: what it is that women truly desire. Seeking the answer to the question that was to stump Sigmund Freud, he travels over the earth, and at length chances on an old and ugly woman who promises to give him the truth if he will marry her. As his allotted year is nearly up, he agrees. She reveals then that above all other things women want mastery over their husbands, the upper hand, the last word—what the Wife of Bath has told us, in her Prologue, she has striven all her married life to get. On their wedding night, the young man refuses to touch the loathly lady, who by turns begs and insists. Finally she asks if he would rather have her as she is, old and ugly and reliably faithful, or young and beautiful and a source of husbandly anxiety. "As you like," he more or less replies, and so by magic she makes herself young and beautiful and absolutely faithful, repaying him for his submissiveness with everything. They live happily ever after.

Such a story—a fairy tale or an old wives' tale, a story about sexual love from the woman's point of view, touched with malice and mockery but respectful of men's status and prerogatives, a generously and even maternally indulgent story—such a story is traditionally a woman's. Men are not surprised to hear it told by a feminine voice; that women's stories are about magic and sex is, to misogynists, evidence of women's narrowness (*i.e.*, women are interested only in sex, and seek entertainment, not truth, being credulous not logical, petty not philosophical). Another kind of story women are "supposed" to tell is such a one as the garrulous Wife's preamble: an earthbound outpouring of circumstantial domestic detail, a litany of memories of all the men she knew, of all the clothes she wore, of all the clever things she said. Another stereotype goes like this: women are obsessed with themselves and their bodies and the facts of their daily lives; they talk too much; they tell tales; they have sharp tongues; they are gossips; they can't keep a secret. The Wife touches on all these accusations in the course of her Prologue.

The two stories the Wife of Bath tells epitomize two of its elements for which the novel has been condemned: romantic fantasy and domestic realism. Both these different characteristics have caused the novel to be disparaged as feminine. The Wife of Bath lived centuries before prose fiction began to be widely produced by women, for women. She was no writer of romance. But women who wrote titillating gothics and sentimental tales of love could be seen as following in distinctly feminine footsteps like the Wife's. While they were condemned on moral and artistic grounds, they were not deemed unfeminine. To write what they did, fantastic and/or personal fictions about women and love, was not to rebel against the condition of women, but rather to conform to it—to confirm stereotyped views about the garrulous daughters of Eve. A literary genre without respectable classical ancestry, prose fiction was not defended from women but rather, condescendingly, granted them.

In French there is no feminine form of the word "*écrivain*," but a woman who writes novels may be called a "*romancière*." A serious writer would not be pleased by the term, any more than a serious male writer would want to be called a "*romancier*." Male and female novelists have struggled since the eighteenth century to distinguish their work from what we call "pulp," to legitimize a bastard genre. Their antagonists, those who question the novel's right to be read and taken seriously, have emphasized, in order to denigrate the form, its connection with women. For female writers of fiction the novel's dubious status as art has been a mixed curse. It has not been necessary for them—as it was for the poets Anne Bradstreet and Anne Finch—to stake a claim to a form that came into the world rather like Tristram Shandy, apologizing for itself. On the other hand, writers like Currer, Ellis, and Acton Bell, and George Eliot, have concealed their sex to avoid being read as "lady novelists," writers of a gender and a genre provocative of contemptuous indulgence or moralizing about women and their poor, merely womanish efforts.

From its beginnings the novel form has challenged the serious writer to reconceive, rewrite, and revise (in Henry James's sense of the word) an upstart form of literature with vulgar connections. A novel is after all only a story about ordinary people, of necessity mired in details of ordinary lives; it is a story like the ones ordinary people have told to pass the time; ordinary people like novels, can read them without knowing very much more than how to read. The novelist, especially one who takes a female subject—a heroine, a woman's life—chooses to dignify and make important things from which Homer averts his eyes, matters at which Virgil only nods.

Today we read novels about women without apology; the form and the subject are accepted as legitimate. A woman's struggle to define herself against stereotyped images is a theme of current

feminist novels and of fiction affected by feminism. And because
women's lives are no longer so predictable as they were when the
novel first shaped itself to the prescribed middle-class female destiny, contemporary novelists not especially interested in women's
issues (I think of the author of *Burger's Daughter*) can still find
the particularity of a female protagonist emblematic of the human condition. Meanwhile, of course, romance continues to be
written, and as always it continues to lap seductively at the edges
of realism, and even feminism. The paperback editions of Margaret Drabble's quite serious early novels about modern young
women feature, on the front, an attractive large photograph, and
on the back a biographical note about "Margaret Drabble, pic-
tured on the cover" to confirm the reader's guess at the identity
of the woman in the picture, and underline the photograph's
importance. Reprinted praise from the *Times Literary Supple-
ment*—"Margaret Drabble, like her heroines, always knows what
she is doing"—further insists that the woman novelist is a feminine ideal, constant, conscious, active, and admirable, interesting
for being literary as attractive women often are. Feminist critics
who find this traditional position of women writers uncomfortable have called for new approaches, new plots. The persistence
of the old ones, and of the old assumptions they reflect about a
woman's literary/sexual nature, suggest how hard it is to alter
formative fictions.

The fiction of the heroine encourages aspiration and imposes
limits. Paradox is at its core: probably that accounts for its power.
The beautiful personal integrity the novel heroine imagines and
stands for and seeks for herself is a version of the romantic view
of woman as a desired object; as the image of the integral self, she
is the inverted image of half of a couple. The literary associations
that halo the heroine keep her in a traditional woman's place.
That self-awareness which distinguishes her from the simple
heroine of romance ends by implicating her further in fictions of
the feminine. On the other hand, in the end I have only self-
awareness—the conscious heroine's pride and prison—to recommend as a solution to all these problems. The classic English
heroine-centered novels (I recommend them, too) do not begin

to offer a blueprint for a feminist utopia; on the contrary, to enjoy them is to experience the pull of a seductive, reactionary dream. But in their complex self-consciousness they are wise, and full of useful information about what must be kept in mind if we would try to change. I suppose I am saying that they are in a way exemplary.

# Notes

## Introduction

Richard Ellmann comments on George Eliot's description of girlhood reading in "Dorothea's Husbands: Some Biographical Speculations," *TLS*, 16 February 1973, p. 166. The passage he quotes is from Gordon S. Haight, ed., *The George Eliot Letters* I (New Haven, 1955), p. 22. The reader inclined to dispute my emphasis, and to argue that women are no more influenced by fiction than men are, might cite Dr. Johnson's confession of his lifelong habit of reading "extravagant fictions" and his belief that they had contributed to his "unsettled turn of mind." (See W. Jackson Bate, *Samuel Johnson*, [New York, 1977], pp. 392–93.)

I quote Freud's "On Narcissism: An Introduction" (1914), in Sigmund Freud, *Collected Papers* IV (New York, 1959), p. 46. Tony Tanner's remark is in *Adultery in the Novel: Contract and Transgression* (Baltimore, 1979), p. 97. Virginia Woolf's 1929 essay on women and literature is *A Room of One's Own* (New York, 1957); her definition of marriage occurs in *Three Guineas* (1938; New York, 1963), p. 6. *The Great Tradition* is F. R. Leavis's influential book which states that "the great English novelists are Jane Austen, George Eliot, Henry James and Joseph Conrad." Adrienne Rich defines re-vision in "When We Dead Awaken: Writing as Re-Vision," *On Lies, Secrets, and Silence* (New York, 1979). Virginia Woolf's description of George Eliot's heroines is in "George Eliot," Virginia Woolf, *Collected Essays* I (New York, 1967), p. 204. Nancy K. Miller makes the point I refer to in "Emphasis Added: Plots and Plausibilities in Women's Fiction," *PMLA* 96, January 1981.

For the novel as opposed to the epic, see Georg Lukacs, *Theory of the Novel*, tr. Anna Bostock (London, 1971): "The novel is the epic of an age in which the extensive totality of life is no longer directly given, in which the immanence of meaning in life has become a problem, yet which still thinks in terms of totality" (p. 56). "The epic gives form to a totality of life that is rounded from within; the novel seeks, by giving form, to uncover and construct the concealed totality of life" (p. 60). On the nonheroic and the novel, a classic work is Mario Praz, *The Hero in Eclipse in Victorian Fiction*, tr. Angus Davidson (Oxford, 1956).

The term "heroine" is even harder to define than "hero" is; I can make no useful preliminary definition, since its problematic nature is my subject. There have been notable attempts to define a female mode of the heroic in recent years, much of it an aspect of the feminist project of redefining both "extraordinary" and "ordinary" women that has influenced my thinking in more ways than I can detail. In *Literary Women* (New York, 1976), Ellen Moers coined the term "heroinism" and described a typology—traveling heroism, loving heroism, performing heroism, educating heroism—in a historical account of women writers and characters from the eighteenth to the twentieth century; her aim was to assert the existence and importance of a female literary tradition and an imaginatively vivid and durable (therefore valid) idea of a powerful, remarkable woman articulated in literature. In *Reinventing Womanhood* (New York, 1979), Carolyn G. Heilbrun called upon women who have been denied and excluded from heroism as men have defined it to look for models among strong men, rather than women, in literature. In an essay responding to Erich Neumann's definition of the mythical Psyche as a model of female heroism (in his *Amor and Psyche* [Princeton, 1971]), Lee R. Edwards argued that there is an ancient idea of the heroic that is gender-free, therefore available as a model to women as well as to men ("The Labors of Psyche: Toward a Theory of Female Heroism," *Critical Inquiry* 6, Autumn 1979). See also Rachel Blau Du Plessis, who like Edwards rejects Neumann's idea of a "feminine" Psyche, proposing a feminist ideal of femaleness and wholeness ("Psyche, or Wholeness," *The Massachusetts Review*, Spring 1979).

My own interest is less in defining a new model or a theory of female heroism than in exploring the paradoxes inherent in the traditional idea of a heroine, or the idea of the anti-heroic that interrogates it from within. The mythic resonances of the word are of course essential, but my concern is with the heroine as a creature of her text. (See, in this connection, Nancy K. Miller, *The Heroine's Text* [New York, 1980], which elegantly compares two kinds of heroines, of two kinds of plots, in French and English novels.) The ambiguity of the idea of the hero is a major theme in literature (see, *e.g.*, *Don Quixote*, *Tristram Shandy*, Byron's *Don Juan*); here I discuss the idea(l) of the remarkable female self as that is thematized. B.M.W. Knox, in "The Medea of Euripides," *Yale Classical Studies* 25, 1977, describes one ancient tragic heroine as an inversion of the hero; perhaps a suggestion of parody hovers over the head of every heroine, as woman's traditional powerlessness and unremarkable, predictably generic nature is set up against the importance, clarity, and transcendent meaning of a central character in a literary work. The ideas of the remarkable individual and the achieved self are presented in novels about women, I think, in such a way as to emphasize the literariness and the limitations of the heroic ideal.

It would be false for me to claim direct descent from particular feminist critics, and misleading to emphasize my differences with them. The ideas in this book have been shaped by reading, listening to, talking with, and reacting to a variety of people who have been writing about women in literature, women writers, and women's lives. Some of the books I list here inspired me, and others disposed me to argument; others, which I read while I wrote or after I finished writing, are products, as my work is, of a shared time, and shared places. In a review article, "Feminist Criticism in the Wilderness" (*Critical Inquiry* 8, Winter 1981), Elaine Showalter distinguishes between "feminist readings" and what she calls "gynocritics." I shall borrow her categories. One kind of feminist critic focuses on women as figures in and subjects of literature. Books in this tradition that have been important to me are, politically and methodologically, a heterogeneous lot: Françoise Basch's *Relative Creatures* (New York, 1974); Mary Ellmann's *Thinking About Women* (New York, 1968); Joan M. Ferrante's *Woman as Image in Medieval Literature from the 12th Century to Dante* (New York, 1975); Elizabeth Hardwick's *Seduction and Betrayal* (New York, 1974); Carolyn G. Heilbrun's *Toward a Definition of Androgyny* (New York, 1974); Kate Millett's *Sexual Politics* (New York, 1970); and Emily Jane Putnam's *The Lady* (1910; Chicago, 1970). Books in the other category, "gynocritics," which is concerned with women as users of language, include those, like *Literary Women*, which describe a female tradition, and those that aim to define the specificity of women's writing. They include Nina Baym's *Woman's Fiction* (1978), about American novels; Elaine Showalter's *A Literature of Their Own* (Princeton, 1977), about British novelists;

Patricia Meyer Spacks's *The Female Imagination* (New York, 1975); and, most recently, Sandra M. Gilbert's and Susan Gubar's magisterial *The Madwoman in the Attic* (New Haven, 1979). In very different ways, these last two studies attempt to locate, in literature, evidence of women's difference from men; French feminists using linguistic and Lacanian analysis address the same problem (see Elaine Marks and Isabelle de Courtivron, *New French Feminisms* [Amherst, 1980], and the Autumn 1981 issue of *Signs*). Showalter's essay, the other articles in the "Writing and Sexual Difference" issue of *Critical Inquiry*, and an essay by Myra Jehlen, "Archimedes and the Paradox of Feminist Criticism" (*Signs* 6, Summer 1981), are evidence of the increasing intellectual vigor of feminist critics who reinterpret and examine the process, and the effects, of interpretations.

Among feminist critics who focus on the female readership, most study popular fiction (see, *e.g.*, Ann Barr Snitow, "Mass Market Romance: Pornography for Women is Different," *Radical History Review*, Spring/Summer 1979); Judith Fetterley, in *The Resisting Reader* (Bloomington, 1978), has addressed herself to the relationship between women readers and "classic" American literature and its received interpretations. The indispensable text on the female readership is Ian Watt's *The Rise of the Novel* (Berkeley, 1957); also relevant are Q. D. Leavis, *Fiction and the Reading Public* (London, 1932; 1965), and Richard Altick, *The English Common Reader* (Chicago, 1957).

For the transition from romance to realism, see, in addition to Watt, J.M.S. Tompkins, *The Popular Novel in England, 1770–1800* (1932; Lincoln, 1961); Arnold Kettle, *An Introduction to the English Novel* (1951; New York, 1960); John J. Richetti, *Popular Fiction Before Richardson* (Oxford, 1969); Ioan Williams, *Novel and Romance: 1700–1800: A Documentary Record* (New York, 1970) and *The Realistic Novel in England* (Pittsburgh, 1975). The classic in the field is Clara Reeve's *The Progress of Romance* (1785; facsimile edition New York, 1930).

For the relationship of the idea of character in literature to fictional form, see Leo Bersani, *A Future for Astyanax: Character and Desire in Literature* (Boston, 1976); W. J. Harvey, *Character and the Novel* (Ithaca, 1975); and an important essay by Martin Price, "The Other Self: Thoughts about Character in the Novel," in *Imagined Worlds: Essays on Some English Novels and Novelists in Honour of John Butt* (London, 1968).

For woman and the form of the novel, see Pierre Fauchéry, *La Destinée féminine dans le roman européen du dix-huitième siècle* (Paris, 1972);

N. K. Miller, *The Heroine's Text*; and Tony Tanner, *Adultery in the Novel*. Myra Jehlen's "Archimedes and the Paradox of Feminist Criticism" states a strong feminist position on the relationship of constraints on women to novelistic constraints.

When I speak of the conscious heroine I have in mind Henry James's definition of "consciousness" as "that reflective part which governs conduct and produces character" ("Guy de Maupassant" [1888], in Leon Edel, ed., *The House of Fiction* [London, 1957], p. 166).

On reading, finally, see Kenneth Burke, "Literature as Equipment for Living," in *The Philosophy of Literary Form* (Berkeley, 1973); "*The reading of a book on the attaining of success is in itself the symbolic attaining of that success. It is while they read* that these readers are 'succeeding.' I'll wager that, in by far the great majority of cases, such readers make no serious attempt to apply the book's recipes. The lure of the book resides in the fact that the reader, while reading it, is then living in the aura of success. What he wants is *easy* success; and he gets it in symbolic form by the mere reading itself. To attempt applying such stuff in real life would be very difficult, full of many disillusioning difficulties" (p. 299). Burke writes this about the Dale Carnegie type of how-to book; the reader of fiction craves not so much actual as symbolic success, which only literature, or life apprehended as literature, can provide.

Freud's essay "Family Romances" (1909) is in Sigmund Freud, *Collected Papers* V (New York, 1959).

# Being Perfect:
# My Life in Fiction

Susan Ferrier's *Marriage, a Novel*, ed. Herbert Foltinek, was reprinted by Oxford University Press in 1971. What Dr. Johnson actually wrote in his *Journey to the Western Islands* was: "But it must be remembered, that life consists not of a series of illustrious actions, or elegant enjoyments; the great part of our time passes in compliance with necessities, in the performance of daily duties, in the removal of small inconveniencies, in the procurement of petty pleasures; and we are well or ill at ease, as the main stream of life glides on smoothly, or is ruffled by small obstacles and frequent interruptions." My source is William K. Wimsatt, Jr., *The*

*Prose Style of Samuel Johnson* (New Haven, 1941), p. 85; Wimsatt cites *Works* X, pp. 338-39.

I quote on p. 6 from Virginia Woolf's "The Niece of an Earl," *Collected Essays* I, p. 220; in the Harcourt, Brace, Jovanovich edition of Woolf's *The Voyage Out*, the description of Rachel Vinrace reading is on pp. 123-24.

Alice's obligation to marry is discussed in Chapter 11, on pp. 140-41 of the Penguin edition of *Can You Forgive Her?* (New York and Harmondsworth, 1978); what I characterize as a Jamesian snort may be found in a short review of *Can You Forgive Her?* in *Notes and Reviews by Henry James: A Series of Twenty-Five Papers Hitherto Unpublished in Book Form* (Cambridge, Mass., 1921), p. 85.

The quotation from Meredith's "An Essay on Comedy" is in Wylie Sypher, ed., *Comedy* (New York, 1956), p. 32; in the Norton Critical Edition of Meredith's *The Egoist* (New York, 1979), Sir Willoughby accosts Laetitia Dale on p. 24; in the Norton *The Portrait of a Lady* (New York, 1975), Isabel's thought about thinking about marriage is on p. 55.

I quote from the Bantam Books edition of Doris Lessing's *The Golden Notebook* (New York, 1973), p. 208 on Jane Austen, and p. 340 on "blood." The squib by Elizabeth Hardwick is on the cover. Claire Sprague's work on Lessing has been helpful to me.

Georgette Heyer's *Faro's Daughter* (copyright 1941) was reprinted in 1976. For some nice distinctions about the romance genre in the early 1980s, see *Publishers Weekly*, November 13, 1981. For Jane Austen as a writer of romance, see the challenging article by Ann Barr Snitow in *Radical History Review*, Spring/Summer 1979. Lillian Robinson writes about Jane Austen and Georgette Heyer in "On Reading Trash," in her *Sex, Class, and Culture* (Bloomington, 1979).


# Being Perfect:
# An Exemplar to Her Sex


Mme. de Genlis is quoted by Patricia M. Spacks, in *Imagining a Self* (Cambridge, Mass., 1976), p. 191. Spacks's point there is that Fanny Burney quoted the remark; her citation reads: "Quoted by Fanny Burney #410, To Mrs. Waddington, 4 April 1801; Journals IV, 483."

The young American diarist is quoted by Barbara Welter, *Dimity Convictions: The American Woman in the Nineteenth Century* (Athens,

Ohio, 1976), p. 9; the passage from Chapter 6 of Maria Edgeworth's *Belinda* (1801; London, 1896) is on p. 84.

For the eighteenth-century novel, the female readership, and the shift from romance to realism, see Kettle, *An Introduction to the English Novel*; Richetti, *Popular Fiction Before Richardson*; and of course Watt, *The Rise of the Novel*. For French heroic romance see Maurice Magendie, *Le Roman français au xvii$^e$ siècle de l'Astrée au Grand Cyrus* (Paris, 1932), and Robert R. Nunn, "Mlle de Scudéry's *Clélie*" (Columbia University dissertation, 1966). I read portions of *Clélie* and *Le Grand Cyrus* in anonymously translated volumes ascribed to *George* de Scudéry (Madeleine's brother and collaborator), dated "London, 1768." See also Clara Reeve's *The Progress of Romance* (1785), criticism in the form of a discussion between a man and two women (like Henry James's "*Daniel Deronda*: A Conversation," of which more later). Euphrasia, evidently speaking for the author, argues that Romance is respectably descended from Epic, that it can inspire to virtue as well as to vice, and that it is different in form from the realistic novel. Among novels she distinguishes between the moral and the nonmoral, and she argues that young men as well as women can be ruined by reading. Appended to *The Progress of Romance* is an adaptation of an Arabian tale about a maiden's triumphant subtlety: Charoba defeats, by magic, the king who would marry her, and dies a virgin after giving over her throne to her also virgin kinswoman. A bloody story hardly encouraging the Christian morality Euphrasia praises, it does not on the other hand encourage overvaluing romantic love, either. Does Reeve mean to imply romance might be found objectionable by men for other reasons?

Dr. Johnson sanctioned moral fiction, insisting that "if the power of example is so great as to take possession of the memory by a kind of violence, and produce effects almost without the intervention of the will, care ought to be taken that, when the choice is unrestrained, the best examples only should be exhibited; and that which is likely to operate so strongly should not be mischievous or uncertain in its effects" (*Rambler* 4, 31 March 1750, in *Samuel Johnson, Selected Poetry and Prose*, ed. Frank Brady and W. K. Wimsatt [Berkeley, 1977], p. 157). But see Charlotte Grandison's counter-argument in Richardson's last novel: "Some of us are to be set up for warnings, some for examples: And the first are generally of greater use to the world than the other" (Samuel Richardson, *The History of Sir Charles Grandison*, ed. Jocelyn Harris, 3 vols. [London and N.Y., 1972], II, p. 264). Pierre Fauchéry argues that the heroine (he writes "*victime*") of the realistic novel has to be sufficiently close to the norm for the reader to identify with her, and on the other hand exceptional and exemplary. He observes that self-consciousness (like Charlotte's) is usual: "*Souvent elles prennent d'elles-mêmes conscience de cette mission*," he writes, of the heroines' exemplary function; "*sinon, d'autres se chargeront de les en avertir*" (*La Destinée féminine dans le roman européen du dix-huitième siècle*, p. 117).

# *Clarissa*

In *Samuel Richardson: Dramatic Novelist* (Ithaca, 1973), Mark Kinkaid-Weekes complained that only a few of his critics "encouraged any student to take [Richardson] seriously" (p. vii). Since 1973 a very great deal has been written about Richardson, much of it by feminists and critics influenced by the women's movement; if Richardson can still be called "the most misunderstood of the pioneers of English fiction," in Kinkaid-Weekes's words, it is impossible now to say he is "the most neglected" (p. 3). My essay on *Clarissa* was finished before I saw most of the latest on Richardson, including Kinkaid-Weekes's extremely sensitive and sensible study. I am most indebted to the early critics who discussed Richardson's novel in its social context: to Arnold Kettle's pages in *An Introduction to the English Novel*, Ian Watt's *The Rise of the Novel*, and Christopher Hill's very important "Clarissa Harlowe and her Times," reprinted in John Carroll, ed., *Samuel Richardson: A Collection of Critical Essays* (Englewood Cliffs, 1969). Other excellent essays on the novel, including Carroll's introduction to that collection, and Dorothy Van Ghent's provocative "On *Clarissa Harlowe*," are useful and/or stimulating. Also valuable is the introduction by George Sherburn to the abridged *Clarissa* in the Riverside edition (New York, 1962).

To an essay by Leo Braudy, "Penetration and Impenetrability in *Clarissa*," in Phillip Harth, ed., *New Approaches to Eighteenth-Century Literature* (New York, 1974), I owe some observations about Clarissa's tomb. Essays in *The New York Review of Books* which appeared later as chapters of Hardwick's *Seduction and Betrayal* and Moers's *Literary Women* influenced my interpretation.

Margaret Anne Doody's scholarly study of Richardson's novels, *A Natural Passion* (Oxford, 1974), includes a useful chapter on "*Clarissa* and Earlier Novels of Love and Seduction." For the epistolary novel (and *Clarissa*'s place within that tradition), see Ruth Perry, *Women*,

*Letters, and the Novel* (New York, 1980). Janet Todd, in *Women's Friendship in Literature* (New York, 1980), offers an interesting analysis of Clarissa's relationship with Anna Howe, a subject to which I pay too little attention here. William B. Warner's study, *Reading Clarissa: The Struggles of Interpretation* (New Haven, 1979), concentrates on Lovelace as a modern man playing parts; it is well worth arguing with.

For clothing in general see Anne Hollander, *Seeing Through Clothes* (New York, 1978). A number of Richardson's critics have interesting things to say about clothing in *Clarissa*. For the relationship of costume to prescriptive articulation of female roles, see an essay by Eugene Waith on Heywood's *Women Worthies* (1640), a book illustrated with engravings. Waith notes of the illustrations that "the impression remains that these ladies are in fancy dress—that they have put on costumes to play the roles of worthies," and that this implies to the female reader that she too "may be a Deborah or an Elpheda," that she could acquire the role as easily as a costume. See Eugene M. Waith, "Heywood's Women Worthies," in *Concepts of the Hero in the Middle Ages and the Renaissance* (Albany, 1975), pp. 234, 236.

The juxtaposition of two statements by Dr. Johnson on p. 61, about letters, I have borrowed from Watt, p. 229. The interested reader might like to see an essay by Frances Ferguson, "The Unfamiliarity of Familiar Letters," in Leonard Michaels and Christopher Ricks, eds., *The State of the Language* (Berkeley, 1980).

The authoritative biography of Richardson is T. C. Duncan Eaves and Ben D. Kimpel, *Samuel Richardson: A Biography* (London, 1971). Cynthia Griffin Wolff, in *Samuel Richardson and the Eighteenth-Century Puritan Character* (Hamden, 1972), places the novelist in his social and intellectual context.

In a brilliant essay that demands to be listed as the last word on the novel, "He Could Go No Further: A Modest Proposal about Lovelace and Clarissa" (*PMLA* 92, January 1977), Judith Wilt makes the irreverent suggestion that in fact Lovelace did not—because he could not—rape Clarissa.


# Getting Married: Jane Austen

The literature comparing conventional feminine behavior to the tropes of novels, and tracing the sources of one to the other, dates back to *The*

*Female Quixote* and Jane Austen's juvenile *Love and Freindship*. In "Silly Novels by Lady Novelists," George Eliot turned the formulation upside down, but that too had been done before, notably by Mary Wollstonecraft, who wrote with disdain of "the herd of Novelists" in *A Vindication of the Rights of Woman* (1792). In our own zealous scholarly times, commenters on these matters are legion; one need only reflect that they include everyone who has written about *Northanger Abbey*.

For the writers before Jane Austen who established the conventions, see F. W. Bradbrook, *Jane Austen and Her Predecessors* (Cambridge, 1966). For a view of another eighteenth-century woman novelist as revising conventions about women, see Katharine M. Rogers, "Sensibility and Feminism in the Novels of Frances Brooke," *Genre* XI, Summer 1978; see also her "Inhibitions on Eighteenth-Century Women Novelists: Elizabeth Inchbald and Charlotte Smith," *Eighteenth Century Studies* II, Fall 1977. Q. D. Leavis, in her influential *Scrutiny* essays on Austen, argued persuasively that the novelist's habitual method of composition was by rewriting. (For a feminist interpretation of Austen's covering her paper with a blotter, and the development of that detail into a critical theory, see Sandra M. Gilbert and Susan Gubar, *The Madwoman in the Attic,* especially pp. 107–86.) Mrs. Leavis connected "that intimate tone with the reader that has made her so popular" and an awareness of a critical audience that produced "self-ironical touches" to the fact that Austen wrote for her family circle. See Q. D. Leavis, "A Critical Theory of Jane Austen's Writings" I (1941), IIb (1942), and III (1944), in F. R. Leavis, ed., *A Selection from Scrutiny* II (Cambridge, 1968).

Mary Lascelles, in *Jane Austen and Her Art* (Oxford, 1939), argued that Austen treated every convention she used critically. Henrietta Ten Harmsel's *Jane Austen: A Study in Fictional Conventions* (The Hague, 1964) explored in detail the links between conventional behavior and conventional fictional form; Jane Nardin in *Those Elegant Decorums: The Concept of Propriety in Jane Austen's Novels* (Albany, 1973) took a similar angle. For an assessment that stresses aesthetic rather than social factors, see, *e.g.,* George Levine, "Realism Reconsidered," in John Halperin, ed., *The Theory of the Novel* (New York, 1974): "Jane Austen, ridiculing the absurdities of the sensational novels of her own day, adopted a style and a subject most appropriate to her own possibilities as an artist: what began as parody became subject and structure" (p. 250). A recent and critically acute book-length study of Austen's art and its relations to the structures of her social and moral universe is

Julia Prewitt Brown, *Jane Austen's Novels* (Cambridge, Mass., 1979). Brown's discussion of *Mansfield Park* is especially good.

Alistair Duckworth's excellent study, *The Improvement of the Estate* (Baltimore, 1971), emphasizes the importance of place in Austen's novels. Other books I have profited from reading include W. A. Craik, *Jane Austen: The Six Novels* (New York, 1965); A. Walton Litz, *Jane Austen: A Study of Her Artistic Development* (New York, 1965); Darrell Mansell, *The Novels of Jane Austen* (New York, 1973); Marvin Mudrick, *Jane Austen: Irony as Defense and Discovery* (Berkeley, 1968); and Andrew Wright, *Jane Austen's Novels: A Study in Structure* (New York, 1973). A valuable collection of documents in the history of Austen criticism is B. C. Southam, ed., *Jane Austen: The Critical Heritage* (London, 1968). John Halperin, ed., *Jane Austen: Bicentenary Essays* (Cambridge, 1975) is a treasure trove of critical comments, including Mary Lascelles's "Jane Austen and the Novel." Ian Watt, ed., *Jane Austen: A Collection of Critical Essays* (Englewood Cliffs, 1963) has in it other important essays, including Lionel Trilling's famous discussion of *Mansfield Park* and Edmund Wilson's "A Long Talk About Jane Austen," from which I quote on p. 110. See also the Jane Austen numbers of *Nineteenth-Century Fiction* (December 1975) and *The Wordsworth Circle* (Autumn 1976).

Psychoanalytic, sociological, feminist, and generally speculative literature documenting and generalizing about the various and rich relationships women have had and can have with other women has burgeoned in the last several years: I will not pretend to give a bibliography. Here I read the heroine's relationship with other women as a clue to, and an image of, her self-awareness. Critics who have pursued the subject of friendships among women in fiction in rather different directions, with interesting and illuminating results, include Nina Auerbach (*Communities of Women* [Cambridge, Mass., 1978]), and Janet Todd (*Women's Friendship in Literature* [New York, 1980]). In *Among Women* (New York, 1980) Louise Bernikow categorized and analyzed kinds of sisterhood among literary women and female characters conceived by women writers.

Of Elizabeth Bennet's conversations with her sister Jane, Nina Auerbach writes that "during the many confidences we see between [them], they talk of nothing but Bingley and Darcy, speculating over their motives and characters with the relish of two collaborators working on a novel" ("Austen and Alcott on Matriarchy: New Women or New Wives," in *Towards a Poetics of Fiction*, ed. Mark Spilka

[Bloomington, 1977]). But it seems to me that Jane Bennet would write another sort of novel than Elizabeth, who would write *Pride and Prejudice*. Jane is more a necessary auditor to bounce off and amuse than a full-fledged collaborator. For a first word on women's talks with one another, see Lady Grandison to Lucy Selby on the subject of the long walks shared by the co-heroines Harriet and Clementina in *Sir Charles Grandison*: "*Heroines* both, I suppose; and they are mirrors to each other; each admiring herself *in* the other. No wonder they are engaged insensibly by a vanity, which carries with it, to each, so generous an appearance; for, all the while, Harriet thinks she is only admiring Clementina; Clementina, that she's applauding Harriet" (Samuel Richardson, *The History of Sir Charles Grandison* III, p. 418).

The reference to Roland Barthes on p. 85 is to *The Pleasure of the Text*, tr. Richard Miller (New York, 1975), pp. 9–10.

The idea that a Jane Austen heroine is the one who knows what a true heroine is I owe to Peggy Brawer. The observation about "the world's wife" from George Eliot's *The Mill on the Floss* I owe to Nancy K. Miller (see her "Emphasis Added: Plots and Plausibilities in Women's Fiction," *PMLA* 96, January 1981).

The quotation on pp. 100–101 from Elizabeth Gaskell's *North and South* is on p. 221 of the Penguin edition (New York and Harmondsworth, 1977); the quotation from *Daniel Deronda* (New York and Harmondsworth, 1967), is on p. 150.

For Freud on the uncanny, see "The 'Uncanny,' " (1919) in Sigmund Freud, *Collected Papers* IV (New York, 1959).

For Lord Shaftesbury on "the natural free spirits," see Anthony Ashley Cooper, Earl of Shaftesbury, "An Essay on the Freedom of Wit and Humour," in his *Characteristics of Men, Manners, Opinions, Times* I (ed. John M. Robertson, London, 1900; repr. New York, 1964), p. 50. Alistair Duckworth connects Elizabeth's style to Lord Shaftesbury's ideas about humor. See also Freud on the humor of the repressed and of the underclass, *Jokes and Their Relation to the Unconscious* (1905), tr. James Strachey (New York, 1960). A sour comment by Lady Mary Wortley Montagu, one of the wittiest women of her time, about Richardson's witty virgin-heroines is worth recalling here: "Anna How[e] and Charlotte Grandison are recommended as Patterns of charming Pleasantry, and applauded by his saint-like Dames, who mistake pert Folly for Wit and humour, and Impudence and ill nature for Spirit and Fire. Charlotte behaves like a humoursome child, and should have been us'd like one, and have had her Coats flung over her

Head and her Bum well whipp'd in the presence of her Freindly Confidante Harriet" (letter of 20 October 1755, in Robert Halsband, ed., *The Complete Letters of Lady Mary Wortley Montagu* III [Oxford, 1965], p. 96)

For intimate conversations within a group, see W. A. Craik, *Jane Austen: The Six Novels*, pp. 37–39. Walter E. Anderson, "Plot, Character, Speech and Place," and F. R. Hart, "The Spaces of Privacy: Jane Austen," both in *Nineteenth Century Fiction*, December 1975, discuss the subject. See also Erwin Goffman, *Behavior in Public Places* (New York, 1966).

Howard Babb, in *Jane Austen's Novels: The Fabric of Dialogue* (Columbus, 1967) writes well about the concept of "performance" in *Pride and Prejudice*, but he sees Darcy as teaching Elizabeth about a difference between truthful and bravura performances; I think the distinction is between performances that are exclusionary and mutually understood performances, which, because they are understood as performances, communicate what cannot be spoken.

G. H. Lewes wrote about marrying Elizabeth Bennet in "The Novels of Jane Austen," reprinted in B. C. Southam, ed., *Jane Austen: The Critical Heritage*. "We may picture her," he wrote of the novelist, "as something like her own sprightly, natural, but by no means perfect Elizabeth Bennet, in *Pride and Prejudice*, one of the few heroines one would seriously like to marry" (p. 151).

For Charlotte Lucas's realistic choice in the context of the actual marriage market, see Lillian Robinson, "Why Marry Mr. Collins?" in her *Sex, Class and Culture*.

# Thinking It Over

For the nineteenth-century heroine, see Patricia Thomson, *The Victorian Heroine: A Changing Ideal, 1837–1873* (London, 1956). For women in society and in novels, see Françoise Basch, *Relative Creatures* (New York, 1974) and Jenni Calder, *Women and Marriage in Victorian Fiction* (New York, 1976). Two collections of essays on nineteenth-century women edited by Martha Vicinus, *Suffer and Be Still* (Bloomington, 1973) and *A Widening Sphere* (Bloomington, 1977) are very useful. Such recent studies as Patricia Beer's *Reader, I Married Him* (New York, 1974), Hazel

Mews's *Frail Vessels* (London, 1969), Susan Siefert's *The Dilemma of the Talented Heroine* (Montreal, 1977), and Anthea Zeman's *Presumptuous Girls* (London, 1977) have interesting things to say about classic novels and the characters in them, which they analyze as if they were actual persons; more or less feminist in emphasis, these books are evidence not so much of something new as of the power fictitious women and women writers have had in the imaginations of women readers since the eighteenth century.

I quote Jean-Paul Sartre on p. 141 from *The Words*, tr. Bernard Frechtman (New York, 1965), pp. 205–206.

Florence Nightingale's *Cassandra* was reprinted by The Feminist Press in 1979; I quote from p. 28 of that edition. The tract is reprinted also in Ray Strachey, *The Cause* (1928; London, 1978), an excellent history of the women's movement in Great Britain.

For Elaine Showalter on heroes, see Chapter V, "Feminine Heroes," in *A Literature of Their Own: British Women Novelists from Brontë to Lessing.* Carolyn G. Heilbrun in *Reinventing Womanhood* presents the view that women novelists have been unable to imagine heroines as strong as themselves; see especially pp. 71–92.

The Clarissa-Harlovian ideal of the single feminine life perfected into art continued to haunt the nineteenth-century woman's Christian, father-fearing imagination. In *Communities of Women*, Nina Auerbach quotes from *A Woman's Thoughts about Women* by the minor novelist Dinah Mulock Craik: "A finished life—a life which has made the best of all the materials granted to it, and through which, be its web dark or bright, its pattern clear or clouded, can now be traced plainly the hand of the Great Designer; surely this is worth living for?" (p. 20).

For Virginia Woolf on Elizabeth Barrett Browning, see *"Aurora Leigh,"* in *Collected Essays of Virginia Woolf* I (New York, 1967), p. 212. For her comments on Eliot's heroines see "George Eliot," *Collected Essays* I, pp. 201–202.

I quote from the Penguin edition of *Middlemarch* (New York and Harmondsworth, 1965), pp. 894, 896.

# Villette

Biographers since Elizabeth Gaskell (*The Life of Charlotte Brontë* [1857; New York and Harmondsworth, 1975]) have found it hard to disengage the life of the novelist from the work, and also to trace their connections: the strong reactions provoked by Charlotte Brontë the woman and Charlotte Brontë the novelist from her time to our own are evidence of the intrinsic, knotty ties of women to fiction. For Mrs. Gaskell's limitations as a biographer, see Margaret Ganz, *Elizabeth Gaskell: The Artist in Conflict* (New York, 1969): she writes that Mrs. Gaskell's tact, personal inhibitions, and determination "to present Charlotte's life to the world as a moral exemplum" led to an idealization of her subject (p. 187). Inga-Stina Ewbank, in *Their Proper Sphere: A Study of the Brontë Sisters as Early-Victorian Female Novelists* (Cambridge, Mass., 1966), writes that "it was Mrs. Gaskell's *Life of Charlotte Brontë* which was most instrumental in changing people's ideas about the supposed coarseness of the Brontës; and it is in reviews of her biography that we first see the very terms of abuse turned into praise" (p. 47). For the life, Clement Shorter's documentary *The Brontës: Life and Letters* (1908; New York, 1969) is an invaluable source; modern biographies by Winifred Gérin (*Charlotte Brontë: The Evolution of Genius* [Oxford, 1967]) and Margot Peters (*Unquiet Soul* [New York, 1975]) contain further information and interpretation. For an excellent feminist reading of Brontë's life and work as a process of self-definition and self-realization, see Helene Moglen's *Charlotte Brontë: The Self Conceived* (New York, 1976); for Brontë's life and work in relation to social factors and forces, see Harriet Bjork, *The Language of Truth: Charlotte Brontë, the Woman Question, and the Novel* (Lund, 1974) and an article by Terry Eagleton, "Class, Power, and Charlotte Brontë," *Critical Quarterly* 14, 1972. Critical commentary by Brontë's contemporaries is collected in Miriam Allott, *The Brontës: The Critical Heritage* (London and Boston, 1974). See also F. B. Pinion, *A Brontë Companion* (New York, 1975). For a criticism of Brontë scholarship, see Tom Winnifrith, *The Brontës and Their Background: Romance and Reality* (London, 1973).

On *Villette* in particular much attention has been lavished by feminist critics since Millett's pages (139–147) in *Sexual Politics*. *Jane Eyre* is arguably still the most widely and feelingly read of Brontë's novels, and Adrienne Rich's 1973 essay, "Jane Eyre: Temptations of a Motherless Woman," reprinted in *On Lies, Secrets, and Silence* (New York, 1979), is a milestone in recent feminist criticism. But the popularity of *Villette* as an object of feminist examination and source of feminist theory has grown enormously. The best and fullest discussion of the novel is the heart of Gilbert and Gubar's *The Madwoman in the Attic* ("The Buried Life of Lucy Snowe," pp. 399–440); their argument that the tropes of women writers are responses to the repression of patriarchy can get no better support than their thorough reading of this text. As Nina Auerbach observed, "the plot of *Jane Eyre* expresses Jane's central conflict, but the plot of *Villette* obscures and stifles Lucy Snowe's" ("Charlotte Brontë: The Two Countries," *University of Toronto Quarterly* XLII, Summer 1973). But its complexity both as a psychological study and as a narrative have made not only feminists more interested in the novel than ever: see, *e.g.*, excellent essays by Robert Colby, "*Villette* and the Life of the Mind," *PMLA* 75, September 1960; E.D.H. Johnson, " 'Daring the Dread Glance': Charlotte Brontë's Treatment of the Supernatural in *Villette*," *Nineteenth Century Fiction* 20, March 1966; Jean Frantz Blackall, "Point of View in *Villette*," *The Journal of Narrative Technique* 6, Winter 1976; and Tony Tanner's introduction to the Penguin edition of the novel (New York and Harmondsworth, 1979).

Winifred Gérin notes that a painting very much like the "Cleopatra" Brontë condemns, and also paintings of scenes of a typical woman's life by a woman painter, Fanny Greefs, were in fact exhibited in the Salon in Brussels when Charlotte Brontë visited it in 1842 (pp. 209–210); she describes, pp. 49–53, the pictorial prototypes of Brontë's early heroines and her early interest in being a painter. Jane Austen's celebrated letter to her sister Cassandra about a visit she made to a picture gallery reveals her conviction that a painter could not capture the charming liveliness of Elizabeth Bennet: she wrote that she was "very well pleased . . . with a small portrait of Mrs. Bingley, excessively like her." Austen says she "went in hopes of seeing one of her Sister, but there was no Mrs. Darcy" (*Jane Austen's Letters*, ed. R. W. Chapman [Oxford, 1979], p. 309). Austen claimed to prefer men and women to paintings; in another letter she writes that "Mary & I . . . went to the Liverpool Museum, & the British Gallery, & I had some amusement at each, tho' my preference for Men & Women, always inclines me to attend more to the company than the sight" (p. 267).

The quotation from Brontë's *The Professor* is from the Everyman's Library edition (1969), p. 214. The famous letter from Charlotte Brontë to Robert Southey is reprinted in Gaskell, p. 175. Brontë's comments on Jane Austen are often reprinted; see, *e.g.*, B. C. Southam, ed., *Jane Austen: The Critical Heritage*, pp. 126, 128. The quotation from Brontë's Roe Head Journal is in Gérin, p. 105. Thackeray and Arnold on Brontë are in Allott, pp. 197–98 and 201. Elizabeth Gaskell, p. 132, quotes Mary Taylor's recollection of Brontë's dream about her dead sisters. Brontë's characterization of Emily is in her "Biographical Notice of Ellis and Acton Bell," in Emily Brontë, *Wuthering Heights* (London, Old-hams Press, n.d.), p. 15. The reflection on "people who have been brought up in retirement" is from Brontë's novelette "Caroline Vernon," in *Legends of Angria*, ed. Fannie E. Ratchford (New Haven, 1933), p. 264. On the juvenilia, see Ratchford's *The Brontës' Web of Childhood* (New York, 1941). The letter to Ellen Nussey is quoted in Gaskell, p. 164. For Brontë's Byronism see Moglen, pp. 26–59; that Charlotte believed she was not entitled to identify with Byron, because she was a girl, seems to me incorrect, though. The appeal of Byronism, to Byron's lovers and his readers, is sexual but promises release from gender. For a brief recollection of Charlotte Brontë by Anne, Lady Ritchie, see James Sutherland, ed., *The Oxford Book of Literary Anecdotes* (New York, 1976), pp. 321–23.

The Vicar of Wakefield comments on his daughters in Chapter 1 of Oliver Goldsmith's *The Vicar of Wakefield* (1766; New York, 1961), p. 12. The quotation from Charlotte Smith's *Emmeline* is on p. 5 of the edition edited by Anne H. Ehrenpreis (London, 1971). For Jane Eyre's being plain on purpose, because creating beautiful heroines was "morally wrong," see Gaskell, p. 308: "I will show you a heroine as plain and as small as myself, who shall be as interesting as any of yours." Kathleen Tillotson, in *Novels of the 1840s* (Oxford, 1956), p. 260, says the novel started a vogue for plain heroines. For the Byronic Zamorna's agreement with the heroine that "adventures never happen to plain people," see "Caroline Vernon," in *Legends of Angria*, p. 257.

The quotation from *Sanditon* is in R. W. Chapman, ed., *The Works of Jane Austen*, VI, Minor Works (London, 1954), p. 391. The quotation from Defoe is from the edition of *Roxana* edited by Jane Jack (Oxford, 1964), pp. 72–73. (Roxana, by the way, is given her name while she dances in fancy dress; she *looks like* a Roxana, therefore becomes one.) See Elizabeth Gaskell's letter to Miss Lamont, January 5 [1849], for her testimony that she changed the novel's name from *John Barton* because of "a London thought coming through the publisher" (*The Letters of Mrs. Gaskell*, ed. J. A. V. Chapple and Arthur Pollard [Manchester, 1966], p. 70).

For Harriet Martineau's decision that *Villette* was "almost intolerably painful," see Allott, p. 172. For Freud on the uncanny see "The 'Uncanny' " (1919), *Collected Papers* IV.

For Charlotte Brontë on Rachel, see Moglen, p. 216; Gérin, pp. 481–82. For Rachel generally, see Jules Janin, *Rachel et la Tragédie* (Paris, 1859); Joanna Richardson, *Rachel* (London, 1956); also Bernard Falk,

*Rachel, the Immortal* (New York, 1936) and Nicole Toussaint du Wast, *Rachel: Amours et Tragédie* (Paris, 1980). Excerpts from G. H. Lewes's "Rachel and Racine" are in Alice R. Kaminsky, ed., *Literary Criticism of George Henry Lewes* (Lincoln, 1964).

For the unsigned review (by Anne Mozley) in *The Christian Remembrancer* about Brontë's seeing life as a school, not a home, see Allott, p. 203.

# The Egoist

For George Meredith's life see Lionel Stevenson, *The Ordeal of George Meredith* (New York, 1953). Diane Johnson's *Lesser Lives* (New York, 1972), a "True History of the First Mrs. Meredith," is also, or is really, about women's relation to the peripheries of literature, which Johnson shrewdly and wittily surveys.

"An Essay on Comedy" is most easily found in Wylie Sypher, ed., *Comedy* (New York, 1956). For Meredithian comedy, see V. S. Pritchett's Clark Lectures, published as *George Meredith and English Comedy* (London, 1970). Although Meredith is still rather "in the trough" of literary reputations, as E. M. Forster put it, there has been something of a little renaissance. See, *e.g.*, Gillian Beer's *Meredith: A Change of Masks* (London, 1970); a collection of essays edited by Ian Fletcher, *Meredith Now* (London, 1971); Ioan Williams, ed., *Meredith: The Critical Heritage* (New York, 1971); and Judith Wilt, *The Readable People of George Meredith* (Princeton, 1975).

In her essay on Meredith's novel in *The English Novel: Form and Function* (New York, 1953), Dorothy Van Ghent drew connections between Sir Willoughby Patterne and Gilbert Osmond of *The Portrait of a Lady*, concluding in James's favor. John Goode in the Fletcher collection discusses the Meredith-James connection further. See also a book-length study of the two novelists by Donald David Stone, *Novelists in a Changing World* (Cambridge, Mass., 1972).

Among those who have noted the relation of Sir Willoughby Patterne to Sir Charles Grandison is A. D. McKillop, who characterized Sir Willoughby as "a Grandison subjected to pitiless scrutiny" (*Samuel Richardson, Printer and Novelist* [Chapel Hill, 1936], p. 210).

For the significance of the willow pattern and a story depicted on it, see Robert D. Mayo, "The Egoist and the Willow Pattern," reprinted in the Norton Critical Edition of the novel. Gillian Beer (pp. 131–32) points out additional facts about what china might have meant to Meredith's first readers.

The quotation from Virginia Woolf on p. 198 is from her essay, "On Re-reading Meredith," *Collected Essays* I, p. 237. Woolf's more famous essay from *The Second Common Reader*, "The Novels of George Meredith," is reprinted in the Norton *Egoist* as well as in *Collected Essays* I. All the critical essays in the Norton volume are valuable; the reader might consult, in addition, Kate Millett's *Sexual Politics*, pp. 134–39.

The biographer of Caroline Norton whom I quote on p. 199 is Jane G. Perkins; see *The Life of Mrs. Norton* (London, 1909), p. xiii. See also Alice Acland, *Caroline Norton* (London, 1948) and Ray Strachey, *The Cause*, pp. 34–40. I am indebted to excellent articles on Diana and Caroline Norton by Jane Marcus, " 'Clio in Calliope': History and Myth in Meredith's *Diana of the Crossways*," *Bulletin of the New York Public Library* 79, and Judith Wilt, "Meredith's Diana: Freedom, Fiction, and the Female," *Tennessee Studies in Language and Literature* 18.

# Daniel Deronda

"Play," in the double senses of gambling (gaming) and play-acting, being the organizing metaphor(s) of this novel, I begin where it begins, and also where it began. Gordon S. Haight, in his authoritative *George Eliot: A Biography* (Oxford, 1968), writes that the sight of a Miss Leigh at the Kursaal in Homburg "proved to be the germ of" *Daniel Deronda* (p. 457). In a letter to John Blackwood describing her vision of the young Englishwoman gambling, George Eliot identified Miss Leigh as "Byron's grand niece"; in his diary, George Henry Lewes described her as "Byron's grand-daughter" (Gordon S. Haight, ed., *The George Eliot Letters* V [New Haven, 1955], p. 314). Haight writes, "whether she was grandniece or granddaughter I cannot discover." Her surname would indicate that Miss Leigh was descended from Byron's sister Augusta, and I assume the rumor that Augusta's daughter Elizabeth Medora was Byron's child accounts for the contradictory identifications. It would appear that Lewes assumed the rumor was true; it is hard to know what George Eliot thought, as she would hardly have indulged in innuendos about what was still a riveting focus for scandalmongers (Harriet Beecher

Stowe's *Lady Byron Vindicated* appeared in 1870) in a letter to Blackwood (or anyone else). In *George Eliot: The Emergent Self* (New York, 1975), Ruby V. Redinger, whose emphasis on the brother-and-sister theme in George Eliot's life and works has influenced my reading, too easily assumes that Miss Leigh was "actually" Byron's granddaughter (p. 474); the line of descent seems at more than one point uncertain. For a recent reweaving of the shreds of evidence in the case of Byron and his half-sister, see John S. Chapman, *Byron and the Honourable Augusta Leigh* (New Haven, 1975).

The significance of Maggie Tulliver's lover's name was pointed out to me by Nancy K. Miller, who writes, "Maggie, previously unawakened by *her* fiancé, Wakem, awakens both to her desire and to what she calls her duty, only to fulfill both by drowning. . . ." See "Emphasis Added: Plots and Plausibilities in Women's Fiction," *PMLA* 96, January 1981, p. 45.

For George Eliot's intentions to reform the attitudes toward the Jews with *Daniel Deronda*, see her letter to Harriet Beecher Stowe (*Letters* VI, p. 301). For Blackwood's advertising plans, see his letter of 17 November 1875 (*Letters* VI, pp. 185–87) and G. H. Lewes's letter of 22 November (*Letters* VI, pp. 192–93).

F. R. Leavis's famous division of *Daniel Deronda* is in *The Great Tradition* (1948; London, 1962); pages 79–126 are about George Eliot's novel and *The Portrait of a Lady*. Henry James's essay "*Daniel Deronda*: A Conversation," reprinted there in an appendix, distinguishes between the vividness of Gwendolen's story and the coldness of "the Jewish part." In *The Novels of George Eliot* (London, 1959), Barbara Hardy observes that "the rejections of the Jewish parts of *Daniel Deronda* are usually aesthetic rejections, it is true, but sometimes they carry an echo of Gwendolen's casual and 'civilized' anti-Semitism. 'I am sure he had a nose,' says Henry James's Pulcheria" (p. 17).

I quote GE's objections to what seemed to her misreadings of her novel from her letter to Barbara Bodichon, *Letters* VI, p. 290. For comments by GE's contemporaries, see David Carroll, ed., *George Eliot: The Critical Heritage* (New York, 1971).

For a brilliant analysis of the narrative complexity of *Daniel Deronda*, which comments on the interlocking worlds of action and prophecy, see Cynthia Chase, "The Decomposition of the Elephants: Double-Reading *Daniel Deronda*," *PMLA* 93, March 1978. Chase's challenging rereading interprets the famous "flaws" in the novel as strengths, and clues to meaning.

For a sound reading of all the novels, see W. J. Harvey, *The Art of George Eliot* (New York and London, 1962).

For George Eliot's "Silly Novels by Lady Novelists," see Thomas Pinney, ed., *Essays of George Eliot* (New York and London, 1963).

John Blackwood's letter of 17 November 1875 is in *Letters* VI, 185–87.

The quotation from Chapter 16 of *Middlemarch* is on p. 189 of the Penguin edition. Commenting on Rosamond's memorable neck, Geoffrey Tillotson refers to *The Memoirs of Martinus Scriblerus*, where the "author," in Chapter X, "charg'd all Husbands to take notice of the Posture of the Head of such as are courted to Matrimony, as that upon which their future happiness did much depend" (Tillotson, *Criticism and the Nineteenth Century* [London, 1967], p. 32). The common masculine interest is in the set of the head as an index to feminine character, presumably in the question of docility; George Eliot's point is that it shows how a woman values herself.

For GE on *Villette*, see *Letters* II, p. 87. *Daniel Deronda* began appearing serially the year after the publication of a book of George Henry Lewes's essays, including an essay on Rachel. I have emphasized the French Rachel, here, as the nineteenth-century incarnation of The Actress, but for George Eliot and *Daniel Deronda* the English Helen (or Helena) Faucit is more to the point. In his biography, Haight notes (n., p. 471) that the novelist told Miss Faucit she thought of her while writing Klesmer's remarks on art and artists in Chapter 23. In a letter of 3 March 1865, GE praised Miss Faucit for her performance of Lady Teazle in Sheridan's *School for Scandal*, writing of "that deep benefit which comes from seeing a high type of womanly grace, to shame away false ideals" (*Letters* VI, p. 25). For the real life of actresses and the ways they were seen in the nineteenth century, see Christopher Kent, "Image and Reality: The Actress and Society," in Martha Vicinus, ed., *A Widening Sphere: Changing Roles of Victorian Women* (Bloomington, 1977). Commenting on Miss Faucit's influence on *Daniel Deronda*, Kent calls the novel "one of the few serious literary treatments of the theatrical profession in the nineteenth century" (p. 100).

The remarks of Pulcheria *et al.* are from James's "*Daniel Deronda*: A Conversation," reprinted in George R. Creeger, ed., *George Eliot: A Collection of Critical Essays* (Englewood Cliffs, 1970), as well as in *The Great Tradition*. James himself discusses Deronda's quality of soul in the Preface to *The Princess Casamassima*, in *The Art of the Novel* (New York, 1934), p. 70.

Deronda's power residing in a massive receptiveness is perhaps akin to "the power of being deeply moved" that was valued by Walter Pater, which, Geoffrey Tillotson suggested, derives from the Wordsworthian ideal of "wise passiveness." See Tillotson's *Criticism and the Nineteenth Century*, p. 113.

Steven Marcus's comment on Deronda's apparent unawareness of having been circumcised appears in a footnote to an essay, "Literature and Social Theory: Starting in with George Eliot," in Marcus's *Representations: Essays on Literature and Society* (New York, 1975), p. 212. He credits Lennard Davis.

Barbara Hardy, in a note to the Penguin edition of *Daniel Deronda*, writes that the sentence beginning "I may awaken a movement in other minds" is "not in the manuscript, and [was] presumably added in proof in order to make Daniel's statement and his political destiny sound more tentative and realistic" (p. 903).

The matter of GE's name was vexed from early on. Haight writes (n., p. 3) that "The Chilvers Coton Parish Register records her baptism as *Mary Anne*, and her earliest letter is so signed. In 1837 she began to write *Mary Ann*, in 1850 it became *Marian*, and in 1880 she reverted to *Mary Ann*." In an 1857 letter signed "Marian E. Lewes," she "renounced" the name *Miss Evans* (Haight, p. 243; *Letters* II, pp. 384–85); by then she had begun writing as "George Eliot." Redinger observes that "in a sense, both the masculine name of 'George Eliot' and the feminine one of 'Mrs. Lewes' were unfounded in reality" (p. 335). GHL's letters to his children allude to her as "Mutter," "The Mutter," or "The Little Mutter." For pseudonyms and Victorian women writers, see Elaine Showalter, *A Literature of Their Own*, especially pp. 73–79, and an earlier essay, "Women Writers and the Double Standard," in Vivian Gornick and Barbara K. Moran, eds., *Women in Sexist Society* (New York, 1971).

GHL's letter to Blackwood about "good honest heart and brain" in boys is in *Letters* VI, p. 159.

The extract from a letter from the American Louisa S. Reid is in a note on p. 51 of *Letters* VI; GE's response is on pp. 51–52. For GHL's letter to Alexander Main, see *Letters* VI, pp. 218–19. For GE's nervousness about "the Jewish element," see *Letters* VI, p. 238; see also a letter of 29 October 1876, from GE to Harriet Beecher Stowe, in which she writes, "As to the Jewish element in 'Deronda,' I expected from first to last in writing it, that it would create much stronger resistance and even repulsion than it has actually met with" (*Letters* VI, p. 301). In the letter to the author of *Uncle Tom's Cabin*, appropriately enough, GE articulates her ambition "to rouse the imagination of men and women to a vision of human claims in those races of their fellow-men who most differ from them in customs and beliefs," insisting on the "peculiar debt" of Christians to Jews.

It is Dorothea Brooke who must experience the "equivalent center of self" that is in Mr. Casaubon; George Eliot writes in Chapter 19 of *Janet's Repentance* of the "blessed influence of one true loving soul on another."

For "unspeakable joy," see, *e.g.*, *Letters* VI, p. 3, quoted in Haight, p. 469: "our unspeakable joy in each other has no other alloy than the sense that it must one day end in parting."

I have avoided the issue of GE's regarding her novels as her "spiritual children" (*Letters* VI, p. 246) as I avoided the same issue apropos of Jane Austen, who wrote of *Sense and Sensibility*, "I can no more forget it, than a mother can forget her sucking child" (Austen *Letters*, p. 272), and of *Pride and Prejudice*, "I have got my own darling child from London" (Austen *Letters*, p. 297). It is well known that many male authors have also spoken of their literary creations in terms borrowed from biological maternity, and I do not wish to suggest that a frustrated maternal instinct caused George Eliot or Jane Austen—or Virginia Woolf—to write novels. While there is a metaphorical relation between the kinds of creating, and the feelings of protectiveness and pride that attend on them, and while it is clear that writing novels was ever hard for mothers who lack the organizational skills of an Elizabeth Gaskell or a Frances Trollope, George Eliot was a genius (as Austen and Woolf were) who demands from her admirers protection from the banalities of simple psychologizing. In Nina Auerbach's "Artists and Mothers: A False Alliance," *Women and Literature* 6, Spring 1978, there is an interesting discussion of psychiatrists' and critics' and writers' comments about maternal and artistic creation, and of George Eliot in this connection.

## The Portrait of a Lady

George Eliot reflects on Hetty Sorrel's reading in Chapter 13 of *Adam Bede* (New York and Harmondsworth, 1980), p. 181. Henry Fielding's review of *The Female Quixote* is in Ioan Williams, ed., *The Criticism of Henry Fielding* (New York, 1970), p. 193. The quotation from Thomas

Hardy's *Tess of the D'Urbervilles* is from Chapter 12, p. 69 in the Norton (New York, 1965) edition. I quote Flaubert from Lowell Bair's translation of *Madame Bovary* (New York, 1959), p. 140.

In Clara Reeve's *The Progress of Romance*, one critic catalogues the evils attendant on romance-reading as follows: "The seeds of vice and folly are sown in the heart,—the passions are awakened,—false expectations are raised.—A young woman is taught to expect adventures and intrigues,—she expects to be addressed in the style of these books, with the language of flattery and adulation.—If a plain man addresses her in rational terms and pays her the greatest of compliments,—that of desiring to spend his life with her,—that is not sufficient, her vanity is disappointed, she expects to meet a Hero in Romance." To which the wise and witty Euphrasia responds, "No . . . ,—not a Hero in Romance, but a fine Gentleman in a Novel:—you will not make the distinction" (II, p. 78). For a discussion of the early attacks on novels, including some which claim the corruption of the minds of young women is in effect a defilement of their bodies, see J. Paul Hunter, "The Loneliness of the Long-Distance Reader," *Genre* X, Winter 1977. See also Ioan Williams, ed., *Novel and Romance*, in particular a 1773 review quoting a French physician who claimed "that of all the causes which have injured the health of women, the principal has been the prodigious multiplication of romances within the last century. From the cradle to the most advanced age, they read with an eagerness which keeps them almost without motion, and without sleep. A young girl, instead of running about and playing, *reads*, perpetually reads; and at twenty, becomes full of vapours, instead of being qualified for the duties of a good wife, or nurse" (p. 279). The concern here seems to have slipped insensibly to the health of *men*. For the other side, see the 1794 comments of Mary Wollstonecraft, who argued that debased language, as given currency by romances, debases the feelings: "the reading of novels makes women, and particularly ladies of fashion, very fond of using strong expressions and superlatives in conversation; and, though the dissipated artificial life which they lead prevents their cherishing any strong legitimate passion, the language of passion in affected tones slips for ever from their glib tongues, and every trifle produces those phosphoric bursts which only mimic in the dark the flame of passion" (*A Vindication of the Rights of Women*, ed. Carol H. Poston [New York, 1975], p. 186).

It is traditional for English novelists to argue that foreign (continental, and especially French) novels are corrupting. Charlotte Lennox does in *The Female Quixote*; part of the joke in *Northanger Abbey* is that Catherine can suppose what she imagines might happen in *England*. (It is perhaps relevant in this connection that Meredith's novelist-heroine, Diana Merion, is Celtic, which is to say not Anglo-Saxon and anti-romantic.)

On the subject of women and serious reading, Jane Austen is always provocative. The author of *Northanger Abbey* declares that "a woman especially, if she have the misfortune of knowing anything, should conceal it as well as she can," but adds "in justice to men" that "though to the larger and more trifling part of the sex, imbecility in females is a great enhancement of their personal charms, there is a portion of them too reasonable and too well informed themselves to desire anything more in woman than ignorance" (Chapter 14). The irony is heavy here, but not in the letter where Austen described herself as "a woman who . . . knows only her own mother tongue, and has read very little in that" (*Letters*, p. 443). The tradition of Austen as an untutored wren warbling her native woodnotes wild began with her own insistence that she had not read much besides novels. She described her whole family as "great Novel-readers & not ashamed of being so" (*Letters*, p. 38).

For a critique of the standard attacks on learned ladies or bluestockings, and general suspicion of feminine wit, see Katharine M. Rogers, *The Troublesome Helpmeet: A History of Misogyny in Literature* (Seattle, 1966).

Sections of Henry James's Notebooks that are relevant to *The Portrait of a Lady* are reprinted in the Norton Critical Edition. The quotation on p. 247 is from pp. 625–26. See F. O. Matthiesen and Kenneth Murdock, eds., *The Notebooks of Henry James* (New York, 1947), pp. 15–19, 29.

The quotation from *The Wings of the Dove* is from Volume II, Book Tenth, on p. 365 in the Norton Critical Edition (New York, 1978).

Leon Edel comments on Caspar's revised kiss in *Henry James: The Master, 1901–1916* (Philadelphia and New York, 1972), pp. 326–27. Edel's more extensive discussion of the novel, from which I also quote, is in his *Henry James: The Conquest of London, 1870–1881* (Philadelphia and New York, 1962), pp. 421–34. He observes the sexual connotations of Caspar's "way of rising before her," and concludes Isabel's American suitor "is in short monotonously male" (p. 423).

The "recent editor" I quote is Robert D. Bamberg, editor of the Norton Critical Edition; in addition to a list of variants from the first edition of the novel and appropriate selections from James's notebooks and the autobiography, this volume includes several excellent essays about James's revisions. The reader who wants to read the 1881 *Portrait* should get the Signet (New York, 1963) edition.

The quotation from James's definition of revision is from his Preface to *The Golden Bowl*. See Henry James, *The Art of the Novel*, pp. 338–339, 347.

James recalls his cousin Mary Temple in *Notes of a Son and Brother*. See the selection included in the Norton Critical Edition of *The Portrait*, pp. 632–37, and James, *Autobiography*, ed. Frederick W. Dupee (New York, 1956), pp. 282–84.

# Mrs. Dalloway

For Lionel Trilling on Mary Crawford, see his famous essay "*Mansfield Park*," in *The Opposing Self* (New York, 1959). He writes, "In Mary Crawford we have the first brilliant example of a distinctively modern type, the person who cultivates the *style* of sensitivity, virtue, and intelligence" (p. 220).

For a succinct commentary on the publishing industry's embrace of Virginia Woolf, by an observer who presumably has not taken into account the literary and feminist journals, see the cartoon by Stevens in *The New Yorker*, March 12, 1979, p. 39.

Leonard Woolf compared Vanessa Stephen's beauty with Virginia's in the third volume of his autobiography, *Beginning Again* (New York, 1964), pp. 27–28.

For Virginia Woolf's life, the acknowledged biography is Quentin Bell, *Virginia Woolf: A Biography* (New York, 1972). The limitations of Bell's point of view as Woolf's nephew and a middle-aged man are very well described by Jane Marcus in a review of Woolf studies, "Tintinnabulations," *Marxist Perspectives* 21, Spring 1979. Marcus's corrective interpretation of Woolf is useful; like other feminist critics, she stresses Woolf's rich relationships with women, and also emphasizes her humor and, most of all, her serious political ideas and her hard work. But the claim that Woolf was not at all a snob or an elitist seems to me to be exaggerated. Marcus disapproves of a feministic biography by Phyllis Rose, *Woman of Letters: A Life of Virginia Woolf* (New York, 1978). In this book Rose makes an attempt to de-romanticize the novelist ("She was almost sixty years old when she died, a fact that always startles me, for I imagine her dying young" [p. 262]). Her view that Woolf was one of the rare "manic-depressives born to culture and terrified of life," who "successfully transformed her life into a life of letters" (p. 266) is unregenerately romantic, however; a conflation of the life and the work is interpreted, in the end, as an artistic and personal achievement, and the ending of the one as a period beautifully put to the other, so as to point its moral. Jane Marcus, in "Art and Anger," *Feminist Studies* IV, February 1978, argues that "Woolf's suicide was the result of an ethical imperative rather than the result of 'madness' or 'despair' " (p. 92); she pleads for "no more ethical suicides" (p. 98). But she links Woolf's to Hedda Gabler's suicide, "angry and rebellious as well as a work of art." Perhaps to conceptualize is inevitably to heroinize; but I think we should look harder at such formulations. For Jane Marcus on Virginia Woolf as an "outsider," an interpretation of the woman and the work that provides the grounds for criticism of Bell and others, see "No More Horses: Virginia Woolf on Art and Propaganda," *Women's Studies* 4, 1977 (a Virginia Woolf issue).

For a discussion of Virginia Woolf's relation to her father that stresses literary rather than psychological influences, see Katherine C. Hill, "Virginia Woolf and Leslie Stephen: History and Literary Revolution," *PMLA* 96, May 1981.

The quotation on p. 275 is from Virginia Woolf, *A Writer's Diary*, ed. Leonard Woolf (London, 1953), p. 138. For the *D.N.B.*'s affecting Adrian Stephen's life and his sister Virginia's head, see *The Diary of Virginia Woolf* II, ed. Anne Olivier Bell assisted by Andrew McNeillie (New York, 1978), p. 277. Rose, p. 17, quotes the sentences about *To the Lighthouse* from Woolf's autobiographical writings collected in *Moments of Being* (Sussex, 1976), p. 71.

The letter to Roger Fry of September 22, 1924, is in *The Letters of Virginia Woolf* III (1923–28), ed. Nigel Nicolson and Joanne Trautmann (New York, 1977), pp. 132–33. Woolf's statement about *Mrs. Dalloway* is in *Diary* II, p. 312. See also Virginia Woolf, *Mrs. Dalloway's Party*, ed. Stella McNichol (New York, 1975). The quotation characterizing Clarissa Dalloway is from *The Voyage Out*, p. 47.

"Mr. Bennett and Mrs. Brown" is reprinted on pp. 319–37 of Virginia Woolf, *Collected Essays* I (New York, 1967); the long quotation is on pp. 330–31. "George Moore," in which the passage on Tolstoy occurs, is on pp. 338–41.

On Virginia Woolf the novelist as a "self" that impinges on the reader's consciousness, this passage from a famous analysis of *To the Lighthouse* is illuminating: ". . . the author at times achieves the intended effect by representing herself to be someone who doubts, wonders, hesitates, as though the truth about her characters were not better known to her than it is to them or to the reader" (Erich Auerbach, *Mimesis* [Princeton, 1953], p. 535). For an author to characterize herself thus is to blur the hierarchical relation of character, reader, author; nonauthoritative and obscure in outlines like her characters (and her readers?) who are sensibilities first of all, this novelist exists within a novel in a new way.

The passage on dialogue is in a letter to Gerald Brenan, *Letters* III, p. 36. For Woolf on "party consciousness," see p. 11 of McNichol's introduction to *Mrs. Dalloway's Party*, where she quotes from p. 75 of *A Writer's Diary*. For "a sensibility" versus "Virginia," see *Diary* II, p. 193. For Virginia Woolf's plan to read *Clarissa*, see *Diary* II, p. 309; the notation was made while work continued on *Mrs. Dalloway*. Anne Olivier Bell observes in a note on p. 309 that an edition of Richardson's *Clarissa* was among the Woolfs' books sold after Leonard Woolf's death.

# Afterword

For Anne Finch and Anne Bradstreet, see Sandra M. Gilbert and Susan Gubar, *The Madwoman in the Attic*, especially pp. 7–11, 62.

The covers on the early Margaret Drabble novels are in the Popular Library editions.

# Index